D1280915

The Moral Economy of the State

This series of publications on Africa, Latin America, and Southeast Asia is designed to present significant research, translation, and opinion to area specialists and to a wide community of persons interested in world affairs. The editor seeks manuscripts of quality on any subject and can generally make a decision regarding publication within three months of receipt of the original work. Production methods generally permit a work to appear within one year of acceptance. The editor works closely with authors to produce a high quality book. The series appears in a paperback format and is distributed worldwide. For more information, contact the executive editor at Ohio University Press, Scott Quadrangle, University Terrace, Athens, Ohio 45701.

Executive editor: Gillian Berchowitz
AREA CONSULTANTS
Africa: Diane Ciekawy
Latin America: Thomas Walker
Southeast Asia: William H. Frederick

The Monographs in International Studies series is published for the Center for International Studies by the Ohio University Press. The views expressed in individual monographs are those of the authors and should not be considered to represent the policies or beliefs of the Center for International Studies, the Ohio University Press, or Ohio University.

The Moral Economy of the State

Conservation, Community Development, and State Making in Zimbabwe

William A. Munro

Ohio University Center for International Studies
Monographs in International Studies
Africa Series No. 68
Athens

Library of Congress Cataloging-in-Publication Data

Munro, William Andrew.
    The moral economy of the state : conservation, community
development, and state making in Zimbabwe / William A. Munro.
        p.   cm. — (Monographs in international studies. Africa
series : no. 68.)
    Includes bibliographical references and index.
    ISBN 0-89680-202-7 (pbk. : alk. paper)
    1. Rural development—Zimbabwe 2. Zimbabwe—Rural condi-
tions. 3. Zimbabwe, Politics and government. I. Title. II. Series.
HN802.Z9C649   1998
307.1'412'096891—dc21   97-46465
                                                                    CIP

For my mother and in memory of my father

Contents

Part Three
The National-Popular State

Acknowledgments

It is salutary but singularly pleasing to be able, in the final stages of preparing a book, to acknowledge the daunting array of debts—material, intellectual, personal—that made it all possible. This book is based on doctoral research conducted under the direction of William Foltz and James Scott, to whom I am deeply indebted for the judicious mix of support and patience with which they guided the dissertation to its completion. In addition, Bill Foltz generously made available a series of research assistantships that pulled me through lean times while allowing me to continue my own work. I am also grateful to both for their continued interest in the development of the project.

In scholarly research, as in other walks of life, institutions matter. Research for the book was funded by the Human Sciences Research Council, the Institute of International Education, and the Yale Center for International and Area Studies. A grant from the African Studies Council at Yale University made a pre-dissertation visit to Zimbabwe possible, and post-dissertation visits were facilitated by the Program of African Studies at Northwestern University. Beyond the material base, the research would not have been possible without the ready and friendly assistance of the staff of the Seeley Mudd Library at Yale University, the Cory Historical Library of Rhodes University, and the Africana collection at Northwestern University. I am particularly grateful to the staff of the National Archives of Zimbabwe and of the Government Documents Collection at the University of Zimbabwe for their sustained and good-humored helpfulness.

A large number of Zimbabweans disrupted their schedules to accommodate my inquiries, in interviews and in conversations. In doing so, they deepened my appreciation of the fine texture of political life and history in Zimbabwe, and I thank them all. Some shared not only their experiences and ideas but also their personal archives. I would like to thank Nick Amin, John Barratt, Bruce Berry, Kathy Bond-Stewart, Derek Carlisle, Ben Cousins, Nick Hodgson, Jim Latham, Alistair MacKenzie, Stanley Morris, Victor Machingaidze, James Murombedzi, Hostes Nicolle, Brigid Willmore, and Bob Woollacott. My greatest debt in Zimbabwe is to Jill Bleakley, who not only shared her lodgings, her car, and her own research work in Chinamora and Mount Darwin communal lands, but gave time and interest to my project far beyond the call of friendship. Without her help the fieldwork would have been far less fun and less productive.

In the course of transforming this work from a long and empirically detailed dissertation into a more streamlined interpretative essay, several colleagues and friends generously gave up time to read all or parts of it in draft form. Interpretation being what it is, none will be fully satisfied with the result, and our arguments will no doubt continue. Without implicating anyone, I would like to thank Leslie Bessant, Jill Bleakley, Bill Freund, Jane Guyer, Norma Kriger, Chris Lowe, Victor Machingaidze, Kathryn Oberdeck, Adolph Reed, Akbar Virmani, Louis Warren, and Professor Crawford Young. I have both enjoyed and profited enormously from long discussions, over several years, with Leslie Bessant and Jane Guyer that have shaped my ideas on colonial Zimbabwe and African development. An anonymous reader for Ohio University

Press offered incisive and helpful comments that forced me to clarify some central points of the argument.

More broadly, I have benefited enormously from the moral support, intellectual camaraderie, and encouragement of a group of friends who, in the age of e-mail, must, I suppose, count as a "network." In many conversations, over food and drink, they have helped me to clarify my ideas, to do good social science, and to keep writing in trying times. This group includes Fred Bartol, Micaela di Leonardo, Jacqueline Dirks, Chris Lowe, Cecelia Lynch, Kathryn Oberdeck, Leslie Reagan, Adolph Reed, Daniel Schneider, and Subir Sinha. It would be difficult to exaggerate my debt to Kathryn Oberdeck, who has lived uncomplainingly with this manuscript for far too long. Not only did she put aside her own prodigious workload to read an embarrassing number of drafts, but she allowed the manuscript to overflow into all corners of our household without losing her sense of humor. I look forward to returning the favor.

One could not ask for a more supportive environment in which to complete a book than the Program of African Studies at Northwestern University. I am particularly grateful to Roseann Mark and Akbar Virmani for their warm friendship and unfailing good humor. Jill Nystrom, Alyce Smith, and Derwin Munroe helped with the final preparation of the manuscript. I would also like to thank Gillian Berchowitz, senior editor at Ohio University Press, for steering the book through the complexities of acceptance, revision, and production in a humane, considerate, and supportive way.

My parents have shown unstinting faith in all my endeavors, and supported this one enthusiastically. My father died during the field research. It is an honor to dedicate the book to his memory and to my mother.

Acronyms

ADA	Agricultural Development Authority
ADF	African Development Fund
AFC	Agricultural Finance Corporation
Agritex	Department of Agricultural, Technical and Extension Services
CAMPFIRE	Communal Areas Management Programme for Indigenous Resources
CIO	Central Intelligence Organisation
CMB	Cotton Marketing Board
CNC	Chief Native Commissioner
CONEX	Department of Conservation and Extension
CSO	Central Statistical Office
CYL	City Youth League
DA	District Administrator
DDF	District Development Fund
ESAP	economic structural adjustment program
FEPD	Finance, Economic Planning and Development
GMB	Grain Marketing Board
GOZ	Government of Zimbabwe

LAA	Land Apportionment Act of 1930
LHA	Land Husbandry Act
LDO	Land Development Officer
LGPO	Local Government Promotion Officer
MCCD	Ministry of Co-operative and Community Development
MCDWA	Ministry of Community Development and Women's Affairs
MLARR	Ministry of Lands, Agriculture and Rural Resettlement
MLGRUD	Ministry of Local Government, Rural and Urban Development
MYSC	Ministry of Youth, Sport and Culture
NAD	Native Affairs Department
NADA	*Native Affairs Department Annual*
NAZ	National Archives of Zimbabwe
NC	Native Commissioner
NFAZ	National Farmers' Association of Zimbabwe
NIC	Newly Industrializing Countries
NRB	Natural Resources Board
PF-ZAPU	Patriotic Front—Zimbabwe African People's Union
PSIP	Public Sector Investment Programme
PV	Protected Village
RF	Rhodesian Front
RO	Resettlement Officer
SIA	Secretary of Internal Affairs
TDG	Tribal Development Group
TILCOR	Tribal Trust Lands Development Corporation

TLA	Tribal Land Authority
TTL	Tribal Trust Land
UANC	United African National Council
UDI	Unilateral Declaration of Independence
UFP	United Federal Party
UNEP	United Nations Environmental Program
VCW	Village Community Worker
VHW	Village Health Worker
VIDCO	Village Development Committee
VIDEC	Village Development Center
WADCO	Ward Development Committee
ZANLA	Zimbabwe African National Liberation Army
ZANU(PF)	Zimbabwe African National Union (Patriotic Front)
ZIPRA	Zimbabwe People's Revolutionary Army

ZIMBABWE

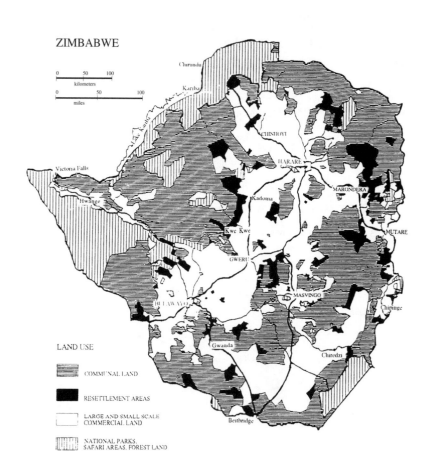

0   50   100
kilometers

0   50   100
miles

Chirundu

Kariba

CHINHOYI

Victoria Falls

HARARE

MARONDERA

Hwange

Kadoma

Kwe Kwe

MUTARE

GWERU

BULAWAYO

MASVINGO

Chipinge

Gwanda

Chiredzi

Beitbridge

LAND USE

COMMUNAL LAND

RESETTLEMENT AREAS

LARGE AND SMALL SCALE
COMMERCIAL LAND

NATIONAL PARKS,
SAFARI AREAS, FOREST LAND

Introduction

The consolidation of nation-states has been one of the most dramatic themes of twentieth-century political history. The politics of "nation building," in which political leaders set out to extend the authority of the national state over territorially defined populations of citizens, gained particular prominence in the era of African decolonization and Latin American revolutionary struggles during the 1950s and 1960s. In a postcolonial world, democracy and development were secured as the key desiderata of political progress in emerging nation-states —though with widely varying ideological inflections and widely varied results. Since the end of the Cold War and the collapse of authoritarian regimes around the world in the late 1980s, the question of citizenship and nationality has been reinvigorated, as fragile new democracies have sought to recast and secure new foundations of political authority.

This new urgency has also been felt in agrarian localities in Africa, Asia, and Latin America, where extended economic crises or environmental decline have fueled endemic rural violence or spawned agrarian social movements that draw heavily on rhetorics of community, citizenship, and tradition. As struggles over rural livelihoods and resources have intensified, patterns of partial proletarianization have made it clear that small-scale agrarian production is not a passing historical phase: in various parts of the world, large rural populations drawing their living at least partly from the land are here for the long run and will play a significant role in shaping national polities and state power. The new farmers' movements that emerged in India in the late 1970s and early 1980s, for instance, have developed a rhetoric that explicitly challenges state authority from a standpoint of "peasant popular culture." In Chiapas, Mexico, leaders of the recent Zapatista rebellion demanded: "What sort of citizens does the government take indigenous Chiapanecans to be? Are they 'citizens in formation'? Does the government still treat them as little children, as 'adults in formation'?"[1] In short, these movements emphasize that if nationality is to be a serious conduit of the relationship between a state and its citizens, rural voices must be heeded. Contrary to the conventional thrust of development theory, agrarian struggles over citizenship and popular allegiance to the state occupy a growing rather than diminishing place on the national landscape of many developing countries. In such cases, states must negotiate the contours of citizenship with their rural populations.

This situation is especially formidable in contemporary Africa, where weak yet authoritarian states and ruling elites appear to perch precariously atop agrarian societies composed primarily of poorly educated and self-provisioning peasants. Yet many analysts of African political development would insist that agrarian citizenship and state authority are not significant issues in African state politics. The thoroughgoing failure of most postcolonial African governments to carry out sustained nation building, or to extend state authority in the countryside, suggests that popular allegiance to the state is of no concern to African political leaders precccupied with personal rule, private enrichment, or ethnic oppression. African regimes are commonly perceived as the principal culprits of conflict and decline, and as "basically untouched by the pursuit of various political visions, especially those of development and democracy."[2] However, students of African political development have been unable to agree on the effective reach of African states, and the extent to which agrarian decline in Africa has resulted from elite political will, state incapacities, or the dogged autonomy and resistance of peasant populations. Their challenge has been to explain how African states could appear *both* as domineering and authoritarian *and* as ineffective, rickety, and porous—"lame leviathans" that appear, to paraphrase Peter Evans, as both too "embedded" (in their ethnic, prebendal, or clientelist character) and too "autonomous" (in the sense of "floating above society").[3]

The main aim of this book is to resolve this conundrum by returning the problem of state-based public authority, as an integral component of the raison d'état of modern political organization, to the center of our understanding of African political development. It is only through a close historical analysis of what states and citizens *have* had to say to each other (and how they have said it) that we can better understand the contours of contemporary state power and properly assess the ways in which African states have been touched by political visions, including those of democracy and development. I argue that in rural Africa, as elsewhere, control of social life has to be negotiated between state agencies and rural citizens in ways that make dualistic conceptions of domination and resistance inadequate. These negotiations involve conflicts over the nature of citizenship and participation in the national polity, which are not conflicts for control of state power but conflicts over the extent and character of legitimate state intrusions in the organization of rural social life. In this book I develop a sociology of state construction that shows how the dynamics of these negotiations interact with the managerial logics of centralizing states to shape the contours of state power and the prospects of political development in agrarian settings.

The extended exploration of state formation in Zimbabwe that forms the bulk of the book shows that state formation, in colonial and postcolonial contexts, involves efforts by rulers not only to rule effectively and sustainably, but also to construct a state, in the sense of securing the overriding public authority of state institutions that manage the sociopolitical order. To do so, rulers try to establish the state as the final arbiter of social and political authority by establishing state control over the distribution of public goods (thereby undermining alternative authority sources), and by controlling the social definition of what counts as a public good (thereby delimiting social expectations of state responsibilities and material outlays for social welfare). These efforts lie at the core of the politics of state-making. The strategies that state agents employ engage what Gramsci calls "the sphere of hegemony and ethico-political relations," through which regimes seek to maintain the sustainable balance of control and consent that lies at the heart of modern state power.[4] They show that in modern politics, domination and resistance are not zero-sum options. It is the dual, and often contradictory, imperatives of domination and incorporation, of control and consent, that provide the analytical key to the politics of state formation from which contemporary African states have emerged.

At first blush, this argument seems counterintuitive. In many cases, the main interest of Third World governments in poor or marginalized rural populations is to keep them socially stable and politically quiescent at the lowest possible cost. To do so, they can—and often do—deploy the coercive apparatuses of the state. But this is a costly and often risky strategy that few postcolonial governments have the political will or capacity to carry out systematically, exclusively, or interminably. Governments recognize the importance of containing social struggle and resistance within the ambit of state authority, and they therefore seek noncoercive strategies to stabilize rural populations and to overcome centrifugal political forces. Several scholars have noted that "development" policies play a central role in such stabilizing strategies. They do so not only by structuring the economic and social opportunities of rural citizens, but also by casting public policies in a technocratic, politically neutral language that privileges ideas of technical expertise and promotes a generalized conception of social improvement. In effect, they depoliticize public policies.[5]

But such strategies go beyond social stabilization. They rest ultimately on a tension between the constraints they place on social actors and the social actions they enable those actors to undertake. When a state sets out through rural development policies to manage the technical and social arrangements for production in agrarian communities, it disrupts local institutions of social security and risk management and thereby becomes the focus of civic responsibility. Since this responsibility carries potential economic costs and political dangers, state agents try to mediate it by defining the limits of legitimate and appropriate state interventions in social life. For instance, when governments change land rights they can radically disrupt the social institutions of agrarian communities. Unless they are willing or able to ram these measures through by authoritarian means, they must present them to rural citizens in terms that invoke the social good.[6] Frequently they try to do both. In the context of developing states, therefore, development is an inherently political process that both lays out measures whereby the state manages society and invokes a normative framework for such actions that connects public goods and social provision to community membership. In as much as they provide the conduits for negotiating control of social life, these strategies are key components of state construction.

These negotiations reveal the moral economy of the state.

In using this term, I draw on the work of E. P. Thompson and James Scott, who have used it to illuminate the culture and politics of social groups at the fringes of (and often against) the state. For these writers, the moral economy underwrites locally understood concepts of property rights, community membership, and the social good (or right) that make agrarian communities resilient in the face of environmental or political stress. Thompson notes that "at the interface of law and agrarian praxis stands custom." By this he means *local* custom —as "ambience, *mentalité*, and as a whole vocabulary of discourse, of legitimation and of expectation." For Scott, the moral economy resides in the close intertwining of the social and the technical arrangements of production that inform a panoply of relations of social obligation and reciprocity.[7] Both writers focus on the impact of expanding capitalist markets on these community norms and expectations. Here I argue that, in the context of social change and state formation in Africa, this perspective can be reversed and applied to the state and its practitioners as well as to popular classes. The practices of state agents assume a general understanding of state authority, a kind of common wisdom of norms and expectations that inhere in what it means to be a state; but the processes of state formation involve the creation of such a wisdom. Most broadly, the transformation of local moral economies by the establishment of market-based national states requires the entrenchment of a wider, more incorporative public realm for which the state itself provides the moral, political, and institutional hub. State authority must be constructed in laying down forms or traditions of social control and management that are understood either as not coercive or as appropriate to the exercise of state power.

There is a burgeoning literature in comparative historical sociology that views the establishment and maintenance of rule as a protracted cultural process as well as a quotidian political process. This trend is in part a response to the explosion of resistance studies during the 1980s, which not only explored the prevalence of "everyday" forms of resistance but declared the capacity of subaltern classes to be the subjects of their own history.[8] Drawing on Foucaultian interpretations of power and Gramscian interpretations of hegemony, this literature has focused on capillary negotiations over domination, identity, and culture; as Lynn Hunt notes in her study of revolutionary France, "governing cannot take place without stories, signs and symbols that convey and reaffirm the legitimacy of governing in thousands of unspoken ways."[9] Such work reminds us forcefully of the need to recognize the active participation of rural populations in political arguments over public authority. Still, in pre-occupations with long-term cultural change or everyday struggles over meaning, the institutional role and identity of the state itself has remained a perplexing problem. If we are to make full sense of the politics of state construction, we must also take account of the institutional, ideological, and political characteristics of the modern state form that profoundly shape the ways in which rulers try to rule effectively. As I argue in greater detail in chapter 1, state formation occurs not only in arenas of "political struggles and discourses" but in the construction, legitimation, and implementation of policies through which states try to shape the social order.

To address the problem of authority, governments set out to structure and define the public realm by structuring and defining the overriding social conceptions of right, rights, and membership that underwrite citizenship. At the same time, states try to control the parameters of this expanded public realm. Such a process of transformation is by nature a political process, characterized by clashing claims and conflicting interests, and never determinate. As David Held points out, "If citizenship involves the struggle for membership and participation in the community, then its analysis involves examining the way in which different groups, classes and movements struggle to gain degrees of autonomy and control over their lives in the face of various forms of stratification, hierarchy and political oppression."[10] African states, occupying a peculiarly uncomfortable (neocolonial) nexus between logics of domination and accumulation, have had to negotiate with their populations the specific conditions of social management and political incorporation within the constraints of national and international economic structures. Such negotiations have been particularly difficult because they both require and presuppose a common political language in which the interventions of the state in social life can be negotiated and legitimated. As such they concentrate the minds of policymakers, politicians, and administrators on the political problem of social control and consent.[11] A state's capacity to resolve this tension affects its capacity to provide consistent administration, to gather and to distribute revenues, to regulate national markets effectively, and even to operate a system of law. It is, broadly speaking, the problem of governance. While it engages the multivalent relations between the state, markets, and civil society, its crux lies in the processes—historically tortuous and often politically betrayed—of constructing state authority. At the same time, as the Zimbabwe case shows, the purposive rationality of the state is not monolithic. Different agencies within the state and government may advance alternative strategies and visions of state building, which make it more difficult to negotiate legitimate state interventions in rural social life.

Chapter 1 provides a detailed explication of this analytical perspective. The chapters that follow explore the mechanisms and techniques through which states pursue hegemonic strategies by tracing them in the making of contemporary Zimbabwe. Zimbabwe does not fit the general model of a stagnant agrarian economy dominated by predatory state elites. It has a rich agricultural base, a well-developed infrastructure, and a diversifying industrial sector. Agriculture ranks third (at 15%) behind services (48%) and manufacturing (30%) in terms of contribution to GDP. But Zimbabwe does demonstrate how relations between the state and agrarian populations shape state formation even in an industrializing and urbanizing economy. Its growing industrial base notwithstanding, Zimbabwe's population is largely rural and will remain so for many years; its rate of urbanization (28.5% in 1990) is no more than average among African and Asian countries. The economy is externally oriented, dominated by old-colonial and foreign capital, and vulnerable to fluctuations in the world price of commodities that hamper economic growth and industrial employment. The unemployment rate is chronically high, estimated by the government in 1988 at some 30 percent of the total labor force. The agricultural sector still reflects the colonial division between a large-scale farming sector dominated by whites who occupy the best farmland, and a small-scale sector where the majority of Zimbabwe's population lives under conditions of traditional or "communal" tenure. In the context of these macroeconomic structures, the populations in the latter sector hold the key to Zimbabwe's political development trajectory.

The small-scale agrarian population occupies 42 percent of the land, much of which is ecologically fragile and subject to increasing land pressure, environmental stress, and frequent drought. But it is not characterized by a relatively homogeneous class of peasant smallholders closely associated with individual plots of land that they work. Postindependence development produced a "peasant miracle" of rapidly expanding production levels. Marketed produce from the communal sector increased from about 10 percent of total production in 1980 to over 50 percent in 1990. Although the large-scale sector still dominates the major cash crops of tobacco (Zimbabwe's principal export commodity) and sugar, communal farmers now produce more cotton and about as much maize, the staple food crop, as the large-scale sector. Nevertheless, this "miracle" excluded the vast majority of communal land dwellers. The rural population is socioeconomically stratified, both on agro-ecological lines, and on interlocking indices of class, gender, age, and lineage that shape patterns of productivity and land access. The urban and rural economies are integrally linked by patterns of migrant labor in which the more productive small-scale farmers tend to draw also on income from migrant remittances. This distribution of agrarian resources undermines food security, especially for the rural and urban poor. Economic downturns, whether occasioned by commodity prices or by periodic drought, have severe effects on local incomes and consumption markets, especially if job creation slows. Dependent on both commodity production and commodity consumption, the rural poor—who are often women, youths, or holders of marginal land—experience a "reproduction squeeze." As rural incomes tighten, fault lines of social conflict in agrarian social relations deepen, putting pressure not only on household and community relationships but also on the ability of the state to manage these populations according to its own political and economic objectives. The provision of hunger relief is a regular demand on the public fiscus. Macroeconomic liberalization exacerbates such tendencies. Consequently, the social economy continues to fluctuate with the fortunes of agricultural production. The structure of agrarian relations and access to productive land thus remains the fulcrum of national political development in Zimbabwe today.

Similar patterns are not uncommon in other developing areas. Even in more highly urbanized parts of Latin America, rural regions have become an expanding "refuge sector for surplus population," despite increasing integration in the labor market and growing pressure on natural resources. In these cases, as the Mexican government discovered so dramatically in Chiapas, changing structures of land access, land use, and food distribution are crucial not only to the organization of agrarian production and the moral economy of agrarian life but also to the ability of states to manage social conflicts and to exercise social control. Even in so-called New Agricultural Countries such as Brazil the existence of a marginalized rural population that can only be sporadically and partially absorbed in urban employment has spawned agrarian-based social movements—such as the landless workers' movement—that pose significant challenges to the authority of the state.[12] Zimbabwe, like other African countries, differs from these cases in the greater role that agriculture plays in the economy and in the livelihoods of the population. But it poses strikingly similar political challenges to the ability of the state to establish rural hegemony. An analysis of rural state formation in Zimbabwe shows that if one is to understand the politics of citizenship in contemporary agrarian settings it is necessary to ask not only why many countries are unable to feed significant portions of their population consistently (a question that has preoccupied development policy analysts) but also how regimes and citizens have negotiated institutions of risk management and social security to secure their respective survivals.

The argument in this book therefore focuses mainly on the political logics and imperatives of the centralizing state. Specifically, it examines the design and implementation of conservation and community development policies through which state agents have sought to shape and manage rural social life in Zimbabwe since early in the colonial period. In colonial development thinking, resource management was inextricable from state efforts to manage rural communities and to regulate their position within the emerging capitalist social order. Colonial governments implemented policies in the name of conservation—such as centralization of villages and adjustment of land rights—to extend state control over peasant populations. Such policies evoked enormous peasant resistance and created a vast reservoir of support for the nationalist cause in the 1950s and 1960s. During the liberation war of the 1970s, and even in subsequent years, anticonservationism was a powerful idiom of rural resistance to the state. Community development policy was conceived in the late 1950s, and implemented by the Rhodesian Front government in the early 1960s, as a strategy to shift accountability away from the state and to press the responsibility for social stability and development onto rural communities through self-help. Nationalists denounced these policy initiatives as attempts to impose a form of apartheid, and used them during the liberation war to orchestrate rural resistance. Students of Zimbabwe's political history, in turn, have viewed them as the political mechanisms of authoritarian colonial domination. Remarkably, however, the postindependence government—whose social base, ideology, and political objectives are very different from those of its colonial predecessor—reasserted "conservation of natural resources" and "community development" as the dominant idioms of rural control and development. Its development policies have resonated markedly with development ideas of the 1950s and 1960s, even while the government has vigorously asserted its political independence from the interests of settler capitalism and stressed its adherence to a development strategy sensitive to the interests of rural citizens.[13]

This continuity can be viewed as evidence of the enduring disdain for development and democracy that characterizes many postcolonial African regimes. Such a reading would be in accord with recent scholarship that traces such disdain to the institutional and ideological legacy of colonial authoritarianism.[14] But it would not do justice to the fragmented and contradictory politics of state formation from which the Zimbabwe state has emerged. An analysis of state construction shows that colonial land reform was not only a mechanism of social control, but also an attempt to reorient public authority in the countryside. And community development was not only an effort to abdicate state responsibilities for rural development, but also a deliberate effort by the colonial state to reshape the social and political identities of peasants. In short, they were efforts to embed specific conceptions of state authority in the countryside. Postindependence policy continuities reflect the same dynamics. Like other African ruling parties at independence, Robert Mugabe's ZANU(PF) acceded to power with a brief to undertake the massive challenges of national development and nation building. The new regime was eager to represent—and be seen to represent—a distinctive new national political order. To do so, it needed to restructure the balance of control and consent in state-society relations, and to inculcate a new state ideology that would represent and legitimate this new political order. In particular, it sought to demonstrate a clean break with the old colonial relations of power, provide a framework for political and economic development strategies, and mobilize popular support for both state and party as the legitimate political embodiment of the new national polity. But the survival of colonial state, economic, and property structures—most notably the division of land between large-scale commercial farming and the peasant communal sector mandated by the Lancaster House independence agreement—constrained the government's development intentions and activities, and therefore also complicated such legitimation.

In effect, Zimbabwe's ZANU(PF), like other nationalist African regimes, found that wielding state power did not mean dominating civil society. Indeed, political leaders found that the postcolonial state itself must rationalize, extend, and legitimate the political order in the face not only of a structural bias toward world markets, but also of rural populations whose political sensibilities had been forged in antagonism to the state. These conditions placed a premium for the emergent leadership not only on political control and social stability, but also on political allegiance. Unwilling to tamper with the entrenched structures of the economy, the new leaders recognized the need to fulfill wartime promises—of land, liberation, and education—made to rural communities. In effect, they faced a dual legitimation challenge: not only did they have to legitimate the new government as incumbents of the independent state, they also had to legitimate the state itself as the overriding locus of political authority in society. As in other emergent African countries, therefore, the Zimbabwe government was eager to secure forms of political authority in the countryside that would incorporate rural communities effectively into the nationally defined polity and economy. In short, it had to negotiate the contours of citizenship with the population.

Without a fuller historical understanding of these efforts, both before and after independence, we cannot properly assess the legacy of colonial authoritarianism and the postindependence regime's relationship to it. By tracing continuity and change in development policies, the chapters that follow map the historical and political terrain on which the politics of citizenship has been negotiated in Zimbabwe. They show that the historical importance of conservation and community development policies in the political development of Zimbabwe was threefold. First, they were strategies for structuring the participation of rural Africans in national labor and agricultural commodity markets. Second, they were attempts to define and structure the participation of rural Africans in the polity. Third, they established the political terrain on which struggles for control of rural social life were fought out between peasants (and peasant communities) and state agents. As pursued by successive governments, these strategies represented repeated efforts to penetrate, structure, and indeed define rural communities. As such, they were attempts to manage not only the relations of peasant communities to state institutions but also social relations within the peasant sector. Each strategy prepared the sociopolitical foundations of the next, and each was devised as a reaction to its predecessor.

Thus, conservation and community development policies, before and after independence, provided a contradictory blend of coercive and legitimating political practices. Through these practices state agencies tried to penetrate and define rural communities in ways that would establish a foothold for state authority in local power structures but also mediate state accountability and responsibility for controls on rural social life. Each policy initiative advanced a distinct, though related, ideology of progress that linked state authority to modernity. These efforts engage the most profound conundrum of postcolonial state construction: the separation of state and society is necessary to secure the overarching authority of the state, but such separation can only be institutionalized on the basis of a common ground of political argument, a normative language of state power and nationality that secures the state as the final arbiter of social order and the public good. Consequently, the separation of state and society rests on the delineation and construction of links between state and society. We cannot make proper sense of political power and development in Africa today without trying to understand regime attempts to secure state authority and to forge national conceptions of citizenship. Such attempts are especially apparent in the ways that the state in Zimbabwe set out over time to define and arbitrate rural land rights and property regimes: under the 1951 Land Husbandry Act as vested in individuals; under Rhodesian Front community development as vested in communities; under ZANU(PF) national-populism as vested in the state. Behind it all was a quest to define for rural Zimbabweans what it would (and should) mean to be a citizen.

Conflicts over public authority are of course significantly shaped by regional variations in ecology, economy, or culture. In Zimbabwe, the peculiarities of resource management politics vary across cattle farming, high land pressure, irrigated and resettlement areas, thereby adding their own specific dynamics to local interactions with the state. So do the different migrancy rates between remote areas in the Zambezi valley and areas with easier access to urban employment. Certainly, the politics of state construction looks different from distinct regional or social vantage points. This point is most dramatically illustrated by the postindependence regime's brutal campaign of terror against rural populations in the western provinces of Matabeleland and the Midlands (strongholds of the opposition nationalist PF-ZAPU party) between 1982 and 1987. This sustained campaign of state-sponsored violence aimed ostensibly to crush an outbreak of antinational dissidence that threatened the fragile nation-statehood of Zimbabwe. But as an action carried out by Shona-speaking ZANU(PF) forces against Ndebele-speaking PF-ZAPU supporters it bore significant ethnic inflections and was an obvious attempt to crush ZAPU. As such it challenges the very notion of a national hegemonic project by invoking the abiding problem of ethnicity in African politics.

But the ethnic core of politics cannot be assumed. Indeed, the Matabeleland security situation casts important analytical light on several aspects of the politics of state construction, which it is useful to mention here. First, it reminds us that hegemony and oppression are not mutually exclusive options or processes. The ability of the government to crush Ndebele-speaking opponents meant neither that it had the residual support of Shona-speaking citizens nor that it could use the same techniques in other parts of rural Zimbabwe. The political roots of the Matabeleland violence are complex (I take them up briefly in chapter 6). But when placed in relationship to other patterns of political violence—including widespread party and generational intimidation at the local level, electoral violence, and struggles over control of resources that were not confined to Matabeleland—it is clear that they did not lie principally in long-standing ethnic rivalries or in the imperatives of ethnic domination. Like other fledgling nationalist parties, ZANU(PF) came to power unsure of its social base. This uncertainty was compounded by the regional strength of its nationalist rival, ZAPU, as well as by South Africa's predilection for destabilizing its neighbors. The government responded to the outbreak of dissidence in 1982 with a "crush and co-opt" strategy through which it hoped to both take control of the national polity and lay the groundwork for a one-party state. While this strategy had the ironic effect of hardening oppositional ethnic sensibilities in ways that are likely to mark Zimbabwean politics for generations to come, its roots lie firmly in the imperatives of regime consolidation. In this light, the Matabeleland situation alone could not define the politics of state formation. Rather, it points toward a broader panoply of potential threats to regime power that reached beyond ethnicity and included traditional authorities, disillusioned youths, and persistent colonial influences within the state apparatus. It was one part of the larger problem of sovereignty.

Second, although the politics of regime consolidation and the politics of state construction are closely associated, they are analytically distinct. Politically insecure regimes always face a tension between sustaining political alliances that keep them in power and shaping national identities. The authoritarian and ethnicizing propensities of the postindependence regime therefore reveal a crucial element of state power in contemporary Zimbabwe, just as racial domination did in the colonial period. But they do not negate the broader quest for agrarian hegemony through which successive regimes sought to structure state-society relations. Indeed, by the end of the 1980s, there were signs in Matabeleland that debates over public authority were predicated on some form of national identity, and that "the most prominent contradictions in society [were] increasingly between democracy and misuse of power and between the different needs and interests of larger groups within the population, rather than between the regionally based 'traditional' power bases of nationalist politicians."[15] In effect, debates over the *use* of legitimate power are not the same as debates over the norms and expectations that establish the realm of legitimacy.

Third, the intricacies and flexibilities of local politics cannot tell the whole story of state making, especially since charges of "top-down" development are among those most consistently leveled against postcolonial states. Local and ethnographic studies have made an enormous contribution to our understanding of agrarian change and popular resistance in Zimbabwe. Inasmuch as these processes constitute what Sara Berry calls the 'inconclusive encounters' that characterize interactions between African states and agrarian populations, they play a critical role in state formation. But local studies of these encounters cannot readily reveal the broader imperatives of state and the larger historical logics of stateness that have shaped the trajectory of political development in modern Africa. Where public authority is at stake, local arguments and conflicts must be linked to centralized arguments of state. In colonial and postcolonial Africa, state policies have been shaped by institutional incoherence and intellectual contradictions as well as considerations of power, domination, and allegiance even before they reach the local level. The bifurcations of state power between urban and rural, civil and customary, central and tribal, that Mahmood Mamdani has analyzed so provocatively, were never static or systematic. They were always in dialectical tension. The center was always to be found in the local. To explain the persistence of weak but authoritarian regimes more effectively, we need first to lay out the logics that provide the framework for local arguments about public authority and citizenship. Thus, it is important to break the prevalent dichotomy between the study of the central state (which tends to focus on the central institutions of rule and dominant social groups) and the study of local politics (in which the central state tends to appear as an overarching and monolithic predatory force).

It is to expose these dynamics of state construction that I have set out to tell a different tale from one that local ethnographies are able to tell.[16] My aim in shifting analytical focus to the state-making imperatives and politics of the centralizing state is to expose the roots and the effects of these state logics on African political development. To start with the state is not to deny that the politics of state construction looks different from different regional or social vantage points. But it is to recognize the importance of national-level sociological processes whose prospects are determined at the local level. Certainly, the politics of citizenship in the rural hamlets of Matabeleland acquired different layers of meaning than those in the land resettlement schemes of Marondera district, or those in the chambers of parliamentary debate in downtown Harare. But in all these locations, the meaning of citizenship and legitimate public authority lay at the heart of politics. All bring different perspectives to the politics of state formation.

The shifting and fractured moral economy of state construction that I trace in this book brings political economy and political argument together to reveal repeated state efforts to remoralize state-peasant relations. It shows that terrains of argument were not only ideological; they were deeply rooted in the material realities of agrarian life and in the dynamics of accumulation at both the national and local levels. These political-ideological strategies cannot be properly understood outside of a structural context of class formation. The vision of a stable yeoman producer class that inspired rural development strategies both before and after independence was a fundamentally class-bound vision and regime attempts to structure state-society relations consistently bore the stamp of politically dominant class interests. At the same time, regime efforts to structure social relations within the peasantry aimed specifically to achieve a particular class outcome—the "class of African 'peasant farmers'" projected in the 1951 Land Husbandry Act. This class orientation created serious political tensions in state-peasant relations. At the local level, a development strategy based on managed class formation required the government to address the social effects of uneven patterns of commodity production (by region, household, and gender) under skewed and stringently limited land holdings. Development policy had to provide security for the rural poor—mainly youths and women—while promoting the interests of middle peasants. Such strategies inevitably engaged community-level social conflicts over income, land access, and gender authority, to which the state had little access.

A growing body of research in Zimbabwe explores state politics, agrarian control, and socioeconomic differentiation within the peasantry. Rural political economists have explored the complexities of changing agrarian structures in which individual farming decisions, patterns of accumulation, and labor management strategies are shaped by variations in access to migrant remittances and urban employment. While the communal property regime continues to secure land for most people, the majority of rural households—particularly relatively young households and those headed by females—

feel the combined effects of land pressure, environmental decline, drought, and unemployment keenly. Patterns of social differentiation are complicated by categories of age, gender, and lineage as well as class or region. As stress on youths and the rural poor has increased, so has the pressure on the state to stabilize the countryside. In addressing this issue, most analyses of rural state politics have focused on the impact of the state on agrarian change, generally through agricultural policy or through the political activities of the ruling party.[17] None considers the impact of agrarian change on state construction, or shows how these fault lines of incipient social conflict have been engaged in the negotiation of public authority and the politics of state construction. It is only when one does so that the importance of these social groups in the structuring of state-society relations can be clarified.

In setting out to explicate these links, I have drawn on an artificial, but heuristically useful, distinction between "agrarian" and "nonagrarian" development policies. In postindependence Zimbabwe, agrarian policies, which addressed agricultural productivity, set out to structure land access, use, and tenure. Based on state-sponsored land resettlement and villagization schemes, they maintained the management of communities as the focus of rural development initiatives. Nonagrarian policies addressed the quality of life of rural citizens by setting out to promote community development. They stressed the importance—and transformative capabilities—of self-reliance. Thus nonagrarian development strategies deemphasized state management of communities. Analysis of this dual approach to rural development shows how state-peasant relations engage not only issues of land and agriculture, or productivity and accumulation, but also definitions of social being, and they run through a variety of institutional forms. In a similar vein, I have retained the term *peasants*, despite the analytical imprecision it invites by lumping together a diverse and fractious population. While the peasantry incorporates a significant range of farming practices, objectives, and levels of productivity (both between and within communities) that differentiate peasant motivations and strategies, the category remains politically meaningful. It refers to a historically, juridically, and politically constructed social category: those people who live and farm in the communal areas of Zimbabwe. It informs the social memories that rural dwellers draw on to gauge their interactions with the state and to constitute their contemporary communities. It is understood and accepted in the everyday political language of Zimbabweans to reflect a distinct social group. It is part of the definition of rural citizenship.

This book is a study of processes rather than structures. My aim is not to trace the features of Zimbabwe state politics under structural adjustment, but to explain the genesis and entrenchment of institutional and ideological constraints on contemporary state formation. The analysis covers the first ten years of independence, and does not go beyond the government's adoption, in 1990, of an economic structural adjustment program (ESAP) underwritten by the World Bank. By the early 1990s, the economy was faltering and party, class, and state control of society all seemed precarious. Against a background of growing external capitalist domination, burgeoning elite corruption, and a tenuous state hegemony, the government became increasingly contradictory and authoritarian in its development policies. While the government adopted the ESAP, which dramatically boosted inflation and consumer prices, it sought to hold the peasantry by calling for increased aggression for land redistribution. But by the mid 1990s, the prospects of most Zimbabwean peasants, as producers and as citizens, appeared increasingly bleak.

The burden of my argument is that these prospects are best evaluated through a historical explanation of the politics of state making, in which state agents and rural citizens struggle over the control of social life in the countryside. In seeking systematic criteria for such an analysis, the book revisits colonial history at some length. It does so on the argument that changes in how regimes approach the project of rule are important, not because they create or follow path dependency in any strict sense but because they give authority and prominence to particular ideas and discourses and because they make particular institutional choices easier than others, especially for resource-poor governments. In Zimbabwe it is clear that social memories of colonial rule, and of the liberation war, have also deeply affected rural citizens' view of the postcolonial state. Indeed, they will use these memories to point out continuities in policy as they engage the state in negotiations over legitimacy. Thus, how political actors explain their actions is an important part of the political process. Such explanations are rooted not only in interests or cultures, but in political and institutional histories. The book sets out to illuminate the role of the state and state power in making those histories. The analysis moves back and forth between national political economy and rural political struggles in order to highlight the action of each upon the other and to explicate the dynamic relationship between state hegemony, rural politics, and agrarian productivity. Thus the essay is structured to reflect the links between history and political process in the making of the state.

Part One

HISTORY, POLITICS, AND THE STATE

In general, the temporality of periods of heightened *political* conflict and *political* mobilization is determined, in the *first* instance, not by the conditions of the local economy nor by cultural factors, but by the activity of all those institutions of government and political order, both legislative and executive, central and local, which in short we call the state.
—Gareth Stedman Jones, *Languages of Class*

1

State Construction and Moral Economy

Any account of state formation must begin with an account of the state. Given the complexities and variations of modern state structures, the problem of analyzing the location of the state within modern social formations remains a central problem of social and political theory. In particular, theorists argue over how to analyze causal relations between state actions, modes of social and economic organization, and historical political processes. But if we recognize that state actions have powerful causal effects on social relations and historical political processes, we need to be able to specify more clearly how the structural relationship between the state and society is sustained or restructured over time. In this chapter, I set out to resolve the tension between structure and process in state-society relations by focusing on state practice. By this I mean not only the actions of state agents but also the political and ideological logics that drive their actions and make them intelligible. Gianfranco Poggi argues that "[f]or all its structural complexity and the vastness and continuity of its operations, the modern state—like any other institutional complex—

3

resolves ultimately into social processes patterned by certain rules."[1] This perspective can be applied not only to the internal workings of the state but also to relations between state and society, for it implies that when state agents act they do so according to patterns of behavior that are socially understood and recognized as appropriate to the state.

Approached thus, state practices have two central logics. First, although state practices involve an enormous variety of frequently contradictory activities, they draw their authority from social conventions that define the location of the state in the social order. By authorizing the state, these social conventions also specify the nature of citizenship as a peculiarly modern form of political identity associated with the nation-state.[2] State actions assume state hegemony. Second, state actions promote the peculiar purposive logics of modern political domination. These logics, which I outline in this chapter, can be usefully characterized in terms of three analytical categories within the parameters of a particular national mode of economic organization: the generation of revenue, the management of society, and the accomplishment of allegiance.

Conceiving of state practice in terms of these logics helps us to better understand the policies that the following chapters analyze, for state practices are realized, in everyday ways, in the design and implementation of state policies that provide the most important conduits of state-society relations. These policies, in turn, help us to understand the politics of state formation. In this chapter, I argue that this conception of state practice also provides a starting point for substantiating the moral economy of the state, for it locates state authority at the core of state practices. The political negotiations over state authority that infuse state practice, and lie at the heart of this book, are the motor that drive the dynamic historical relationship between political economy and political argument that defines the moral economy of the state. My argument proceeds cumulatively in five parts that focus, throughout, on emerging states in modern agrarian, and particularly African, settings. The first part sketches the modern state's distinctive features. The second and third parts explicate the twin logics of state practice sketched above. The fourth places these logics in the historical context of African nationalism. The fifth explains the moral economy of the state in the context of African agrarian development.

The State and Modernity

In modern social formations the state is the principal institutional locus of political power.[3] Modern states typically have particular defining characteristics, including a centralized administration, security apparatus, and judiciary. The state bureaucracy comprises a complex ensemble of organizations, each with its own distinctive tasks, but all operating according to both the dictates of party power and regular bureaucratic rules. The state is seen as the legitimate provider of specified political goods, over which it has sole and universal jurisdiction, on the basis of a national collectivity. It seeks revenue on the same basis. This state also draws on the ideological and normative postulations of territoriality, nationality, and sovereignty.[4] The capacity of modern states to exercise effective control over social life is fundamental to their character as states. On this basis a set of institutional administrative and legal relations are brought into being that establish a separation between state and civil society that is critical to the exercise, and understanding, of state power in modern societies.

In developed countries, economic life and political life are understood as separate and civil society is developed, diverse, and highly institutionalized: relations of power are mediated by a plethora of social, cultural, economic, and political institutions—such as the family, church, schools, cultural and economic associations, and markets for goods and for labor. These institutions embody the forms, processes, and requirements that shape social reproduction. They not only establish the link between mode of domination and mode of production, but also constitute the link between state and society. These institutions are neither simply the conduits of political or economic power, as Althusser's formulation of "ideological state apparatuses" implies, nor are they simply the crucibles of freedom, individuality, and social justice, as some civil society theorists suggest. Liberal and marxist scholars alike have pointed out that the institutions of civil society are related to capitalist economies in complex, and often contradictory, ways. As John Keane has noted, it was the role of these institutions in modernization that provided the focus for the emergence of the nineteenth-century debates about the relationship between the state and civil society in modern social formations.[5] From these debates emerged the argument that in an essentially consensual social climate—that is, one in which institutionalized structures and processes of political power are not disputed, although control of them may be—the state can become universalized and come to express an authority that is socially understood as independent of ongoing political (class) struggles.

It is this idea of universality that gives modern state power its overarching authority and legitimacy, and separates the state from civil society. While arguments about the abuse of state power, and about the legitimate extent of state power are frequent in both political theory and everyday political debates, the concept of state power itself constitutes part of an accepted understanding of what states are. In this sense, the modern state has a historical meaning that is larger than its agglomerated institutions, their incumbents, or the social groups that dominate society through it. The authority of the state underpins relations of political domination, social control, accumulation, and property at the level of society: the state is socially *constituted* as the proper domain of politics, and in this sense plays a pivotal role in the historicity of particular societies. This constitution of the state, however, means that it cannot be the rational "actuality of the ethical Idea," as Hegel conceived it. States are rooted in the material bases of social power and, as Habermas points out, the quest for universality is a purposive political quest for legitimation, pursued through political-ideological processes.[6] Where the capacity of the state to establish a domain of universal authority or dominance over society is compromised or limited, state power is compromised.[7]

Stateness in Africa

In African countries, it seems clear, the ideological hegemony of this state form—imposed as part of the "organizational revolution"of colonialism—is at best far from secure. The power base of the state tends to be narrow. Social and political power is a shifting mixture of new and old forms of domination, status, and social control. State power, itself the subject of internal tensions and struggles, has to vie with preexisting idioms of sociopolitical organization for ideological dominance. The political process is largely constituted in diffuse and cross-cutting networks of patronage relations between political, economic, and social elite groups. Civil society is discrete and fragmented.[8] This does not mean that these states are weak, or that state institutions are marginal to the construction of historicity. Where politicians are able to stay in power, even by force, corruption, or murder, it is not compelling to call them weak. To the extent that states are able to generate revenues, to service the demands of political and economic elites, or to sustain a coercive apparatus, they are not weak. All states are able to tell their citizens what to do in at least some ways, and no states dominate their citizens entirely. States can continue without making extensive claims on civil society provided they can hold on to key resources of accumulation and coercion. In this light, S. N. Sangpam and Achille Mbembe argue that African states are neither dysfunctional nor weak, but that they are "overpoliticized" or based on systems of "improduction" through which they actually fulfill the ends of their peculiar political logics.[9]

Yet the establishment of modern state structures had an enormous impact on the processes and logics of African politics. With the establishment of the modern state form in Africa, the formal institutions of state authority became the principal channels through which political domination was exercised. Although relations of power and domination have widely taken on forms of patronage and clientelism, it is through these formal institutions that patronage is dispensed and social control is organized on a national basis. Colonial states were constructed institutionally—and, in the minds of administrators and settlers, ideologically—on the assumptions and premises of the modern European state. They were centralized and centralizing states which introduced a permanent coercive apparatus, a permanent bureaucracy, national taxation, codified law (albeit often applied in a rather haphazard fashion), and a unified and regulated market. They were also monetized and revenue-seeking states, founded upon a peculiar rationality of property, exchange, ownership, and administration.[10] They relied on the collection of revenues to sustain their own economic viability, and on their ability to extend management structures over the entire population to entrench their political viability.

Colonial administrations did not of course have democratic pretensions. Their first impulse was to establish control over a defined territory in order to facilitate the profitable extraction of natural resources. The political ideas and institutions of the modern state were carefully attenuated and tailored (often with the help of strong social Darwinist convictions that enjoyed vogue in Britain and the United States in the first decades of the twentieth century) to meet the requirements of colonial domination, extraction, and accumulation. The success with which they achieved these goals varied widely. But the institutional ensemble of the state provided a framework within which the normative postulations of territoriality, nationality, and sovereignty could be laid down at decolonization. These postulates underpinned the notions of citizenship and accountability which informed the nation building and development rhetoric of newly independent African states. They provide the political currency for the upsurge of appeals for democratization in recent years, for the repeated calls under military regimes for a return to constitutional civilian rule, and for the popular disaffection evoked by political or financial corruption within the state. Most importantly, they constitute the institutions of the state as the legitimate domain of political and legal authority. The ideological dimensions of the modern state form do thus exercise considerable political currency in African states. They are, as John Lonsdale puts it, "part of the moral calculus of power."[11]

Further, the modern state form played a key role in the construction of new epistemes of progress. Its ministries employed experts—botanists, ecologists, geologists (and later anthropologists)—to collect data, to map and survey and plan, so that the government could properly manage the environment.[12] The planners of Africa's political future, both within decolonizing powers and newly independent governments, all envisaged that the state would play the key managerial role in political development and nation building. The state was the symbol of the nation—the 'political kingdom' which, once gained, would provide. Moreover, under the conventional development wisdom of the day, planning, public investment and government regulation were regarded as the core principles of development, and crucial vehicles of progress.[13] For the decolonizing powers, participation in planning—along with aid financing—allowed them some say in the construction of postindependence institutions. For newly independent governments, it provided a sense of control over the process. And in general, planning and regulation placed technical expertise and scientific knowledge at the core of development discourses.

Given these institutional, ideological, and epistemological influences on political formations in contemporary Africa, how should we tackle the problem of analyzing African states? An influential body of recent literature stresses the structural separation of the state from society and privileges the role of the state as an autonomous actor in (and on) society.[14] In this view, the political demands of security and the domination or control of society are the quintessential raisons d'état. Using this approach, scholars have tried to measure state "strength" or "weakness," cast principally in terms of the degree of state autonomy from societal interests and state capacity to manage society. For some, these categories provide measures of stateness.[15] For instance, Thomas Callaghy's influential analysis of neopatrimonial state politics in Zaire characterized state-society relations as a struggle and argued that the aim of politics in such regimes is to secure a ruling group in a fragile polity. Focusing on the institutional structure of the Zairian state, Callaghy demonstrated its tendency toward caprice and bureaucratic coagulation at the center, and its ineffectiveness in the countryside, where local politics dominated and local notables ruled supreme. Thus he showed state power to be ambiguous, wavering between subordination to an authoritarian coalition on the one hand, and the political autonomy (and caprice) of a neopatrimonial ruling cabal on the other.[16]

This state-centered work demonstrated that the state-society separation must be taken seriously. But it cannot be taken at face value. Other scholars working in the same tradition have shown the value of understanding long-term economic ties between political officeholders and commercial elites, as well as the murky internal networks of "informal" politics and markets.[17] As Timothy Mitchell points out, a proper understanding of the state requires that we investigate *how* the state comes (or appears) to be autonomous. One of the principal paradoxes of African polities is that their state structures were externally imposed, yet "those modern techniques that make the state appear to be a separate entity that somehow stands outside society" have not yet been fully institutionalized.[18] To understand state formation in Africa it is necessary to understand the efforts of African regimes to deploy such techniques.

Assuming state autonomy without adequately addressing this dimension of state power has given rise to two methodological problems. The first is a failure to adequately conceptualize the links between the state and the social formation as a whole. To make sense of how the state is both separate from and part of the social formation, we have to take account of the "paradox of state and society" that arises, as Bob Jessop points out, from "the fact that the state is just one institutional ensemble among others within a social formation, but it is peculiarly charged with overall responsibility for maintaining the cohesion of the social formation of which it is a part."[19] This paradox has a political core, which has been marvelously articulated by flight lieutenant Jerry Rawlings, president of Ghana:

> People talk about capitalism as one mode of development and communism or socialism as another mode, but at least they're both on the move, using different paths. They have something in common, namely a certain level of social integrity, a certain national character, a demand for accountability. All of which is miss-

ing in most of the third world. But without it, your capitalism or your socialism, or whatever it is, isn't going to work.[20]

Here Rawlings highlights two central points about the state. First, the state as a historical entity is not definable separately from national modes of production and accumulation. Second, the state is not definable separately from ideas and traditions of accountability that constitute its historical links to society. The character of states is thus determined both by political economy and by political argument. The former establishes the structural relations between accumulation and domination. It is in the latter that relationships of domination and reproduction are ultimately fought out. It is in their efforts to bring these two dimensions of stateness together that the purposive logics of modern states can be traced.

The second problem with assuming state autonomy is a tendency to either advance a notion of the state as a monolithic political and ideological actor (as in the personal rule model) or to present the state as an arena in which conflicts between interest groups get worked out (as in neocorporatist and pluralist models). But, as Michael Mann has noted, the modern state is both actor and space.[21] Indeed, the term *state* today has two referents that are conceptually inseparable. The first is the modern unit of sociopolitical organization, allegiance, and identity associated with the nation-state, defined and bounded by its sovereign authority and by international territorial borders. The second is the set of institutions and their incumbents that administer, manage, and act on society within those boundaries. As a political actor the state is categorically distinct from the government, and, as Mann argues, can be disaggregated and disunited, even at odds within itself. But the term *state* is unavoidably aggregative; it provides an explanatory and legitimating umbrella for the actions of its various institutions and agents when they act *as the state*. To this extent the state presents a disaggregated unity that informs the actions of its agents and underwrites a unifying logic of state practice.

This logic of "disaggregated unity" suggests that state agents acting as the state draw on a particular set of authorizing assumptions. They assume that the authority of the rules and regulations whereby the state manages society underwrites their actions. They also assume an institutionalized quality of community membership that accords membership rights to citizens and constrains how they may be treated. Finally, they base their actions on the configuration of political power that informs the programmatic intentions of the regime (such as distribution of resources according to party support, ethnicity, etc.). These assumptions provide the explanatory and legitimating framework for state practices. They reveal that the state is not simply a discrete political actor in society with interests and actions defined by its autonomy, for they can contradict each other and create incoherence within the state. The logic of social management embodied in the state as a public institution and the interests of elites in sociopolitical domination are never hermetically congruent; nor is domination ever absolute. It is indeed in the interstices of state logic and political power that the character of the state must be sought.

These interstices specify the public realm, which is historically the realm of citizenship.[22] This realm can be understood to encompass both public institutions (the institutions of the res publica and the institutions attached to the *rechtstaat*, which embody the idea of the disinterested state) and public discourse (the realm of popular participation by voice). In the ill-formed agrarian social formations of postcolonial Africa, the state plays a central role in defining this sphere, but it does not always control it. It is for this reason that one cannot think about agricultural producers outside of "development" practices, institutions, and discourses. African agrarian producers are who they are today at least partly because of the particular patterns of agricultural modernization that have been implemented—albeit, in many cases, with a high degree of failure—throughout the twentieth century. In turn, "development," as it has come to African farmers, cannot be disarticulated from modes of accumulation and regulation that are both national and international in scale.

The authorizing assumptions that underwrite state practices indicate that state power rests not only in coercive capacity or in the influence of dominant social groups but also in political and ideological traditions of control and consent that are not socially fixed. At the level of the social formation the state underwrites relations of work and production, property, and domination. Consequently, the links between the state and society are multivalent and complex. They run not only through the regime and through the economy, but also through the institutions and discourses of the public sphere. In this light, the core problem of governance and state authority is how to incorporate people into a polity and economy in such a way that they accept the particular forms of political and legal authority that center on the state. Most broadly, governance depends on the diverse ways in which the various realms of civil society are made subject to the ultimate jurisdiction of the state through its legal and administrative institutions. This process occurs by historically determined patterns of force and persuasion. Critically, however, it engages the problem of making people into citizens. A proper historical understanding of the state thus requires that we reinterpret the term *state* to take account of the "moral calculus of state power" that defines the nature of citizenship.[23] As I argue in greater detail below, such a moral calculus requires the grounding of a theory of government, a normative language of state power and nationality, that secures the state as the final arbiter of social order and the public good.

Philip Corrigan and Derek Sayer show persuasively in their work on English state formation that the emergence of such a state-centered social order is a protracted and complex cultural process in which states attempt over time to define concepts of right, to regulate property rights, and to underwrite the nature and membership of communities. Thus, state formation involves extended political struggles to effect shifts in social consciousness. In England, for instance, capitalist relations of production came over time to be underwritten by the "enforced legitimacy" of private law and bourgeois property rights. But as Douglas Hay and others have shown, these transformations generate intense social conflicts by challenging popular moral conceptions of property that are permeated by cultural expectations of security and need. It may also take centuries, Corrigan and Sayer suggest, before new conceptions of social being linked to property rights are settled.[24] This view of state formation as a protracted cultural process accords with Bayart's conception of African "historicity," through which Africans are forging their own modernity. For Bayart, modern African politics is "a system of historical action whose origins must if possible be understood in the Braudelian *longue duree*"; to analyze it we must understand "the concrete procedures by which social actors simultaneously borrow from a range of discursive genres, intermix them and, as a result, are able to invent original cultures of the State."[25] On these accounts, stateness is ultimately the outcome of protracted political and discursive struggles over the terms of social order.

This emphasis on historical process is indeed essential to an understanding of state politics in contemporary Africa. But as we have seen, the structure of modern states reflects more than process. It also promotes structural goals of social stability, accumulation and domination. While it is neither straightforwardly a deus ex machina that acts on society nor a complex social relation that reflects the arrangement of economic forces in society, it does follow political imperatives and institutional logics that inhere in the modern state form itself. These logics determine the broad goals of state practice, and must be the foundation of an analysis of state formation in modern Africa.

State Interests and Agrarian Development

State agents interact with citizens in making and implementing the policies through which they exercise governance. The range of such policies is vast, but they are all predicated on three core purposive principles that establish and sustain the state's institutional separation from society, and provide the essential components of governance. The first principle is the generation of revenue that sustains the state, and that includes assumptions about promoting accumulation and distributing the social product. The second principle is the management of society in order to suppress social conflicts and to sustain social stability. The third is the accomplishment of popular allegiance to the sociopolitical order by securing a concept of national citizenship. Broadly, these policy principles may be described as predatory, managerial, and hegemonic. On this basis we can generate a simple heuristic model of state interests, development strategies, and governance institutions that might illuminate processes of state making in modern Africa, and in agrarian contexts more broadly.

Revenue

All modern states extract revenue from their citizens, directly and indirectly. In her theory of predatory rule, Margaret Levi argues forcefully that the extraction of revenue is the central characteristic of a state's relationship with society.

The uses to which rulers put these revenues—personal en-richment, altruism, social transformation, and so forth—are irrelevant; the ability to attain them from society is all-impor-tant. For Levi, arguing from a social choice perspective, state authority and state legitimacy derive from that ability and do not underwrite it.[26] This conception of a "revenue imperative" underlines a central tension in the structural relationship be-tween a state and the citizenry: to the state, citizens appear at least in part as sources of revenue; to citizens, the state ap-pears at least in part as the provider of public goods. How this "revenue tension" is resolved, socially and politically, will define the contours of state power in significant ways.

This view of the state carries considerable weight in the context of colonial and postcolonial Africa, where the extrac-tive propensities of rulers have been direct, transparent, and frequently brutal. Colonial administrators, consistently under pressure from their metropolitan masters to reduce the costs of colonial administration, passed those costs on to agrarian populations by appropriating massive surpluses; they were quintessentially predatory. Postcolonial regimes are notorious for their rent-seeking, prebendal or even "kleptocratic" ten-dencies. Moreover, it is the decline of their extractive capabil-ities that has enabled scholars to map the failures of African states through their inability to "capture" the peasantry, to regulate formal markets, and, in the view of some analysts, to become irrelevant to citizens' conceptions of public goods.[27]

Yet the revenue tension also indicates the importance of considering what revenues are for. States do not only pursue policies that extract resources from their populations. They also provide collective or public goods and promote entrepre-neurial or "developmental" activities, either by the state itself or by private actors. As Peter Evans has noted, for most states, "the balance between predatory and developmental activities is not clearcut but varies over time and depends on what kind of activities the state attempts."[28] Marxist scholars have long insisted that since states depend on employers and producers for their revenues, their interests cannot be disarticulated from broader class interests. More particularly, in a world of finite resources, it is the state that manages scarcity. The scarcer the resources in a particular society, the closer the relationship is between extraction and distribution, for it raises the premium on social compliance and social stability. For instance, in agrarian contexts agricultural commodity production from which the state derives revenues can actually create social hunger along regional, class, or gender lines by pushing resources toward the market or toward state repositories and away from social need. Such conditions caused the Chinese famines during the Great Leap Forward and also sustain everyday hunger in parts of Africa and Latin America.[29] State policies to alleviate such social costs are the obverse side of revenue extraction.

Thus the generation and the distribution of the social product are inextricable components of the revenue imperative. In the light of these interconnected policy domains, it is useful to draw on Michael Mann's concept of despotic power and begin analysis of the revenue imperative not with the state's extractive capabilities but with its distributive power over civil society.[30] This approach enables us to specify the revenue imperative more clearly according to three broad policy domains: predatory, developmental, and hegemonic. The predatory domain comprises policies that secure state revenues directly through taxes, fees, levies, and so on. The developmental domain comprises macroeconomic policies that promote state revenues indirectly by stimulating productivity and economic growth. The hegemonic domain comprises policies of "unproductive social spending" such as state-provided welfare benefits.

Hegemonic policies play a critical, though much neglected, role in state revenue imperatives. Their salience is most clearly demonstrated, as John Keane has noted, in the current politics of reassessing state-society relations in European welfare states.[31] But they also played a central historical role in modern statebuilders' efforts to displace preexisting networks of social power and to locate the state at the center of social organization. They shape both the generation of revenues and the use of revenues because they are a crucial element of government efforts to limit the propensity of particular social groups (notably the urban or rural poor, but also sometimes the aged and infirm) to become either a systematic drain on state resources or a source of social instability. Thus, debates over the right and capacity of the state to extract revenues cannot be politically untangled from debates over the responsibility and capacity of the state to underwrite public goods. Crawford Young has noted the tension in the welfare ideology of late colonial states, advanced as a doctrine of legitimation while the state remained "external to the citizen, an alien and predatory other."[32] In contemporary Africa, the salience of this link is poignantly demonstrated by Ghana's program to mitigate the social consequences of adjustment (PAMSCAD), implemented to maintain social stability under the conditions of economic instability that accompanied structural adjustment in the 1980s. More dramatically, the thoroughgoing breakdown of this link in Sierra Leone inspired Paul Richards to describe the recent civil war as a "drama of social exclusion."[33]

For rural populations in developing countries, these policy components have a powerful local impact, for they converge on rural development strategies that aim to improve their quality of life either by alleviating rural poverty or by stimulating rural incomes. Such strategies are always determined by the dominant political vision within the state of how the small-scale agrarian sector fits into the national (and international) political economy. As Gavin Williams notes, states tend to *do* rural development *to* peasants. But it is also in this light that we can best interpret the differences and similarities between different development models and their effects on state-peasant relations in Africa.[34] The propensity of African governments to treat peasant populations as a cash cow, transferring agricultural surplus either to the industrial sector (through import substitution industrialization) or to the state (through taxes, levies, and the notorious marketing boards) has been extensively documented. States respond to an array of pressures, including the political demands imposed by international markets and powerful social groups, their own fiscal requirements, and regime ideologies. While trying to establish the national market as the linchpin of economic life, governments have continued to regulate markets for peasant produce in order to secure their own political-economic advantages: generating revenues and rents, distributing surpluses for political purposes, keeping urban food prices low, creating a labor force, and so on. Consequently, although revenue-dependent states are generally aligned with large-scale agrarian and industrial interests, and their patronage systems tend to favor urban constituencies, these biases entail extensive state interventions in the social processes of peasant production.

As we shall see, interventionist and extractive state strategies create demands for ameliorative strategies that not only alleviate rural poverty but deflect state accountability for constraints they place on peasants, and do so cheaply. It is these contradictory pressures on the state that make hegemony essential, and that place community development and self-reliance strategies at the heart of an analysis of agrarian state construction. An excellent example is Kenya's self-help strategy known as Harambee, which was originally designed to shift the cost of providing social services to the peasantry but which has come to profoundly structure state-society relations and, on some accounts, to enable rural citizens to bargain with the state for greater resource transfers.[35]

The extractive tendencies of African states have their roots in the exigencies of colonial capitalism. Early colonial administrations tended to be instrumental and rather rudimentary, content on the whole to meet the demands of capitalist interests—local or metropolitan—with the minimum expense and effort. The processes and effects of this project varied, according largely to the nature of the colonizing agency and the nature of the resources it sought to exploit. But in all cases colonial powers sought to secure capitalist and market-oriented economies, dominated either by settlers or by European commercial interests. Colonial governments played an active role in efforts to secure the market as the linchpin of economic life. In some cases they took on the task almost single-handed, becoming deeply embroiled in producer, consumer, land, and labor markets, in order to secure accumulation opportunities favorable to political and economic elites.[36] In pursuing these objectives, colonial states both deployed "labor-repressive mechanisms" and appealed to traditional relationships of power, authority, and law.[37] These contradictory strategies propelled a protracted process of rural transformation in which state actions disrupted patterns of local authority, status and stratification, tenure and property rights, and the division of labor. Thus the organizational revolution of the colonial state embraced major incursions into the very fabric of African social and economic life and conditioned the possibilities for political development and state formation.

Several writers have stressed the lasting impact of these incursions on African political formation. Mahmood Mamdani argues that the overriding principle of colonialism was the "native question"—the need felt by administrators to establish effective mechanisms to control indigenous populations—which left a powerful legacy of "decentralized despotism" that postcolonial governments have been unable to bring under control. Crawford Young argues that they embedded traditions of "Bula Matari"—rule by naked force, terror, and rapacity. Similarly, Bayart and Mbembe argue that the "habits" and patrimonies that came to characterize postcolonial states were formed under the European administrative system, which was characterized by a close symbiosis between the worlds of administration and business, and by morally lazy, ignorant, and naive administrators who allowed the logics of coercion, extortion, and public authority to become hopelessly confused.[38] Yet, capricious and violent as colonial administrations often were, their extractive capacities and oppressive reach was never comprehensive. They lacked humanpower, adequate agrarian information, and technical knowledge. If one takes the state's ability to exercise surveillance as a yardstick for state power, as Foucault and Giddens suggest, colonial African states were generally quite unsuccessful. Despite the well-documented success of primitive accumulation policies in colonial Africa, it is not clear that the political balance in the countryside was ever settled by colonial states, or is settled now. For this reason, a historical account of state efforts to construct rural hegemony is essential for an understanding of agrarian state formation.

Predatory policies, it has often been noted, have detrimental effects on peasant productivity. They also sour state-peasant relations. In Africa, where such policies frequently involve state control of commodity markets, peasants have often become pitted directly against the state, and the market itself has become an arena of political struggles. The state's strategic resources for controlling markets are institutional—pricing policies, subsidies, credit facilities, marketing boards, and the like. But to control market institutions does not mean to regulate participation in them, especially where the state does not exercise effective control or authority over labor relations at the point of peasant production. Peasants have adopted a variety of "exit" strategies—evasion, changing crop mix, smuggling, and so forth. To exercise comprehensive control over the peasantry, therefore, the state must have either the strength or the legitimacy to assert its will. In short, attempts by African states to secure viable, legitimate, and integrated market societies rest on deep-seated political tensions.

A consideration of these tensions must go beyond the immediate purview of the market and agrarian strategy since, as we have noted, the right and capacity of the state to extract resources cannot be divorced from the responsibilities and capacity of the state to underwrite public goods. The revenue imperative cannot be pursued—or understood—separately from government efforts to structure not only appropriate agrarian development strategies but also public authority. As the extended analysis of community development policy in later chapters shows, this problem reflects the contradictions of state formation most profoundly. Resource-poor and predatory, colonial as well as postcolonial regimes have sought to displace the main responsibilities for improving the quality of rural life onto rural communities themselves, thereby defining the state's own responsibilities rather narrowly. They have done so precisely through such strategies as community development, cast in terms of self-help, self-reliance, or Harambee, which have provided the discursive and institutional conduits through which states have set out to define the parameters of state accountability and citizenship in the countryside.

Social Management

As Foucault, among others, has pointed out, the capacity of the state to penetrate social life is a hallmark of modern polities.[39] Modern states coordinate the social life of their populations through complex administrative and legal apparatuses, planning expertise, and control of the national purse. As the *fons et origo* of political authority in modern polities, states are charged with the task of controlling and ultimately suppressing social conflicts within the parameters of a particular mode of economic organization; it is partly for this reason that states have the monopoly on legitimate coercive force. At the most general level, social management engages a range of technical management strategies to secure a stable national labor force, regulate urbanization, feed the nation, distribute national water resources, and so on. Such strategies involve the structuring of labor, land and commodity markets, and are frequently coordinated through National Development Plans.

It is in this sense that it is most useful to think of state-society relations as a mode of regulation. Urban geographers and constructivist social theorists have argued that state planners design social policies such as education, housing, and transportation systems in order to structure the social spaces within which the national labor force can be deployed to meet the class-based objectives of economic efficiency and social stability.[40] Such efforts are most directly discernible in state strategies of industrial decentralization, the designation of export processing zones, and the development of industrial parks. Housing and transportation policies are important because they structure the physical and social spaces that workers must traverse between their homes and their jobs. Education policies are particularly potent instruments, not only because they allow educators to inculcate systems of authoritative knowledge and to shape cultural meanings, but because they enable the state to define the workforce through the management of skills training, the provision of preschools, day-care centers, and so forth.[41] In agrarian settings, such broad management imperatives have particular local meanings, for they demonstrate that rural development is never only a process for improving rural livelihoods or promoting economic development; it is also a political process whereby states set out to manage rural populations in accordance with macro-level intersectoral development plans. Rural development plans invariably take this external framework as a starting point.

Inevitably, states use both their power resources and a variety of justificatory techniques to manage society. Governments are able to deploy the coercive apparatuses of the state, but they are generally reluctant to do so on a systematic basis, partly because such actions undermine legitimacy, and partly because technical management strategies reinforce a particular rule-bound rationality of state. Even in cases of the most brutal and capricious expropriations, states tend to act through what one might, paraphrasing Bayart, call the "shadow theater of technocracy"—a miasma of sanctions that invoke the overriding authority of legal and technical precision, rather than the capacities of their coercive agencies.[42] In many twentieth-century agrarian settings, government management efforts have been constrained by tenuous or unreliable state capacity in the countryside. Local elites are often able to co-opt state strategies and to entrench their own patronage networks that might be at odds with state objectives. These conditions have sometimes resulted in what Prasenjit Duara calls "state involution," whereby a state becomes both weaker and more coercive at the same time.[43] In promoting capitalist development, centralizing states in Latin America, Asia, and Africa have tried—with varying degrees of brutality and success—to overcome centrifugal political forces, and to secure the state as the final arbiter of social and political authority. They have done so, largely, by setting out to establish state control over those levers that determine the distribution of public goods, and also by trying to control the social definition of what is to count as a public good.

Where states lack, or have not yet established, sophisticated cultural techniques of social management, they rely more heavily on coercion but also on more mundane instruments such as planned development, the supply and management of services, and land reform to manage their populations. Indeed, in agrarian settings, these techniques are critical dimensions of state construction. Perhaps the single most important social management instrument deployed by developing states in the twentieth century has been land reform. In agrarian societies, the linchpin of social relations is the relationship of people—as individuals and as communities—to the land that sustains them. Therefore, regulating people's access to and use of land establishes the possibility of creating a link between resource management and social management. Social choice theorists, drawing on the Lockean argument that the state's principal raison d'état is to protect property rights, have made this point suggestively. For instance, Margaret Levi argues that the development of new forms of property subject to laws governing possession and exchange increases rulers' control over coercive resources. This occurs because the consequent creation of more elaborate courts and policing institutions increases the dependence of constituents on rulers. Following this logic, some analysts view the adjustment of property regimes as the key to managing social change and promoting modernizing development. As Robert Bates puts it, in what is to date the most extended and sophisticated application of this approach to Africa's political economy, "to alter property rights is to redefine social relationships."[44]

By dictating rural citizens' rights of land access and land use, developing states have sought to manage their participation in national labor and agricultural commodity markets. Such management strategies take a number of forms, ranging from South Africa's iniquitous bantustans, through collectivization and state farms, state cooperatives and *ujamaa* villages, to strategic resettlement and state protection of *ejido* land. In each case, the state acts to direct, manage, or guide the access of rural citizens to particular economic resources by manipulating property laws and tenure systems. In some cases, the state determines what land may be used for and by whom. By doing so, states can exercise a certain degree of control over the mobility of citizens and their location within a national mode of production.

Post–World War II modernization in developing areas of the world rested on the ability of regimes to transform or to control the popular agrarian sector. Indeed, the most intense struggles for social transformation in the twentieth century, as well as a generation of scholarship on revolutions, were profoundly shaped by the "agrarian question."[45] As the protracted sagas of agrarian conflict and land reform in Latin America attest, managing rural populations often depended on the deployment of massive coercive force by the state or by agrarian elites. Postrevolutionary China, where the communist government used the land reforms of 1947–52 not only to excise the landlord class but to thoroughly penetrate and manage the lives and livelihoods of rural citizens, shows most dramatically the capacity of states to use property regimes to manage populations. But the degree of effective control has varied. Today, scholars comparing the developmental successes of east Asian NICs with the failures of postcolonial Africa routinely point to their different histories of land reform. Whereas Taiwan and Korea carried out extensive land reforms after World War II that enhanced the autonomy of the state vis-à-vis agrarian elites, this did not happen in Africa, where control of land is highly fragmented and contested. In Latin America, the prevalence of agrarian social movements and rural rebellion testify to the limited ability of states to control either elites or peasant populations through land reform.[46] A vast literature today documents the abilities of peasants to resist or to circumvent state predations and to cling, with what James Scott calls "Brechtian tenacity," to the vestiges of autonomy.[47] In short, the relative capacity of developing states in the twentieth century to manage agrarian economic transformation not only reveals patterns of state weakness or of elite power, it places agrarian politics at the center of an analysis of state formation.

Allegiance

As I have noted, political leaders in emerging states must not only legitimate their own incumbency of state office, they must also legitimate the state as the overriding locus of political authority in rural society. The distinction between these two dimensions of legitimation is necessarily imprecise. It varies with the relationship between the state apparatus and the ruling party. In developing countries, this relationship has tended to be close. Both nationally and locally, the spoils of party control over state power have been massive, and the relationship between party largesse and *public* goods intimate. Nonetheless, the analytical distinction is important because it highlights the different political dynamics of party power and state power. The latter dynamic, which is frequently neglected in analyses of development politics, focuses on establishing the Rules of the Game, which secure the authority of the state. It specifies what is to count as a public good, and what access people gain to civic resources by virtue of being citizens.

Establishing such Rules has been a field of intense political struggle in colonial and postcolonial Africa. Rural development has played a key role in these struggles. Colonial administrators had no coherent political appeals to make to rural dwellers. The externality of the colonial state, and its central historical role in mediating political interests and relations, made it very difficult for governments to completely transform or capture local relations of authority, and to establish ethico-political structures that could replace preexisting linkages of social cohesion and reproduction. The fragmented efforts of colonial governments to transform or manipulate the agricultural practices of African farmers generated severe political contradictions. Over time, market participation by rural cultivators was encouraged and choked off at the whim of rural administrators, local elites, or metropolitan merchants. The dissemination of new codes and symbols of social and political authority was blocked by administrative fiat, by the contradictions of direct rule, or simply by a shortage of humanpower. The principles of rural administration fell between the stools of formal, common and traditional law, between centralized control and local devolution. Systems of indirect rule frequently required the mobilization of preexisting linkages of political authority while undermining those linkages in the market place. Complex and highly integrated webs of preexisting community and domestic power relations were challenged and disrupted—though frequently not destroyed—and irrevocable changes were wrought upon existing social and political structures. Even where regimes attempted to retain and use existing structures, they transformed them to meet the demands of colonial domination and extraction. The result was a confused history of expropriation and encouragement, of the deterrence of agrarian class formation and the promotion of class formation, as the balance of power in the countryside was fought out.

Political interactions in rural Africa took place to a significant extent outside of representative or incorporative political organs in specific institutional settings: the market, local administrative offices, and state management strategies such as development programs, land apportionments, and labor control mechanisms. In an important sense, African politics grew up outside of and against the state, partly in struggles against state predations and partly in struggles over domestic power in communities that were excluded from the Political Kingdom.[48] Thus, although founded on universalist premises, the state could never, in its colonial form, be anything more than a partial state—administrative, bureaucratic, coercive, and without roots in civil society.[49] In settler colonies, where the state was mired in its own partiality, the contradictions deepened into profound political crisis. In most colonies, the solution was sought in formal decolonization and extension of the Political Kingdom.

Independence could not wipe this slate clean. At independence, nationalist parties trying to establish their own political domination and leadership found that wielding state power did not mean controlling a civil society. State authority was not fully constituted, and these leaders had to start by entrenching state control over society and *constructing* legitimate state authority. The difficulty of this challenge has been reflected in the tendency of regimes to shift uneasily between the broad strategies of rural repression and appeals to traditional authority, in the sustained political salience of ethnicity, in the partial involvement of peasant communities in the market, and in their frequently partial subordination to the state or to ruling classes. It is true that the composition of the state, and of the political community, changed dramatically at independence: new wealthy and powerful indigenous groups emerged, bringing to bear a range of new political and economic interests. In some cases, under the impact of mass populist-nationalist political movements, the politically dominant visions of the state's role in ordering society shifted. But despite the shift in constituencies, contests over social and economic power that took shape under the colonial regime and were mediated by state institutions have been central features of the emerging national polity. The establishment of highly bureaucratic state structures in colonial Africa imposed institutional continuities on the process of state development that constrained the ability of governments to meet changing political and economic conditions. African states inherited a set of political structures in which administration was highly institutionalized but political participation was not. States themselves remained central, dominant protagonists in strategic processes of testing and negotiating power relations in society.

At the same time, indigenous power structures have remained politically resilient despite the transforming effects of colonial domination. States have found their capacity as claimants limited by the strategic negotiating strength of social groups that have remained substantially beyond the authoritative reach of the state. Under the impact of economic stagnation or endemic food crises (or both), their capacity to maintain social cohesion and carry out political tasks has been challenged. Consequently, establishing the state as the final arbiter of economic and political authority relationships has been a peculiarly intricate and difficult task. As Thomas Callaghy has pointed out, authoritarian forms of rule "result not from high levels of power and legitimacy, but from the tenuousness of authority. The quest for sovereignty takes place within the context of poorly organized states with limited power resources," leading to centralist and authoritarian strategies. It is precisely because relations of control often become dissipated further from the political center, and because the local level of the state is unable to assert its importance, that the role of political institutions such as the party is central to patterns of political recruitment, control, and patronage.[50] In short, the institutional and structural dimensions of the modern state form exercise considerable political currency in postcolonial Africa but its social and ideological roots are shallow.

In this respect, it is notable that a large number of African states set out after independence to systematically restructure land tenure arrangements and to place the state at the center of authority and control over land, often by vesting its ownership in the state or the people, with ultimate authority exercised by the president on their behalf. One of the most salient processes whereby governments try to put the stamp of state authority on rural communities is by taking control of and manipulating property regimes. For centralizing states, it is important to codify an effective land management system in accordance not only with the interests of agrarian elites but also with state-based institutions of law and sanction. Polanyi showed vividly that the transformation of property rights and capitalist market formation was made possible by "continuous, centrally organized and controlled interventionism" by the state.[51] But to the extent that "the law itself [became] now the instrument by which the people's land is stolen," as Marx put it, there was more at stake than the creation of markets or the ability of rulers to bargain with their populations. If the law became the main instrument for managing property rights, the transformation of property rights also provided a means for entrenching the law as the ultimate arbiter of social relations. In effect, the transformation of property regimes was also part of a broader rearrangement of the structures of social authority. Efforts by states to lay down a legal regime that secures the public authority of the state are of particular moment in such processes. It is in this sense, as David Zweig notes in his analysis of rural China, that "the battle over land is tied to both policy and morality."[52]

Thus, there is a dialectical historical relationship between the reconstruction of property rights and state construction in agrarian settings; the "land question" and the "national question" are intimately connected. Control of land enables states to try to manage populations in accordance with the demands of social stability and the distribution of national resources, on the one hand, and to secure the authority of the state as the final arbiter of the social order and the public good, on the other. Yet causal lines between property rights and social relationships (or economic interests) cannot be taken for granted. Africa's modern history shows that control of land is a particularly delicate and volatile focus for state-society relations. Property regimes on the ground tend to be flexible and dynamic—both the subject and the source of intense political conflict.[53] Thus, adjusting property rights is by no means a straightforward political task, since state management efforts may conflict with local contingencies arising out of social change (or political transition) and transactions costs are understood by individuals and communities in cultural terms. Much comparative research, including the present work, shows that, in processes of social change associated with colonial and postcolonial development, property regimes and the forms of social authority linked to them have frequently fragmented rather than transformed.

Such processes have complicated the hegemonic projects of posttransition governments. They highlight an important conundrum of state construction in agrarian contexts: although it is a central part of the national question, the land question is also a source of potential conflict in restructuring social authority. In Africa, tensions between statutary law and customary law, and tensions between scientific knowledge and local practice, have served to intensify this conundrum, for they have highlighted the contradictory tendencies of African nationalism.

African Nationalism and State Authority

Under the tacit agreement of state managerialism, post-independence African regimes were, with a few exceptions, committed to state-led social transformation. The ideologies and strategies of governments varied, but their ideologies were all essentially nationalist in the sense that Plamenatz terms "eastern nationalism": a unifying ideology of colonized or dominated social groupings with weak overarching solidarity and low organizational capacity.[54] This form of nationalism, rooted in Western imperialism, reveals the deep ambivalence that characterizes the political and cultural dilemma of postcolonial regimes setting out to construct their own (autonomous) political cultures. The historical roots of African nationalism lie most deeply in a demand for political inclusion—that is, for an expansion of the public sphere understood as the realm of citizenship and res publica—and in a demand for national and cultural self-determination. Having adopted nationalism as an ideology of progress, these regimes' vision was tied to the dominant concepts and institutions of the modern European state form; but they felt a compulsion to demand progress under their own terms. Theirs was a vision of a noncolonial world that tried simultaneously to look both "forward" to a state-centered polity and "backward" to the cultural integrity of tradition.

It is in attempts to carry out this dual transformation that we can trace the construction of postcolonial political institutions in populist development strategies and the rhetorics of primordial African socialism, in tendencies toward state authoritarianism and control over functional organizations such as trade unions, and especially in one-partyism and organic-statist ideologies that stressed a fundamental consensus between nation and state in promoting the common good.[55] For these governments, organic-statism meant more than a strategy for managing national development or controlling national populations. It was part of a political project whereby regimes pursued their transformatory aims (or were seen to pursue these aims) and tried to entrench national political identities in society, while also trying to maintain their often tenuous hold on the state institutions that are the fountainhead of power in the postcolonial context. One-partyism was wholly consistent with the principle of inclusion that was the first impulse of colonial-era nationalism. The organic-statist impulse is further apparent in the extensive penetration of society through youth brigades, women's organizations, community and cooperative development initiatives, and the like. Tanzania's 1962 constitution, for instance, emphasized "the active participation of the government in the nation's economic life," and Zaire's cultural policy stressed the primordial role of the state in the creation, preservation, and encouragement of culture. Attempts to secure the power of the state through such strategies were frequently accompanied by practices of political control in which the party became located within the state, or by policies of decentralization that aimed to dispel perceptions of a distant, domineering, urban-based state in the colonial mode. In short, this was a project of managing the relationship between social control and political incorporation. As Rene Oyatek has argued with reference to Burkina Faso: "For the cultural and ideological references that for centuries structured the political make-believe of the existing social formations, the [regime] had to substitute its own."[56] In other words, postcolonial regimes had to "create traditions," not only traditions of "culture" but also traditions of "state."

This project, as I have argued, required that regimes develop a normative language of government that would provide the currency for negotiating sociopolitical relationships of control and consent, and ground the modern state form as the ultimate arbiter of social order. Constructing such languages was an extraordinarily difficult political task. As Atieno Odhiambo points out, colonialism's political heritage was "an admixture of two traditions": a tradition of political struggles (which encouraged skepticism of state pronouncements), and a tradition of leadership (which represented efforts to accede to the state).[57] But neither the history of colonialism nor the aspirations of nationalism provided a substantial terrain for political argument upon which to reconcile these traditions politically. (Development theory did very little to resolve this situation.) As a result, state rhetorics of legitimation were fragmented and contradictory; they rapidly became mired in the tensions between sociopolitical incorporation and sociopolitical control in which the constitution and dissemination of knowledge took on deep political importance. Attempts to create "traditions" of state rationality, on the one hand, appealed to the epistemological status of scientific-technocratic knowledge and the administrative-managerial traditions of the colonial state. Such appeals invoked the virtues of planning, precision, and standards for measuring the achievements of government. They were therefore attractive to both external funding and planning agencies and to still insecure state agencies. But they narrowed the bounds of accountability because they rested on a narrow ground of expertise and took the final appeal of accountability further from the public realm. Inevitably they represented systems of control and the established (colonial) "way of doing things." Structuring legitimacy required additional, sociocultural, languages of accountability. Attempts to appropriate cultural knowledge, however, frequently availed themselves of ethnic, religious, or patrimonial symbols that undermined their national and inclusive character.

These traditions have provided the principal idioms of power and legitimacy in postindependence Africa. But they have made it very difficult for regimes to institutionalize those modern techniques whereby the separation of state and society is accomplished. The creation of tradition is a difficult, uncertain, and generally protracted process. Moreover, attempts to create traditions are invariably ambiguous, partly because both interests and beliefs are at stake, and partly because those engaged in the process seldom have a monolithic vision. In Africa reliance on fragmented technocratic and sociocultural or ethnic development languages threw up contradictions in the development processes and institutions by generating different understandings of development within and outside the state. The following chapters trace the political effects of such contradictions.

The relations between state and society are structured by the state's predatory, managerial, and hegemonic imperatives. As we have seen, states pursue these goals through a variety of policy frameworks, but their institutional and ideological resources are constrained by historical conditions. It is here that the nexus of state power and class power in postcolonial African states is forged. The interventions of the state in the market and its policies of rural administration are closely linked. They provide a focus for political transformations: overturning of property rights, subversion of family controls on labor, orchestration of labor supply by taxation, enforcement of wage labor, production quotas, controlling political competition, cementing alliances between local bureaucrats and local elites, and so forth. But it is also in these specific arenas that states have been weak and partial. In the case of state-peasant strategies and struggles, political resources center on the institutions of administration (courts, services, local government, etc.) and exchange (pricing policies, subsidies, credit facilities, marketing boards, and the like). These arenas have become spheres of contestation over control of social life that are crucial to the nature of African states and to the process of political development. Indeed, they are readily identified as such in state rhetorics and programs of "institution-building for development" or "self-management." But the rural social base of postcolonial states has tended to be insecure. The lines of power and authority in rural African communities have remained fluid and fragmented, and the predominance of the state is by no means a given.

This tenuous authority has had a crucial and enduring effect on the location of the state in the social order. The political conflicts that condition African state development are not confined to social groups contending for state power, or to dominant classes, but also reflect a tenacious defense of individual or collective autonomy by social groups remaining partially outside the state. Of particular importance in this fluidity are rights of access to and use of land, and the sociopolitical organization of rural life at the village level, where control of those rights has its most politically meaningful locus. It is at this level that the division of labor is most fundamentally organized in agrarian societies, and is embedded in a textured web of kinship, clientage, and age relationships that provides the framework for political and economic power.[58] The survival of customary law, even in an attenuated form, helps to sustain this web even as it unravels under the impact of national markets and the world capitalist economy. In short, forms of political authority within rural communities are at best unsettled and at worst at loggerheads. How these struggles unfold shapes the unfolding character of the state.

African states, then, require more comprehensive and incorporative forms of control. But here they are not in a strong position. The "officially sponsored capitalist transition" that began with colonialism and was to have been consolidated in the process of decolonization and the establishment of the universal national state is far from complete. Although preexisting relations are being eroded and transformed under the impact of the market and the state, continuities in forms of social and economic power persist and must be taken into account. As Lonsdale notes:

> men cannot so easily detach themselves from old identities and associations in so uncertain a world, nor cease to be troubled by the problem of evil. Individuals they were, members of a class perhaps, but also human beings tugged at every step by all the cultural symbols with which their elders had taken such pains to endow them.[59]

The central developmental problem of African states today is to establish some control over this process of transition.

The Moral Economy of the State

The nationalizing project of African regimes has, quite clearly, had its smallest ideological impact on rural communities. In his influential formulation, Goran Hyden argues that peasants have remained "uncaptured" because their independent access to land and a kin-based "economy of affection" provide an "exit option" as well as a "civic public realm" that is beyond the reach of the state.[60] But this view fails to capture the fluid political texture of state-peasant relations. We have noted that the imposition of national markets and the extension of the colonial state inevitably transformed social relations on the ground. This has two important effects on state-peasant relations. First, local and domestic relations of power and production within the peasantry have shifted as a result of new labor patterns (sometimes migratory), new opportunities for accumulation, local proletarianization, and economic stratification. As Steven Feierman and others have noted, these shifts have been negotiated partly on cultural terrain.[61] Second, states have attempted to regulate processes of rural class formation in line with broader national development policies and the interests of dominant elites. These two effects are connected. As Lonsdale points out, "Any concept of an African mode of production which insists on the durability of community and the fragility of rule, yet which also maintains a rigid separation between the communalities of production and the administrative level of the state, cannot begin to explain these interconnections between politics and societal change and dislocation."[62] Like African states, African peasantries are in a process of formation.

Peasants tend to have localized political interests, centered on their concern with conditions of production and tenure, access to markets, and local autonomy. While they are frequently able to assert their relative independence from state predations, their readiness to take on the costs associated with the exit option (such as withdrawal from the market, entering migrant labor, and entering the informal sector) suggests that peasants make these choices within a wider panoply of relations and negotiations over the control of social life. Moreover, these choices also influence power relations *within* communities at the point of production, and vice versa. The state is able to exploit these local relations in negotiating with peasant communities, for state initiatives can be pegged at both the community and the individual level. Farmers, for their part, are able to counter state strategies. By changing their farming objectives, for instance, they can mitigate the impact of government incentive packages or sanctions that are based on the state's own economic rationality and geared toward the regime's interests. The state is then vulnerable if it depends on increased peasant productivity, whether for political or economic gain. The peasantry is able to flex some muscle. The rural development history of Zimbabwe presented in this study is one largely of the flexing and counterflexing of muscle.

Clearly, peasant options are limited. They are limited by the level of individual resources, and by community-level constraints and power relations such as lineage and kinship ties. But so are state options. They are limited by the anomalies inherent in its historical relationship to society and its capacity to overcome them, and by the degree of ideological cohesion within the state. This is revealed in a succession of direct struggles between state and peasant communities that demonstrate both the need for the state to "capture" the peasantry, and the difficulties that it faces in doing so. Strategic choices— at the level of both peasant actions and state policies—are made on the basis of understood constraints; but they are made also with a view to creating new spaces for political maneuver. When a state becomes administratively ineffective, it is unable—for structural, ideological, or political reasons—to create that space.[63] The problem for the state is not in the mode of domination (which is established) nor in the mode of production (which is also established), but in social reproduction—that dimension of social cohesion (the political-ideological) in which the balance of coercion and consent becomes crystallized. It is this realm of social power that culminates, as Gramsci puts it, in the symbiotic relationship of "force and consent, authority and hegemony, violence and civilisation, agitation and propaganda, tactics and strategy" that characterizes relations between states and partially or unincorporated classes.[64] Thus it engages the moral economy of the state.

Power relations within societies are not settled because the chain of social causation is not determinate; people simply do the best they can.[65] Political actors deploy the political resources at their disposal in order to promote or protect their interests. As Charles Tilly points out, how this happens depends substantially on the nature of the resources available, and on the opportunities to deploy them.[66] But opportunities do not simply happen; they are made in the processes of testing and negotiation between protagonists. In such negotiations people do not choose their courses of action freely. The range of choices open to them is constrained both by the relations of power in society and by the ways in which they understand those relations. There is thus no fixed standard of rationality against which to measure these actions. Individuals and groups exercise political strategies and choices within the bounds of their everyday understanding of what is politically possible.[67] The articulation of interests, power, and cohesion within peasant communities are deeply conditioned by their relations within and to a wider social formation and specifically, in colonial and postcolonial African societies, by the relationship of the community to the state itself, which stands exposed as the central and overarching institution of domination and control.

Clearly, the purposive rationality of peasants, individually and collectively, might vary from that of the state or its agents, thereby narrowing the ground for common political argument. Indeed, this is a common argument against top-down technocratic development. Yet by the same account the purposive rationality of the state is also multivalent, porous, and limited by ideological considerations. A narrow base for political argument constrains the range of strategic and nor-mative appeals that the state can make without losing coher-ence. Indeed, as we shall see, within the broad rubric of acting as the state, regimes standardly make contradictory appeals and arguments. Thus, where the common base for political ar-gument is narrow, and the range of advantages and benefits offered by the state is limited, the state may face significant difficulties in establishing hegemony. Such difficulties are fre-quently manifested in cultural forms. Historically, the most dramatic struggles over cultural transformation have been forms of millenarianism. But more everyday political difficul-ties are also widespread. In Zimbabwe, for instance, land re-settlement has been hampered on occasion by settlers' insis-tence that their new allocations are occupied by antagonistic spirits. And in a world of a rampant AIDS virus, compromises with traditional healers over regulating people's lives have taken on considerable political urgency.

Political interactions in these arenas do not, of course, take place on an equal basis; dominant classes or groups have a greater capacity to control interactions. The rules and para-meters of negotiations are entrenched and institutionalized in a variety of ways, from formal institutional guidelines to moral and ethical codes, or what Pierre Bourdieu calls "le-gitimate culture."[68] This illuminates some important features about the control of peasantries. First, it is extremely important for those who wield social power to institutionalize their power within a "legitimate culture" or, as Stanley Greenberg puts it, to find "common principles in social organization."[69] Second, disjunctures can emerge between institutional guidelines and legitimate culture. Such disjunctures will profoundly affect strategies of political negotiation and may lead to political crisis. The politically subordinate have political effectivity to the extent that they are able to negotiate political impositions and evaluate political benefits. Often, space for negotiation may be confined to a minor adjustment of one's personal situation. But even if these negotiations do not threaten the structures of control and domination in any immediate sense, they cannot be ignored by political analysis and explanation, for they are constantly in process and therefore constantly challenge, reconstitute, and shift power relations. The analysis in this volume is largely about attempts to manipulate and mend such disjunctures.

In areas where administrative institutions lack popular support or local legitimacy, their effective jurisdiction is often limited. In colonial Zimbabwe, chiefs without formal judicial authority preempted the formal courts of the Native Commissioner by continuing to hear cases in their district. In independent Zimbabwe, the government has recently agreed to return chiefs' local judicial powers to them. In both Zimbabwe and Zambia, legitimacy of local institutions has often depended on a lack of central political control; central control has meant lack of legitimacy. In Tanzania, imposed bureaucratic zeal was instrumental in the rejection of *ujamaa*. Nevertheless, these administrative institutions are the focus of state-peasant political interactions where democratic mechanisms and other vehicles of hegemony, such as the rule of law, are weak.[70] Therefore they provide a central arena for political negotiations of various forms.

Peasant communities (like states) are more than economic communities; they are also political and moral communities. This does not mean that they are closed moral units to any greater extent than other kinds of communities. It means simply that communities constitute themselves through a kind of "language of memory" that grounds the structure of beliefs, traditions, and conventions of the community.[71] Such a language articulates, among other things, ecological and social norms through such vehicles as taboos, totems, and sacred groves. Thus it provides the currency for local concepts of Right, rights, and community membership in which moral expectations of need and security are embedded. For politicians and state functionaries to extend the hegemony of the state, they must insert the presuppositions of state authority into that language and remoralize the political forms of local authority so as to place the state's institutions at the center of the community. In a sense, if the village is to be brought within the state, the state must be brought into the village. Regimes must establish what Benedict Anderson has termed an "imagined community," in which state universality can be secured so that it becomes part of the commonsense reality of village life.[72]

To do this requires a nuanced political-ideological project whereby the state sets out to reorient the settled social practices of villagers so as to incorporate the village into a wider public realm. As Ian Shapiro points out, "political languages are embedded in the real world and instrumental in its reproduction."[73] Attempts to generate new imagined communities are most readily discernible in the decisions by postcolonial states to take thoroughgoing control of property relations in regulating access to land, in state-directed villagization policies, such as the Ujamaa projects in Tanzania; in attempts by states to regulate domestic relations of production and control through women's rights laws, as in Zimbabwe; and by widespread attempts by postindependence states to establish new forms and institutions of political participation and representation at the local level. These attempts have involved states in self-conscious and determined efforts to (re)structure the public sphere—the sphere of citizenship. As we shall see below, such a project has ideological, procedural, and institutional dimensions. Ideologically, it entails attempts by state agents to secure the state as the final arbiter of Right, property rights, and community membership (citizenship) at the local level. Procedurally, it generally entails the spatial reorganization of living arrangements and social practices, often couched in terms of planned development. Institutionally it involves the co-optation or creation of local institutional structures as the locus of accountability.

Not surprisingly, such attempts have faced overwhelming sociocultural and political obstacles. They have met resistance from holders of economic or symbolic power at the local and community level. Different forms of local power, and sources of authority, may of course also be a source of political conflict within a community. Control of community symbols is sometimes more important than economic power at the local level since it allows a stronger voice in a language of tradition. Incipient conflicts may be exploited by the state in undertaking ideological interventions, drawing on mixtures of the languages of tradition and modernity. This means that ideology is not merely epiphenomenal. Political struggles have an ideological dimension because they are fought out at least partly on the terrain of language, memory, and meaning. The state sets out to root its hegemony in local social relations through the language of tradition while at the same time attempting to transform that language. This is not only a postcolonial phenomenon. In Zimbabwe, as in other African countries, the traditions of social management were laid down over an extended period in ongoing dialogues between state officials and rural dwellers over traditions and citizenship. These dialogues are by no means over.

The fluid and fragmented character of both the state and rural society in Africa shows that individuals and groups are not simply the bearers of particular social relations; nor are the institutions of civil society either separate from the state or the legitimating structures of ideological state apparatuses. They are real arenas of political contestation in which the dominated have some room for effective maneuver in shaping the relationship between control and consent in African societies. This is the core of ideological and political struggles between states and peasant communities, which shape the performance, nature, and limits of state power. For a political regime, the challenge of hegemony is to establish a common language or terrain of political argument that will ground a new theory of government to provide the currency for what Gramsci calls "the sphere of hegemony and ethico-political relations," in which contests and struggles over control of social life become defined and obtain an extra-coercive dimension.[74] Such a language typically has particular constitutive features:

1. The object is to legitimate the state (not its incumbents), and to substantiate claims to impartiality. The principal convention of the normative language of authority is that the state is the final arbiter of social provision and social order which is secured by the relationship between law and right. Civil-private authority also derives ultimately from the impartial authority of the state. At stake is a concept of national citizenship as a form of political identity.

2. Such a language invokes the public good. It contains four discursive elements that are not always in harmony: an epistemological element, which invokes the authority of knowledge; an element of social need and material produc-

tion, which invokes the need to sustain society; an element of right, which invokes principles of justice and desert in distribution and redistribution; and an element of power, which refers to the regulation of society by state apparatuses.

3. This is a public language. It provides a public transcript of the government's programmatic initiatives, and thereby articulates its efforts to structure state-society relations. It is thus both explanatory and legitimatory.[75]

4. Such a language does not sustain the authority of the state on its own; state authority still rests (in Weber's classic formulation) on the legitimate monopoly of force.

The language of state, thus conceived, directs an analysis of state formation to an interpretation of negotiations over legitimate state interventions in social life (individual and collective) and the specific contexts in which the state becomes socially understood as the appropriate underwriter of public goods. In the context of developing agrarian societies such an analysis focuses on the confluence of technical and social arrangements for agrarian production. It stands at the intersection of ideology and interest, history and politics, that which is tolerable and that which is not. Thus it offers us a moral economy of the state. But it can only be understood in the historical context of state making. The following chapters offer an extended analysis of such processes.

2

Establishing the State, 1890–1950

The Ambiguities of Colonialism

State formation is a contested process in which different social groups and different forms of authority contend, compromise, and coexist over a period of time before a definitive new political order emerges. It is thus difficult to specify the political moment at which a state comes into being. Certainly, the process of laying down the lines of power and authority that produced the definitive features of the Rhodesian state was tortuous, protracted, and politically contested. Early state construction in Zimbabwe reveals the emergence of an increasingly busy and administrative state, progressively extending legal and political mechanisms in the service of racial domination and colonial capitalism to control the African population. The efforts whereby the administration pursued these goals—separating the races through land alienation and reservation, implementing discriminatory marketing regulations, and developing infrastructural, institutional, and financial support for the white economy—laid the broad parameters for subsequent political-economic development. This application of state power had definitive implications for state-peasant relations over time, for it determined that the links between peasants in the countryside and the social formation as a whole ran directly through the state.

Zimbabwean scholars have discussed the impact of the colonial state on rural African populations in two principal ways. First, writers in the underdevelopment tradition have argued that state mechanisms systematically and willfully suppressed the African peasant farming sector in the process of imposing strict social and economic control over the African population, and driving African labor into the employ of white settlers.[1] Second, Terence Ranger has argued in his important work *Peasant Consciousness and Guerrilla War in Zimbabwe* that peasant loss of control over life-opportunities through state exactions fostered a deep-seated, simmering tradition of resistance that ultimately boiled up in the 1970s into the liberation war. The burden of these arguments is to show that the state itself, as the unmediated agent of social control, became the principal focus of social conflict. As such they provide a useful starting point for analyzing the historical construction of state-peasant relations and the political trajectory of the Zimbabwean state. Yet neither argument seriously analyzes the character of the colonial state, viewing it respectively as a mechanism of underdevelopment controlled by colonial capital, and as the adversary that defined peasant struggles. Consequently, they neglect a central dimension of the extremely complex process of rural contestation and struggle that they address. For these struggles were defined in part by the character and limitations of state power, which conditioned not only the political strategies available to peasants but also the strategies of domination available to the state.

A closer focus on the character of state power and resources of domination offers a clearer understanding of the political dynamics of state making under colonialism and its legacy for contemporary Zimbabwe. As elsewhere in Africa, the early colonial administration was predatory and managerial, its main tasks being to secure market advantages and cheap African labor for the white-dominated mining and agricultural industries. But over time, the demands on the administration to manage rural society changed as the interests of elites shifted from the desirability of a migrant labor force to the desirability of a settled industrial labor force and a stable, productive peasantry. At the same time, there was always a tension between the state's objectives of managing rural society, on the one hand, and its tenuous control of rural African communities, on the other. The administration responded to these pressures through a succession of strategies that sought to manage the economic and political lives of rural Africans without resorting to systematic coercion and without deploying significant material resources. These efforts, which are the subject of this book, required the state to pursue hegemonic policies through which it could reorient local concepts of rights and community membership to meet broader structural goals of accumulation and social management. The following chapters argue that these attempts to remoralize state-peasant relations lie at the very core of state construction in Zimbabwe. First, however, it is necessary to sketch out how their political and ideological parameters were laid down during the early years of the colony in the racial definition of land rights, the ambiguities of state power in the countryside, and the impact of agrarian change on the settled social practices of rural Africans.

Land and Domination

The creation of African reserve areas to supply cheap labor and to regulate African agricultural competition has been extensively documented. By regularizing labor migrancy and managing the mobility of workers to and from the workplace, the system involved the state actively in structuring the workforce. Initially, forced labor *(chibaro)* was widespread, but over time this crude mechanism was replaced with a range of extra-coercive measures—hut taxes, dog taxes, poll taxes, dipping fees, grazing fees, and the like—to press Africans into wage labor relations. The most far-reaching mechanism for structuring African participation in the economy and polity, however, was the set of measures adopted over time to regulate African access to land. The Land Apportionment Act (LAA) of 1930, which divided the land resources of the country on a strictly racial basis, laid down the parameters of land, property, and citizenship rights most starkly. The land reserved for African domicile and agriculture was mainly in the poorer ecological zones. As the African population in these areas expanded, especially with increasing evictions from white farms after the 1930s, the African reserves became increasingly crowded.

It is difficult to exaggerate the definitive impact of land apportionment on the social, economic, and political development of Zimbabwe. It provided the state with an extremely powerful instrument to oversee and structure the character of the economy and the polity by controlling mobility and domicile. In stark physical lines, it drew the parameters of political identity and citizenship through strict racial segregation. Similarly, it drew the parameters for economic identity and participation through strict segregation of property rights. Within the reserves, Africans occupied land under traditional tenure systems controlled by local "royal" lineages; outside the reserves, with the exception of the small African Purchase Areas, Africans were prohibited from owning land, and could at best be tenants. By a system of passes the state regulated the influx of Africans into towns. Moreover, the LAA provided a constitutional framework in which agricultural development and market participation could be regulated by judicious apportionment of resources and outlets. State bureaucracies, statutory bodies, development initiatives, and the legal structure made strict sectoral distinctions between African agriculture and European agriculture. This institutional separation became particularly important in the 1930s, when the government passed the Maize Control Acts to shield white farmers from the effects of the Great Depression by favoring them in the market against both large-scale growers and African farmers.

Throughout the colonial period the LAA provided the state's principal political instrument for pursuing the dual tasks of structuring the economy and managing society. Over time, it became the greatest symbol of colonial oppression and a focus for African resistance, rebellion, and ultimately war. Its legacy still dominates the political landscape. But land control was more than a catalyst of conflict in state-peasant relations. The contours of state power in the countryside dictated that it provide the normative terms in which administrators negotiated state interventions in rural social life. The ways in which it has done so over time illuminates the processes of state construction in Zimbabwe.

The Ambiguities of State Power

The willful suppression of the African peasantry by state action cannot be taken at face value, for peasant decline was in part an outcome of conflict. Nor indeed can state domination of rural communities be assumed, for the ways in which state officials expressed and understood domination were rooted partly in the process of conflict. Colonialism disrupted African society massively but it never transformed relations of sociopolitical power and authority in a fundamental or comprehensive way on its own terms. Nor indeed was the colonial administration ideologically or politically monolithic. Consequently, there was always an ambiguity to colonial domination that created the political space for rural contestation.

The pace and process of social disruption of African communities in the early years of colonialism varied across region and ecological zone, and tracing the patterns of uneven development falls outside the scope of this study. But two basic trends can be identified. In the first place the early colonial state did not have the will, the interest, or indeed the capacity to determine social and economic relationships within African communities. While the rule of law was the yardstick of state penetration of white civil society, this objective was not pursued with any conviction in the African areas. Once the primary objectives of producing labor and reducing agricultural competition had been achieved, the administration was content to let existing relationships of power and authority in African reserves be. Its objectives of control, therefore, were clear but strictly limited. In the second place, regulating economic behavior by manipulating market mechanisms contained inherent contradictions. On the one hand, control of the market choked off economic opportunities; on the other hand, the existence of the market created them. The tension between opportunities created and opportunities reduced made social and economic control always incomplete, opening up for peasants strategic possibilities for contestation. As a result of the curious historical interplay between these two trends—ambiguous political domination and uncertain market opportunities —control of society came to be cast by the end of the 1930s less in the sociopolitical terms of legitimate political authority than in the technocratic terms of controlled land-management.

Rural administration in the first half of the century was a rather ad hoc affair, vested in the Native Affairs Department (NAD) and embodied locally in Native Commissioners (NCs) who presided over administration and tax collection in the reserves. The terms of reference for the NAD and its officers were vague and the department was able by and large to go its own way.[2] The form of administration in different areas was determined largely by the personality of the NC. For early NCs, as one NC memorialized romantically, life was not trammeled by heavy responsibilities:

> A tranquil, almost idyllic, life wherein the commissioner's greatest problem was probably the uncertainty of being able to shoot enough meat for his porters on month-long foot safaris in the Zambezi valley! These were days when postal communications were erratic, telephones and radios virtually non-existent and the government's senior representative in the field was a law unto himself—unchallenged by white or black man.[3]

In African administration it was a time of flexibility (characterized, in Joy MacLean's coy phrase, by the "humility" of NCs).[4] The head office in Salisbury would rather not hear about the problems of the districts. Before the 1940s, development money was almost completely lacking, and NCs would occasionally run vaccination campaigns to make a little pocket money for themselves. In general they dealt with problems as they arose, priding themselves on their independence, initiative, and flexibility, and rationalizing their authoritarianism as pedagogical or pragmatic.[5]

Underlying this "flexibility" of social management, however, was a curious emerging ideology of guardianship that over time became the central self-identification of the entire edifice of African administration.[6] The ideology had two broad strands. One was the "civilizing" mission that was associated with the imperialist vision of men such as Rhodes. The other was a vision of "protecting" Africans from the domination and demands of white settlers. Such protection took the form mainly of trying to ensure that Africans retained access to reasonable amounts of productive land where they could develop "along their own lines."[7] The Native Department supported the LAA to provide a statutory safeguard for Africans against the white appetite for land, and they opposed the United Party's proposal to scrap the LAA in the early 1960s for the same reason. In an age of imperialist ideology, rampant social darwinism, and value relativism, "protecting" the interests of Africans rested on an ambiguous notion of stemming the disintegration of the tribal system.[8] The ambiguity of the notion lay in its inherent tensions between thoroughgoing protection and thoroughgoing control.

The general style of rural administration was what the NAD was pleased to call "benevolent paternalism." NCs relied heavily on a personal style of administration, and most were proud of their capacity to work with and through local traditional authorities and to get the job done, although this was frequently not a consultative arrangement. As a senior NAD official described the situation (without acknowledging the caprice and bullying tactics that characterized the personal style of many NCs):

> You know, whatever was the official policy—and I don't remember ever reading anything about that—it all depended on the District Commissioner, or Native Commissioner in those days. Some worked entirely through chiefs, others looked upon them as useless. It depended on each Native Commissioner's own opinions. . . . So I think there was a tremendously varied policy towards the chiefs, but happily the chiefs carried on whether there was external influence or not. The surprising tenacity and the strength of the indigenous institution remained, whether it was hastened by one DC or it was depressed by another. But it was never eliminated, no matter what the official policy was.[9]

This structure of governance and administration remained essentially unchanged throughout the colonial period.

NCs varied widely in the zeal and efficiency with which they carried out their appointed, and self-appointed, tasks. In fact most NCs realized that administrative control was really quite tenuous, that administrators were too remote from most settlements to know what was going on, and that most rural Africans "went their own independent ways, paying scant attention to authority in the form of administrators or police with white skins. . . ."[10] Tellingly, the Chief Native Commissioner (CNC) remarked in 1954 that "[w]hile it is disappointing to know that little direct assistance is given to the administration by Chiefs and Headmen, there is no doubt whatever that their mere presence has a stabilising effect upon their people and this in itself is of great value."[11] Robert Blake argues that rural African administration was emphatically a system of direct rule based on the native commissioner but, as one senior NAD official confided in an interview, "so far as I know most Native Commissioners didn't really know what happened on the ground. . . . This so-called direct rule is really very noticeable for the lack of it."[12] Thus NCs in fact represented less the overweening power of the state than the ambiguities of local politics and state penetration of rural society. These ambiguities were reflected in the Southern Rhodesian Native Regulations, which aimed to both break the power of chiefs and incorporate them into the administrative hierarchy by assigning them constabular rank, paying them, and requiring them to report such occurrences as crimes and offenses, deaths, suspicious disappearances, diseases, and epidemics.[13] Rural administration was a curious mixture of authoritarianism, flexibility, sometimes complete inaction, and occasional brutality. But most significantly, if local state agents knew so little about their constituents, central state policymakers had to work almost completely in the dark: African demography and production techniques were little understood, and knowledge of the extent of African production was scattered. Throughout the colonial period, policymakers wrote sweeping, and often draconian, social management policies on the most impressionistic evidence.

The tenuousness of rural control had two important effects on the political ideology of guardianship and on state-peasant relations over time. Firstly, NCs had a powerful sense of their own geographical and political isolation. This made them very protective of their position as local representatives of the state and very sensitive to potential threats against the order and stability of their district. In interviews, several former native commissioners declared that they knew little about what went on in other stations; but they would generally close ranks in support of a colleague facing disciplinary action for exceeding his authority in dealing with local Africans. In the end, for NCs, the guiding principle of guardianship was the maintenance of order, and in defense of that principle they fiercely pursued their independence from other branches of the state, struck up alliances with amenable local authorities, bullied others, and opposed state policies that they believed might be disruptive. Thus they insisted on independence also from the wider demands of the state. This insistence was central to the ambiguities of rural power and control as they unfolded during the colonial period.

In addition, the tenuousness of social control demonstrated that the yardstick for social progress could not be sought in the transformation of *social* relationships. Social management as exercised by NCs in the countryside gave them little or no moral purchase on the sociopolitical or sociocultural dimensions of rural life. Instead, the yardstick became a set of relationships that the administration believed it could control and use to mold the character of African citizenship: the relationship of people to their land and their technical expertise as farmers. This has remained a lasting and powerful theme in the politics of Zimbabwean citizenship.

As early as 1913, the CNC stated in his annual report, "The conversion of Native land tenure from the communal to the individual system is the true basis on which the progress of the natives is to be evolved. . . ."[14] Indeed, NAD ideology drew close connections between progress, civilization, segregation and land. In 1923 H. S. Keigwin and H. N. Wilson stressed these connections in the first edition of the *Native Affairs Department Annual (NADA)*:

> We may educate the native with education—literary, industrial, religious, liberal and vocational; we may bombard him with progress and souse him in Chindamora; we may uplift him until individual natives are on a plane with Booker Washington; but unless we have some field of activity to which he may pass on we shall not only break the machine, but we ourselves shall be buried under the debris.

For Wilson such a terrible fate could be avoided in "a system whereby the development of the native should be combined with as great as possible a measure of segregation of interests."[15] And, as Keigwin echoed, the key lay in the land:

> As we think on these things it becomes abundantly clear that this "sacred trust of civilization" is also a plain duty of self-preservation. There being no-where else for these people to go, it is incumbent on us to see that they are taught without delay to make the best of the land on which they live. It is not merely a case of counselling them; there must be an organised scheme of progressive instruction.[16]

In the political-ideological context of the day, then, Native Department ideology of progress and development came to focus not on citizenship and sociocultural development but on production and technical development. The point is most strikingly made in Joy MacLean's description of NCs' tasks as "merely to learn all they could and to report back; to learn the language and customs of any people in their areas, and to start the process of civilising *both land and people*."[17] Thus land and property came to provide the central connection between the flexibility of local dynamics of political control and the ordering impulses of the larger state project of national hegemony. And the state established a tradition of social management that continues to define state development and state-peasant relations in Zimbabwe.

This focus drew heavily on current European and American concepts of economic growth, productive efficiency, and social worth. In Southern Rhodesia they were substantiated most profoundly in the person of Emory Alvord, an American-born conservationist missionary who was appointed Agriculturist for the Instruction of Natives in 1926. Alvord hewed to a "gospel of the plough" based on the belief that the moral and cognitive transformation necessary to secure the social progress of Africans must begin with the inculcation of modern rational agricultural practices. Under his leadership, the yardstick of African progress in the period preceding the Second World War became the efficiency of land management and production. Significantly, official language prior to 1961 referred to rural Africans as "producers" or "cultivators," and African social development was associated consistently with urbanization.[18] African rural progress was understood primarily as a technical question, to be pursued by force of the example set by successful progressive farmers selected and trained by Alvord's staff of agricultural demonstrators. From the mid-1920s to the early 1940s, agricultural development was separated from the administrative branch, initially in the Department of Native Education and subsequently in the Department of Native Development, a situation that was much resented by NCs, who saw it as a threat to their control. Indeed, this separation created lasting tensions and suspicions between rural administrators and rural agricultural developers. It was in fact part of a growing imperial trend of ecological managerialism, in which the acquisition—and then the application—of scientific ecological knowledge became a powerful conduit for "civilizing both land and people" in the colonies. As Fiona Mackenzie suggests, it allowed colonial officials to subjugate local African knowledge as "unscientific" and entrench the environment as "both a discourse of knowledge and a discourse of power."[19]

The centerpiece of Alvord's mission was to promote scientifically optimal land use, which in his view rested on the fixed separation of arable, grazing, and residential land.[20] From the late 1920s, he pursued this aim through a policy of "centralization," which involved separating arable land from grazing land and consolidating it into blocks of permanent fields, improving agricultural techniques under state direction, and implementing conservation measures. The success of this policy depended largely on the capacity of agricultural demonstrators to persuade or coerce African farmers to follow their advice. The policy was highly intrusive in all three of its aims, and was not implemented systematically until the late 1940s.

First, the scheme required a large-scale reallocation of arable holdings and the removal of many homesteads to new residential sites, usually in extended lines along the edges of the blocks. The allocation of permanent holdings seemed to farmers to reduce economic opportunities and to create land shortages, for it limited the amount of arable land under cultivation. It also inhibited their access to patches of wetland (most important in periods of drought) where these fell within a grazing block, and reduced access to grazing resources. Villagers resented "going into the lines," especially as perceptions of land shortage increased, because it disrupted the patterns of village life and frequently left them further from their land.[21] It also disturbed locally specific cultural inflections of land use by ignoring sacred ridges, trees, and propitiation sites through which communities processed their relations with ancestors and rainmaking.

Second, improved agricultural techniques focused on crop rotation and control of stocking levels. For producers on the fringes of the capitalist market, both measures appeared as excessive controls on their economic decision making. Many farmers wanted, or needed, to produce maize every year because it provided the best market returns. This reflected both their increasing dependence on cash incomes to meet taxes and fees, and the fact that maize was less labor-intensive than millet or groundnuts.[22] Development officials found this behavior exasperating. In 1944 the NC Mazoe exploded:

> These natives are so wedded to their maize, which they can always sell for cash, that now an effort is being made to make them rotate their crops for the benefit of the soil it is very difficult to persuade them to do so. They are so anxious to get a surplus crop of maize to sell, that the necessity of growing other crops in rotation in order to preserve the productivity of the soil is lost on them . . . suffice it to say that compulsion seems to be the only means to employ, but it is difficult to prosecute thousands of land owners for neglecting to rotate the 6 acres allotted each of them.[23]

Indeed, rotation policies only intensified for peasants the link between state domination, permanent holdings, and land shortage.

Finally, conservation measures involved labor-intensive activities such as de-stumping, filling gullies, and constructing contour walls. This labor not only disrupted the organization of farming activities, it had to be supplied by villagers for little or no recompense. Conservation labor was ordered by the NC and recruited by the chief, thereby placing local authority relations under considerable strain. This situation was exacerbated by the 1942 Compulsory Labour Act, which was passed to help meet new wartime demands for agricultural production. Moreover, as Ken Wilson points out, arable blocks were often moved in successive land use exercises, so that arduous de-stumping tasks not only proved pointless when the government redesignated land for grazing a few years later but proved ecologically destructive.[24] Although the colonial government took ecology increasingly seriously (eventually producing an ecological map of the country that divided it into five "agro-ecological" zones), it was much less interested in micro-ecologies, which local people understood well and used effectively to manage the effects of periodic drought or other disasters. For all its genuflections toward scientific and rational agricultural management, local implementation of this "authoritative" agrarian knowledge depended rather heavily on how it was refracted through the mind and energy of the NC in residence. Local rules changed as NCs changed, or as they changed their ideas. Not surprisingly, centralization generated considerable local resistance. By the end of 1933, Alvord had become convinced that conditions in the reserves could only be remedied by making centralization compulsory.

As relations between the colonial administration and the rural population grew increasingly adversarial in the 1930s, the government tried to depoliticize and mediate state controls by creating Native Boards comprising "tribal" and "elected" representatives under the chairmanship of the NC. Under depression conditions the boards failed miserably. In 1936 the CNC, Charles Bullock, called for a renewed initiative, arguing that "more concerted effort [from the Africans] is badly needed— something in the nature of group co-operation—something which can form, and utilise also, Native public opinion."[25] In 1937 the boards were replaced with Native Councils, on the idea that councils would evolve gradually as a means whereby local people might take action to improve their own conditions. Under an amendment in 1943, the councils were given powers to levy taxes for the construction of roads, conservation, sanitation, education, and other functions. The system was designed to mediate the impact of the central state on rural communities. Councils would sustain and bolster social control but depoliticize state management of social life and market access. As we shall see in the next chapter, councils were a thoroughgoing failure, the harbinger of conflict rather than cooperation.

Rural politics thus reveals a fundamental tension in colonial state power between the state's broad structural objectives and its local management of rural communities (a tension that informs any attempt at state construction). During this period, state management strategies aimed less at suppressing the peasantry and creating labor supplies than at securing the future of marginal white farmers and workers. But by structuring African domicile, mobility, and access to markets, and pushing Africans out of the rural market economy, the state made its noncoercive, authoritative, purchase on their lives increasingly tenuous. Its resources to stabilize and control the peasantry in accordance with its own objectives of social management and economic structuring were limited and ultimately authoritarian. Within the reserves, social management efforts lay mainly in a turn by development officers to increasingly hardheaded implementation of centralization and conservation programs. But these programs increased the antagonism of the rural population to the state, and provided a ready terrain upon which they could engage the state in struggles for control of rural social life.

Colonialism and Agrarian Change

Over time, the political structure of colonial capitalism created two intensifying strains on rural African communities. One was the limitation of African access to land. The other was incipient agrarian stratification within the reserves. As increasing numbers of African tenant farmers were forced off white land, pressure began to build on the land resources of the African areas, where land was often of inferior quality and agricultural produce more expensive to market. This pressure was exacerbated by the emergence of wealthier peasants early in the twentieth century, responding to market opportunities and using new technologies to increase production. Just as these farmers wanted to increase their land holdings, their opportunities were curtailed by the increasing influx of people into the reserves, as well as by local ecological variation. Ranger documents at length the emergence of the beginnings of an "entrepreneurial class" of farmers who were greatly expanding their area of tillage and the amount of grain they were marketing. But administration officials opposed the creation of either a landless class or a group of major African landowners. As land pressure grew, Native Commissioners began to report a growing differentiation in plot size and to warn that if plow farming and market production continued to be encouraged a landless class could rapidly emerge and destabilize rural society.[26] This threat to their control was one reason for their surliness towards Alvord's agricultural staff.

Wealthier peasants were often able to ignore government directives that limited their arable and cattle holdings. Supported by the patronage of village heads, some managed to retain extensive plots. Nevertheless, differentiation of land use provided the context for growing perceptions of land shortage both within the administration and within rural communities. In September 1937 the Agriculturist to the Natives wrote to the Chief Native Commissioner that "certain more ambitious Natives are hogging large areas of the best land and producing crops for sale . . . many others cannot find suitable land on which to grow their food. We must enforce a redistribution of lands in the Reserves and these men who farm for profit should be requested to buy land in the Native Purchase Areas."[27] At the same time large numbers of poor peasants became substantially disengaged from the market, and many set their production objectives at the level of subsistence and survival. In 1949 the NC Gwanda remarked, "Owing to the distance from rail-head and resultant lack of markets there is little incentive to grow more grain than is required for personal consumption."[28]

In many areas, poor farmers were pushed out of the cash market altogether by their dependence on local traders or store owners who preferred to pay in kind and at the lowest grade. The rural economy in some cases became substantially demonetized. Poor peasants were forced into the migrant labor market in search of cash incomes. The response of poor peasants to the cumulative strains on their lives was to develop a "subsistence ethic" with regard to production, in which food security and access to land were the central principles— conditions that persist today among many poor households. The produce market became a secondary consideration in their farming decisions, off-farm employment—either on white farms or in urban areas—being the preferred and frequently the only accessible source of cash income. Over time, these pressures inculcated in rural citizens a powerful desire for education and skills that might improve their position in wage labor markets; for many education became a major object of household investment. As Leslie Bessant and Elvis Muringai point out, by stressing self-sufficiency in their production objectives, peasants were able to increase the flexibility (if not the range) of their production and marketing choices.[29] By discretionary participation in the market peasants were able to effectively narrow the range of noncoercive appeals that the state could make for their cooperation.

These developments had manifest effects on local relationships of power and authority. In the first place, they placed considerable strain on the local labor economy. As in many other African farming systems, labor as a factor of production was chronically in short supply in the reserves. When production increased, labor demands changed: fields were enlarged and kept in cultivation longer, which required increased weeding, and larger crops took longer to harvest. The migrant labor system exacerbated pressure on rural labor resources. In the early 1970s A. K. H. Weinrich remarked that the majority of migrant workers were young, and the majority of landholders were old. The bulk of agricultural work was carried out by women and children.[30] Control and deployment of labor was thus a serious concern in the organization of household production. However, noting the voracious demand for education among rural Africans in 1957, the CNC also remarked on the fact that the desire to go to school had changed the distribution of rural labor.[31] Youngsters frequently sought remunerative off-farm work, not only for family income but to loosen family controls on themselves.[32] There is evidence too that rural women tried to loosen the bands of domestic control, leading local patriarchal authorities to appeal to the state for help "in stopping our younger women wandering about the country whoring with any man."[33] The 1925 Morris Carter Commission, commenting on the shift from hand cultivation carried out by women to draft power by oxen, suggested that women were no longer inclined to display the energy and determination with which they had previously applied themselves to the hoe, and presented this as a possible explanation for decline in agricultural yields.[34] The CNC's annual report for 1949 remarked that "[i]ncreased use during the year of female labour for casual work on farms and, to a lesser extent, in domestic service, is indicative of the gradual emancipation of African women, which however involves relaxation of traditional controls and moral standards as evidenced by the increasing flow of single women to the towns."[35] In addition, as the century progressed, local wage labor markets began to emerge as poorer households—who often were unable to engage in migrancy—began to sell labor to wealthier households—who often used remittances to purchase labor.

Incipient tensions were also exacerbated by the dramatic increase in the number of African-owned cattle during this period.[36] Shortages of humanpower could be offset by the increased use of cattle. Shortages of oxen could be offset by pooling labor resources. However, individual cattle holdings were highly skewed within peasant communities. Access to cattle was increasingly a requisite for the accumulation of agrarian wealth, less as a source of cash income from beef production than as a source of draft, manure, and transport. But in the eyes of officials, increased ox-plowing not only created the "threat" of African agricultural competition with whites, it raised the specter of land shortage and ecological degradation due to overstocking and overcropping. In 1938 the assistant agriculturist, referring to Chiweshe farmers, reported:

> Some Natives have the idea of being progressive farmers by ploughing these areas all up and down the slope, planting maize every year and reaping very small returns from it. Other Natives have no land and very small patches so naturally never reap sufficient grain to see them through the year. If these farmers were made to till smaller areas and a rotation of crops [enforced] everyone would be very much happier because there would be sufficient land for all and better yields reaped. . . . these Natives are running wild with their ploughs and ruining the Reserve.[37]

But for individual farmers, introducing livestock into the system potentially allowed them to increase yields and to reduce labor requirements at key periods in the season. This development put a premium on cattle ownership and became the crux of complex local relationships of power, reciprocity, and rights to grazing, manure, stover, draft, and labor.[38] The hub of these relationships, in which kinship, bridewealth, and inheritance laws played a central role, was rural labor.

In the communal lands today, ownership of sufficient livestock for draft purposes is limited to about 30 percent of farmers, and a sizable minority of communal area households—over 40 percent in almost all parts of the country—have no cattle. Expanded agricultural production is closely associated both with livestock ownership and migrant remittances.[39] Non-stockholders have to obtain draft power by borrowing, hiring, or by work sharing. Pressure on farmers to enter draft arrangements is exacerbated where transport shortages have forced them to haul their produce to marketing depots on scotch carts and sledges. In some areas farmers deal with this problem through a group approach to draft exchange. In others informal cooperation and exchange is not the norm, and labor performed by nonfamily members tends to be paid for, at a local rate. Commercialization of draft has become a lucrative source of income for stockholders, and this places an increasing strain on cooperative relationships.[40]

Over time, then, access to cattle (and its regulation) has played a pivotal role in transforming agrarian relationships. Families who lack cattle find not only that they are denied the benefits of livestock, but that their crop husbandry is also debilitated by limited access to draft and manure.[41] It is likely that the relationship between stock ownership and labor supplies influences crop selection and production patterns. Where large stockholders are local businessmen, access to draft and local consumer credit sometimes becomes linked. Where there is severe population pressure on the land, cropped areas encroach on grazing areas with the effect of reducing carrying capacity without increasing marketable surplus. Thus, as Lionel Cliffe points out, there is a paradox in the national land question whereby there are too many people and cattle on the land at the same time as there is a shortage of labor, underutilized land, and not enough oxen to till the land.[42]

As recent research has shown, differentiation occurred along lines of region, household, and gender from the earliest days of colonialism.[43] Inevitably, the gradual emergence of new relations of local power and reciprocity, incipient economic stratification, and the advent of labor migrancy as an alternative source of cash income created social strains in rural communities. These strains are directly related to patterns of incorporation into the capitalist economy, as unequal access to land, livestock, technology, and agricultural capital have widened gaps between households with differential capacities to generate agricultural surpluses. The relationship between commodity production and commodity consumption in the countryside has created a "reproduction squeeze" for the rural poor, especially in poor agro-ecological zones. But these strains were not the results simply of spreading market relations. They were greatly exacerbated by government policies that aimed to protect white farmers during the Great Depression.

In particular, the Maize Control Acts of 1931 and 1934, designed to favor small white farmers by establishing a two-pool pricing system, seriously impaired the economic flexibility of African producers by requiring them either to deliver their produce direct to Maize Control Board depots at railheads, or to market it through registered traders (known as trader-producers), who were often white. While few African farmers had the cash resources at the beginning of the pool year to bag and transport their produce, trader-producers were able to dramatically reduce the prices paid to African producers in the controlled areas. Moreover, trader-producers preferred to offer Africans trade goods rather than cash in payment. As African cash incomes diminished, they faced increasing cash flow problems, which forced them to produce more maize, to sell more than their marketable surplus early in the season, and to buy back food before the next crop was ready. Fifty to 70 percent of African maize marketed was actually retained by traders and sold back to Africans in the dry season, while less than 10 percent was delivered at places on rail for transporting to central markets.[44]

African farmers had access to several strategies to counter the effects of this control. First, they could withhold their produce. This strategy could only succeed if they could meet their cash demands by other means, such as migrant labor. Second, they could try to evade formal market channels and continue to ply their traditional outlets. Third, they could resist government policies in other spheres—such as conservation and land management policies—to create political spaces in which to bargain with the state over the control and autonomy of everyday rural life. We shall see below how African farmers resorted to all these strategies in ways that established profound and enduring traditions of political contestation and negotiation between rural communities and the state. Most strikingly, peasants viewed growing social pressures less as the outcome of social stratification (and local injustice) associated with skewed land and livestock holdings than as the outcome of state control and management policies, most notably centralization (state injustice). Peasants deeply resented the large discrepancy between the price they received for their produce and that paid to Europeans, and they deeply distrusted government motives. They linked social dislocations ultimately to state-induced land pressure and deepening perceptions of absolute land shortage. This had a profound political impact on their relationship to the state and on the contours of rural power. For instead of agrarian accumulation becoming the focus of rural social conflict (as administrators feared) peasants turned their anger against the state. Rural dislocation was attended by stiffening resistance to state-directed programs of land management, intensified production, and conservation. These traditions lie at the very heart of the processes of state formation in Zimbabwe.

State, Peasants, and the Control of Social Life

As noted in chapter 1, regulating people's access to and use of land establishes the possibility of creating a link between resource management and social management. In the 1930s the Southern Rhodesian state was forging just such a link. But it was an ironic link, for the perceived land degradation that provided the context for intensified management was part of a peasant response to those very policies. It could only be negotiated at the local level, where flexibility was the rule of thumb. But frustration within the administration with peasant behavior also fueled a conflict between technicist central state policy-makers, who sought stricter control and uniformity of policy, and NCs, who were afraid of losing control of their districts.

African farmers opposed state-directed notions of efficient farming in part out of a deep suspicion of government motives. In 1935 the assistant agriculturalist reported:

> Before the [Maize Control] Act came into force in the Fort Victoria and Matabeleland area, the demonstration work was really going ahead in leaps and bounds, and in certain areas the demonstrators were unable to cope with the large numbers of natives interested in the better methods of farming. There were 141 plot owners in the Zimutu Reserve last year, and I regret to report that this year there are only 67. I have spoken to the natives to try to encourage them to continue with the better methods of farming that they have been taught, but they simply refuse and say "Why should we grow crops and sell them at less than we used to," and another remark is "Yes, we told you when you first brought demonstrators onto other reserves that they had come to try out our land, and later the government would either take it or our crops."[45]

In Matobo, where Africans could not sell their surplus maize as a result of the Maize Control Act, the Matobo Native Board "wanted to know why Native Demonstrators had been sent into the Native Reserves to teach them modern methods of growing maize."[46] Between incentives to produce more efficiently and strictures on their market position, peasants drew a troubling conclusion: "My fear is that if I were to go to a demonstrator and be taught, my land would be cut and I will be given a very small area to plough. . . . We feel that if we follow these people there is a danger that some of our land will be taken away."[47] It was a deep and lasting suspicion, fueled by veterinary controls on the movement and sale of African-owned livestock, which peasants interpreted as part of the authoritarian and discriminatory controls arising out of the Cattle Levy Act. Disaffection was deepened by strains that state conservation and management programs placed on the local labor economy. As one chief, cited by MacLean, put it:

> [F]irst of all we are told it is not right to plant at the bottom of a vlei or on the streambanks. This is ridiculous for it is damper there and it is easier for the women to water the crops if need be. These are the best places to plant. Then we are told to manure our lands with cattle manure in order to get bigger crops—but who is to spread the manure on the land? . . . The lands round our huts belong to many different people. How can we decide who will put on the manure?[48]

Over time, conservation labor created increasingly stressful pressures on domestic relations. Given the labor shortage in the reserves, and the increasing importance of off-farm incomes, African farmers had little incentive to expend their labor resources on conservation measures. Especially as state marketing policies reduced the returns, expensive and labor-sapping conservation measures were simply not worth it. When required to provide such labor, farmers handed the tasks to subordinate family or kin members, such as junior women and youths.

State strategies for controlling or reducing the numbers of

livestock in the reserves met similar responses. Because of the pivotal role played by cattle in local socioeconomic relations, any state initiative to regulate the use of cattle became a very touchy subject. Larger stockholders had little incentive to reduce their holdings because cattle were a source of local power or patronage: poorer farmers needed them for draft. Poorer farmers wanted to retain cattle in order to mitigate such relations and to avoid dependence on labor-intensive hand implements. Also, cattle were a source of security against drought for they could be sold for emergency cash needs or traded for grain.[49] Thus, both poorer and wealthier farmers had (and continue to have) reason to offer combined resistance to state stock control projects.

The combination of state policies and resistance to these policies evoked perceptions of increasing land pressure in the minds of both the rural population and state officials. But the political weight of these perceptions was very different. State officials viewed land pressure as an aspect of poor land-use practices associated with Africans' traditional land allocation system and their relationship with nature, which administrators considered to be driven by superstition, witchcraft and ignorance. In the view of the African population, land shortage was a result of state policies that threatened the very fabric of community life, for land occupied a central place in the moral scheme of Shona-speaking communities.[50] As in many African societies, ultimate political authority in Shona-speaking society resided in the ownership of the land, which was vested in the guardian spirits *(mhondoros)* of ancestors who first lived there or were ancient conquerors. Political authority was actually wielded by a chief, who was the leading member of a patrilineal lineage that claimed descent from those spirits. The accession of particular chiefs, and consequently their claims to public authority, was legitimated by the *mhondoro* through the voice of his spirit medium *(svikiro)*. The domain of chiefly authority was the *nyika*, which was defined both by territory and by spirit domains. The *nyika* was further divided into areas presided over by headmen, and the smallest social unit, the village, was a kinship unit.[51] Lineages were grouped in clans, which were distinguished by clan names (totems), were exogamic, and were generally associated with a particular geographical region. Consequently, individuals felt strong psychological links to the ancestral territory. Not all residents of an area (in some cases not even the majority) were of "royal" lineage; they were "outsiders" or "strangers" residing in the area for a variety of reasons, prominent among which were marriage ties. Such individuals faced the problem of trying to be incorporated into local social structures. Descent was not available to them but they could acquire clan membership by working the land in that territory and taking part in the communal rituals of the agricultural cycle. Thus, as David Lan puts it, social identity was "a question of action not of essence." "All the *vazukuru* of the *mhondoro* think of themselves and of others as such because they all live within the same spirit province, they all work the same land and they all take part in the same rituals that maintain its fertility."[52]

On this account, land is central to the social identity of Shona-speaking communities. The exogamic clan structure required that outsiders be constantly brought in. For outsiders the possibility of clan membership was linked to their ability to become *vazukuru* (recognized as descendants), which depended on land-based spiritual allegiance and land-based toil. Public authority was closely associated with land allocation and land access in local moral economies. This moral scheme also provided the context for cooperative and reciprocal laboring arrangements at the household and village level, whereby villagers combined efforts on specific tasks such as clearing bush, plowing, weeding, or reaping. Seen in this light, a threat to land access also constituted a threat to the capacity of communities to compose and recompose themselves. This had both psychological and material effects. Most immediately, pressure on land directly threatened the livelihood of *vazukuru*, who could never become members of a royal lineage and could therefore never achieve the status of chief or headman with land-allocating authority. More broadly, it disrupted community and household relationships of reciprocity and power in the deployment of labor, along lines of age and gender as well as class, as junior siblings have seen the opportunities of land inheritance narrow, and unmarried women's claims to land allocations have become less secure. Over the long term, one apparent effect was to politicize the social significance of witchcraft, as communities came under increasing strain.[53]

Over the course of the twentieth century these effects have played a pivotal role in the unfolding of state-peasant relations and, as we shall see, have prompted successive governments to design hegemonic strategies aimed specifically at women and youths in their efforts to manage the politics of rural citizenship. The public authority of traditional leaders, intimately associated with land allocation, has been undermined without being comprehensively replaced by the authority of the state. As elsewhere in Africa, the establishment of capitalist markets powerfully disrupted agrarian social relations, but it did not transform those relations in any linear way into capitalist relations. As Ben Cousins and others have noted, there are some factors that promote differentiation and some that retard it, and the balance not only varies spatially and socially but is unclear everywhere.[54] The communal property regime tends to constrain economic stratification by (still) securing land for most people. But the parcels may be very small and not very productive. Lineage elites still allocate land in many communities, and land tends to be allocated to older people. Increasingly, young families have to wait for a land allocation or receive it through inheritance. Kinship relations remain important for securing access to critical production resources. At the same time, expanded agrarian production is positively correlated with urban wage labor. Rural social relations are therefore deeply implicated not only by access to land, but also by the size and direction of the national labor market, opportunities for education, and ties of kin-based community. These changing conditions deepened social cleavages in the countryside, especially as youths and the rural poor came under increasing pressure. Their effects on state-peasant relations became increasingly prominent from the 1930s on. Their overarching, immediate, and lasting, impact was to intensify the politics of land control between the state and the peasantry.

Development, Social Control, and Hegemony

As strains on the rural economy and rural society intensified in the early 1940s, the political pressures on the administration to manage and control rural socioeconomic life shifted to meet new economic interests. Southern Rhodesia emerged from World War II with a broadening and growing economy. Although the economic base remained narrow and heavily dependent on mineral and agricultural exports (especially the expansion of asbestos and chrome mining and the postwar tobacco boom) the domestic market was expanded by a rapid increase in the urban African population and in white immigration. Competition from overseas was disrupted and local companies, especially those that used local resources (such as food-processing industries) were able to expand.[55] The white Rhodesian establishment of large-scale commerce, industry, and agriculture, represented politically by the ruling United Federal Party (UFP) under Godfrey Huggins, expressed a new enthusiasm for industrialization and a new op-

timism and confidence in the growth potential of the Rhodesian economy.

This new vision entailed ideas about development that centered on a desire to join the ranks of the developed, integrated,
"mature" capitalist economies. The conventional wisdom that
mature economies required state regulation and planning, "to
avoid the worst abuses of unfettered free enterprise," was applied also to the Southern Rhodesian state. It became government policy to "step in and ensure the adequate development"
of important industries where the private sector had not taken
the lead.[56] Several commissions were set up to coordinate and
regulate development, including the Natural Resources Board
(NRB), which imposed strict conservation standards on farmers. Especially after the Unilateral Declaration of Independence (UDI) in 1965, the state provided massive investment
and subsidy support to industry, developing infrastructure,
expanding social services for whites, and helping businesses
bust sanctions.[57] Consequently, the state was heavily dependent on capital input and revenue. Yet throughout the period
tax concessions, especially to white farmers, remained very
generous. The generation of revenue for development purposes became, and remained, a deep-seated constraint on state
rural investment.

Given its commitment to white agriculture and industry,
expenditure on rural African development came last on the
government's list of priorities. At the same time, three closely
related political-economic factors were pressing the government to reassess the role and participation of rural Africans in
the national economy and polity. First, the labor demands of
the colonial economy were changing and industry was calling
for a steady, stable and guaranteed supply of productive labor.
This situation was complicated by a postwar upsurge in African worker militancy that culminated in a general strike in

1948.[58] Control of labor was therefore as important a political consideration as supply of labor. Second, a new interest was growing within both industry and the state to boost African productivity. This interest was rooted partly in a concern that low levels of African production limited the state's ability to subsidize European agricultural prices through such mechanisms as the Maize Control Act, and partly in fears that the progressive decline of the African peasant sector would destabilize the African rural population. Also, the government wanted a revenue surplus to release to Britain for postwar reconstruction aid.[59] Thus, whereas peasant participation in the market had been reduced during the early part of the century by means of "primitive accumulation" in order to push a labor force out of the rural population, a reversal of this trend occurred in the late 1940s: the demand for labor came to be seen as closely linked to the reestablishment of settled African agricultural productivity. Third, for a state heavily dependent for economic resources on its capacity to generate capital for investment and development, and politically reluctant to become a generous provider, it became increasingly important to place the onus of regenerating African agriculture on the peasant sector itself. African producers, therefore, should develop a stake in the system. In the face of peasant decline and "routine resistance" this imperative required a more co-optive approach to peasant producers, individually and collectively.

In order to meet these pressures the state had to bring economic development and social management together under its own direction. Its responses to this task established the political terrain on which rural struggles over state domination were played out. They are examined in detail in the following chapters. Here it is sufficient to sketch the contradictory political currents that they aimed to negotiate in managing labor, regulating African agrarian class formation, and entrenching state authority. Taken as a whole, these currents cast a critical light on the shifting contours of state power.

Labor Supply

In the formative years of the colonial political economy, the Southern Rhodesian state had played a pivotal role in securing labor supplies for industry and white agriculture. But in the 1940s industry began to oppose state direction and allocation of labor. Industry's principal demand was not that the state should ensure the cheapness of labor, but that it should ensure a regular, efficient, and sufficient supply of labor. Employers and labor bureaucrats, who were reluctant to use political mechanisms to direct labor, began to argue that an orderly end should be made to the migrant labor system, and a permanent industrial labor force settled in urban areas, to increase the efficiency and stability of industrial labor.[60] This argument amounted to a call to bring about a clear separation between the rural and urban African populations, thereby dismantling the migrant labor system, on the view that "this country is destined to become very highly industrialised. . . . We cannot escape from the fact that the great majority of natives will in future have to seek an outlet in industry and not in agriculture. . . ."[61] While the Land Apportionment Act remained inviolable, Native Department officials began to call for African tenure security. In the wake of the 1948 general strike, Chief Native Commissioner Powys-Jones argued that "quiescence and regard for law and order" among Africans could not be relied upon indefinitely "unless conditions of housing and security of tenure are stabilised."[62] But the government, dependent on white votes, was reluctant to act. Only in 1960, by the Land Apportionment Amendment Act, was African freehold tenure allowed in urban townships, thereby opening the door for the development of permanent urban

African communities with secure land tenure. After UDI, the Rhodesian Front government, under pressure from urban white constituencies, tried anew to limit and regulate the growth of the urban African population.

The changes in labor demands meant that the state had to turn around a system of labor supply it had brought into being in the colony's early years. To do this it would have to restructure the forms of control and domination it exercised over rural communities. In 1951 the government enacted the Native Land Husbandry Act for this purpose. I take up the issue in detail in chapter 3.

African Productivity and Agrarian Class Formation

The pressure to improve the labor supply by substantially "freeing" it was attended by pressure to improve productivity in the African reserves. The threat of declining African production increased vulnerability to drought and hunger in the reserves, exacerbating urban pressure and the difficulty of controlling labor flows. In 1948, for instance, the Director of Native Production and Marketing estimated that although African production had produced a record crop, the African areas had managed to meet only 93 percent of their subsistence crop requirements. But the pressure to expand African agricultural production was also a response to the fact that since the early 1940s Southern Rhodesia had been a consistent importer of essential foodstuffs, notably maize. The cost of importation created a serious and unwelcome fiscal burden at the same time that many white farmers were reducing maize production to concentrate on tobacco. The government began to look to the African agricultural sector to meet the shortfall between the maize production and the maize requirement of the colony. Also, urban businesses wanted to expand African production in order to keep food prices low and to extend the domestic market for agricultural and household requisites and other commodities. Indeed, throughout the later colonial period, and increasingly after UDI, business interests called for strategies to increase the earning and spending power of rural Africans.[63]

In the view of state officials, therefore, it was imperative to create a positive incentive for African producers and to stabilize African agriculture. In the late 1940s NAD officials began to stress the need to improve marketing facilities for African producers. In 1956 the Department of Native Economics and Marketing was created as part of the reorganization of the Native Department and as a response to the need to reform marketing arrangements. A standing liaison committee of the executive of the African Farmers' Union and officials of the department was set up in the hope that "this committee will do much to secure the co-operation of the African farmer."[64] But stimulating African productivity was a politically sensitive business because the interests of small and large white agriculture, urban consumers, and the government fiscus were not congruent. While the government wanted to limit expenditure, it did not want a potentially volatile proletariat in the African areas, nor did it want to promote agricultural competition with small European farmers. Large farmers, in turn, wanted easier access to international markets and opposed state regulations that small farmers supported. Under these conditions, the regeneration of African agriculture could not be left to the operation of market forces. Price and marketing controls seemed to offer a solution. Since it was clear that the Maize Marketing Act would have to go, European farmers brought great pressure to bear on government to provide stability for the industry by means of a five-year guaranteed price.[65] Urban consumers supported this demand for stability as a kind of compromise: the state marketing board could sell to the urban areas at relatively low and controlled prices while still meeting farmers' demands. For the state, manipulation of prices could provide a source of revenue to meet these political demands and to fund African development through the African Development Fund. But price stabilization would only be feasible if there was a viable African agricultural sector to provide a buffer against low world prices. Thus pricing and marketing control as a political strategy had one crucial weakness: it depended on African rejuvenation actually taking place. If African markets were not expanded, neither the security of white agriculture nor low consumer prices in urban areas could be sustained. Wages in urban industries would be pushed up and the expansion of consumer markets curtailed.

Significantly, the government did not intend to plow resources garnered from African agriculture back into African development. Instead, it created a mechanism for African rural development to be funded by Africans themselves through the African Development Fund (ADF), which was to be used, under the control of Native Affairs, to promote agricultural production and marketing. The bulk of the fund derived from levies on produce marketed by African farmers. Although officials admitted early on that this system cut into the resources of producers and reduced the amount of capital that could be plowed back into improving production, the ADF became and remained throughout the colonial period the principal source of funding for African agricultural development. In effect, this system of funding meant that improving conditions for production depended on expanded marketing, which depended in turn on increased production. Most particularly, African producers themselves would bear the cost of development.

These actions illuminate the delicate political problem of rejuvenating African agriculture. The process of agricultural decline set in train in the early part of the century would have to be turned around, but at the same time the process of agrarian class formation must be carefully limited in order to restrict African proletarianization and agrarian competition. Securing the cooperation of African farmers was a task that only the state could undertake and it would require a reassessment of relations of state domination and control. But much depended on the response of African farmers. The managed development of the rural economy rested on several factors— including the monetization of the economy, the nature and distribution of rural incomes, the nature and source of rural savings, the objectives of production, and the decisions on which the disposal of a rural surplus is based. Under the impact of economic stratification and labor migrancy these factors were changing. Any reassessment of state-peasant relations would have to take account of these transformations, at the level of both individual producers and rural communities.

State Power, Development, and Hegemony

The economic and ecological decline in the African reserves that had attended the expansion of the colonial economy had created tense and adversarial relations between the state and rural communities. The 1944 Godlonton Commission on Native Production and Trade declared agricultural practice badly wanting, especially in the sphere of production, but also in trade and marketing. It stressed the need for drastic action, recommending more compulsion and more rapidly applicable agrarian and marketing laws to supersede the cumbersome Natural Resources Act of 1941, as well as new laws to enhance the power and prestige of chiefs and to provide greater overriding powers for rural administrators. In the wake of the commission, the Native Affairs Division began to abandon its earlier noninterventionist strategy of agricultural demonstration and to devise a policy "that made conservation and change in land-use the dominating interest of native commissioners and the Native Agriculture Department."[66] This ushered in the "phase of progress by compulsion," of which the Native Land Husbandry Act was to be the centerpiece.[67]

William Beinart has pointed out that the adoption of

conservation as the keystone of managed rural development
was not simply a racial strategy. It was part of a larger attempt to manage agrarian economic development that initially
aimed at white farmers, and used the Natural Resources Act to
end white subsistence farming and raise agricultural output.
Nevertheless, the increasingly central role of conservationist
ideas in the management of rural African populations had a
peculiar political cast, for these ideas were inextricably tied to
hierarchical conceptions of civilization and social progress,
and to intensifying concerns about the uncertain status of
public authority in the reserves. In 1934, Alvord argued that
the greatest handicap to improved African farming was the
lack of marketing facilities, rather than agrarian decline. Only
in the following year, after an extended visit to the American
midwest, and a tour of conservation and extension projects
among African-Americans and Native Americans in the
southern and south-western states, did he become more intensely interested in systematic conservation. The Department of Native Agriculture started systematic soil conservation well before its white counterpart, and it was the sense of
dissipating administrative control and African agrarian intransigence in the ensuing years that led development officials
to start demanding "progress by compulsion" in the early
1940s.[68] In fact, neither the example of European conservation
techniques nor "progress by compulsion" was necessarily the
best way to rejuvenate African productivity. One major difference between white and African farmers was that the former
had a powerful political voice, as well as abundant access to
credit, capital, and technology. The lethargy, indifference, and
lack of responsibility and discipline on which the Godlonton
Commission blamed rural decline was not a function of the
"natural turpitude" that the commission attributed to
Africans. It was part of a political response to the forcible creation of a labor force and the immediate predations of the state

on rural society, especially in terms of regulating marketing and trade. Such resistance typically took the form of noncooperation and opposition to imposed agricultural techniques. This raised the problem not only of how to compel peasants to become "progressive" farmers but of allocating the financial burden of providing the infrastructure for such progress.

The envisaged answer was to increase the commitment of African farmers to market-oriented production and to inculcate new forms of civic responsibility. These objectives became more urgent as African political dissent increased in the 1950s and the voices of nationalist opposition and labor protest became louder.[69] The government became increasingly (and unsuccessfully) determined to keep these sentiments out of rural African areas by giving rural Africans a stake in agricultural development. Yet it consistently hedged on the question of who was to bear the political and economic costs of "bringing in" the peasantry, generally placing its faith in the ADF. Between "progress" and "compulsion" lay a multitude of political tensions. While peasants could conceivably be compelled to adopt conservation measures, it was infinitely more difficult to manage their participation in the market. With little reason to trust the state and every reason to distrust the market, peasants retained a discretionary option on participation.

In short, by the end of the 1940s, the colonial administration faced a new array of structural and political imperatives to modify the forms and processes of state controls over rural African society. Controls could be negotiated in several different arenas: regulation of the market (the sphere of exchange), regulation of land (the sphere of production), regulation of power and authority (the sphere of reproduction). The following chapters examine the negotiations between the colonial state and rural communities for control of rural life in these spheres and show why it was essential for successive governments to pursue their managerial objectives through hegemonic strategies that sought to remoralize state-peasant relations and secure state authority. The remainder of this chapter shows why market regulation itself provided an inadequate basis for bringing in the peasantry.

Markets, Management, and Social Control

Among development experts it has been conventional wisdom in recent years that state regulation of markets impedes economic incentives among small farmers, and therefore tends to constrain development. Rural development in postwar Rhodesia illustrates both the strengths and limits of this argument. Rhodesian development officials recognized that reserve economies could be stimulated by bringing African farmers into formal markets. But establishing secure markets is itself a political act. National commodity markets are structured by the national political economy and class relations at the national level—in this case the power of European agrarian capital and the revenue demands of the administration. Peasant incentives, however, are determined by local economic interests and power relations. It is the interplay between these two levels that determines peasant participation in markets and necessitates extramarket hegemonic strategies to promote economic development and manage society.

The postwar administration presented rural market controls as institutional supports for African farmers. They would rationalize the national market to offset the ecological precariousness of much of the African reserve area, and they would secure developmental revenues through levies on marketed produce. The Grain Marketing Act of 1950 was designed to stabilize producer prices, encourage poorer peasants to grow low-value food crops rather than maize by providing a guaranteed market, and to provide an efficient marketing and distribution service through the Grain Marketing Board (GMB). Revenues would be secured by deducting an ADF levy, a transport charge and a handling charge from the guaranteed producer prices paid to African farmers. The government noted that these deductions would offset "unfairness" to European producers, who had to bear the cost of delivering their produce to the market.[70]

As a way to manage agricultural markets, generate revenues, and promote economic development, this was a fragile initiative. The success of the ADF depended on the effective operation of the GMB. This in turn depended on the cooperation of trader-producers, to whom most African peasants sold their produce. Trader-producers systematically cheated African farmers by pricing their crops only at the lowest grade, or by adjusting their scales or the size of their bins to systematically undervalue African produce.[71] Furthermore, since the ADF was a national fund, greater market participation did not ensure greater local ADF disbursements. In a classic free-rider scenario, farmers who marketed through the board subsidized those who did not. In 1962, the Secretary of Internal Affairs acknowledged:

> The levy system itself is a tax on the productive sector of the African economy and when the expressed aim is a conversion of the subsistence economy into a cash economy, it would appear to be somewhat contradictory to tax those producers who, by their efforts, shift into the cash economy. A levy can, therefore, be seen as a retarding influence as long as it only applies to those who produce for the market and leaves untouched those whose effort remains in the subsistence field.[72]

African farmers resented this system at every level, and evaded or manipulated it wherever possible. Price stabilization and producer levies together provided both sellers and independent buyers with incentives to enter direct-consumer transactions. Many Europeans living close to African areas purchased their grain requirements in this way, consuming an estimated 30 percent of African crops. In 1953 a subsidy was placed on grain consumer prices to discourage direct consumers from bypassing official channels, and thereby losing the subsidy. Moreover, African producers had an interest in evading trader-producers, with the result that competition developed between registered and unregistered buyers in African areas.[73] When the government cracked down by specifying that controlled products marketed by Africans be sold only at designated locations, peasant resentment of the marketing system, and particularly of trader-producers, deepened.

Thus, despite the state's stress on the need for an orderly marketing system to ensure orderly production, its ability to regulate patterns of production and marketing was weak. The CNC's annual reports hinted that the department really did not know the extent of African production, since its reports were based on disposals through legal channels only. Over the years, the degree of control over various crops was shifted back and forth in order to protect the Grain Marketing Board rather than to protect producers. In 1952 the NC Mazoe noted a range of problems attached to the rise of an independent rural market: the price structure for all farmers was being undermined, the ADF was losing thousands of pounds of revenue, honest farmer-consumers or trader-producers were being squeezed out of the market.[74] For the state, the problem was that African agricultural activity that remained outside the formal market not only undermined the market (and the state's capacity to regulate it) but also undermined the revenue base for the state's rural development strategy. Market control could not bring in the peasantry.

The livestock market was a particularly conflictual arena of state-peasant relations. Throughout the colonial period, the administration's attempts to control African stocking levels as a conservation measure depended heavily on its ability to persuade or coerce Africans to sell their cattle at state-run sales. NAD administrators argued that if African stock numbers were to be maintained at their correct level there should be a market for surplus stock at attractive prices. But African farmers recognized that this market was stacked against them by favoring European cattle in pricing and grading structures that were regulated by the parastatal Cold Storage Commission. They also resented veterinary controls which restricted the movement and sale of cattle, and affected the price. They were aggrieved at state pressure to destock in order to protect land when overstocking was a clear result of state prohibitions on grazing their cattle on crown lands. African stockholders found themselves in the unattractive position of being under stringent pressure from NCs to sell stock but unable to secure good prices.[75] Consequently, as Native Commissioner Allan Wright vividly chronicles in his memoir, the cattle auction itself became an arena in which peasant resentment and resistance to the state was enhanced by "[s]uspicion of buyers, suspicion of price lists and, unfortunately, even suspicion of those incorruptible officials whose duty it is to organise sales."[76] At the sales the NC, cattle grader, buyers, and the NC's field staff would all camp together at rest houses while the African stock owners congregated at the nearby sales pens. This segregation, Wright argues, created among the sellers the belief that the whites were conspiring to ensure that African-owned cattle were sold at the lowest possible price. Their suspicion was deepened if the buyers decided to form a "ring" for the sale. Africans would also blame NCs, who arranged cattle sales, for low prices.

Perceiving the state and market as deeply entangled, African farmers responded by boycotting sales that they thought were irregular. Frequently, they would bring cattle long distances to the auction, only to spurn offered prices and trail them home again—an environmentally destructive practice.

Refusal to sell was a strong bargaining chip. Indeed, as land pressure became more serious in the 1960s and 1970s, African cattle sales tended to decrease. It is likely that this reflects the increasing importance of cattle as a source of security for poor farmers against a sudden cash need. Yet it does not explain why Africans were prepared to bring cattle to sales only to withdraw them in large numbers.[77] In fact, it appears that African farmers were playing a more complex market game. They were quite willing to participate in the cattle market provided the price was right. But they also used the market to establish cash values for their cattle so that they could negotiate, in a separate economic sphere, local relations of accumulation, trade, and patronage with shopkeepers, butchers, and kinfolk.

Under these market conditions, control of the cattle market accorded the state very little purchase either on stocking levels in the African areas or on the economic decisions of African farmers. Indeed, the tenuousness of that purchase led the state to impose compulsory destocking sales between 1943 and 1947 under the Natural Resources Act and to strengthen measures for limiting stocking levels under the 1951 Land Husbandry Act. As we shall see, these measures failed but had significant effects on subsequent political development. In the short term they exacerbated the adversarial relationship between the state and peasant communities. In the long term they created an environment for new incorporative political structures in the countryside.

The tenuousness of state control over rural markets demonstrated that the market was an inadequate mechanism for managing economic change and manipulating the production practices of peasant farmers. As elsewhere in the Third World, Zimbabwean peasants saw, perhaps more clearly than government officials and development theorists, that the state and markets are not separate institutions, nor are they particularly rational. Peasants could manipulate markets not only to create opportunities for accumulation but also to negotiate broader state interventions in the control of rural social life. The state's strategies, on the other hand, were constrained by its desire to regulate agrarian transformations to meet the changing demands of the expanding economy. Yet the political impact of economic change on rural society was intensifying. Land shortages were becoming increasingly visible, and differential access to cattle for draft and fertilizer was becoming a new focus for domestic and community power. These developments influenced peasants' production decisions and their participation in migrant labor markets. If the state was to establish some purchase on these aspects of rural social life, more nuanced strategies of state intervention would have to be devised.

Conclusion

The costs of early political initiatives to squeeze out African agricultural competition and secure a cheap labor supply were high. By the late 1930s, the reserves were becoming ravaged by the combined effects of labor-inducing policies, peasant resistance to market inequalities, and state intervention in production. State officials articulated these political processes and their impacts in terms of ecological deterioration and what appeared to be incipient social disintegration within rural African communities. Government officials and peasants were at loggerheads over conservation and "good" farming practices. Administrators regarded the problem as one of "inefficiency" and "backwardness" leading to fragmented and unproductive holdings. The Godlonton Commission perceived Africans as lethargic, irresponsible, and unable to grasp the concept of cooperation. It concluded that "the maximum benefit both for the state and for the natives . . . can only be obtained by compulsory planned production. . . ."[78] But peasants viewed the problem as resulting from state policies. The more urgently development officials tried to push through centralization plans, the more peasants regarded this as a ploy to reduce African land holdings. There was virtually no common ground for political argument between administration officials and rural citizens.

But these conditions also generated incipient conflicts within the state, both between local administrators and central policymakers, and between those officials most concerned with rural governance and those most concerned with resource management. The process whereby African rural development came to focus on land rather than on Africans was not merely an outcome of the precarious character of the state's outer reaches and the contradictory civilizing ideology of the Native Department. In the early 1940s technicists in the central civil service, frustrated with the flexibility of local administrators, whom they perceived as insensitive to the fragility of the environment, forced conservation to the very center of social management policies.[79] As demands on the state to manage economic and political development shifted to meet new national conditions, this uncompromisingly authoritarian and directive vision provided the framework for state-society relations in the countryside.

At the same time, new socioeconomic conditions of production were emerging within the African reserves. Most salient were land pressure and the regularization of migrant labor, for they intensified the problems of local labor control, and established structural links between local labor, cattle holdings, and the market that has had a lasting impact on sociopolitical relations in rural Zimbabwe that no government can afford to ignore in its attempts to manage its citizenry. The interplay of these local socioeconomic conditions with the structural objectives of state policies created an enduring tension between state intervention and nonintervention in rural life.

Changing political-economic demands in the 1940s impressed on the administration the increasing political need to reassess its strategies of social management in order to consolidate social and political control over rural society, to stabilize the rural population, and to root the authority of the state in the rural areas. The peasantry had to be brought into the national agricultural economy as an essential factor in the market, in a way which would not threaten white farming interests. Also, the spread of nationalist appeals from the urban centers had to be preempted. All this demanded a reassessment of the relationship between political domination, social control, and citizenship. But state-peasant relations had come to be defined in adversarial terms, and state incursions into the patterns of rural life were limited, contradictory, and coercive. As the demands of rural control shifted under the impact of economic and political change, this tension gained political intensity and led the colonial state down a politically contradictory path. For while it created the need for more hegemonic state strategies it also made such strategies very difficult to implement.

Part Two

THE NATIONAL RACIAL STATE

We have before us an unparallelled opportunity to perform a great sociological undertaking, in accordance with scientific concepts. We have a sound legal and constitutional basis for this task and we have an enlightened public opinion. There is, however, one vital factor that may easily dash all our hopes and plans to the ground—that factor is the soil; our mother-earth which is being lost forever at a terrifying rate, and without which we must quit the earth.

—R. G. Haw, in *NADA* 1950

3

Extending the State, 1951–1962

Conservation and the Control of Land

When the Minister of Native Affairs introduced the Native Land Husbandry Act (NLHA) in the Legislative Assembly early in 1951, both sides of the House hailed it as one of the most important pieces of legislation ever laid before them. Indeed, the act is perhaps the most extensively discussed legislation in the history of development in Zimbabwe. Designed to establish a "class of peasant farmers" with individual freehold tenure on "economic land units," the policy drew the interest of development specialists throughout the world because it addressed the problem of managing rural populations under conditions of industry-led development. It fit the prevalent post–World War II preoccupation with land reform in the Third World, and it conformed to a specific model of rural control that was gaining prominence in other settler-dominated African economies. Throughout the 1950s, all other rural development plans in Southern Rhodesia were officially subordinated to the Land Husbandry Act (LHA). Students of Zimbabwe's development history have understood the act as first and foremost a blueprint for controlling the peasantry within the parameters of the Land Apportionment Act. It also became a nexus of state-peasant conflict that generated credence and support for the nationalist cause in the countryside. As peasant resistance to the act exploded in the reserves, state control of the rural population became increasingly tenuous. The irony of the LHA is that it began as a mechanism of social control and ended as a catalyst of liberation.

But an analysis of the Land Husbandry Act that begins and ends with its coercive propensities cannot do justice to its place in the politics of constructing state hegemony in postwar Southern Rhodesia. In his social biography of a Kalanga family, Richard Werbner suggests that local conflicts over land use planning and the implementation of the act were not only conflicts over the control over social life, but also conflicts over the meaning of legitimate public authority and constitutional order. They were, in other words, not just political battles but also ideological battles.[1] Werbner's account focuses on the intimate political context of the village. But struggles over the meaning of public authority were not only local. They were part of the broader sociopolitical intent of the act. In his annual report for 1951, the CNC declared:

> The new Act does more than merely make good husbandry methods compulsory and control stock and grazing; it gives power to give individual farming rights which can devolve to an heir, and so make the right-holder more land-conscious; the power for provision of labour to ensure soil conservation in the communal grazing areas; and the power to set aside townships and business centres, in which outright title will be granted, to cater for the landless African . . . and it will ensure that all those who *do* till the soil or raise cattle will obtain from the good earth the highest yield made possible by modern skilled husbandry methods.
>
> In short, the provisions of this Act give us the opportunity of changing for the good of themselves, and of the Colony, and of

Africa as a whole, the social and economic structure of the Africans of Southern Rhodesia.[2]

Thus the act represented a highly intrusive strategy to manage transformations in the social and material relations of property, power, and authority that structured the everyday realities of rural life. By establishing a new rural property regime, the formulators of the act sought to inculcate new conceptions of personal and civic responsibility that would reorient local concepts of Right, rights, and community membership. Moreover, since chiefs were accountable for the behavior of their followers, these new forms of responsibility would be linked to political accountability. In effect, the act aimed to do more than manage rural African populations within the parameters of the postwar colonial political economy. It aimed to remoralize social management. As a "development" strategy, it relied on the depoliticizing terms of rational and responsible resource use to perform political tasks, in ways that James Ferguson has superbly analyzed elsewhere.[3] But in doing so, it also sought to secure new categories of agrarian knowledge, moral understandings of rights, and agrarian social practices that could provide the framework for settled membership in the polity.

A full understanding of the Land Husbandry Act's place in the historical production of modern Zimbabwe must therefore go beyond its role as the vehicle of "coercive development," which etched the battle lines of liberation into the countryside, and take account of its efforts to transform rural social relations in the context of state making. This chapter shows the state-building impulses that drove this initiative, and the profound political and institutional tensions that undermined it. By the end of the 1950s, as the LHA loosened rather than strengthened rural control, the normative language of the colonial administration shifted from stressing responsible resource use to stressing the "paramountcy of human relation-ships," and administrators began to realize that the institu-tional crux of rural citizenship lay in local government struc-tures and new conceptions of community membership.

Technocracy and Social Being

The Land Husbandry Act was formulated by senior agricul-tural and administrative officers in the Native Affairs Depart-ment who conceived the act, together with the Native Devel-opment Fund Act and the Grain Marketing Act, to form "the tripod upon which the future satisfactory development of Na-tive agriculture and production rests."[4] The LHA provided for the demarcation of villages into "economic" arable and graz-ing units based on individual security of tenure and individual grazing rights. These units would be based on a technical cal-culation of the quality of soil and other natural resources. Though grazing areas would remain communal, stocking lev-els would be limited to the carrying capacity of the land in re-lation to individual arable holdings large enough for sustain-able agriculture. The designers of the act anticipated that by ending the fragmentation of land holdings in the reserves, the act would create "a class of African 'peasant farmers'" that was stable in both size and mobility—settled, satisfied, relatively homogeneous, and noncompetitive with European farmers. Simultaneously, implementation would release a reliable and steadily increasing labor supply for industrial development. The five-year implementation plan estimated that if the act was implemented on schedule 20,000 to 25,000 male workers would "come forward annually" and move into industry. Gov-ernment rhetoric repeatedly stressed that Africans must "make a final choice" between being "farmers or industrialists."[5]

Thus, although the LHA was a rural and technical act, its

rationale was urban and political. By revitalizing rural productivity it would bring the migrant labor system to a coherent end, ensure a stable urban proletariat for industrial
development, and cement the provisions of the Land Apportionment Act. Significantly, as the Director of Native Agriculture acknowledged, the act *presupposed* that industrial development would occur:

> The implementation of the Act stabilises the land and the cattle
> position but we must face the fact that it cannot do that without
> stabilising the rural population and additional families cannot be
> accommodated in the reserves and special native areas. Only
> through industrial development can employment be found for
> this expanding population and living standards raised.[6]

But if industrial development did not meet expectations, or if
the migrant labor system could not be brought under control,
rural Africans might challenge not only the Land Husbandry
Act but the Land Apportionment Act itself. Ten years later,
the crash from power of the party that represented most profoundly the misplaced faith in industrial development marked
the state's failure to bring off this initiative in social management.

As an attempt to redefine the relationship of rural Africans
to their land, the LHA was a massive technical undertaking,
which involved surveying the reserves comprehensively, planning infrastructural development, and demarcating individual
land holdings. It was also massively disruptive. White politicians and administrators recognized from the outset that such
a far-reaching attempt to make agrarian policy the linchpin of
social management could only be effectively implemented with
the cooperation of rural Africans. Even before the bill was
passed, African farmers had sought unsuccessfully to make
representations against it, and one MP predicted that, given
these sentiments, NCs would be unable to implement it. One
senior NAD official remarked:

[W]e have to interfere with all the Native cherishes. Not to do so means erosion and famine, but in doing so we arouse hostility, suspicion and political ferment. It is a very grim choice, and there has never been a time when closer contact with the Native Department and the Native has been more needed and it has never been so difficult for the Native Department to do it.[7]

Nevertheless the Land Husbandry Act was conceived with a peculiar technocratic confidence that brushed aside these qualms. In later years colonial administrators and technocrats would insist across the board that the act had been a superb technical measure defeated in the end by cultural obstacles and ham-fisted implementation.[8] Indeed, this argument would provide the rationale for a move away from a technocratic vision to a more incorporative conception of social management. Yet to the act's implementers, it was not simply a technical exercise. They saw it, in Haw's words, as "a great sociological undertaking" and a vehicle for social progress that would change the relationship of rural citizens to the law, public authority, and each other. This vision of modernity and development can be traced in the conceptions of land rights, land politics, and rural economic transformations that informed the structure of the act.

Concept of Land Rights

The technocratic development vision of the LHA rested on a deep tension between an appeal to individual property rights as the foundation of modern social being, and state activism in regulating rural production patterns. White politicians and (with a few exceptions) administrators believed implicitly in the empowering capacity and progressive nature of individual property ownership. They saw progress as linked to personal incentive, and personal incentive as rooted in individual rights of property and exchange. This belief provided the pivotal philosophical assumption of the LHA, articulated most cogently in arguments for individual freehold tenure. To CNC Powys-Jones, secure tenure offered the only potential guarantees of "quiescence and regard for law and order." Founded on a principle of rights in which property ownership was the basis of value, the LHA posited free and equal exchange of property as the key form of social interaction, and personal incentive as the basis of personal responsibility with regard to occupation, employment, and use of land. In effect, this vision linked responsible citizenship directly to responsible land use, and responsible land use directly to private property. The incentive structures associated with individual property rights would undermine the "superstitious" elements of African agrarian organization, and thereby establish a new ethico-political terrain for securing state authority. Public officials counterposed a rhetoric of "free enterprise" (linked to individual tenure) directly to "communism" (linked to communal tenure). Introducing the bill in the House, the Minister of Native Affairs argued:

> Here we have a legal recognition of security of tenure in the reserve. We entrench the rights of the individual and from that basis there is a splendid opportunity for development as the native advances and wishes to adapt the system to his rising standards. Now, without this framework, in which to design and carve out his future way of life, the native must continue to face a jostling state of communal frustration with no clear definition of his personal rights. Under such conditions—and this is the important point—under such conditions, the frustration occasioned by insecurity of tenure in the communal system, there can be no sustained personal incentive to improve and develop as the man should and would if he had security of tenure.[9]

Thus the LHA would inculcate a concept of social being that officials believed was appropriate for social stability and progress. The corollary was that once African economic life came to rest on a liberal market concept of individual utility, African participation in the national cash market would be stimulated. And a stronger, more extensive national market was both the hallmark and the keystone of progress.

According to this vision personal development and social development were inextricably linked, and both were promoted by the LHA's insistence on individual ownership and responsibility. On this uncompromising appeal to possessive individualism, the proponents of the act believed, a conceptual framework would be erected to transform the African rural economy, to structure the relationship between the state and rural communities, and to ground a new concept of citizenship that could ensure political stability, progress, and hegemonic development. It was a boldly asserted faith:

> rapid implementation of government policy by application of the Native Land Husbandry Act right throughout all the Native reserves and areas is vital to establish and ensure a contented and progressive Native peasant who, having been divorced from the present communal system of land tenure will, with his individual allocation of land become aware of a new pride of ownership and aware of a new incentive to adopt better husbandry methods for his own progress.
>
> Inevitably he will disregard the political sirens of the industrial areas, who themselves are making no headway with their self-aggrandisement schemes.
>
> In the urban areas attention to the living conditions and amenities of the urban native will lead to more political contentment and a desire and ability to progress.[10]

Officials saw two ways in which to promote this vision. One way was to curtail the ability of individuals to move between access to land ("semi-loafing in the Reserve") and access to employment in order to meet their everyday desires. This strategy would involve extensive state regulation of people's mobility by defining and controlling their rights of access to fixed property either in the townships or in the reserves. Thus the state would be the ultimate repository of property rights, strictly policing social life by deciding where people could live or own property, and under what terms. The other way to promote this development vision was to advance a conception of the state as noninterventionist and nonregulatory, encouraging individuals to "make their choice" by reducing a panoply of civic actions and relationships to an economic nexus. As the CNC expressed it in 1961,

> [L]ooking at the problem in an even wider context, all the blueprints of agricultural development and technical extension to promote increased production and a change from a subsistence economy to a cash economy, will remain largely ineffective as long as the only incentive to effort is a personal target objective (a bicycle, a dress or other trade goods which can be acquired in the labor market) and the really massive and continuing communal needs of health and education are catered for by free issue, or nearly free.[11]

In this respect, the state would appear simply as the arbiter of rights in a more Lockean sense, allowing citizens to pursue their well-being in the market by purchasing the trappings of progress. According to this hands-off approach to development, "The primary need is the promotion of the desire for progress, and of self-reliance in achieving it," and the language of African development became the language of initiative and responsibility from within, of "self-development."[12] In the context of the colonial polity, and the entanglement of state and market outlined in chapter 2, this conception of the state as both the repository of rights and the arbiter of rights was politically contradictory.

The contradiction was fully realized in the LHA, which reined in the operation of possessive individualist concepts of rights, value, and property by limiting the size of land holdings and by limiting land alienation that farmers were allowed under the act. The allowable size of land holding was limited by the concept of an "economic unit," which was calculated by agricultural officers according to the ecological condition of the land (ecological zone, state of the soil, and rainfall). Technically neat, this formula actually imposed on farmers an unrealistic uniformity that took little account of existing production systems or social relations already being transformed under the impact of the colonial economy and the migrant labor system. Local officials often had only the sketchiest knowledge of local ecologies or the logics of agrarian practices. The size of an "economic" holding may be different depending on whether it was calculated in a good year or a drought year. Moreover, the migrant labor system ensured that the size and demographic profile of the available labor pool varied by household and season, requiring an agrarian flexibility that the idea of an economic unit could not capture.[13] In addition, the act restricted the land market by limiting the amount of land an individual could buy and prohibiting individuals from renting grazing or cultivation rights.

These limitations on the potential achievements of individual initiative and enterprise were articulated in terms of the need to end fragmentation of land holdings for reasons of land conservation (especially overstocking and overpopulation) and economic efficiency. But the rationale was political. Flexibility in land allocation or land access would reduce the capacity of the state to control the process of labor stabilization. Moreover, the LHA was formulated not only in conformity with the absolute strictures of the Land Apportionment Act but also in compliance with European farmers' demand for noncompetition by Africans. Consequently, the act provided for controls over land alienation to preclude not only fragmentation of holdings but also their consolidation. There was to be no rural African middle class or any marked degree of stratification in the reserves that might create a threat either to white farmers or to local political authorities. The policy aimed only at limited, stable, rural proletarianization.[14] But given the shortage of land and the declining size of allocations even this was an unrealistic hope.

The Land Husbandry Act, then, was not a liberating or empowering action (despite the enthusiasm with which it was promoted) but a controlling action. As Garfield Todd pointed out in the Legislative Assembly, the act actually militated against maximizing production:

> This is a limiting Bill. It is another restrictive measure. It is another instrument designed to take things away. Admittedly, it is going to conserve our natural resources. We know that, but how is it going to do it? It is going to preserve our natural resources by cutting down the holdings of the people and limiting the possibility of production of the native families. It is going to conserve our natural resources by limiting the probability of the average native family in the rural areas to live a good life. I believe that what we want today is legislation which will grant rights, not take them away.[15]

In short, the act stood revealed as a vehicle for control rather than a harbinger of rights. It demanded both state intrusion and state extrusion in rural social and economic life, an exercise that required a stronger, more coherent, ideological base than the Rhodesian state could muster.

The Politics of Land

The LHA's proponents ignored the fact that the land question had already been established as the focal point of rural opposition and resentment toward the state. It was impossible for the state to appear noninterventionist when its main activities, in the eyes of Africans, were to uphold the LAA and to impose farming controls that were often ecologically insensitive and interfered with their agrarian decisions. While the state could present the controls represented in the act as technically rather than politically necessary by casting them in the language of conservation, the myth of the nonregulatory state was unsustainable so long as the LAA remained in place. But for the government the tenure principle of the LHA was inseparable from the LAA as a mechanism for protecting European farming areas and relocating African "squatter" farmers from European areas. Nevertheless, as the 1950s progressed, the inability of the state to regulate the rural population on these terms became increasingly apparent.

The limited political vision of the LHA was revealed in two related underlying assumptions. First, in arguing that the real key to stability lay in security of tenure, the act assumed that land pressure was the result of population increase "brought about solely by [the benefits of] Pax Britannica" rather than by the political strictures of the Land Apportionment Act.[16] Further, it assumed that farmers and migrant laborers were two distinct and separate social categories, and that the provisions of the act presented both cohorts with real, and even attractive, choices. Poorer farmers would "be given the choice of entering the market economy through proper land use"; migrant workers would "be likely to move to full-time industrial occupations."[17] Both these assumptions were faulty. The designers of the act had thought about land essentially as property: a commodity, a means of production. But for African farmers land was not simply an economic resource; it was, in important ways, the keystone of their moral, political, and economic world. The principles of the LHA cut at the very roots of social ties and land rights that this ethico-political world substantiated. By custom, as Holleman stressed, an individual's security lay in his (in the political arguments of the day citizenship was always gendered) vested right as a member of the community to claim a share rather than in a relationship to a specific holding in perpetuity;[18] villagers who worked the land did not have the right of alienation. This understanding entailed powerful social, emotional, and economic bonds between individuals within the community, which also set up a powerful reciprocal relationship between community and land: as long as an individual was able to maintain ties with the community, he knew that he would have access to land; and as long as he had access to land, he could lay claim to some community status. Werbner shows how these issues were central considerations in local structures and meanings of public authority. They were also fundamentally patriarchal; women's rights and status were generally defined by their relationships to men.[19]

For the LHA to succeed, these bonds had to be severed. But that was a politically difficult task. The act ignored the fact that for poor peasants farming and migrant labor provided different and complementary forms of security on the fringes of the colonial economy. As in other contexts of agrarian social change, rural Africans had to negotiate access to land, labor, and cash in complex and shifting, but interrelated ways. For them, the final allocations of land under the act, which were made by NCs to individuals they designated as occupants on the day of allocation, were arbitrary and exclusive. The philosophy of private property rights cut directly across the precepts of customary public authority expressed by lineage groups, chiefs and spirit mediums. Africans across the social structure deeply resented and resisted state attempts to transform their moral and material world. Yet their economic world was already being transformed by the exigencies of colonial capitalism. One of the fundamental ironies of the Land Husbandry Act was that it failed to recognize the impact of these transformations. As a result its strategies for land and stock control not only compromised its broader objectives of ending the migrant labor system and controlling agrarian class formation, but created the conditions for political resistance. This becomes clearer in the light of emerging economic relationships between land, labor, and livestock.

Economic Transformations: Land, Labor, and Livestock

The provisions of the Land Husbandry Act were based on colonial perceptions of the rural economy, which failed to appreciate not only the structural connections between farming and migrant labor but also the increasingly central role of cattle in the local economy. Destocking was one of the principal measures of the LHA. Yet it rested on concern for arable rather than animal husbandry. Land allocations were to be linked to the total number of cattle sustainable, and the act took no account of the social effects of skewed stockholding patterns at the local level.[20] This approach intensified the politics, outlined in chapter 2, of both "formal" livestock markets and local political economies. State-imposed stock control cut directly across emerging local relationships of power, security, and survival at the community and household level, and thereby exacerbated strains on social and economic relations. One aspect of increasing strains was the emergence of informal "markets" in land as larger farmers began to renegotiate land use arrangements with poorer neighbors. Although land alienation was prohibited in customary law, by the early 1960s land holdings were being "sold" by alienating permanent improvements such as buildings and planted trees. There was also an increased reliance on off-farm incomes and concomitant pressure on rural labor resources. Most peasant farmers relied on cooperative labor arrangements. As Weinrich notes, migrant workers would often try to plan their absences in such a way that there was always one of an extended group in the reserve to preside over matters of kinship. Migrant workers also tried to return during the harvesting period to participate in the daily work parties held in each village. Yet this system was beginning to crumble gradually where farmers who could afford it began to hire labor.[21]

Taken together, these conditions reveal a direct relationship, resulting from state policies, between the effects and politics of destocking on the one hand and the persistence of migrant labor. Not only did peasants across the board resist destocking but poorer or stockless peasants could avoid dependence on stock-holding neighbors by entering migrant labor. It was, indeed, an irony of the act that although it was designed to increase rural incomes, it increased the reliance of poor families on off-farm sources, which made it important to maintain ties with urban family members. Rural ties were equally important for urban workers. Urban policy under the LHA was "to encourage and assist in the proper accommodation of natives in the native urban areas within the European areas."[22] But this policy depended on the ability of urban Africans to make stable and adequate incomes, on the willingness of white urban authorities to provide the resources to house urban African families in reasonable conditions, and ultimately on the political will to ensure these conditions. None of these conditions was met.[23] Consequently, access to rural land remained an important source of security for urban Africans. The land allocation procedure of the LHA threatened to cut off this access. When the LAA was finally amended in 1960 to allow Africans freehold tenure in the townships, control was left in the hands of local authorities, and no significant change took place. And by then it was already becoming clear that the migrant labor system could not be broken. Only in 1973 did the government, desperate to strengthen its influx control measures, consolidate central government control over urban African affairs through the Urban Councils Act.

In sum, the philosophical and political underpinnings of the LHA undermined its objectives of managing rural society and regulating socioeconomic development because they embodied a stark political paradox: by concentrating the forms and processes of control and authority on the relationships of peasants to their land they brought the shortage of land and the power of land allocation into sharp political focus. Rather than mitigating and containing the impact of socioeconomic transformations on rural political life, they exacerbated that impact. Indeed, focusing social management on land challenged African cultural sensibilities that centered on land-based ancestral communities. It was, consequently, inevitable that the implementation of the act would intensify the political tensions in state-peasant relations.

Politics, Resistance, and Social Authority

Implementation of the Land Husbandry Act was a cumbersome and protracted process for which the government lacked adequate resources. By 1956 no Farming Right Certificates had been issued, and the Land Board still did not know when they would be able to start. In 1960, the Director of Native Agriculture reported that of the 27 million acres of African land proclaimed under the act, 91 percent had been surveyed but allocation of land rights had been completed in only 33 percent, of stocking rights in 28 percent, and of residential sites in 13 percent.[24] The LHA was implemented under conditions of great agrarian confusion. Government officials had a poor knowledge of both production levels and patterns of overcrowding in the reserves.[25] Moreover, evictions under the LAA expanded the cohort of land seekers at the very time that the state was trying to regulate allocation of land within the reserves. The result was that demarcation of holdings was frequently contentious and poorly controlled. On-the-ground implementation of the act was entrusted to the Native Commissioners, to whom the act extended wide-ranging powers of land and stock allocation as African farmers became increasingly hostile. Some NCs undertook allocation zealously, ignoring local authority structures; some left the job to their Land Development Officers, and simply passed on complaints or requests to the LDOs; others worked closely with chiefs, subchiefs, and village heads and bent the rules to make the act work. Many simply indicated where the division between arable and grazing was to be, and left the rest to the chiefs and headmen.[26]

As most commentators have noted, this was a recipe for political disaster. For rural families, the implementation of the act was a deeply traumatic experience, not least for the increased uncertainty that it injected into their lives. A large number were denied land. Many were resettled. Not knowing when the act was going to be implemented in their area, they often refused to practice improved agricultural methods, such as crop rotation and winter plowing or manuring of fields, for fear that they would raise the fertility of their soil only to find their fields allocated to someone else. Conservation became more coercive, and *chibaro* labor increased. Arduous conservation tasks were often assigned to the poor, women, and children, and this exacerbated intrafamily and intravillage tensions. Where LDOs took over land allocation, they undermined the domestic authority of elders by taking control away.[27]

This implementation strategy resulted in intensive and sustained rural opposition. Peasants stoned cattle dip tanks, burned hide sheds, encouraged grass fires, and destroyed government property. They ignored or actively opposed conservation measures. In 1956 the CNC reported instances of plowing across demarcation contours, of moving beacons, and of plowing outside allocated plots but regarded this as "only natural in the settling down stage." By the next year he was calling for an increase in staff to implement the act and to counteract these activities.[28] Resistance was particularly heavy in areas that were already overcrowded and overstocked, and land shortage became the pivotal issue of struggle. By the end of 1956 it was becoming clear to the government that the number of people entitled to rights should be stabilized immediately, for "as the Act became known many natives who originally had no intention of taking up land were flocking to the reserves and special native areas to put a plough or hoe into the ground so that they would be entitled to farming rights."[29] By the early 1960s, individual arable allocations were being pushed into communal grazing areas, thereby breaking the golden rule of the LHA. At the same time the government slowed down allocations and called a halt to compulsory destocking.

Yet the question of land shortage was a complex one, as much about politics as about agrarian decline. Some of the opposition to the policy came from migrant workers who had either lost their farming rights or feared that they would, or from young urban nationalists trying to mobilize rural support. Some opposition came from farmers having to make do with allocations on poorer land. Some of it was an expression of resentment by families who found the increased distance between their land allocations interfered with their labor allocation practices. And some opposition lay in the frustration of wealthier farmers who wanted to open up new lands for cultivation.[30] Indeed, a land shortage could be said to exist by virtue of the allocation process itself. The NAD blamed the land shortage on overuse of allocated lands, leading to a decline of soil fertility "in many cases to a level where the subsistence requirements of the farmer cannot be met."[31] But overuse of land could mean any one of three things. Either the farmer was "overcropping" the land, in which case he or she must be producing a significant surplus and actively participating in the market; or the allocation was too small to provide the subsistence requirements of the farmer except under intensive farming techniques; or the land was actually overcrowded. In each case, it was inadequate to blame the situation on "tribesmen who have impoverished the land allocated to them," and in all cases the allocations could be represented as state interference with the life opportunities of peasant farmers. Peasants generally did view it as such. As the Provincial Native Commissioner for Midlands acknowledged, "As long as there are large tracts of unused land in the European area, there will be resentment by Africans of legislation such as that proposed."[32] Thus, in Holleman's words, "being discriminatory and restrictive and agrarian the Act became almost inevitably associated with the Land Apportionment Act, one of the most hated symbols of white authoritarianism and exclusiveness to the African political mind."[33]

The situation also meant that the political stakes of local-level land control were highest for traditional authorities who, under the impact of economic and political change, found themselves situated most centrally in the vortex of struggles for local power and authority. As elsewhere in Africa the local standing of chiefs and headmen was undermined by their partial and ambiguous incorporation into colonial law and government. Although executive and judicial agents of the state, their authority was strictly delimited and subordinated to the NC. A chief's appointment had to be ratified by the NC and, although appointments continued in general to be regulated by spirit mediums, NCs became incessantly involved in succession struggles arising out of the collateral form of succession (and sometimes out of the NC's disapproval of the chosen candidate).[34] As land shortages became more pressing, jurisdictional struggles between chiefs also embroiled NCs. In 1951 the state reorganized chiefdoms, scrapping minor ones, increasing pay for upper level chiefs, and creating Provincial Assemblies for chiefs where they could receive the wisdom of Provincial Commissioners. At the same time the NC's magistrate's courts tested chiefs' judicial authority by establishing an alternative outlet for grievances. Indeed the two courts operated according to different principles of procedure and law of evidence yet the magistrate's court acted as an appeal court.[35]

One effect was that the deliberative, participatory, and consensual character of decision making in the headman's *dare*—which greatly frustrated NCs for its protraction and much impressed them for its effectiveness—was compromised. This effect was intensified by the increasing social strains accompanying economic change. As a tool for social control, customary law was always ambiguous: it restricted the authoritative domain of tradition, but also secured a domain of authority beyond the reach of the state, which could be used for resistance.

Chiefs and headmen also found themselves confronted by the emerging economic power of wealthier farmers and local businessmen. With increasing land shortage, their inability to provide more land threatened to push wealthier farmers seeking to increase their land holdings into the informal land market. At the same time, local notables began to seek accumulation opportunities in other avenues, such as retail outlets and transport operations. Such activities secured these notables considerable status and power as providers of consumer goods and local credit. Many used the local council to secure their businesses, often against the wishes of the chief. Generational conflicts also intensified as young men with upper primary or secondary education began to challenge the authority of chiefs and headmen. Thus traditional authorities felt threatened by emerging, though still fluid, local elites, sometimes organized in "leaders' associations."[36] The resulting conflicts drew NCs increasingly into matters that previously would have been dealt with by the headman's council, thereby deepening the ambiguities of traditional authority.

In this situation, the locus of political and judicial authority at the local level tended to fragment. Local power and authority relations came to rest largely on the personality of the NC and on the effectiveness of chiefs and headmen. Chiefs and headmen clung to their judicial power, continuing to hear criminal and civil cases that by statutory law fell outside their jurisdiction. Some also continued to hear witchcraft cases, which was an effective way to sustain their authority.[37] But they also relied on the state, to which some owed their positions, and the loss of their power to allocate land under the LHA was a severe blow. Pressed from several sides that occasionally merged, traditional leaders had a political stake in declaring a shortage of land because it provided a way in which they could consolidate the concerns of both landless and wealthier peasants against the state while ensuring that they retained the power of land distribution. They were frequently at the forefront of resistance to state land policies, often blaming councils (rather than the state) for implementing and financing the LHA. A great deal of opposition to the act came from chiefs and headmen who used their personal authority to persuade people who had received allocations to return their receipts.

The most famous case was that of Chief Mangwende of the Mrewa [Murewa] district, who was deposed by the government in 1960 for behavior "obstructive and detrimental to good order and progress" and for "virtually paralysing" the Mangwende council. Chief Mangwende had been very successful in carrying out development tasks—including resettlement, destocking, and labor supply—until the mid-1950s. When his capacity to maintain independent leadership and authority was challenged by a new NC and by the implementation of the LHA, however, he became deeply recalcitrant and led the council in obstructing the state, at the same time maneuvering to maintain his prestige *within* the community. Variations on this situation were not uncommon, and they compromised not only the LHA but also the local councils.[38] But this strategy was risky because chiefs and headmen were also charged with implementing conservation programs. They risked either the wrath of their constituents for doing so, or the wrath of the state for not doing so. Thus chiefs' contradictory but indispensible role in the administration's efforts to inculcate new conceptions of civic responsibility through its conservation strategy actually heightened the anomalies of public authority at the interface of state and society. Chiefs engaged in increasingly complicated and difficult negotiations, often psychologically very stressful, with their constituents and with the NC. Werbner recounts how Chief Bango "both 'co-operated' and resisted the colonial state [but] never ceased trying to embody *buxe*, in its richest sense of legitimate public authority over land and people." Ironically, Bango was murdered after independence, during Five Brigade's brutal campaign in Matabeleland.[39]

In a situation where bending the rules was the best guarantee of successful implementation, it was frequently unclear who precisely controlled land allocation. But by the end of the 1950s it was clear that the state did not. Questions of land use, land rights, and conservation were "aggravated by politics and intimidation," and rural administrators found themselves faced with a situation of escalating political discontent and spiraling economic decline. In his annual report for 1961, the Secretary of Native Affairs remarked on "the apathy, neglect, and sometimes hostility which face the extension agents, both Europeans and Africans, on the ground." He expounded at length on the intensive "underworld campaign conducted by ruthless and furtive gangs from the towns intent on spreading fear, confusion, hostility and breakdown" by preventing farmers from selling cattle, preventing women's clubs from meeting, wrecking cattle dips, arson, inciting "freedom ploughing" (ploughing in areas designated by NCs or LDOs as unsuitable), and intimidating chiefs and headmen.[40] Yet the 1961 Robinson Commission noted that prosecuting people for failing to implement conservation measures brought its own problems because "there are signs that the feeling is growing that imprisonment for defiance of certain statutes is an honour entitling the prisoner to some such title as 'prison graduate.'"[41] At the end of 1961 the Minister of Native Affairs told the House that no directed cropping was being undertaken at all in the African areas. By 1962 control of land use and occupation had slipped inexorably from the state's grasp. In 1963 allocation of land and farming rights under the LHA was done only when specifically requested by African farmers. In 1964, acknowledging a fait accompli, the Secretary of Internal Affairs reported that the LHA had been suspended, pending the introduction of the proposed Tribal Trust Land Act, which would formally recognize "traditional tribal authorities as the land authorities in the tribal areas, with powers to control the allocation of land in their areas."[42]

This death knell of the NLHA signifies the failure of the state's attempt to remold the ethico-political relations of production and accumulation in rural Rhodesia, and its failure to secure the state's own authority as the final arbiter of those relations. A 1964 government report observed that the act:

> has *not* achieved what it was designed to achieve. It has *not* created a free market in land and cattle rights in the tribal areas. It has *not* resulted in rights of cultivation of arable land being transferred, whether on a permanent or a temporary basis, to those best able to make the land produce more. On the other hand, it *has* created a landless class. It *has* created a great deal of ill-feeling among that class towards agents of government. It has disturbed social stability.[43]

Indeed the collapse of the act signaled an incipient and growing crisis in the capacity of the state to manage the transformation of rural society.

Social Management in Crisis

The failure of the LHA not only fueled rural resistance, it also undermined the central mechanism for regulating the supply of urban labor and demanded a new normative language of social management and state-society relations. During the recession of 1958–59, rising unemployment began to pose increasingly pressing questions about the appropriate mechanisms for securing social and political stability. This demanded a serious reassessment of rural policy to tackle the problem of regulating a mobile population. As the Minister of Labour argued in the House of Assembly,

> the question of African unemployment is not only one which relates to economic policy alone; it is very much bound up with the question of land and the land problem. . . . All the developments in relation to the land must be related to part of the Government's problem to deal with the whole question of stability of people, and to deal with this question of unemployment because—I have said before and I repeat—we will never solve the problem of unemployment in the towns alone.[44]

Once again, then, the migrant labor system was under scrutiny, but this time under conditions of economic recession, less confidence in the rate of industrial development, and rapid economic disintegration in the African reserves. This problem has never abated and remains the central concern of rural development strategies in Zimbabwe.

Once again the pivotal factor was land. In 1959 the government set up a Parliamentary Select Committee (the Quinton Committee) to reassess the land question. The committee concluded that the LAA had outlived its usefulness, was now actually retarding development of the country's natural resources, and should be repealed. It called for urban freehold tenure for Africans and the rapid establishment of an open, nonracial, rural land market. These conclusions concurred with other commission reports of the time that further state regulation of the labor force would not work because the state lacked both the humanpower and the fiscal resources to exercise effective control.[45] They amounted to a recognition that the state was unable to exercise control over the lives of the population at large within a political system which demanded such control.

In fact, by the end of the 1950s, there was a growing opinion among policymakers that control over the economy and the labor force could only be maintained by raising national productivity "to manage the flow of Africans to employment," expanding "the opportunities for African participation in the money economy" and boosting the national market. The 1962 Phillips Committee on Economic Development stressed that the only way to do this was to raise "the productive efficiency of the pastoralists, the cultivators and those engaged in simple mixed farming," because otherwise "the migration of rural inhabitants to the towns will be accelerated, the level of wages in urban and related activities will remain depressed, there will be a continuance of a social structure slowing down an expansion in the demand for consumer goods except of the simplest and cheapest kinds, and finally the market will not be sufficiently widened and varied."[46] These arguments were supported by a 1962 report on African school-leavers.

In this view, the key to popular quiescence and a well-regulated society lay in increased earning and spending power, and this depended on economic growth in the rural areas. It was attended by arguments for a shift from state control and the policing of African occupational, geographical, and social mobility to state support and encouragement of self-help, through such means as local government, education, cooperatives, improved credit facilities, and marketing. In particular, administrators began to view education as the social instrument for promoting ideas of self-help as well as social stability. A 1962 confidential report by the Joint Committee on Technical Education declared the importance of expanding rural education for both social and geographical stability:

every effort should be made to increase the amount of investment in rural education so as to enable every African to become literate; Otherwise there will continue to be widespread dissatisfaction with the differential opportunities for those living in the towns and those living in the country, and a consequent drift to the towns of those seeking more education. Indeed there is evidence of whole families moving to the towns in order to obtain better facilities for education. Moreover, with education limited to Standard III, as is the case with the majority of Africans in rural areas at the present time, there remains a large body of young people who, when they become adults, will be incapable of thinking for themselves and will be at the mercy of political extremists.[47]

But this increased official interest in educating rural Africans was also a co-optive strategy to harness the vociferous African demand for education to broader sociopolitical purposes. Access to education was the most strident demand of rural Africans, and the lack of control over education was one of rural communities' most searing indictments of the African councils. It was also a source of great conflict between communities and NCs, who appeared unsympathetic to rural Africans' educational aspirations—a conflict exacerbated by the fact that rural Africans had to pay school fees, although urban schools were free. Outlining an impending crisis in African education in February 1962, a memorandum from the Native Education Department argued that "we are faced with both a political and moral obligation to expand the service, and the consequences of failing to make some provision for the most pressing additional needs could only entail a diversion of funds from education to police." The opinion of the 1962 Judges Commission on Native Education was more cynically co-optive: "Policy . . . must be to encourage an attitude so that they will readily recognize their responsibilities and accept opportunities to participate actively and imaginatively in programs that add to their amenities, increase their productivity, and thereby their prosperity. It is in the field of education that this spirit of conscious involvement finds a most ready expression. . . ."[48] Thus state officials viewed African education not as a keystone of modernity but as a mechanism to mediate the relations of control and participation between state and rural communities by both inculcating and exploiting values of civic responsibility.

The underlying vision of social and political development reflected in these arguments was one in which state interventions in everyday life were limited and individual incentives for progress and collective action, associated with the market, were privileged. But to move to the domination of market relations, in the context of a racial colonial social order, posed serious political difficulties. First, the government would have to secure white electoral support for whatever strategy of disengagement it pursued. Second, state control in the rural areas was already tenuous in the face of discontent, resistance, and economic decline. Third, turning that decline around demanded an enormous fiscal commitment not only to salvage African agricultural productivity, but also to provide for a meaningful increase in rural education. Thus political, fiscal, and technical factors had to be carefully integrated in a new hegemonic strategy.

In the early 1960s, the United Party began to move tentatively to deracialize the social and political order gradually on the basis of what the Minister of Local Government—somewhat high-mindedly and not a little disingenuously—called "a mentality that is imbued with reverence for the individual, for the dignity of the human person." This shift demonstrated the emergence of what Duncan Clarke calls "'liberal reformism' built on an ideological base of paternalist welfarism."[49] It included the removal of racial distinction in labor conciliation under the Industrial Conciliation Act of 1960; the nonracial Apprenticeship Act of 1960; the nonracialization of the civil service in 1961; the encouragement of African business and of individual tenure rights for urban Africans; attempts to impose the minimum wage requirements of the Industrial Conciliation Act on European farmers in 1960 and again in 1962; the gradual extension of the African franchise; and, most important, the proposed removal of the Land Apportionment Act. The logic of this shift was to evolve an increasingly inclusive concept of citizenship. Its irony was that it was predicated on the emergence of an African middle class, and represented an overwhelmingly urban response to an overwhelmingly rural crisis.[50] It also spelled the political doom of the United Party in 1962.

It was in this situation that Prime Minister Whitehead decided in June 1960 to adopt community development—which he described as "almost a new science"—as the foundation of a coordinated rural policy toward the African population. This new policy approach would follow an agreement laid down with the US government:

> That the people of each local community are given responsibility for their own development in specific fields, a responsibility which can only be discharged through communal organisation formally or informally for democratic planning and action. These bodies of organised communal self-help will have to make their own plans to meet their needs and solve their own problems, and execute these plans with maximum reliance upon resources found within the community supplemented, where necessary, with administrative and technical advice and assistance and financial and material assistance from Government and other agencies outside the community.[51]

The policy was intended to end "progress by compulsion," to give rural Africans a stake in the physical and political development of their community that would both dampen political militancy and ease the fiscal responsibilities of the state, and to withdraw the overweening presence of the central state in the everyday lives of rural people. This shift also signaled a new emphasis in official thinking about how to inculcate civic responsibility and incentives for stable social progress among Africans. No longer would such attempts focus primarily on the relationship between individuals and their land; they would now focus on social relationships and the attainment of social skills—including education, which was to be the responsibility of "local government and its constituent communities." Given the tensions in state-society relations, this was not a clear-cut or wholehearted shift. Most particularly, however, this shift illuminates the vulnerability of state authority in rural society.

Managing the Crisis: Power, Authority, and Administration

Managing economic and social transformation in the countryside required appropriate political machinery. By the 1950s such machinery was looking woefully rickety, and the state faced the most penetrating dilemma posed by the LHA: how to structure and present its (legitimate) role in overseeing rural transformation. In the late 1950s the government embarked on an attempt to restructure relations of accountability between the state and rural communities by moving away from the technocratic strictures of the LHA and stressing the importance of human relationships. In the political climate of the day this effort faced deep-seated political obstacles from two quarters. The first was the adversarial relationship between the state and rural communities. The second was the outbreak of internal tensions within the state as a result of the deteriorating political situation. These two sets of obstacles converged on the office of the Native Commissioner, and on the reluctance of the NAD to relinquish overriding control over the varied tasks of administration, governance, and agricultural development.

As we have noted, the government had set up Native Councils to mediate political accountability. In official language, councils were intended to inculcate a sense of participation, cooperation, and corporate responsibility:

> It is in the democratic operation of little things with the comprehension and genuine interest of the people that the real values or a council lie . . . [providing] at the grassroots level of community life a tremendous educational influence in corporative responsibility, problem-solving and decision-making, all carried out within a democratic code of orderly discussion and decision with a public opinion genuinely interested in the background.[52]

This initiative was not successful. Councils were reluctant to become the outer bastions of an overweening colonial state. They were powerless to deal with problems that concerned them most, such as *chibaro* labor, local schools, grain prices, African wages, or the level of the poll tax. They had no interest in self-taxation or promoting unpopular development initiatives since they could leave that to NCs. Some were dominated by local notables who used them, sometimes corruptly, for their own particularist interests. In 1952 the CNC reported:

> More disturbing for the future than apathy and lack of initiative, which can be attributed largely to ignorance of the nature and function of local government institutions, is the complete refusal of even old-established Councils to accept responsibility or make decisions which might court unpopularity. . . . Time and again, it is seen that Councils refuse to reach decisions on even trivial matters without referring them back to the people, and the Native Commissioner, Mrewa, speaks of the failure of numerous attempts to make members of the Councils take on responsibilities.[53]

By the early 1960s, state control in the rural areas appeared to be rapidly dissipating. Councils were collapsing everywhere. Their capacity to collect rates had dropped considerably, many were moribund or paralyzed by public hostility, and some were abolished at their own request. Dominated by NCs, lacking the financial resources to carry out any meaningful development activities, they either lost all credibility or actively opposed the district administration. In what NC Allan Wright describes as "the surface ripples of general rejection of the authority of government," NCs themselves were "heckled and abused" at community meetings.[54]

The character of African resistance was not of course unrelated to the character of the state it confronted. The NAD had taken upon itself, and defended jealously, the onus of reconciling the two often contradictory demands of rural development: on the one hand, regenerating African agriculture within the constraints of white political and economic interests; and on the other hand, maintaining effective and legitimate political control. These tasks fell almost entirely to the NCs, whose administrative, political, and ideological resources were limited but whose administrative powers were extremely wide. They collected taxes, set wage rates, operated magistrates' courts, appointed local chiefs, and ran councils. They controlled settlement and resettlement of entire communities, regulated the movement of nonlocal Africans into and out of their area, and could prohibit meetings. They also controlled the fiscal administration of agriculture, overseeing soil conservation, water development, physical communication, extension services, grain marketing. They were empowered to mobilize African labor, often through the hated *chibaro*, for the protection of collective resources, even though they often did not understand the ecologies they were working with. Under the LHA their power to destock was extended to allow seizure and sale of stock which strayed from grazing areas. In 1961 the Robinson Commission commented, "It will be apparent that there is little which the native commissioner may not do within the above framework to regulate the ordinary life of natives living in the reserves and Special Native Areas." Little wonder then that relations between NCs and locals were frequently characterized by "resentment and suspicion."[55]

By the early 1950s, morale in the NAD was sagging. One NAD official argued that the department was going through a crucial period of transition "because it is trying to change over from a system in which the Native Commissioner is a kind of benevolent autocrat to something which the Native can build up on his own."[56] Yet this perception offers a sanguine view of the real political interests of most NCs. NCs relished their autonomy in exercising administrative power and guarded it jealously, even against their own superiors. Many NCs regarded councils merely as vehicles for carrying out development activities. In 1958 the chairman of the Native Councils Board inveighed against two prevalent attitudes among NCs: first the idea that "if the people are contributing in cash, labor or discussion they are therefore 'participating' and the rest of the operation can be safely left to the Native Commissioner"; and second the idea that "a council is a kind of extension service of central Government, another agent among the people through which plans and decisions made by departments can be implemented."[57] Thus, what NCs really felt in the 1950s was that the mounting pressure of administration, and especially the implementation of the LHA, made them office-bound and unable to keep their finger on the pulse of everyday local life (with their own preferred level of benevolence or autocracy). Though the NAD had "come to be regarded as the author of, and instrument for, all oppressive legislation," the LHA vividly demonstrated that the state lacked either the power or the authority to regulate rural development.[58] Indeed, the act not only failed to bring about stability and productivity, it promoted economic decline via political resistance. It also created a fertile seedbed for the spread of African nationalism, and added urgency to the state's need to regain control over rural development. But to do so, the state had to find ways to change its relations with rural citizens, to both accept the power of chiefs and use it to manage social and economic transformations. In short, it required a new look at state hegemony. Consequently, in the mid-1950s, the government brought renewed vigor to its attempts to establish the councils as mediating institutions of accountability and responsibility.

The main responsibility for drafting guidelines to institutionalize rural African politics and administration was passed to H. R. G. Howman. Howman was a singular character in the department. The son of an NC, he had joined the Native Department in 1928 and in the late 1930s had been sent to London to study anthropology and sociology at the London School of Economics. Studying under Karl Mannheim, he became deeply influenced by current theories of community relationships and their importance in determining individual identity and behavior. This influence was deepened by a visit to the United States, where he was exposed to ideas of community development and the communitarian qualities of American pragmatism. During the 1950s he conducted an exhaustive and authoritative study of local government in colonial Africa for the NAD. Regarded as something of an egghead within the department, he became the principal theoretician of local government and community development in rural Rhodesia.

Under Howman's direction a new self-consciousness was injected into the state's attempts to accomplish political-ideological change in the countryside. Howman had a conception of communities as organic units in which the whole is larger than the sum of the parts and he believed that both peace and prosperity could best be secured by fostering such organic identities. Thus he argued, "If we can but resurrect a sense of community and cooperation we will find law and order inhering in the process and that highly intractable material we work with, the wills of men and women, will no longer baffle and stultify our efforts." He stressed "the need to work through groups, build up new groups around the individual, use them as the machinery of social control" because, he believed, "leaders are molded by the groups out of which they emerge and take on the attributes and roles expected of them by their followers. If then we can foster the corporate life of the Africans and design wisely the devices whereby leaders emerge, we may influence very greatly the kinds of leaders we shall have to face in the future."

Howman's intention was to lay the ground for future ethico-political development by appealing to existing traditions, identities, and legitimate authority structures, while remolding a sense of belonging through a "local sense of community with its own loyalty, responsibilities and organic leaders." This project involved a self-conscious transformation of traditions. Howman repeatedly stressed that the policy was not to try to return to a traditional form of government, but to create the political institutional machinery to promote economic growth and market participation. Indeed, Howman believed that "[t]ransformation, no matter how painful, how strongly resisted, in both attitudes and institutions cannot be avoided," and that "[i]nstitutional change—and that includes the functions of a chief—is inescapable." The entire initiative was based on a recognition of the intimate connection between politics and productivity in the rural areas of colonial Zimbabwe.[59]

It is apparent that there were tensions between the individualist presuppositions of the LHA and the communitarian presuppositions of this new incorporative strategy. The LHA demanded extensive and authoritarian state incursions into rural life in order to transform economic and social organization, and thereby inculcate new social moralities. The local government strategy stressed the essential role of organic community leaders in mediating state power and authority. While there is no principled reason to consider these tensions as irreconcilable, implementation of the LHA showed that politics and productivity placed different political demands on both the state and citizens. Howman believed these tensions could be resolved through a determined and sympathetic policy of community development, an argument he continued to press with vigor and enthusiasm until his resignation from the department in 1969.

The argument received its first political airing in the CNC's annual report of 1961. In this report, which reflected Howman's influence, Secretary of Native Affairs S. E. Morris presented a remarkable admission of the comprehensive failure of rural control and development policy, and an acceptance of the need for a new state hegemonic project:

> It is this factor of mass apathy or cultural resistance which, in spite of the catalogue of achievements each year, should receive the most serious thought and lead to a re-assessment of the whole method of approach. . . . More and more it is being recognised in national planning that the development of African agriculture, or as it is called in the current phraseology, the conversion of a subsistence economy into a cash economy, must receive the highest priority. What is not sufficiently recognised is that this involves a highly complex and illusive problem of human and institutional changes that will not be solved by resort to increased and more dynamic agricultural extension services and more agricultural credit. Both these factors are, of course, highly important but are unlikely to bring about any significant changes in the tribal way of life—as distinct from the few individuals who may respond for a shorter or longer period to the new teachings, and cash incentives—unless a comprehensive approach, which seeks to transform the community as a whole, its institutions, patterns of leadership and social structures, is adopted.

With this statement, Morris aimed to nudge the government in a new policy direction. "It is now obvious," the CNC declared, "that imposed technical planning has had its day." The problem should be tackled "as a psychological and sociological one."[60] In June 1962 this argument bore fruit when the prime minister accepted community development as the core principle of rural development policy.

To secure the support of his staff, the CNC took pains to explain in his 1961 annual report that the principles of community development could be traced in the traditions, history, and philosophy of the NAD. But the concept itself had come into vogue in United Nations, United States, and British development circles on the eve of decolonization. As the UN Economic and Social Council saw it, community development represented a process "in which the efforts of the people themselves are united with those of governmental authorities to improve the economic, social and cultural conditions of communities, to integrate these communities into the life of the nation, and to enable them to contribute fully to national progress." The theory of community development stressed the worth of the individual as a responsible, participating member of society. Its keystones were community organization, education, and social action, and its aim was to encourage self-help efforts to raise standards of living and to create stable, self-reliant communities with an assured sense of social and political responsibility. Most broadly, community development was regarded as a process of nation building, and a harbinger of citizenship.[61]

It was community development's claims to the possibilities of managed social transformation that appealed to CNC Morris, Howman, and a small group of Rhodesian administrators. In March 1959, Morris circulated a Colonial Office publication, *Community Development: A Handbook*, to all NCs. In June the department solicited the aid of the International Co-operation Administration of the United States (later USAID), and secured the services of a community development consultant, Dr. James Green, who in the next year drew up a comprehensive community development plan. But the first step along the road of community development had been taken with the African Councils Act of 1957. This act aimed to eliminate the sense of state domination and regimentation that had become the hallmark of rural administration and to replace it with new hegemonic forms of political administration. It was designed to foster a sense of community and citizenship among the inhabitants of a locality, to promote their initiative and a sense of responsibility, and to stimulate participatory development and economic progress. The act stressed flexibility so that the establishment and structure of a council should rest upon the expressed interest and the needs of the particular community. The council would mediate relations of dominance and control, allowing the state to withdraw its overweening presence in the lives of rural citizens.

This was both a co-optive measure and an ideological measure. It would not only involve community members actively in development initiatives, it would inculcate new forms of authority and accountability. But its success rested heavily on the success of local councils that, as the NAD admitted, represented "the only communal instrument of self-help and responsibility we know."[62] Most important, this stress on the importance of the council demonstrates a belief by Howman, Green, and others that the "community" was the unit of sociopolitical identity, where social transformation and social management must begin. As the 1958 Plewman Commission noted, advocates of community development "contended that the function of the state is confined to one of stimulating and encouraging such development, but that the community itself is the body that must give purpose and happiness to the persons which comprise it."[63] The council should coincide with the parameters of that identity. These planners took this idea so seriously that they assigned a team of anthropologically minded Native Department officials to carry out a country-wide community delineation exercise to determine the precise boundaries of every African community's sense of identity. The principal criteria used by this team, which carried out its task between 1963 and 1967, were territoriality and political allegiance.

In the eyes of these senior officials it was essential to make councils work and to relieve the central state of the administrative and fiscal burdens of accountability for rural conditions:

> The guarantee we seek must be a public opinion not only ready to support councils but encouraged to do so, and indeed forced to do so because of the absence of any other machinery for communal development. This, in concrete terms, means a firm policy imposed on every developmental department of only helping those communities who help themselves and a system of governmental operations which, having drawn a line between central and local government functions, throws real responsibility for organized communal action on the local community. It implies a very carefully co-ordinated and comprehensive approach to the local communities and very strict control over the manner in which central finances, in the form of grants in aid, are made available. Unless such rearrangements are made, councils will never become firmly rooted in and nourished by public opinion; African local government will be a bogus affair; and responsibility an empty platitude.[64]

In this view not only would the council become the principal nexus of state-community power and authority relations but, by returning "a considerable measure of initiative and control to the people where it belongs," responsibility would be shifted from the state to the community. In the House, the prime minister echoed these arguments in language that was to find new resonance in postindependence development planning:

> [W]e must realise it is part of our political duty to obtain support from every village in the country . . . we are up against very formidable dangers on the other side. To make democracy work we have to make the ordinary man in the street, whatever his race, feel that he has a voice in the planning in the early stages of decisions and in building his future. This is something that in the past history of this country has never really been the case, but we are now up against a very formidable and dangerous enemy ideologically from beyond our borders, and unless we can really carry the genuine and wholehearted support of the people—and I mean by that all races—we are going to be in for very serious trouble in resisting these pressures.[65]

But the initiative was doomed to political failure. The LHA had so soured relations between the NAD and rural communities that it was very difficult to build any trust in new state initiatives. Moreover, this initiative was accompanied by a move to revamp chiefs' powers through the creation of a Chiefs' Council and Provincial Chiefs' Assemblies, despite the tensions between chiefs and councils over authority and jurisdiction. This move reflects the government's fear of losing their direct institutional line of access to rural communities. Administrators did not know how much confidence they could place in the councils, and this made them nervous. Chiefs, however compromised, were a known quantity that both administrators and local populations could work through. Neither the Council of Chiefs nor the provincial assemblies received any executive powers. They were there simply to provide a conduit between the state and rural communities, or—more specifically—to legitimate the broad policy directions taken by the government. To mark this shift toward a deeper recognition of traditional authority, references in the official language of policy to rural Africans changed from "producer" or "cultivator" to "tribesman," a nomenclature retained throughout the remaining years of colonialism.

Yet a strong appeal to tradition would not necessarily achieve the entrenchment of state authority at the local level. With considerable insight the independent MP Ahrn Palley poured scorn on the initiative:

> [T]he hon. member . . . is only too aware of the invidious position in which native commissioners found themselves when on the one hand they had to administer an unacceptable Act—the Native Land Husbandry Act—and in the next instance decide disputes arising therefrom. No matter who it is—be it chief, native commissioner, or anyone else—this clash of functions must lead to friction and problems . . . the dilemma of the native commissioner was not solved . . . and now Government is thinking it can shunt this problem across to the chiefs. I think the same problem will arise there and Government will have the same problems; I do not think it will help the native commissioners and it certainly will be one of the steps to destroy the influence of the chiefs.[66]

Indeed, the government was groping toward a solution to the complex problem of securing coherent forms of social and political authority in the countryside. The problem of defining forms and spheres of local authority in relation to the state itself informed all the shifts in rural development and social control strategies over the next two decades as the state struggled to puts its stamp on rural transformations. It was the crucible of rural political struggles, and the focus of state political-ideological failure.

But the problem was not only one of state domination over rural society. It was also a result of unresolved tensions within the state that came to a head in the atmosphere of heightened political tension and insecurity that accompanied the upsurge of urban African nationalist activity in the late 1950s. At that time the NAD, and the NCs in particular, were beginning to feel increasing political and psychological pressure. This pressure was rooted not only in the tenuousness of rural control and incipient rural crisis, but also in the sense of political identity and bureaucratic autonomy within the state apparatus that the NAD proudly fostered. The threats to the department came on two fronts. First, the City Youth League (CYL), a militant group of young nationalists, launched a national campaign to challenge the paternalistic and authoritarian forms and symbols of bureaucratic power as exercised by NCs. The campaign was limited in both extent and form since it involved little more than CYL members refusing to show customary deference and respect to NCs.[67] Nevertheless, it bolstered "everyday" forms of resistance by reinforcing emerging patterns of noncooperation, and challenging the immediate personal authority of NCs as well as the cherished paternalist traditions of the NAD. NCs were unable to tackle the problem effectively because the challenge was urban-based. As a result, while the campaign fueled undercurrents of rural resistance, it also strengthened the resolve of NCs to represent unshaken authority to their rural subjects.

The second threat came from within the state itself as the white establishment grew increasingly alarmed at growing social turmoil in the African townships. Several ministries began to voice long-standing resentment of the NAD's "bureaucratic imperialism," which many believed impeded social development and technical progress. The relations between NCs and officers of other ministries were frequently strained, and the failures of the LHA increased those strains. Many NCs insisted on controlling agriculture department officials in their area. This often led to poor relations between NCs and their LDOs. Some neglected conservation works almost entirely, others enforced these works vigorously and sometimes technically incorrectly. Some employed their agricultural demonstrators on nonagricultural administrative tasks, reducing their credibility. Senior officials in other departments referred to them as "tin-pot gods;" agricultural extension officers found them frequently overbearing and an active hindrance to agricultural cooperation.

But NCs, jealous of their autonomy and protective of their traditions, guarded their domain feverishly. When Prime Minister Todd tried in the mid-1950s to break the NAD's power by fragmenting its duties, they closed ranks. CNC Morris declared, "[o]nly those who grow up in daily contact with the Native evolution, can hope to administer Native efforts to the mutual benefit of both races. At no stage should those unversed in Native affairs be permitted to encroach on this field. . . . Just as in the districts there must be co-ordination of all work and projects by the Native Commissioner, so it is vital that co-ordination of all aspects of Native agriculture and administration should remain under one hand at the top of the tree."[68] In 1961, defending the department against growing criticism from other ministries, he pointed out that "[t]he Department has never claimed that all was well in the rural areas and the only unrest there due to outside agitators. Over long years it has been only too aware of the grim choice between goodwill or co-operation and the need to make drastic efforts to conserve the soil. It has tried to reconcile the two. . . ."[69] This curious sense of benevolence and commitment epitomized the tensions within NAD ideology: a recognition of the need to cede responsibility, but an inability to cede control. It was the hallmark of NAD esprit de corps.

The effect of this solidarity among NCs was a curious mixture of pride in their autonomy and resentment at their isolation. Under fire for the collapse of rural control in the 1950s, NCs felt themselves put upon by politicians and other civil servants, especially those stationed in Salisbury, who they believed had only a vague notion of the NAD's functions and of the difficulties of their job. This sense of isolation fueled great bitterness among NAD personnel and, according to MacLean, drew members of the department together to form the Native Affairs Department Association "to safeguard the interests of its members."[70] By the end of the 1950s, the NAD was in disarray, embattled, frustrated, and disgruntled. With morale low, recruitment was difficult and by the end of the decade the department was so short of qualified and competent staff that the CNC declared administration to be "on the verge of a breakdown."[71] Having gathered to itself and husbanded as many dimensions of rural social control that it could, the department had become at once extremely lean in administrative competence and extremely bloated in administrative power, not only unwieldy and inefficient but a liability to the state.

Against this background of increasing administrative confusion and conflict a number of important commissions of inquiry made their reports in 1960–61: The Mangwende Commission, the Robinson Commission on the administrative and judicial functions of the NAD, and the Paterson Commission on the organization of the public service. All agreed that the state had to be deracialized and restructured to break the monolithic power of the NAD. The Robinson Commission recommended breaking up the NAD into a Department of District Administration to deal with administrative and judicial affairs, and a Department of Native Agriculture to deal with agriculture, conservation and extension. In the event, the NAD was renamed the Ministry of Internal Affairs, Native Commissioners became District Commissioners (DCs), and African agriculture was removed from the purview of the department, being brought ultimately under the control of a unified Ministry of Agriculture in 1964. Internal Affairs personnel resented this split deeply. They fought hard to regain control of agriculture, finally achieving it under the Rhodesian Front in 1969.

These tensions indicate the devastating logic of the state

structure in colonial Zimbabwe. In creating a dual administrative structure, in which the Native Affairs Department could become what Blake calls "a sort of *imperium in imperio*," the colonial state created a monster. In the 1950s, the NAD had become something of a maverick, unwilling to respond to broader demands of and on the state, and unable to respond to the policy initiatives of its own planners. These tensions within the state made it difficult to manage the rural crisis of the 1950s, and further undermined its capacity to regulate and manage the social order. As the next two chapters show, they contributed deeply to the colonial state's spiraling crisis of social control.

Conclusion

By the beginning of the 1960s, the Rhodesian state was moving into a profound and comprehensive crisis in its capacity to manage the social order. This crisis was multidimensional. First, it was a crisis of political control, arising out of rural dissatisfaction with state demands, uncontrolled urbanization when there was a massive housing backlog in the African urban areas, burgeoning unemployment when the economy was slowing down, and political instability in the townships as a result of increasing nationalist activity. Second, it was a constitutional crisis as the Central African Federation was collapsing, white Rhodesians were demanding independence, and the question of extending African political rights was becoming unavoidable. Finally, it was a crisis of administrative capacity in which the structure of the civil service itself appeared to inhibit the state's effective operation.

The core of the crisis lay in the struggle between the state and rural African citizens to define the character of public authority in the countryside. State efforts to redefine land rights as the conceptual foundation of citizenship had so challenged the moral, political, and economic structures of rural social life that it was massively rejected by the rural population. Indeed, as an attempt to construct an ethico-political framework for controlled development it not only proved unappealing to rural villagers, but laid bare the rickety political, ideological, and philosophical base of state authority and established new arenas for contestation over the control of social life. The most prominent of these arenas were conservation policies as a locus of control, and local government policies as a locus of participation. The crisis was complicated by the fact that neither the state nor rural communities presented a cohesive front, thereby establishing the central political paradox of state-peasant relations: as the state was pressed into a managerial attitude, the shifting politics of rural communities made management more difficult.

This crisis pushed the government to embark on a new hegemonic project based on a thoroughgoing reassessment of the structure of the state and its relationship to society. The UFP government's response involved the first tentative moves to deracialize the social order, a prospect so shocking to the white electorate that they effectively scuttled it by electing the Rhodesian Front in 1962. This victory had a powerful effect on the lives and prospects of the disenfranchised, and especially the rural, African population of Rhodesia for in the early 1960s it brought a fundamental shift in the logic of state politics and rural policy.

4

Elaborating the Racial State, 1962–1972

Culture, Identity, and Community Development

The electoral victory of the Rhodesian Front (RF) in November 1962 came as a surprise to most white Rhodesians. The United Party, which had traditionally stood at the controls of the Rhodesian political machine, seemed well ensconced and few if any expected to see it precipitately toppled, especially by a rather hastily assembled and fractious opposition grouping. The RF leadership appealed stridently, though somewhat vaguely, to "certain standards of honesty and justice," "standards of Civilisation," and a "Rhodesian way of life" and espoused a loosely populist political vision in which local organizations were prominent and the role of the central state was curtailed. But this vision stretched little further than the small white towns and communities of rural Rhodesia. There was little of it to be found in RF policy on rural African administration. The new government immediately declared that it would adopt community development as the organizing principle of its African rural policy, although senior cabinet members acknowledged that they did not really understand what community development was. Yet from these inauspicious beginnings, the RF set out over the following ten years to consolidate its electoral power and to entrench a stringent racial policy of social control in the countryside that aimed to achieve the political objectives of the LHA without giving up the LAA. In its electoral goals, the RF was spectacularly successful. In its others it failed miserably. By the 1970s the policy had not only reduced the state's capacity to manage rural society, but had fragmented rural authority in ways that provided ready routes of access for the political and ideological appeals of the nationalist guerrilla armies.

The United Party under Whitehead had turned to community development as a policy vehicle to reestablish the control over rural society that had been lost during implementation of the Land Husbandry Act. The RF followed the same imperative. But the distinctions between their approaches are as important as the continuities, and help to expose central characteristics of the late colonial state's political dynamics. In general, scholarly depictions of the "colonial settler state" have implied a cohesion, continuity, and institutional effectiveness that an analysis of rural development policy calls into question. The vision of community development and its political utility that provided the core of rural state-society relations highlights not only a growing incoherence and ineffectiveness of social control strategies, but also a state profoundly weakened by internal tensions. It also reveals significant reversals in state strategies that press us to reevaluate the hegemonic logics of stateness. Community development was not only cooptive. It also exhibited the reliance of the state on rural cooperation, and in that respect provides an index of state vulnerability.

The RF government rejected the impulse to transform rural "imagined communities" that informed both the LHA and the liberalizing policies of the United Party. Instead, it set out to reinforce local political identities by appealing to the strength of traditional social authority. In this sense, the policy set out deliberately to *re*politicize development strategies that previous technocratic approaches had sought to depoliticize. In effect, it aimed to create the separate civic public realms that Peter Ekeh and Goran Hyden have associated with the relative autonomy of the peasantry. It seized on the community development language of "self-reliance" to disengage the state from rural development and to refract accountability through traditional authorities by focusing local conceptions of rights and civic responsibilities on those authorities. But it did not loosen the bonds of strict social control by DCs. Consequently, this policy intensified rather than mitigated local political struggles, resulting in policy paralysis. Under the cumulative weight of its own contradictions the policy was doomed to fail. It did so in ways that illuminate the deep-seated political incoherence of the late colonial state.

Politics, Culture, and Social Control

Community development theory offered a set of normative terms through which the state could define the appropriate limits of state intervention in rural life and also pursue its political goals of social control. As such, it played a central role in the RF government's efforts to establish state hegemony. But the language of self-reliance and local responsibility rapidly acquired particular political meanings that exacerbated the tensions between the state's propensities for control and its declining ability to obtain cooperation. We can uncover these meanings by considering state officials' own understandings of community development's uses, the political preoccupations of the RF, and the ideology of cultural separation that it deployed.

Arguments within the State

Within the central government, administrators advanced a variety of rationales for community development as the appropriate vehicle for restructuring political authority in the countryside. One rationale was that it would inculcate a new conception of citizenship and participation. Another was that it would give communities a material stake in development activities and reduce the responsibilities of the state. A third was that it could act as a form of sanction. These rationales intersected and overlapped. They all reflected in part a fear of losing control of rural society altogether, and in part a recognition that control could not be retained without the active participation of local community members. They also reflected a recognition among technocrats that stabilizing the population and the movement of labor, as well as rejuvenating the national economy, depended heavily on arresting rural economic decline. Taken together, they produced a vision of community development as the key link between political and economic development.

The first rationale was advanced by Howman and the USAID advisor Green, who were the real ideologues of community development and believed in it as a vehicle for social progress. In a 1969 article, when the argument for community development as a harbinger of citizenship was becoming increasingly embattled within Internal Affairs, Howman made several arguments for a community development approach.[1] First, he pinpointed two "divergent interpretations of the problem" of African development and social change that were prevalent in state thinking. One was a culturalist argument that traditional social structures were effective (despite new conditions), so valuable that they should not be changed, and in any case resistant to change. The other was a technocratic argument that, recognizing evidence of change already under way, wanted to "push on" with greater investment in extension services and credit facilities to achieve a "breakthrough." In what was almost certainly a reference to intense internal debates—particularly between the Ministry of Agriculture and the Ministry of Internal Affairs—over how to proceed with African development, Howman argued that these views could be reconciled by community development. He proposed to substitute the Land Husbandry Act's language of "sociological revolution" with gradual, organic change in which the cumulative build-up of small changes "brings about enormous changes of attitudes" that infiltrate and change deeper social structures and institutions. Second, Howman argued that community development was an integrating process upon which links between local communities and the central government could be constructed through a bottom-up process, focusing on "the social organism as a whole, to develop its capacity to think and feel and act, as a collective body, on a basis of communal organised self-help and self-control." Third, Howman argued that a community would only plan and act on development if it could define its own goals, interests, and priorities so that "its social structure is drawn into action, and all the elements of that structure—new roles, new statuses, new powers, new norms and new beliefs begin to exercise an influence." The outcome of such a movement would be a local government body—specifically the council—operating under central legislation, but expressing a new sense of community solidarity and cohesion.

Under the Rhodesian Front, community development policy systematically contradicted all these arguments. Politicians and administrators showed little interest in the argument for using the organic nature of communities as a starting point for transforming concepts of belonging, obligation, and citizenship within the community and the national state. These ideas would reemerge in postindependence development strategy. Under the RF, policymakers set out to reinforce rather than transform community institutions. But two aspects of Howman's arguments evoked considerable interest. These were the idea of self-responsibility, which would relieve state agents of the onus of planning and implementing development schemes, and the idea of self-help, which would relieve the state of the burdens of paying for development. For a government with limited ideological, material, and human resources, these ideas were particularly attractive because they would contain community expectations at the level of their own resources. The most immediate political advantage, as Whitehead stressed, was that community development should quell the rising African demands for education, which they would now have to fund and organize for themselves at the community level. Further, by giving community members a material stake in the system, self-help and self-responsibility would create an incentive to protect their investment against disruptive political influences, either local or from the urban areas.

Even before the RF took office, civil service working parties had emphasized the importance of an "integrated approach" to district administration and development that both recognized that "human relationships are paramount," and used local capital and labor. This development approach involved a shift "from centrally directed development to local initiative, from central planning and direction to local discussion and collaboration, from spoon-feeding to a financial system geared to the response and resources of the local community" and "a change in the psychology of the people and a translation of existing governmental procedures into practical action for building self-reliant communities willing and able to play an active part in their own development and using intelligently the financial and technical resources provided by Government."[2] Most importantly, this approach could be entrenched by mobilizing rural Africans' intense desire for education. In 1963 the government handed all responsibility for primary education in African areas over to the African councils on the idea that demand for education would help secure the authority of councils. But as a co-optive strategy this action was inherently unstable. It altered relations of authority within communities according to who had the resources, initiative, or skills to promote schools, it introduced teachers as a destabilizing element, and it heightened the pressure on state-community relations, for ultimate control of education remained with the central state.[3]

A final rationale within the state for community development was the argument that it could provide a form of sanction. This argument was based on a collective action model whereby collective participation is sustained because the benefits accrue only to participants. Thus, if community participation in development activities tended to stabilize communities, government aid might be made available only to those communities that were prepared to help themselves and take responsibility for their own development. As the Robinson Commission argued:

> It is possible that a different method of compulsion may be applied in the light of the fact that the offender is a member of a tribal community and that traditionally his actions affect the whole community. If, therefore, the community or its leaders cannot discipline one of their members any sanctions should be imposed on the community as a whole. While we do not go as far as to suggest that existing amenities such as schools, roads and clinics should be closed we recommend that any request for an extension of amenities should be considered on the willingness of the community to discipline its members to ensure that conservation measures are adopted and maintained.[4]

Once communities accepted the responsibility for development, competition might be generated between communities over the extent and speed of development, and the energies of communities concentrated on nonpolitical goods such as physical and infrastructural development.

It was this mixture of stick, carrot, and ideology that made community development an attractive replacement for the technical, coercive thrust of the Land Husbandry Act as the principal idiom of rural control when the RF came to power. The RF added its own political preoccupations and ideas to provide a framework for the construction of rural policy that shaped the direction and character of state-peasant relations but undermined its hegemonic capacity.

The Triumph of Politics

The Rhodesian Front came to power by mobilizing a coalition of disgruntled renegades from the political establishment, working-class and petit bourgeois whites, and marginal groups such as new immigrants, who resisted the notion of liberalizing the polity or the economy and coalesced largely around demands for stringent state control of the African population. While sympathizing with these groups, the RF also recognized the overriding interests of large business in a "free enterprise economy" where government's principal role was supportive. In addition the RF capitalized on discontent within the administration, notably in the Ministry of Internal Affairs.[5] This disparate political base resulted in a curious and shifting coalition of racial and class interests that party leaders could only manage by pouring an excessively large amount of political energy and economic resources into white society, especially after the Unilateral Declaration of Independence (UDI) in 1965. The effect of this strategy was to deepen the crisis of rural social management as the government sought to reconcile divergent pressures for national economic development and for separate development in addressing the political and economic conditions of the reserves (known after 1962 as Tribal

Trust Lands [TTLs]). Community development policy was its main response to this dilemma.

Following UDI and the imposition of sanctions, businessmen and industrialists began to pressure the government to boost African agricultural production and rural incomes in order to extend the market base. According to one estimate, the relative productivity of African agriculture had declined significantly between 1954 and 1964, and that decline showed every sign of continuing.[6] In 1968, a former Secretary for African Education, C. S. Davies, urged in the pages of *NADA* that the distinction between "tribalism" and the "cash economy" be broken. "Tribalism in its economic sense," he argued, "is a luxury we cannot go on enjoying very much longer." Africans must be encouraged to pursue "a world of individual ownership, individual responsibility, of property and possessions, of pride in workmanship and payment according to ability and capacity . . . a world far removed from subsistence tribalism and its communal safeguards."[7] Such arguments for TTL development all looked to revitalizing the economy by opening up economic, political, and social structures. They looked to freehold tenure for Africans. But this was anathema to the more xenophobic party rank-and-file already made jittery by rising unemployment and the government's failure to control the mobility of the African population. To them, rising and unmanaged urbanization made a mockery of the party's separatist ideology and of the Land Apportionment Act. They demanded a clarification of the government's concept of "separate development."[8]

Under contradictory political pressures, the RF government, which lacked intellectual leadership and expertise, procrastinated. In the absence of a coherent policy vision, the construction of rural policy drifted and agrarian decline deepened, while the state became increasingly dependent on African productivity to fuel the domestic economy. The situation was complicated by the upsurge of African nationalist political activity in the 1960s, which monopolized the attention of the state's coercive apparatuses. Continued rural resistance and the early flickerings of nationalist guerrilla activity in the rural areas added urgency. Although this activity was quelled, the armed struggle henceforth had to be a serious policy consideration.[9]

In 1967 the government finally appointed a South African economist, J. L. Sadie, as a one-man commission to report on economic development. Sadie stressed the importance of "modernizing the subsistence sector" to raise its productivity, and of generating employment opportunities outside that sector. In his view, modernizing peasant agriculture required effecting a psychological change in the rural African population in order to generate the "need-to-achieve" motive associated with individualism and the market. Such a change could be brought about, he argued, by increasing the importance of cash in rural relationships.[10] Thus, the Sadie report hewed closely to the standard—and racist—colonial evolutionary ideology that naturalized African poverty as an effect of pre-modern social organization. It ignored the history of colonial primitive accumulation strategies and the processes of struggle for control of social life that they had motivated, though these were the very struggles that the commission was supposed to address.

The Sadie report suited RF objectives. In its wake, the government finally declared its intention to rehabilitate the tribal areas and bring them into the cash economy. This intention was publicized in 1968, in a series of articles in the *Rhodesia Herald* titled "The Other Rhodesia," which explained the thrust of government policy:

> [T]he policy towards the Tribal Trust Lands—the old Reserves—has taken its third leap forward. Once the policy was such that its effect was to keep them as quiet, taxpaying, reservoirs of labour. Now it is to develop their full potential: first into

self-sufficiency; then into exporters of grain, beef and (through the big mining companies, whose exclusive prospecting areas straddle the hills) minerals; and finally, into agricultural and industrial rivalry with the European areas, to the economic benefit of the country as a whole.

The government energetically propagated this image of its commitment to development.[11] But the commitment was strictly limited. The decline in the African areas made an increase in productivity dependent on massive financial input that the government, committed to subsidizing white farmers and industry, did not intend to deploy. It held consistently to the argument that national development could only be maximized by making the most resources available to those able to utilize them most efficiently—European farmers. Consequently, it never took a commitment to the primary development of the reserves very seriously. Instead, it poured much of the effort and material resources that it might have expended on the physical development of the reserves into preparing remote resettlement areas. In short, politically committed to the success of UDI and separatism, the RF government had neither the political nor the economic will to seriously pursue development of the TTLs according to its stated policy.

As the 1960s progressed and rural resistance intensified, profound political contradictions developed between the government's promise to develop the TTLs "into agriculture and industrial rivalry," its intention to abdicate that responsibility as far as it possibly could, and its determination to maintain strict control of the countryside. Under increasing political pressure, the RF government had to find some way of defining the state's role in rural development that would obscure these tensions. In short it faced the challenge of defining the appropriate parameters of state-society relations to reconcile the contradictory objectives of state activism in rural control and state disengagement in rural development. To do this the government set out to entrench a legitimating ideology that would reconcile the pervasive statism of the racial state with an antistatist vision of national—and local—development. This state ideology was based on a revamped concept of cultural relativism and an appeal to "community development."

Culture and Identity

Lacking intellectual vision, the RF defined its political vision in 1962 through two arguments: opposition to "forced integration" (a slogan upon which it had fought a vociferous election campaign) and allegiance to the notion of "partnership."[12] But the RF concept of partnership stood in direct opposition to the liberal paternalism of the UFP, harking back instead to the "two-pyramid" racial policy of the 1930s. No sooner had the party come to power than the UFP's policy of partnership was halted, and the new government turned its hand immediately and almost exclusively to protecting and entrenching the LAA, a task it pursued with single-minded vigor until the transitional government of 1978. In RF eyes, the central historical task of the LAA was to sustain racial separation. Its sanctity provided a definitive yardstick for the moral and political outlook of state, and was simply not negotiable. As R. C. Haw put it in a Ministry of Information publication, "There is today a widespread feeling amongst Europeans that *they* need the protection of the Land Apportionment Act, just as the Africans feel they need their tribal areas to be protected. This is really not a question of colour but of cultural differences. All over the world people feel it needful for their happiness to be amongst those of their own cultural blending."[13]

This political vision represented little more than an appeal to the status quo. But as a political program it demanded extensive state action in structuring civil society, and an elaborate state ideology to legitimate it. Over time, the RF sought to contain the contradictions of its rather rough-hewn political understanding by molding, honing, and hardening it into a variant of the apartheid philosophy of its southern neighbor, to whom it looked for much of its theoretical guidance.[14] It advanced a culturalist philosophy in which the state acted as the arbiter not (as in the liberal tradition) of individual rights and values, but of the rights and values that accrue to groups. As the party's published principles put it: "The Party opposes compulsory integration and believes that the peaceful co-existence of people can only be achieved when communities have the right and opportunity to preserve their own identities, traditions and customs, and therefore recognizes the obligation of Government and respective communities where necessary to ensure the provision of such separate facilities as will make this possible." At the same time, the state would provide the "political shell" for capitalist development.

As in South Africa, this dual commitment to capitalism and sustained racial separatism demanded a pervasive and systematic statism. Under the first commitment, the regime applauded individual enterprise and initiative; under the second commitment, it determined to direct civil society extensively. There is, of course, no insuperable contradiction between these two commitments, but it requires a state that is either physically powerful or hegemonically strong. As we saw above, and subsequent colonial history confirmed, the Rhodesian state was neither. Thus RF philosophy reveals the deepest irony of state attempts to dominate society: it made a hegemonic strategy both imperative and impossible. As in South Africa some twenty years later, the government needed increasingly to "legitimate the illegitimate." But the gap between pervasive state direction of society and the language of state disengagement remained an arena for political contestation in the rural areas.

RF views on cultural distinction were encapsulated in a

forty-three-page booklet published by the Ministry of Information, Immigration and Tourism in 1969, titled *The Man and His Ways*. This publication marks an important shift in the language of policy in which the new political-ideological strategies and directions of the state were articulated. Giving the nod in passing to the fact that "we have to go on living together and are, in fact, dependent upon each other," the booklet stressed the fundamental differences between Africans and Europeans. Most important, it stated, "Except in trivial matters the African, unlike the European, does not regard himself as an individual distinct from the rest of the group. He feels himself to be part of a unit, be it tribe or family, and to that unit he owes certain obligations in exchange for which he derives many benefits." This philosophy drew heavily on a sustained conceptual separation between two economies, the "subsistence economy" and the "cash economy" based on entirely different—indeed exclusive—understandings of the world. It rested on several racial myths: the African's subsistence mentality, high leisure preference, and communal orientation. And it stressed the solid and stolid resilience of the traditional tribal structure and its capacity to resist the imposition and influences of the external and alien structures of European society.

The "high leisure preference" that was a feature of this resistance was explained by a peculiar mix of rational individual choice and the psychological grip of tradition. By virtue of the communal tribal structure, the African "lives in an intricate network of kinship bonds, of rights and duties assigned by that network and he does not exercise his freedom of choice as an individual to make his own self-interests, judgements and choices." Therefore, "the ordinary economic factors that dictate and influence European behaviour, planning and reaction, cannot be explained when dealing with the African operating under a tribal communal structure."[15] On the other hand, African producers see no point in producing a surplus, since as soon as they do so most of it will be claimed by an ever-increasing cohort of family members claiming their right to sponge off the producer.[16] On this argument, the desperate need for fertilizer, seed, insecticide, and implements in the African rural areas was only a secondary problem of development. According to the government, African farmers were not acculturated to receive high levels of capital inputs. Although *The Man and His Ways* denied the myth of African laziness as the crux of the "African way of life," it did project Africans as lacking initiative. Thus the real need was "to get people steeped in tradition and custom, which places a high priority on leisure, to change their ideas and adopt improved farming techniques."[17]

But under the separatist philosophy, there was a contradiction between the demands of development and respect for the sanctity of tribal authority structures. For by this philosophy the necessary attitudinal changes neither could nor should be wrought by state action. The ultimate argument of *The Man and His Ways* was that, given the cultural oddities of "the African," it was important to "remember his background and treat him with patience and courtesy" and to "never forget the need for careful explanation." Thus, appeals to this philosophy allowed the state to effectively sidestep the question of a development strategy for the African rural areas by placing heavy reliance on its own interpretation of community development philosophy: "The only solution appears to be to transform the approach to farming of the community as a whole. . . . The chiefs and headmen will be given the opportunity and the legal power under this legislation to lead their people from a subsistence economy to a cash economy. It will be up to them, with the assistance of the administration and the extension services, to improve the lot of the people."[18] The state was able to abdicate in large measure responsibility for rural development by drawing the boundary of legitimate state initiative at the provision of administration and extension services.

At the same time the stress laid on Africans' group orientation had powerful political ramifications. It provided a final rejection of the philosophical underpinnings of the LHA, which had been predicated on a belief in the propensity of individuals to maximize economic utilities. Many Internal Affairs officials, having long disliked the interference and naiveté of extension officers who expected improved conditions to result from technically improved opportunities, supported this rejection wholeheartedly. In his 1961 annual report, the Secretary of Native Affairs noted "how extremely doubtful administrators have become of this line of thinking" and pointed out how "it has all been tried before. A revolution of subsistence agriculture is unlikely to be achieved by extension methods appropriate only to a European context with no cultural barriers to be surmounted. . . ."[19] The new policy presented the subsistence economy of the African areas as entirely a function of culture, and offered no intention of surmounting cultural barriers. This language directly refuted the hegemonic appeals that the previous government had begun to make prior to its demise.

The refurbished state philosophy translated readily into a two-pronged policy whereby the state would (a) stimulate rural Africans to build and expand their own community life through community development, and (b) secure political control and management by revamping the powers of the chiefs and traditional lines of authority. Thus it provided a rationale for state withdrawal from the structures of society in the African areas in terms of both development strategy and political incorporation or control. This ostensible withdrawal of the central state from rural African life could of course only take place at the level of political language, for to actually withdraw would indeed be to relinquish control. Not only did DCs refuse to allow this, but the state had to manage the LAA, population mobility, resettlement, and squatters. This raised the pervasive irony of rural administration in Rhodesia: the withdrawal of the state could only properly take place if the rural African population accepted community development and chiefly control as hegemonic devices. But would they do so?

The State Politics of Community Development

Under the Rhodesian Front, community development policy was designed to take up those concerns that had become most urgent in the wake of the LHA: land control, political control, economic development, and provision of social services such as education and health. In all these areas, the policy represented a reduction of state responsibility for securing public goods or arbitrating public authority. In addressing the closely related problems of managing the land question in the African areas, regulating the mobility and supply of labor, and resolving the rural crisis, the RF rejected the recommendations of the Quinton Committee and the Phillips Report to relax social controls on the labor force and ease the migrant system. Yet more assertive control meant more extensive state intervention in society, and the failure of the LHA had already demonstrated the political dangers inherent in such strategies. The divergent objectives of controlling African mobility while reducing the state's developmental role in the countryside led the government into increasingly contradictory and incoherent attempts to define the parameters of appropriate state interventions in rural social life. These efforts are revealed in the efforts of the administration to remoralize land politics and administrative control.

The Politics of Land

The poor performance of the economy and the failure of the LHA had demonstrated that migrant labor could not be ended. At best, it could be controlled, and this was the guiding objective of the government's development policy in the TTLs. Specifically, it aimed to provide livelihoods for "a growing African population which cannot be absorbed in industry and elsewhere," create off-farm employment for the poor and landless, and open new areas for settlement and production.[20] These objectives placed resolution of the land shortage at the epicenter of the broader development strategy.

The government vigorously promoted the argument that economic decline in the TTLs was not a function of land shortage, but of the "subsistence mentality" and "resilient traditionalism" of Africans. In 1972 the DC Chipinga [Chipinge] reported that "all in all, the African areas as a whole have access to adequate markets, but lack the will and drive to become productive," and TILCOR's annual report for 1969–70 stated that agricultural productivity was constrained by "disincentives" stemming "from poor utilisation of available land, resulting in poor yields, lack of communications and inadequate marketing facilities all of which are compounded by the high leisure preference of the tribal African."[21] While these arguments may fit the preconceptions of white settlers they were not compelling to African land seekers and farmers already hostile to state interventions in land use and production practices. To deal with these oppositions, the government saw the need to redefine the state's relationship to property rights in a way that would be less politically confrontational and yet would not relinquish control. It found its solutions in a thoroughgoing attempt to harness the power of tradition.

The RF government stressed that rural development planning would be guided by three principles. These principles were communal land tenure, central government participation in administration, and tribal traditional authority in respect of judicial issues, land occupation and use, local government, spiritual and political matters. The first principle lowered the flag officially on the state activism of the Land Husbandry Act. It showed the government's determination not to be seen to intervene in timeless traditional tenure arrangements. This involved a fundamental reconceptualization of property rights in official language. The government now laid stress on what one agricultural official termed the right of avail, a "bundle of rights" to various community resources (residence, tillage, pasture, water, firewood, etc.) held by the community but participated in automatically by every community member on the principle that "tribal land 'belongs to the whole community, the living, the departed dead, and the countless generations as yet unborn.'"[22] Emphasis on the right of avail recognized that rights of access to land were part of a wider panoply of cohesive social relationships within the community that constituted an "effective system of social control," and that individualizing rights disturbed those relations. It also stressed that those rights could be adjudicated only by the community itself. Thus, the state sought to withdraw from direct confrontation with the African population over access to land by locating the definition of land rights outside the province of state jurisdiction—with the two notable exceptions of policing the LAA and carrying out resettlement.

The principle of enhancing traditional tribal authority showed the modus operandi for effecting state withdrawal. Aware of the resistance Land Husbandry Act land allocations had generated, the government was eager to abdicate this responsibility to local traditions and laws, if not to the market. The allocation of land through village head, ward headman, and chief took place on the whole outside of the ambit of central state control, although in some cases the chief would consult the DC. This meant that it was up to the local "authority" to make an allocation or not, and to decide on its size and location. The government based this strategy on a conception of African communalism that stressed the community as the most fundamental social unit in African society. As Secretary of Internal Affairs W. H. H. Nicolle argued, "The traditional African society has never emphasised the free individual. It has comprehended individuals only in the context of the community, protecting them within a cocoon of finespun relationships."[23] A chief's acceptance of a newcomer and his family (as his subjects) implied that they were entitled to participate in the right of avail in that particular chiefdom; they were, or had become, part of the community. If the chief refused to accept the land seeker, it was because he was an outsider to the community.[24] Whether one was part of a community or not was not a matter of state jurisdiction.

The object of this policy was to create constituencies of outsiders and insiders that would bolster the position of traditional tribal authorities as agents of social control. Many land seekers, coming from a depressed urban existence or being resettled across the country, were indeed outsiders. In order to get land and enjoy community rights they had to become insiders. The authority for excluding or including a person in the community carried with it considerable power, and was seen by Internal Affairs officials to have the effect of encouraging members to conform to locally accepted mores.[25] As land pressure grew, however, it became increasingly difficult to move between communities. The fine distinction between royal and nonroyal lineage groups (articulated in clan totems) became increasingly significant, for it was the chiefs and headmen who controlled land allocation. In the early 1960s the community delineation teams noted many instances in which local authorities made land allocations only to local people.

The government's strategy aimed to draw in both parties. Chiefs would continue to allocate land to insiders because the maintenance of their authority depended on it; they might grumble about the shortage of land but they would find it. To sweeten the pot, chiefs received (over and above their basic allowance) an allowance based on the number of their followers, and a personal allowance "having regard to such factors as the personal attributes of the chief concerned, his administrative ability, his co-operation with the administration, his tribal importance, leadership, control and authority over his people."[26] People would continue to respect the authority of the chief because their access to community rights depended upon it. Thus, the strategy would both mitigate the generational conflicts that were finding expression in the burgeoning urban-based nationalist movement and act as a brake on rampant urbanization. In one sense, therefore, the strategy of the government was to *create* community-oriented individuals by forcing this orientation upon them. To this extent, we might talk of the creation of Africans' "resilient traditionalism." It was institutionalized in the Tribal Trust Lands Act of 1967, and was further entrenched by the African Law and Tribal Courts Act of 1969, which returned to traditional authorities their juridical powers under customary law.[27] These acts in turn provided the political and ideological core of the Land Tenure Act of 1969, which replaced the Land Apportionment Act, and was the RF's last-ditch constitutional stand on racial land apportionment.

This policy aimed, very clearly, to secure a rural regime based on what Mahmood Mamdani calls the "decentralized despotism" of late-colonial states. However, it created a wide range of conflicts and compromises at the local level, partly because the community integrity it assumed was not a seamless web, and partly because the government itself violated that integrity at will by implementing the LAA, resettling Africans, and establishing irrigation schemes where the state took over land and allocated plots. Resettlement in particular had a severe impact on the formation of communities, and on relations between chiefs, people, and the state. It required land, and therefore often either increased pressure on land already occupied, or settled people in arid or tstetse-infested areas, which would mean a poor and difficult existence. Many resettlement areas were far from markets. Many settlers were placed under alien chiefdoms, and many headmen and chiefs were moved into areas already under the jurisdiction of another. The strategy resulted in resentment on all sides and the emergence of a panoply of local struggles between people, chiefs, and the state.

Resettled farmers frequently only moved under protest or under arrest.[28] Where chiefs were at loggerheads over spheres of jurisdiction, community development and local government initiatives did not receive a hearty welcome. In Umvuma and Gokwe districts, some chiefs simply refused to cooperate unless they received more land for allocation. In some areas where people were resettled with cattle the sudden rise in livestock population increased pressure on arable and grazing resources. The disintegration of communities thus resettled weakened informal bonds of reciprocity and cooperation that had facilitated local rules for controlling stocking levels. In one section of the Chilimanzi TTL, headmen resisted the government's decision to settle a chief and his followers by rapidly allocating as much land as possible, so that, as the delineation team reported, "Hunyani is today grossly overpopulated and overstocked, the people are fully aware of these facts, and they look to the Government for relief." In short, the question of who was responsible for land shortage, land degradation, and land allocation remained one of vigorous political conflict, to which the government responded by resettling large numbers (sometimes thousands) of "squatters."[29] Nowhere was this more dramatically and brutally demonstrated than in the removal of chief Rekayi Tangwena and his people from the Gaerisi Ranch area in the Nyanga highlands. This eviction produced a three-year running battle between the chief and the state, of which the Secretary of Internal Affairs concluded, "If some people were hurt in the process it was their own fault. Government provided excellent alternative land for them and transport to move them to it. For the most part they declined both." Tangwena, for his part, became a popular hero and a symbol of resistance in the liberation struggle, creating a powerful local social memory of struggles with the state that continues to inform negotiations over development and public authority today.[30]

The question of rights of access spilled over into questions of land use, which the state was also now eager to declare outside its sphere of jurisdiction. With the LHA effectively dead, the implementation of conservation measures slumped badly in the mid-1960s. Besides the persistence of local resistance, there was a massive shortage of qualified agricultural staff at all levels, which "completely inhibited all efforts at an extension program." In fact, after 1969 there was no real agricultural extension service; there was only a number of agriculturally trained personnel on the staff of rural administrators.[31]

The government had set out to reestablish state control of rural society without bearing the burdens of direct accountability and without committing large manpower and financial resources. This was the political core of "community development" based on traditional authority. In 1967 the government passed the Tribal Trust Lands Act, which gave legal recognition to Tribal Land Authorities (TLAs) with the right to make bylaws governing "the use and occupation by tribesmen of the land in the tribal area for which it is established." But this strategy too contained inherent contradictions. On the one hand, legislation now recognized that "the people of the Tribal Areas are responsible for the land they use." On the other hand, government land-use planners insisted that "*a measure of discipline is needed* in those aspects of land use which are vital to continued settlement."[32] Between fostering local responsibility and imposing discipline, lines of authority on the ground were confused and contradictory.

The legislation laid down neither the composition nor the precise functions of TLAs. Many agricultural officials, accustomed to centralized direction of land utilization, assumed that the TLAs would be government agencies and, in some cases, wanted to nominate the membership of TLAs themselves. Local authorities, for their part, often weren't quite sure why they were creating a new body or what that body really represented. The TLAs were hesitant to draw up bylaws, and indeed their authority to enforce them was unclear especially in areas where Tribal Courts had not yet been created. Guided by Internal Affairs officials and Agriculture Department officials, most TLAs became implementers and enforcers of natural resource legislation. But in doing so, as Hughes has pointed out, TLAs appeared as little more than an arm of the state, and lacked any real moral purchase on land use practices. Their effect was not only to exacerbate resentment against the state but to draw the chiefs more tightly into the spotlight of rural anger and resistance. They also strained community relationships by their attempts to implement conservation requirements. On one hand, TLAs hired young men to peg lands for conservation, paying them out of money levied on local farmers. On the other, they added conservation to the labor commitments of subordinates such as young women.[33]

Thus, the government's responses to decline in the African rural areas were deeply contradictory. While maintaining that the state was agnostic on local forms of public authority and property rights, it remained capriciously interventionist and absent, both fostering "communities" and displacing rural citizens. Without the co-optive and stabilizing effects of community development it could not possibly succeed. Yet the RF's vision of community development, mired in the fundamental ideological contradictions of RF separatist philosophy, was irreducibly authoritarian and managerial.

The Politics of Administration

The RF was content with any rural policy that would preserve the LAA, maintain political stability, and present at least a semblance of legitimacy for its racial policies. A tradition-based community development strategy fit these loose requirements easily and, once adopted, the government was generally happy to leave the Ministry of Internal Affairs to its own administrative techniques. Its only demand was that the Internal Affairs leadership should be committed to the LAA and to UDI. This approach to policy construction had two effects with long-term implications for state-peasant relations. First, agrarian policy drifted and rural economic decline deepened. Second, the Internal Affairs leadership moved to strengthen its political hold over rural society.

In 1965, Ian Smith appointed W. H. H. Nicolle, an efficient but deeply conservative administrator who greatly admired South Africa's homeland system and wholly supported UDI, as Secretary of Internal Affairs. Nicolle was perhaps the truest ideologue of Rhodesian separatism, and he became increasingly powerful within the government. But the vigor of his conviction contained the seeds of severe conflicts in the politics of rural development, for he always harbored a deep suspicion of the development efforts and interests of other ministries. Throughout his tenure as Secretary of Internal Affairs (1965–72), Nicolle used his political influence to guide state rural development policy toward two political objectives: fostering a cultural and separatist approach to rural authority, and rebuilding the internal empire of Internal Affairs in rural Rhodesia. For Nicolle, the main value of community development policy lay in the extent to which it facilitated these two projects.[34]

Nicolle believed that community development could promote social control exercised by a monolithic and comprehensively co-opted elite of traditional authorities. In his 1966 annual report, he stated baldly:

> Community development as it is known and applied in other parts of the world is a premature concept for Africa. I believe that the only kind of development which will bring community progress and social advance is through the Africans' own known, tried and understood system—the tribal structure of organization and leadership. It will be a slow process and one full of imponderables and pitfalls. . . . All along we shall have to "play it by ear" without trying to impose a set of hard and fast rules or creating a set kind of policy.[35]

In political terms, this was a cynically co-optive vision in which chiefs would be openly bought off. Nicolle expounded this argument in a 1966 article, which is worth quoting at length:

> In the initial stage each area under the control of a chief will be delineated and in respect of this area the Chief and his Headmen will operate a Tribal Court. The Chief, Headmen and selected advisors will operate a Land Authority. The Chief, his Headmen and selected members will form the nucleus of a Local Government Authority (Council).
>
> If these three types of authority are to work satisfactorily it is essential that there be a permanent headquarters staffed with the necessary executive staff. It would seem therefore that in each Chief's area a suitable headquarters must be established consisting in the initial stage of a Court Room/Council Hall, an office for the Chief, the Council Secretary, Council Treasurer, Clerk of Council and other Council or Tribal Authority employees. Housing for these employees will also be necessary. . . . One of the most important functions that will operate in the Chief's Tribal Area will be his local government. This will have a wide range of

responsibility but it will be principally concerned with Education, maintenance of roads and water supplies, conservation of natural resources and the general development of the area. . . . In addition, Government has provided a further £25,000 which will be utilised to set up a school for the sons of Chiefs and Headmen to train these potential leaders in the work that will fall on their shoulders when in due course they assume the office of Chief or Headman.[36]

As a co-optive strategy this vision can be fruitfully contrasted with the postcolonial vision quoted on page 309 below.

Nicolle's second objective for community development was to enable Internal Affairs to press its own claim as the overriding and authoritative conduit between the state and communities, and to subordinate other ministries in directing rural development and control. By insisting on local-authority accountability for development, Internal Affairs was able to lift the direction of technical development such as conservation out of the hands of the Agriculture Ministry and reappropriate it for themselves. In July 1969, Internal Affairs formally took over responsibility for conservation and extension, as well as the staff and responsibility for cooperatives and the African agricultural loan scheme. The Department of African Agriculture was abolished, and all technical staff were brought under the authority of Internal Affairs. Though many of the most able and experienced agricultural development experts remained with the Agriculture Ministry, Nicolle reported that "[t]his unified control of staff employed in the development of the Tribal Trust Land has simplified the execution of Government policy and there is clear evidence of co-operation and interest by tribesmen, particularly in regard to the conservation of their land."[37]

In fact, "simplification" of government policy simply meant shoring up the central political position of DCs in rural control. Senior agricultural staff no longer controlled grassroots personnel of supervisors and demonstrators. DCs liked Nicolle because he looked to results rather than means, rewarded administrative initiative, and was fiercely protective of his personnel against outsiders. Moreover their overriding local power was bolstered by the Prime Minister's Directive of 1965, which was the principal government policy document on rural development. Its central point is worth quoting, for it was to echo in postindependence policy:

> The district commissioner, as the representative of Government in his district, is responsible for the approach, as a whole, of all ministries in so far as they impinge on the local communities. All ministries share in the process of community development—for it includes better education, conservation of the soil as well as conservation of the community in its capacity for collective action and control—but the district commissioner is the guardian of the process of community development and is charged with the task of fostering, and supporting, local government. In this task he should be able to rely on the willing co-operation of all officers of Government and he will . . . use his powers of guidance and co-ordination on the basis of what is most conducive to supporting the plans and priorities of the councils and community boards, not his own beliefs and preferences.[38]

DCs took to community development because they thought of it as something that had always been there (*pace* the CNC's 1961 statement) and could therefore be readily adopted as state policy. They perceived less readily that as soon as they made it policy it became anathema to locals who recognized it as a strategy of state domination.

Repeated genuflections toward the importance of "willing co-operation and appreciation of the people" and the need for "careful co-ordination" notwithstanding, DCs continued to regard themselves as the spearhead of rural control and development, guiding and directing local authorities and brandishing the Prime Minister's Directive to keep other ministries out of their bailiwick.[39] The community development section, although it held responsibility for councils and was committed to a steady, incorporative process of social transformation in the Howman mold, remained small and politically marginal within the ministry. Consequently, the implementation of community development policy was lackluster. The section's main activities were to carry out research and to run training courses for ministry personnel at all levels. In reality, as the 1971 Memo on community development stressed, "the *district commissioner* is the guardian of the process of community development and is charged with the task of fostering, and supporting, local government."[40] After 1971, the cabinet coordinating committee and its working party became inactive because no systematic basis had ever been provided for community development within the public service. As Ian Cormack has suggested, community development declined within the government because of "a general lack of understanding of what needed to be done and, flowing from this, a lack of interest and an abdication of responsibility."[41] This was certainly often true at the local level. When the British community development expert T. R. Batten visited Rhodesia in mid-1965 he reported, "Everywhere we have been in Rhodesia we have found people's ideas about community development 'woolly' and unclear. . . . "[42]

Against this background of internal government politics and ideology, the central government articulated the stringent limits on its commitment to developing the African rural areas in the political-moral terms of community development. But in the absence of state rural hegemony the character of state domination created profound tensions between self-management at the local level and a domineering, administrative, and regulative state apparatus centered on the DC's office. The result was an array of shifting and cross-cutting lines of control, authority, and power in which the overriding authority of the state became increasingly tenuous at the local level.

The Local Politics of Community Development

If the rural economy was to be stimulated and the rural population stabilized, peasant farmers required capital resources, infrastructural development, and social services.[43] As we have seen, the dilemma of the racial state was that it had every interest in effecting these changes to stabilize the rural population, but it had no interest in committing significant resources to the task. Thus, it needed a workable strategy to promote local-level collective action for development by targeting the most appropriate social groups to undertake it, and by establishing the most appropriate institutions of local governance to manage it. Once again, it found its solution in a policy of state disengagement, couched in the political-moral terms of self-reliance, community development, and civic responsibility focused on tribal authorities. This approach rested on a linear vision of the political process. The promotion of community development projects under the aegis of councils would lead both to the formation of more councils and to stronger feelings of identity by "the tribal people" with their local council. Councils, in turn, would be founded on the social authority of traditional chiefs.[44] Together, chiefs, councils, and community development would provide a resilient institutional framework for sound and stable governance in which the accountability and the responsibilities of the central state would be mitigated. But in the context of a local state apparatus driven by the overbearing administrative sensibilities of DCs, the fiscal stinginess of the treasury, and a deepening security crisis, this policy could not succeed. It deepened, rather than mitigated, the crisis of social authority in the countryside.

Community development theory lays great stress on self-reliance and self-help as vehicles for human development. Not least, according to the theory, self-reliance fosters a sense of responsibility and commitment to society that provides the foundation not only for material progress but also for sociopolitical progress. The theory stresses community choice in selecting local development projects. Accordingly, the Rhodesian government stipulated that development tasks should be confined to the "felt needs" of the people because these were the needs that they would be willing to work for. This principle was politically attractive for several reasons. First, by making state development assistance contingent on communities identifying development projects, it forced communities to either initiate their own development activities or stagnate. As the government's chief land planner baldly put it, "Economic pressures will exert a helpful influence where the basic 'wants' such as health and educational services, have to be paid for from the income obtained from livestock or crop sales."[45] Second, by making all projects contingent on the deployment of *local* financial and labor resources, the government made the policy cheap and easy to administer. Third, by making development projects (material development) the focus of local development activity (and the index of development)[46] the state could structure intracommunity cohesion and intercommunity competition in such a way that local government could be contained and managed at the council level. Thus, community development remained paradoxically an administrative and managerial policy, fundamentally at odds with its theoretical objectives of sociopolitical incorporation.

"Self-Reliance": Community Advisors and Community Boards

Rhodesian community development policy envisaged two main protagonists in promoting local development. On the

side of the state were community advisors, government employees who were deployed in rural communities after a short
training course to "teach people to help themselves and to
make their own decisions and plans." Their primary brief was
to promote community boards and councils, but they were
also expected to "promote and assist all forms of voluntary associations, special interest groups, clubs and organised self-
help" including "youth clubs, women's clubs, guides, scouts and
other organisations with an ideal of self-reliance and service
to the community."[47] These functionaries were not employed
as extension agents, and were instructed not to get in the way
of extension workers. On the side of the community were
community boards, who were to undertake or coordinate community development activities. Their composition and constitution was not patrolled by government, but they had to be
recognized by the DC. The government argued for "flexibility
within a minimum of rules" on the principle that "the assistance given by Government should be sufficient to stimulate
interest and achieve certain limited goals while at the same
time always emphasising that the only really satisfactory way
to achieve major goals is through formal local government."[48]

In effect this strategy amounted neither to a "nondirective"
policy for development (which was one of the watchwords of
community development theorists) nor to a noninterventionist state approach. The government was right to recognize
that community development, as a strategy for managing society, could have only very limited effects unless it was associated with effective local government. But it could not act on
this recognition because of the sustained tension between the
central government's preoccupation with tribal control, DCs'
determination to control their districts, and an absence of any
serious government commitment to rural development. In the
first place, the number of community advisors deployed by government was woefully small: 222 to serve a rural population of

over 4 million.[49] As agents of the state assigned from outside the community, community advisors frequently met with suspicion or noncooperation. Where DCs used them for administrative tasks such as contour pegging, their credibility was severely compromised. In mid-1964 the community delineation officer for Gwanda reported that community advisors' work was inhibited by the lack of follow-up or material assistance from the DC's office. As rural resistance to the state became more intense in the late 1960s and early 1970s, community advisors leaving the service were not replaced.[50]

If the state's commitment to community advisors was minimal, community boards were not effective either. Most boards came into being to carry out a particular project and either died en route along with the project or were disbanded at its completion. In 1972 there were 287 recognized community boards, of which Michael Bratton estimates 97 were inactive.[51] There is no data available on who in rural communities promoted specific kinds of projects, and it is therefore difficult to determine to what extent development projects really were community projects. Boards were flexible in membership, although in the vast majority of cases headmen participated, and the number of people involved in a project ranged from a group of families to the people of an entire chiefdom. Even council projects, such as schools, did not necessarily promote cohesion. Undoubtedly, mobilizing rural Africans' intense desire for education facilitated the implementation of community development policy by generating local involvement. But when thwarted, as it sometimes was, by the state's determination to exercise ultimate sanction over schools, this intense desire often became a focus of local opposition. Furthermore, the government did not offer financial assistance to community development projects, confining its aid to materials, machinery, specialized skills, and advice. But the attempt to extricate the state from accountability by passing responsibility on to local bodies was compromised by the fact that the main source of development financing remained the ADF levy on African marketed produce, which peasant farmers resented deeply. The ill will caused by the levy prompted a number of politicians and officials to argue in the early 1960s that local authorities should be allowed to decide for themselves whether to opt for the levy as a source of local revenue. The interministerial working party on agriculture noted not only that the ADF levy system "however beneficial is a discriminatory form of taxation upon a racial basis," but that it distorted local markets by necessitating "differential forms of marketing to ensure its collection." Under these conditions, it acknowledged, any attempt by the state to appear nondiscriminatory would require the abolition of the ADF levy. Secretary of Internal Affairs Morris argued that the levy was incompatible with the policy of community development, and that "the time has come to vest responsibility for those aspects of the scheme which are not of national importance in the hands of the local people to preserve, reject, modify as they think fit through their local governments. . . ." But this approach was never adopted since most local authorities would be likely to reject the levy, thereby deepening the difficulty of rural control or throwing the onus of financial inputs back onto the government. The RF viewed this prospect as unacceptable.[52]

The policy of state disengagement in fact caused considerable hardship in poor rural areas where development resources were scarce. In very poor communities, where survival was struggle enough, the paucity of local resources made it impossible for people to give their time and effort to community development projects. In these areas, development simply did not take place. In Dibilishaba TTL, Gwanda district, for instance, the community delineation officer reported,

> The inhabitants are more concerned with their existence and their battle against the elements than they are with communal

projects. Their first *need* as they see it is that of existence, and with a reported three crop failures in five years, and then in some cases depredation of their crops in the successful years by elephant, these people have no time to consider outside projects. An inhibiting factor is also that of economy. . . . this community cannot provide any substantial economic contribution to such "luxuries" as community schools, clinics, roads, dips and other necessary institutions.[53]

It was also very difficult for poorer families already dependent on the external disposal of their labor power to contribute to development projects. This sometimes led to their exclusion from the benefits, created tensions within communities, and helped to push young poor people into the liberation armies. In the lower ecological zones, sparser settlement made cooperation on community projects more taxing. Few community boards emerged in these areas. In some areas, such as the Ndanga TTL, the local population refused to identify any felt needs other than more land and stock rights, and some traditional authorities took the opportunity to bargain with the government by refusing to participate in local government until the land question in their area had been addressed. In early 1964 women in the Tanda TTL refused to dip their cattle as a protest against the lack of government services, leading to the arrest of 300. In Mondoro the council, unable to get the degree of control over roadworks that it wanted, refused to take responsibility for any roadworks at all.[54]

Thus, in the context of an inviolable racial land apportionment, community boards were not the harbingers of local government. In 1968 the Secretary of Internal Affairs acknowledged that the community boards and councils were feeding "very little grist . . . into the machine."[55] In fact, community development became a focus of political contestation rather than a focus of sociopolitical integration and cooptation. The state increasingly had to exert pressure on local communities to undertake community development. In 1969 the government decided to start making water supply—the most essential of public goods—the responsibility of communities themselves. In the next year, despite a severe drought, the government kept drought relief below R$100,000 as a part of its policy of promoting irrigation schemes. In effect, some rural dwellers were forced into community development projects at considerable cost to the participants. In 1970 the government cut aid and services to mission schools and forbade missions to expand primary education in an effort to stimulate African self-help.[56] In 1972 a Ministry of Health policy statement stated, "In the primary or lower level of health, such as the curative services, medicines, clinics, maternity services and so on, we feel the African will have to start providing his own services. This could best be achieved by forming medical aid societies or as a matter of community responsibility."[57]

Such initiatives drew widespread opposition. Some communities rejected them because they believed that "this was one way in which a Council would be forced upon the people."[58] They were right. In his 1970 annual report, the Secretary of Internal Affairs, noting a rise in the number of operating councils from 94 to 105, declared, "The sudden withdrawal by most missions from the educational field is the catalyst that has precipitated matters, but it is the untiring efforts and admirable patience of district commissioners, district officers and community advisors over the past few years which should be given full credit for the spectacular surge forward that is taking place."[59] But communities that already ran community schools saw government withdrawal as an inroad upon their autonomy, an extra hardship, and an increase in racial oppression. African schoolteachers in some cases themselves led opposition to community development. As early as 1963, the chair of the parents' association at a mission school in Chiweshe stated African resentment forcefully:

> It has been clearly shown that Government is imposing Community Development because it has failed to build schools for its people. Anyone who sides with this policy is a black European. . . . We know well the people of Zimbabwe are against this because the African people have no money. Anyone who tries to make this policy work is like putting a load of Rapoko on someone's back and making him walk five miles.[60]

Thus, the idea of self-reliance as the harbinger of community integration and incorporation under the concerned but removed eye of the state had quite the opposite effect: it exacerbated local antagonism to the state, and it dragged the state into stricter, sometimes coercive, management of rural communities.

Income Generation: "Capturing" Rural Youth and Rural Women

To make self-reliance work as a way of stabilizing rural populations, the community development strategy had to mobilize both local capital and local citizens for development. For peasant farmers, access to capital was a severe difficulty, partly because of the paucity of credit facilities available to them. The African Loan Fund, their only source of credit, was unpopular because loans were administered by district committees chaired by the DC, and the DC was responsible for loan repayment. Throughout the 1960s, the government remained reluctant to extend credit facilities to Africans, preferring a strategy that would engage community resources and initiative. To this end, it promoted a range of community cooperative organizations: cooperative societies, master farmers' associations, young farmers' clubs, and women's groups. Such groups, T. A. Murton argued, would provide "a continuous process of . . . formal and informal education" that would motivate people "to *want* better production and better profits."[61] In effect, they would change the social and economic aspirations of rural citizens.

But these initiatives delivered neither pedagogical nor developmental results in any significant measure. Co-operatives encompassed a very small proportion of the farming population, and did not necessarily promote the development of communities. For many farmers, cooperatives represented both carrot and stick. While membership provided access to credit through the African Loan Fund, it also meant that they had to market through marketing boards, which considerably reduced their marketing flexibility. For maize farmers on the Gutsa irrigation scheme in the Dande valley, for instance, maize could be sold locally at prices ranging from £2 to £2.5s. a sack. Selling to the GMB at the nearest railhead, 110 miles away, would net the grower about 15s. Moreover, The marketing boards administered the much-resented ADF levy, which for many farmers offset the advantages of a secure market. In these circumstances, producer cooperation remained generally at the level of wealthier, more productive farmers. The government decided that such farmers provided role models who would draw others into greater production through emulation. Accordingly, it promoted Master Farmers' Associations, and designed drought relief packages to "compensate the better cultivator for the loss of input costs."[62] But this was not a successful strategy. Master farmers remained a very small proportion of the farming population. The failure of the demonstration strategy in the 1930s and the phase of "progress by compulsion" had shown that peasants could not readily be lured by a state which they regarded as overweening, capricious, or untrustworthy. A strategy that helped the better-off to help themselves was likely to exacerbate the strains within rural communities; it was unlikely to solve the problems of broadening the rural market base significantly, of stabilizing the African population, and (from the latter half of the 1960s) of stemming the trickle of young Zimbabweans across the borders to join the liberation armies. If it was to deal with these problems, the state needed to come up with a rural development policy that could engage the cooperation of at least some of the rural poor.

In the early 1970s, under the rubric of a strategy "oriented towards a community or tribal approach using group methods more suited to tribal people," the state began to target two social groups that state officials believed could be engaged to develop local resources and increase the operation of the rural cash market.[63] These constituencies were women and youths. Administrators recognized that, in the context of a national economy based on migrant labor, these were not residual social categories. In fact, they were centrally important to the task of managing rural society because they were demographically preponderant in the rural population and played key roles in the rural economy. Under conditions of severe unemployment among school-leavers and increasing nationalist political activity, rural youths provided a potentially discontented and volatile social group. Younger brothers, in particular, faced the prospect of receiving increasingly small or poor land allocations. Women, who ran the household and did most agricultural work, needed cash to meet running costs and therefore could be stimulated to income-generating activities.[64]

The state set out to incorporate rural youths through the establishment of Young Farmers' Clubs and Natural Resources Clubs, which aimed to provide prevocational training to "help them to earn a living . . . [and] to help young people become capable and self-reliant members of the community."[65] Club members received instruction from community advisors, agricultural demonstrators, women's advisors, or other workers in agricultural techniques and various forms of animal husbandry, or in a wide range of handicrafts, for the production of salable commodities such as basketwork, matwork, leatherwork, curios, and clothing. The government hoped that by giving young people an economic stake in their community it would both keep them in the countryside and encourage them to engage in agricultural and infrastructural betterment projects. Club members were also instructed in "the wider aspects of living, how government functions, how the different races can live together and help each other, how the law works, budgeting, and how to be responsible citizens." In effect, the initiative aimed to inculcate concepts of responsibility in the social consciousness of rural youths that would secure their political quiescence.

It is difficult to assess the success of this initiative. By 1972 there were 1,108 young farmers' clubs with a total membership of some 23,000 youngsters. But funding, which came mainly from the government, was poor at only about R$14,000 a year. The state retained little purchase on the character of these groups. In 1972 and 1973 the Secretary of Internal Affairs noted the need for greater supervision and organization. According to Hughes, clubs "proved acceptable to local tribal authorities, and the people in general, primarily because they are essentially locally controlled and serve a very real felt need."[66] But they could not respond to the land question that exacerbated both state-peasant and intracommunity tensions. Certainly, as guerrilla activity in rural Rhodesia gathered momentum in the mid-1970s, the youth as a social constituency moved increasingly out of the authoritative ambit of the state.

Women constituted a crucial group for co-optive development because of their pivotal position in the domestic economy. In his annual report for 1971 the Secretary of Internal Affairs noted that it was women who most appreciated the facilities, services, and consumer goods that some cooperatives provided. At a 1972 congress on rural development, two senior community development officials, B. D. Elkington and R. C. Woollacott, noted the fluidity of the male population and stressed the advantages of targeting women for developmental activities because of their willingness "to spend their leisure in constructive pursuits" and their "almost insatiable desire to learn all they can which can be of benefit to their family and home."[67] The readiness of African women to enter cooperative institutions for improving their economic situation was not a new phenomenon. Already in the mid-1950s the CNC had remarked on the remarkable growth in the number of women's clubs, their vitality and their cooperation with European women. In the 1960s, the state turned its attention to harnessing the "great and powerful potential force" of rural women by "carrying the message of self-help into the Tribal Trust Lands of Rhodesia." In 1964, Internal Affairs appointed a Community Development Officer (Women) and in 1966 it established a community development section for women.[68]

This strategy aimed to secure a sound social base for integrating rural populations into the national political and economic order. Its objectives were twofold. On the one hand, it aimed to involve women in community and civic affairs in a way that would promote credible participation in councils and community boards and generally undermine perceptions of the state as predatory. On the other hand, it sought to stimulate a local cash-based (if rudimentary) consumer goods market in which local people would have a stake. These objectives were linked by concepts of self-help and self-*responsibility*, most proudly declared in the ten-year retrospective survey of the women's community development section's achievements: "All over the country self-help projects have come into being as rural communities begin to accept responsibility for their own development and the individual accepts her responsibility to pass on newly acquired knowledge and to work for the community as a whole."[69] The women's section set out to "co-ordinate the activity of Government and voluntary community development for rural women" by providing a support system for local initiatives and engaging the most qualified people for particular projects. The plan included a countrywide network of African Women Advisors, married women of good standing in their community working from their own homes to "help the tribal women assess their own needs and find ways to meet them." They took training courses in project planning, community development, club management skills, and were identifiable by smart checkered uniforms. They promoted nutrition, health care, adult literacy, and preschool programs in order to improve the quality of rural life.

The rural self-help strategy also aimed to stimulate the cash economy by providing local women with income-generating skills such as pottery, basketry, crochet, embroidery, knitting, and dressmaking. To promote savings and local productive investment, the government joined NGOs such as missions and voluntary organizations in promoting savings clubs in the rural areas. In the government's view, deploying local resources through savings clubs made it possible to "link together the essential elements which are required for success in . . . development programmes: finance, inputs, information, necessary local organisation and group support," while at the same time releasing the government from "at least part of the financial burden and responsibility for development."[70] These advantages made savings clubs particularly attractive to the state, for they forced cooperation and cohesion on local groups if they wanted to improve the quality of rural life. Group involvement and group action, the government believed, would promote the stability of rural communities.

There was a political point to this activity. It aimed to create community bonds that would promote social and political stability without involving the state in providing costly services. By promoting self-responsibility it would relieve the

state of accountability and mediate the adversarial relationship between the central state and rural communities. As the
state's hold on the rural population weakened in the 1970s,
this project became increasingly urgent. In the mid-1970s, the
government created a new category of grassroots worker, the
Development Worker, to tackle the problems of social control
in protected villages (controlled settlements set up as a response to the guerrilla insurgency in an effort to keep the population and the guerrillas apart). In government rhetoric, these
workers were to help rural citizens who were forced to "leave
behind their traditional life" to "make a new one" by teaching
skills and motivation, opening up new interests and "working
their own small miracles." As with Women Advisors, the self-
congratulatory Internal Affairs publication *A Decade of Challenge* indicated, the strategy aimed directly to depoliticize rural
citizens.[71] However, as Sita Ranchod-Nilsson has noted, women
had their own reasons for participating in community development activities: they learned skills that enabled them to
carve out some domestic autonomy, and they formed gendered
comradeships that helped them cope with the vicissitudes of
daily drudgery and poverty. These comradeships provided the
basis for support groups and cooperation with the guerrillas
of the liberation armies as they infiltrated in the 1970s.[72] In
this respect the political effects of community development as
a strategy for state empowerment were deeply ironic.

Rhodesian community development policies, in fact, rested
on a central political tension. They presented the state as distant and supportive rather than overbearing and intrusive in
everyday life. But this was at odds with both the reality of
colonial rural life and the theory of community development,
which stressed a close association between material development and sociopolitical development. By stressing local self-
responsibility and denying state responsibilities, these strategies actually provided a prohibitively narrow foundation for a

credible social contract. At the same time, the local state in Rhodesia simply would not be wished away, especially as the security situation deteriorated from the late 1960s on. The mediation of state-peasant relations that the state sought in community development policy would thus not be achieved unless the dilemmas of local government were resolved. But it was precisely on the question of local government that Rhodesia's community development policy conflicted with community development theory.

The Politics of Local Government

As a co-optive project, community development aimed to promote civic responsibility. But the RF policy of state extrusion and tribal enhancement ran deliberately counter to this objective, for its aim was to focus civic responsibility not on state authority but on tribal authority. Each form of authority compromised the other in ways that mutually undermined their moral suasion. Ultimately, by setting out to strengthen the social control capabilities of traditional authorities the state contrived to increase the political pressures on councils, rather than securing them as conduits of social stability.

Councils provided the only regular source of development finance in the TTLs. This funding came mainly from government block grants, which were calculated as R$1.00 per R$1.00 rate collected to a maximum of R$5,000, as well as designated grants from the ministries of health and education. Thus finance was not only tied to the capacity of councils to generate local revenues, but it placed a ceiling on the incentive to collect rates. The government made provision for ad hoc grants to meet contingencies such as disasters, emergencies, or special development needs, but disbursement of these grants was discontinued in July 1971 in order to enhance the power and authority of councils by increasing community dependence on them.[73] In the late 1960s government grants-in-aid were made contingent on the creation of a council. This perhaps accounts in part for a brief upsurge in the creation of councils (30 in 1971).[74] But it also suggests that Africans established councils for instrumental reasons.

In fact, communities depended less on councils than councils depended on communities. Council projects depended on community support and participation—especially in rates and labor—and their funding from government was so low that they had little to offer community projects. Council projects and "community" projects were sometimes separate and where community projects succeeded without council aid the arguments for allegiance to the council were diminished. Projects undertaken by women, and often supported by NGOs or by the ministry of agriculture, were not even strictly community projects. Such projects were occasionally resented both by men and by the council because they drew female labor away from agriculture or other communal activities. Rural citizens tended to be deeply suspicious of local government, and of councils in particular. In some cases the cavalier domination of the council by local state agents, or by local notables, had created deep-seated resentments. In many areas, the council was compromised by a firm local belief that council rates had been used to finance the implementation of the LHA, or that the council was simply a government agency doing things for government "which it is too busy to do itself," or that it had done nothing at all for the people except take their rates. One of the principal, and most effective, forms of resistance to councils was rate-defaulting. Nationalists and chiefs who opposed councils fostered these beliefs. Where traditional authorities could use the council, they supported it; where they regarded it as competition for power and authority, they opposed it. Any council closely associated with an unpopular chief suffered; any council at odds with a strong chief was likely to suffer.[75]

In the political context of the day, rural Africans' overwhelming rejection of councils expressed the central dilemma of community development policy as a co-optive strategy: without effective and incorporative local government structures community development could not work; but without community involvement local government could not take off. The chief delineation officer stressed that the only way to build up local government as an institutional base for incorporating the rural population was to work through the existing, understood and trusted relations of the headman's *dare:* "Local government, to be lasting, popular and effective, must work through this strong social system (which is based on the community), and by so doing, harness and guide it into an orderly and structured pattern of social change."[76] But for many citizens, community development was the government's way of harnessing them into another form of council. It was a situation that the state was unable to resolve. At the same time that it became more coercive in its attempts to press communities into community development, it began to identify councils and community boards increasingly with the person of the local traditional authority. Some DCs would not support councils and boards unless their members had been approved by the chief. Thus, while they became less participatory they also placed traditional authorities in an invidious political position.

In 1971 the government tabled the African Councils Amendment Bill in an attempt to "maintain vital flexibility but also ensure the continued co-operation between traditional and elected leaders." The bill, which became law in 1973, reflected an increasing desperation in the government's efforts to manage rural society. It strengthened the power of chiefs to control discussion within councils, extended to chiefs the power "to direct a council to defer its deliberations on any matter for consultation between the council, himself and such other bodies or persons as he may indicate," provided for purely nominated council membership, and tightened DCs' control over councils. It also excluded from participation persons who had been restricted or detained for more than six months.[77] No other government action could have expressed the comprehensive political failure of community development policy more eloquently.

Conclusion

As a strategy for co-optation and control, RF community development policy was actually geared away from communities toward leaders and institutions whose capacity or will to promote popular support either for development or for the state had been proved increasingly tenuous over the previous two decades. This strategy resulted in a proliferation of local institutions—TLAs, community boards, councils, and (after 1972) Tribal Development Groups—in which the directions of state intervention and state extrusion were incoherent and frequently contradictory. Lines of local authority and control were deeply tangled. By the late 1960s, the government's ability to guide these lines was increasingly tenuous. Just how tenuous, and how misguided the government's belief in its own capacities, was demonstrated by the outcome of the 1972 Pearce Commission (on the "acceptability" of the Smith-Hume constitutional proposals):

> Mistrust of the intentions of the Government transcended all other considerations. Apprehension for the future stemmed from resentment at what they felt to be the humiliation of the past and at the limitations of policy on land, education and personal advancement. One summed it up in saying "We do not reject the Proposals, we reject the Government." This was the dominant motivation of African rejection at all levels and in all areas.[78]

By 1972, then, the government's policy of community development, as a strategy for managing rural society, had ground to an ignominious halt.

But it had never carried the political weight to succeed. Politically, it was mired in the conflicting interests of the RF's disparate political base. On the one hand, these interests pressed the government to control African society, and this provided the underlying rationale of UDI. On the other hand, to soften the blows of UDI, government had to buy off large industrial and commercial interests with a variety of subsidies. Responding to these pressures, the government retained very limited economic, political, and ideological resources to expend on African rural development. This inhibited its capacity to manage rural society. The government found itself therefore in an invidious political position of its own making. Increasingly, it relied on rural development and productivity to secure social and political stability; but it depended on social and political stability through community development to secure rural development. Thus, the balance of rural power lay ultimately not with the state but with the willingness of rural Africans to cooperate in community development policy. Structurally, however, the state was mired in an adversarial relationship with rural African society, which had its roots in previous government policies of social management, culminating in the Land Husbandry Act. Ironically, of course, it was the political struggles occasioned by these very policies that had both launched community development into the choppy waters of social management, and placed the RF at the political helm.

This historical conjuncture rendered the state's hegemonic project both imperative and impossible. For the RF government was mired in an ideological contradiction between the thoroughgoing statism through which it pursued its separatist philosophy and the thoroughgoing disengagement that drove its appeals to the authority of tribal tradition. In a sense, the RF had misunderstood the project it had itself engaged in. To build state authority in rural society it *was* necessary to appeal to tradition. The political failure of the Land Husbandry Act's individual contractarian assumptions had demonstrated that. But it was also necessary to *transform* traditions in order to secure state universality. Howman had realized this, arguing,

> There can be no question of laissez faire or leaving the African to stew in his own juice or struggle out of it by his own resources. There can only be wishful thinking among those who, believing in some kind of golden age of old custom, seek a solution in the famous words "according to customary law" or the restoration of "traditional authority."[79]

Yet this kind of wishful thinking lay at the very core of government policy. The state could simply not be defined out of rural authority relations. At one level, the panoply of social controls centered on the Land Apportionment Act intensified the politics of land, both between communities and the state and within communities themselves. At another level, the local politics of control that centered on the DC's office made a mockery of self-responsibility, community development, and the authoritative reach of traditional leadership. In these conditions no form of authority was able to maintain an overarching hold in rural society, and authority itself became a terrain of political struggle. That it was a craggy and broken terrain, difficult to hold, was shown by the increasingly desperate efforts of the state to shore up the chiefs. At the same time, its brokenness made it hospitable terrain for the nationalist guerrilla movements. In 1971, opening the intensified and final phase of armed struggle, the liberation armies stepped onto it.

5

Interregnum, 1972–1979

The Collapse of State Authority

As the 1960s gave way to the 1970s, the sociopolitical crisis of the Rhodesian state deepened dramatically. In 1968 the RF faced an internal crisis as party rank and file demanded a more coherent and effective influx control policy to stem the mobility of the African population. Yet rural control was desperately precarious. The rural African population's overwhelming rejection of the proposed Smith-Hume constitutional settlement in 1972 came as a terrible blow to the government. All the suppositions of rural control were revealed as deeply suspect, for the DCs had campaigned vigorously for a yes vote. Against this background, the liberation war intensified toward the end of 1972. Thus, the capacity of the colonial state to manage the social order was showing cracks. The one ray of hope to which the RF clung was the economic boom associated with its import substitution drive. But economists and businessmen recognized that the boom could not last under existing economic structures, and by 1974 it was over. Over the course of the decade the capacity of the state to contain social and political disintegration eroded steadily. The guerrilla war escalated and spread. In 1978 the Interim government was created. In 1979 the Lancaster House independence agreement was signed, and on 18 April 1980 Zimbabwe was finally born.

As the RF government lost control of the economy, it lost its capacity to manage the labor market. This capacity had of course long been tenuous, and had been a central concern in successive hegemonic strategies. Colonial administrators recognized that the solution to regulating African labor lay in the countryside, and as its ability to do so waned, the RF felt increasing political pressure to assert its control over rural society. But during the 1970s, with the increase of guerrilla conflict and the increasing coerciveness of the state in rural Rhodesia, rural authority and power came up for grabs. The rural civil order fragmented into competing forms of civil authority, leaving an ambiguous political legacy for the postcolonial state. This chapter shows the historical paradox of this collapse: in its last-ditch efforts to mitigate its crisis of social control, the colonial state threw up political structures and institutions that would subsequently be consolidated by the postcolonial state as it set out in 1980 to establish its own hold on rural society.

Economic Decline, Influx Control, and State Power

The collapse of the rural state is best understood in the context of economic decline, which increased political pressures on the Rhodesian Front government and shaped its attempts to manage rural society. The apparent economic boom of the late 1960s and early 1970s masked the real precariousness of the economy. Rhodesia's balance of payments deteriorated sharply, making it difficult to meet the costs of imported equipment and forcing the government to tighten control on foreign exchange resources. This inhibited the establishment of new industries, and made it difficult for industry to plan ahead. The international oil crisis of 1973, followed by the withdrawal of South African economic support in 1975, came as a tremendous blow. The European agricultural sector slumped, and after UDI farm sales and farm indebtedness increased progressively. The poor economic outlook was exacerbated by the rapid increase in the costs of security as the liberation war intensified. At the same time chronic unemployment worsened. Although African employment rose by 197,000 between 1969 and 1973, the number of African school-leavers was over 330,000.[1]

Against a background of falling state revenues, increasing unemployment, and decreasing productivity, the disparate social bases of the RF government (and indeed of the colonial state more broadly conceived) began to tug in different directions. Going into the 1970s, the RF government found itself facing an array of contradictory political pressures. Firstly, it needed to oversee the economic development of the African rural areas in order to expand the national market base. Linked to this was the need to secure greater political and social control in the rural areas, especially in the light of a reported guerrilla build-up on the Zambezi. A third imperative was to establish a greater level of control over the mobility of the population to assuage white demands for influx control. The final, overriding political imperative was to tackle these inextricably linked demands of political and economic development through a policy "in which neither group is forced to live under a system or in a manner alien to the group concept."[2]

In the late 1960s and early 1970s the RF spelled out its response to these pressures in terms of two strategies for social management: a strategy for political development cast in terms of "provincialization"; and a strategy for industrial development cast in terms of "decentralization." As strategies for comprehensive control of the African population, they were the closest that the Rhodesian government could come to emulating South Africa's homelands policy. As is often the case with state management strategies, these policies contained contradictory impulses in structuring state-society relations. On the one hand, they aimed to break down the opposition between state and society through greater political and economic incorporation of Africans, notably by co-opting traditional authorities in rural areas. On the other hand, they sought to impose greater state controls on the population through more stringent influx control measures in the rural areas.

The provincialization policy aimed to provide the political substance to fill the framework of the Land Tenure Act. It was presented as a policy of devolution and decentralization, and as an extension of the community development philosophy.[3] Thus it was an attempt by the government to demonstrate its commitment to "the process of divesting central government of its involvement in the day to day life of the people, and of encouraging local people to run local affairs." As such, the policy was co-optive. One of its principal objectives was to reduce rural resistance and to stabilize the rural population by legitimating and entrenching traditional structures of authority:

> These provincial administrations will provide an excellent training ground in the art of government and an avenue for responsible political ambition. . . . These authorities will participate in and assist in the implementation of our development programmes for the Tribal Trust Lands, which are designed to bring these areas into the cash economy and to maximise the job opportunities for African professional, business, skilled and semi-skilled persons at a pace and in an atmosphere suited to their traditional requirements.[4]

The plan envisaged the creation of two provincial councils, one for Mashonaland to cover the TTLs in the eastern part of the country, and one for Matabeleland to service the TTLs in the western part. These councils would lie between central government and local government, and would oversee and coordinate the activities of local government authorities. Ultimately, the RF argued, the relationship of provinces to central government would be analogous to that of the cantons and the federal government in Switzerland.

In political rhetoric, this policy was designed to reduce the overweening domination of society by the central colonial state. In fact, it reflected a decision to locate government control of rural development at the provincial level.[5] The eight Provincial Authorities coordinated development policy for the councils in their area. But even these were strictly controlled: policy decisions were passed through a coordinating committee, chaired by the deputy minister of Internal Affairs and including the chairmen of the two Cabinet Councils (senator chiefs) and senior officials of ministries directly involved in development.[6] This structure was very nearly replicated in the post-independence Provincial Development Committees.

But the full political meaning of provincialization is revealed by its obverse—the extension of influx control measures. The RF rank and file were jittery about uncontrolled African urbanization and job competition. A 1968 report by municipal officials on the homeless and unemployed in Salisbury recommended that legislation be introduced to control the numbers of unemployed people in urban areas and to restrict the number of hawkers. In August 1972 the RF mouthpiece, *Rhodesian Forum*, noted that it was becoming increasingly difficult for Europeans "of limited skills and capacity" to find employment, a difficulty compounded by pressures to provide an ever-increasing range of jobs for "the developing African." This, it argued, was an intolerable situation that exacerbated racial friction and demoralized "less fortunate Europeans." It called for more stringent control of the influx of

African into white urban areas.[7] This required a tighter state control of the labor market, and inevitably a sustained state involvement in the day to day life of the African population.

Influx control had aspects of both stick and carrot. The stick came from legislation for controlled urbanization. In 1972 the Africans (Registration and Identification) Act was amended, requiring Africans to carry registration papers on their person at all times. The issuance of such papers, for which holders had to pay, was tied to job opportunities and work permits, and control was exercised through labor exchanges in both European and African areas. Employers were liable to prosecution if they engaged unauthorized labor.[8] In December 1972 the Vagrancy Amendment Act was passed, to give authorities powers to remove "undesirable elements" from urban areas. In March 1972 new bylaws were approved providing for demolition of squatter housing next to townships, and demolition proceeded immediately.

As a further measure for controlling the flow of Africans into the urban areas, the RF Congress decided in 1972 that future urban African township development would be concentrated in the Tribal Trust Land areas nearest to European development areas. This, they believed, had obvious advantages: future housing development and amenities for those employed in the European areas would be channeled into tribal trust land, where local authorities could be called upon to assist with financial support. With the establishment of townships in the African areas, ownership of land could be promoted, which would not only provide a source of revenue for tribal authorities but would provide a disincentive to uncontrolled influx into European areas. The possession of a permanent home would also alleviate the need for Africans to claim TTL land against their retirement and old age, thereby overcoming in part the "rather ridiculous parrot cry" of land shortage. The stimulation of African agriculture by the presence of large townships would help to overcome the stagnation of the TTLs. With industry more or less equidistant from its sources of European and African humanpower, this arrangement would also conform to the concept of decentralization and perimeter development.[9]

The "carrot" side of influx control looked to the intensive and rapid development of the Tribal Trust Lands, coupled with more attractive conditions for agricultural employees in European farming areas, to siphon off part of the flow of rural Africans to urban areas.[10] To achieve this, government argued, it was necessary to "artificially stimulate" the rural economy, and this task would fall to private industry and to the parastatal Tribal Trust Lands Development Corporation (TILCOR). Industries established on the perimeters of TTLs under the decentralization policy would stimulate TTL development by providing local spending money. TILCOR would establish urban nodes within the TTLs to provide a focus for off-farm employment, a local cash market, secondary industry, and services. These "growth points" should not only be market towns for farmers, they should be attractive to young people seeking education or employment by having "a bright light syndrome ie. sporting facilities and sophisticated entertainment." As the TILCOR policy statement put it rather optimistically, "If the area's hope is centred on the Growth Point for schooling, for job availability, for sophisticated entertainment, it will tend to hold the community, increase its effectiveness and finally the community's total contribution to the Gross National Product."[11] According to this argument, border development and TTL development would be concurrent, providing the basis for a planned and balanced economy.

This policy, founded on the RF's separatist ideology and the demands of its racial social base, was ill-conceived and politically incoherent from the outset. In the first place, the government's perception of African in-migration to urban areas was exaggerated. In the early seventies squatter settlements tended to be small and relatively stable. The urban housing problem was to a significant extent a product of the growth of a second generation urban population. Only in the mid- and late 1970s did in-migration escalate dramatically under the impact of the rural war.[12] People squatted either because they were ineligible for housing (in which case they would hang around town trying to establish their credentials) or because there was no housing available. Consequently, urban removal not only created resentment among urban Africans, it created the problem of where to remove them to, and increased the pressure on rural land without significantly affecting urban conditions. It was ultimately a self-destructive policy, based mainly on xenophobia.

Moreover, the policy was implemented in poor faith. The government undertook almost no planning, ignored the recommendations of the Select Committee on Decentralisation, and declined to designate specific areas as growth points because it wanted to avoid "the clamour of parochial ambitions and competing claims for favourable treatment."[13] The decentralization policy was also prohibitively expensive and administratively overtaxing in terms of moving people to new township sites, of constructing new residential areas, and of laying the means for transporting workers the increased distances to and from work. In fact, senior officials in the Ministry of Internal Affairs themselves found the policy unworkable and opposed it, often successfully, at every turn. Equally importantly, the government lacked the political resources and the will to tell industry what to do or to initiate industrial decentralization. Consequently, decentralization depended on industrial companies' own willingness to move into remoter areas where communications, infrastructure, and services were poor, and the market base was tiny. Reliance on the private sector, therefore, snagged on a basic economic dilemma: the private sector would not get involved until a market existed, and a market could not be created without extensive capital inputs. Despite Prime Minister Smith's cry that it was "absolutely essential and imperative for us artificially to stimulate development in the African areas," such initiatives never extended much beyond the input of TILCOR. But TILCOR's industrial investment remained concentrated on a few large complexes (Seke, Zimunya, Ntabazinduna), on irrigation schemes such as Chisumbanje, and on the tea and coffee estates of the eastern highlands. The vast majority of rural Africans remained untouched. In 1978 an Internal Affairs study of business in the TTLs noted that the policy had failed not because of insecurity of tenure, or because there had been no European investment in the African areas, but because there had been no productive investment.[14] But by that time the rural war was at its height, and market participation of any kind had been largely supplanted by survival.

The link between the provincialization policy and influx control is clear. Their mutual objective was to control African participation in the labor market by pushing them out of the cities, stabilizing the rural African population through rural economic development, and promoting political control and stability through co-optation. Furthermore, both were intended to keep the financial burden of African development off the shoulders of government and on the shoulders of the African population. Political and economic co-optation was central to this objective: creating a sense of participation and self-determination would both help stabilize the rural population and stimulate Africans to pay for their own development.

It is in this respect that the government regarded provincialization as an extension of community development policy. Speaking in the House, the Minister of Internal Affairs presented provincialization as a vehicle

> which would give the African people, and in particular their leaders—and I mean their leaders, the chiefs—a greater and growing responsibility for the provision of the larger range of social services that are required in the African areas of the country, including the African purchase areas and the Tribal Trust Lands, to provide the social services which the growing population of the African needs and which he must, in a large measure, recognise that he must provide for himself—with the assistance of Government but definitely with a large contribution on his own account.[15]

This call for rural self-responsibility was matched in urban policy, which also aimed to retract direct state regulation, "to encourage African participation in the local government of the African residential areas and to seek an evolving form of local government in the African townships."[16] At the same time, however, the government expanded the power of Internal Affairs in the urban African areas, passing regulations in 1971 to place the control of stand allocation and housing construction in the hands of the ministry.

Ultimately, therefore, the contradictory political objectives on which the state's social management policies rested became increasingly obvious. While the government was eager to control the participation of Africans in the labor market, a prerequisite for doing so was to encourage their participation in the commodity market. But the government refused to expend material or political resources to promote rural markets. Such markets were to be both the result and the harbinger of self-determination and self-responsibility. In a deeply ironic speech in Parliament, Finance Minister J. J. Wrathall declared: "The concept of a central planning authority with overriding powers is contrary to the entire concept of grass roots planning and fragmented, specialized responsibility. It implies of a reversal of the process and the adoption of a 'from the top downwards' concept. Government does not accept that a single authority can possibly hope to deal efficiently with the multitude of problems which arise on a national basis."[17] This strategy relied on the ability of the state to persuade rural Africans to participate in state development initiatives. This point was poignantly made in a *Rhodesia Herald* editorial:

> because more or less any devolution of authority, any decentralisation of government, is to be welcomed—and because the Government's ordinary revenue cannot cope with the problems caused by the soaring African birthrate without full development of the TTLs—we hope the tribal Africans will do their best to make the new scheme work. This support naturally implies that real authority will be devolved and that the Authorities are not cast for the role of screen between a Government that should provide services for all its people but does not, and the deprived section.[18]

But the domineering, administrative presence of Internal Affairs remained undiminished in the rural areas.

The concentration of political power in the hands of the central state made rural co-optation extremely difficult. But if Africans were to pay for their own development and rural society be stabilized through a sense of participation and self-determination, the "decentralized despotism" of existing arrangements was also untenable. It revealed that the state was politically vulnerable to the noncooperation of rural Africans. Ironically, the clearest recognition of this vulnerability came from within Internal Affairs. In August 1968 Roger Howman, then deputy secretary, wrote a minute to the minister in which he stated bluntly: "It is difficult to decide how to criticise the RF proposals because they ignore so many economic, administrative, moral, cultural and political aspects in their narrow, short-term, single purpose concern to achieve separation of the races as a guarantee of European preservation and control."

Howman went on to argue that the plan rested on a "crazy interpretation of the relationship between politics and economics" and that the "disastrous complacency with which it is assumed that 'co-operation, trust and goodwill' will be promoted by these proposals" rested on a "defiance of African aspirations."[19] Howman had discerned, quite rightly, that the plan undermined the credibility of the councils and exposed rather than masked the domineering intent of central government. He elaborated these arguments in subsequent minutes in September 1968 and March 1969. But, in the face of RF intransigence, it was a thin and unheeded protest.

By the late 1970s the structural weaknesses of the late colonial state, and the contradictions of RF ideology had been laid bare. As the Smith government began to move tentatively toward a political accommodation with conservative African groups led by Bishop Abel Muzorewa, powerful groups within the private sector and the civil service saw an opportunity to challenge the government's development perspective and secure their own survival in the case of a transition to majority rule. The Agricultural Development Authority and the Whitsun Foundation, a private organization of business and professional leaders, began to resurrect an agrarian development vision based on an integrated, industry-led economy. Accordingly, they moved the stress in arguments about social management and rural development away from separation and stabilization to economic integration and transfer of Africans to the cash-wage economy.[20] These arguments represent a pivotal political moment in the development trajectory of Zimbabwe. In the first place, they involved an effort by the commercial and industrial private sector to establish itself as the indispensable pivot of any national development scheme (regardless of the government in power) on the grounds that only this sector had the flexibility to generate the investment and employment from which other aspects of a development plan would flow. Moreover, they were ready to negotiate an alliance with the state to pursue this end. In short, the relationship of business to the state shifted from "close" to "uneasy" as business (including commercial agriculture) loosened its ties and strengthened its own position.[21]

Furthermore, these arguments represented an effort by technical ministries to take back the initiative for rural development from Internal Affairs, which had not only failed to stabilize or develop the African rural areas but was fighting a losing battle against rural resistance and guerrilla armies to maintain any kind of authoritative presence in the countryside. In July 1978 the Department of Agricultural Development was created within an enlarged Ministry of Lands, Natural Resources and Rural Development by the transfer of African agriculture from Internal Affairs. The new department's brief was to expand agricultural extension, and to plan and implement agriculturally based rural development. The aim was to put in place a rural development infrastructure which would set the agenda for development under majority rule.Finally, these arguments represented the reascendance of the principal philosophical and technical orientations of the Land Husbandry Act, for they were premised on the permanent transfer of laborers from the rural and migrant economies to the industrial wage economy.

As orientations for policymaking, these arguments provided the core of the 1978 *Integrated Plan for Rural Development,* which began to lay down the development structures from which a postindependence government would have to set out on its own development path. The plan took the commercial agricultural sector as the mainstay of the economy because it was the largest foreign exchange earner in an externally oriented economy. It counseled against economic nationalization and the expropriation of white farming land for resettlement. However, it stressed that once the future of the commercial farming sector was secure, it was essential to tackle the socioeconomic conditions of the African farming areas to boost production in the small-scale agricultural sector.[22] Thus, the structural and institutional separation of the agricultural sectors would be retained.

As the sociopolitical crisis deepened and the government began to marshal the white community into an ever tighter (and increasingly belligerent) ideological circle, significant sections of the white establishment recognized, therefore, that state policies to deal with the crisis were not only ineffective but were part of the problem. They began to look beyond the current structure of state-society relations, to distance themselves from RF state ideology, and to present their interests as politically agnostic—essentially technical or entrepreneurial. They looked beyond the horizon of political transition in order to secure their position in a postindependence political order. This was a fatal blow to state cohesion. It left those elements of the state that were most deeply mired in state ideology and social management policies trapped in the political contradictions of state-society relations and exposed to the winds of revolt sweeping across the veld and forests of the Zimbabwe countryside.

The Breakdown of Civil Authority in the Countryside

In 1974 the DC Mount Darwin, C. J. K. Latham, wrote, "The chief in Shona society has unfortunately been included of late in the ideological war that is being fought over Rhodesia."[23] In fact, this struggle was part of a multifaceted fragmentation of authority in the countryside. It was rooted in the strains on rural communities created by government policies and in the escalation of guerrilla activity in the early 1970s. The complex link between these two sets of roots was, once again, the land.

It was partly to regulate the strains on rural communities that the state had moved to a thoroughgoing strategy of enhancing and reinforcing "traditional tribal authority." But one of the deepest political contradictions of this policy was that the *institutional* enhancement of such authority undermined the *moral* authority of the chiefs and reduced the state's capacity to regulate authority in the countryside. Agrarian differentiation and resistance to conservation created severe social strains. The conservation-resistance ideology of "free farming" provided wealthier farmers with opportunities to expand their holdings.[24] Control of stocking rates had disintegrated. As economic decline in the African areas deepened, poorer families held onto their cattle more desperately as security against emergency spending. During the war, the confiscation of cattle had become a favorite punitive tool of the administration, and there is some evidence that cattle became the focus of intracommunity resentments. To manage these incipient conflicts, the state had to find chiefs willing and able to enforce "progressive" agrarian policies. However, it also had to appoint the "traditionally appropriate" chief. The result, as Ranger has shown, was that the state became dependent on chiefs, and vulnerable to their weakness or strength. A strong chief could—and would—continue to allocate land at will, ignoring government injunctions, because that was where his power lay. To remove such a chief was not only to risk increased rural opposition and resistance, but indeed to compromise the government's policy of adhering strictly to tradition. A weak chief, on the other hand, could not prevent farmers from plowing as they saw fit. Replacing such chiefs presented the state with exactly the same dilemma as strong chiefs.[25] Boundary disputes between chiefs demonstrated the contradictions of government policy perhaps most profoundly: determined to adjudicate such disputes and to lay down the law, district administrators found themselves compromised by their own policy of defining traditional authority outside the state's province of jurisdiction.

Under these conditions, the Tribal Land Authorities rapidly proved a failure. As early as 1968 a CONEX working party reported that it was difficult for agricultural officers to manage large unwieldy areas associated with TLAs and suggested that TLAs ought to be persuaded to devolve specific powers for controlling land use to smaller subgroups within TLA jurisdiction. In 1973, Internal Affairs was persuaded to shift the focus of management away from chiefs to community-based units known as Tribal Development Groups (TDGs). The administration encouraged these groups to claim definite Rights of Exclusion over precisely defined areas, including grazing areas, and even to fence these areas. This agrarian policy cut directly across the lines of tribal authority enhancement that the state clung to in political affairs. It passed control of land directly to farmers themselves. But it did not appeal to the principles of self-interest that had informed the Land Husbandry Act, for government was concerned that poorer farmers, subsistence families, and nonfarming members of communities should not have their community-based rights trampled by those who held local economic power. In the government's eyes, TDGs were not to be "interest groups" of farmers; they were to be territorially defined, traditionally recognized as groups with a real sense of group identity. As A. J. B. Hughes describes it, "The whole TDG concept, and the philosophy underlying the legislation setting up Tribal Land Authorities, is that tribal groups *as wholes* should play a greater part in planning their own economic future."[26]

This policy is significant less for its success (which was minimal) than for its historical location in more broadly unfolding relations between the state and rural communities. In the first place, it demonstrates how lines of authority and control over land had escaped not only state control but indeed the control of any one institution or authority. Chiefs, it seemed clear, could not control the use of land, and could not implement "progressive" agrarian policies. Nevertheless, they could block devolution of specific land use powers by refusing to countenance it. As Hughes points out, all a disapproving chief had to do was decline to punish in his tribal court breaches of land use regulations laid down by TDGs.[27] By law, the state was powerless to intervene to uphold such regulations without the chief's sanction. Such interventions could be, and were, challenged successfully in the Appeals Court.[28] In the event, no TLA or chief actually gave any TDG a clear mandate to exercise control over grazing or any other form of land use. At the same time, socioeconomic differentiation in rural communities was creating severe strains on social relationships. But the state lacked institutional conduits to regulate these incipient conflicts. Its appeal to "tribal groups as wholes" to undertake agrarian planning was a somewhat forlorn hope given the long history of state-peasant antagonism. In practice only a few scattered "management committees" and grazing schemes emerged, dominated by village headmen and local notables. But this initiative is intriguing, for it not only reflected and highlighted the collapse of state authority in rural Rhodesia, it contained the seeds of a state strategy for managing rural society through participatory, community-based institutions. After independence, as we shall see below, the nationalist government took up this challenge.

The social strains associated with government rural policies and agrarian decline had wider ramifications that enfeebled the moral authority of chiefs and entangled the lines of social control. By the late 1960s the role of chiefs and headmen in receiving tribute and redistributing it as relief in bad years had broken down almost entirely, especially where land allocation had slipped away from them. Many traditional authorities had become economically dependent on government subsidies and allowances. In many cases villagers close to the margins could no longer rely on traditional relationships to secure them some form of social security in lean times. Many had to sell their produce early in the season to local shopkeepers to meet cash flow needs, and had then to buy back toward the end of the season. This kind of dependence often created resentment against shopkeepers, who were frequently successful farmers. Weinrich notes that most villagers depended on credit from local store owners and that rural dwellers also frequently made an association between witchcraft and success in business.[29] The rural poor were the most vulnerable to climatic disaster, and droughts were frequently associated with the practice of witchcraft in the area. In a time of heightened social stress, the importance of controlling witchcraft was intensified for rural dwellers.[30] But at that very time the capacity of the established power for dealing with witches was weakened. Although the Rhodesian Front government had set out to deepen the jurisdictional powers of chiefs, the colonial state had outlawed the adjudication of witchcraft cases by chiefs' courts. Moreover, as Werbner has shown, both the security forces and the guerrillas manipulated local terror of witchcraft to advance their cause with the rural population. Unless chiefs were prepared to defy the government and continue to hear witchcraft cases, desperate people would go elsewhere to find that power.[31]

Thus, by the early 1970s, the Rhodesian state had become deeply dependent on chiefs who could only sustain their moral authority if they defied the government. This situation not only made the lives of chiefs very difficult, it also complicated the selection of chiefs. One result was that state officials realized that if they could no longer appeal to the authority of living chiefs they would have to go to the ultimate source of political authority in Shona society, the chiefly ancestors: the government would seek the sanction of the ancestral spirits *(mhondoro)* who, in Shona cosmology, are the guarantors of fertility and rain and the true owners of the land.

It was into this situation of shifting and vacillating forms of authority that the soldiers of the liberation armies moved in 1971. The Pearce Commission reported in May 1972 and district officials were well aware of increasing restiveness among the population. Acutely aware of its tenuous control over the rural population, the administration took up seriously the task of bringing the spirit mediums under its umbrella.[32] In 1972, Internal Affairs appointed Latham, who had coordinated the community delineation program in the early 1960s, to the position of Research Officer (Anthropologist) with the task of identifying the major spirits "of functional importance throughout Rhodesia," their mediums, and their cult centers and sacred places. What ensued in the early and mid-1970s, was an increasingly intense struggle between the state and the guerrillas to gain the support of the mediums or spirits. Guerrillas needed the support of mediums because they were not local (it was ZANLA policy not to deploy its soldiers in their home territories) and needed local sanction and legitimation, especially for their violent activities. Similarly, the state wanted to deny them that succor. As Latham puts it, "Throughout the districts affected by the insurgency offensive, mediums were being contacted or referred to, by the guerrillas. I was involved in a sort of a personal race with them to identify those of importance."[33] In effect, this race represented a recognition by state administrators that their faith in the chiefdom as the pivot of rural social management was misplaced: social authority lay at a higher plane, and the ironic effect of the administration's tribal enhancement policy was to exclude the state from access to that authority. Latham himself demonstrated this dilemma in a 1975 article:

> it is obvious that succession to chieftainship is largely dependent upon the pronouncement of the titulary shade *(Mhondoro)* . . . it demands little imagination to appreciate the influence which the medium can assert. In fact it is not uncommon for chiefs to be reminded by their *Masvikiro* that it is they who put them in positions of power. Socio-political clashes are therefore not uncommon between *Svikiro* and chief. . . . The strength of the chief lies in the spiritual sanction placed upon him by his *Svikiro*.[34]

The state could not interfere without undermining the chief. Yet to be the source and final arbiter of social authority it had to interfere. Tribal enhancement, as a strategy for social management, had reached a final impasse.

The struggle over the mediums and social authority was a messy, complex, and frequently tragic conflict, whose real historical significance is the subject of emerging debate.[35] Lan and Ranger (writing in the immediate aftermath of liberation) argue that this conflict resulted in a fundamental and apparently permanent shift in political and moral authority away from chiefs and the state, toward spirit mediums and guerrillas. In their view, this shift created a foundation for a postcolonial social and political order in which Zimbabwean peasants would find control over their lives returned to them. Lan argues persuasively that political authority "was not so much achieved by the mediums as thrust upon them" by ordinary people's rejection of the colonial state's authority and their recognition that the chiefs' authority had become inextricably connected with that of the state. Thus, ordinary people transferred their allegiance from the chiefs of the present to the chiefs of the past. Mediums conferred the authority of the ancestors on the guerrillas.[36] Chiefs had lost the power of land allocation; guerrillas promised the return of the "lost lands."

Chiefs had lost their capacity to control witchcraft; guerrillas happily went witch-hunting.

In fact, however, a fragmentation rather than a shift in political authority occurred. After independence, spiritual authority over the land continued to clash with government decrees, power struggles between chiefs continued to be intense and dangerous, and witchcraft continued to play a large role in the social lives and mores of rural citizens. While Lan's account of the spiritual, religious, and ideological world of the Shona is richly textured and compelling it is curiously disembodied from the everyday lives of peasant villagers. In particular, Lan virtually ignores strains within the community that might spur particular social groups to participate in or support revolutionary activity. Yet in processes of state formation such spurs are extremely important, for revolutionary conflict results in the replacement of one state by another, and the prospects of that state depend substantially on how the revolution was made.[37] It is therefore necessary, before moving across the divide of independence, to make two final, related, points about the collapse of the colonial Rhodesian state. First, the war was extremely brutal. Second, the most important shift in political and moral authority was not the emergence of new morally compelling forms of authority but the disintegration of state cohesion and authority.

The brutality of the war has been widely documented. Without doubt the guerrilla armies enjoyed enormous rural popular support. They based their ideological appeals largely on a cultural nationalism to which the rural population had been exposed, in varying degrees, since the early days of the nationalist movement, and bolstered their legitimacy with appeals to the mediums and ancestors.[38] But the nationalist movement was not united. Partly as a result of feuds among leaders and different external alliances, the armies of ZAPU and ZANU came to draw on increasingly distinct ethno-regional support bases. ZAPU's ZIPRA, based in Zambia, operated mainly in the west and drew its support mainly from the SiNdebele speakers of Matabeleland. ZANU's ZANLA operated out of Mozambique in Shona-speaking parts of the country. By the end of the war, the two armies were at loggerheads and interarmy battles were quite common. Furthermore, peasant support for the guerrillas was never universal and not always wholehearted. Recent research shows that the relationship between guerrillas and peasantry was a complex and shifting one in which generalized coercion and incipient tensions within peasant communities found expression.[39]

Not only guerrillas but peasants themselves were able to use charges of witchcraft or selling out to intimidate their fellows, to exact punishment, or even to have them killed. No research has shown that support for the guerrillas broke down according to particular social groups. Nevertheless, as Norma Kriger has demonstrated, the lines of power within communities and households were disrupted (although not broken).[40] Local youths were drawn extensively into support organizations—running errands, keeping watch, cooking for guerrillas, and acting in a variety of ways as their auxiliaries. Many of these youngsters used these new opportunities to carve out greater independence from the authority and control of their parents and elders, sometimes using their access to guerrillas to extort money, food, or goods from older people, to accuse them of selling out, or to beat them.[41] The result was that rural social relationships became complicated: youths became feared, respected, resented, and admired. The war also created new opportunities for women to assert greater control over their lives, especially by joining the party or the army. These women later pressed the ruling party to live up to its commitment to gender equality, thereby decisively placing gender-based cultural struggles over household and community power on the postcolonial state-building agenda.[42] Further, Kriger argues that the war allowed poorer and less educated rural dwellers to "vent their resentment against the uneven distribution of wealth among rural Africans" by denouncing those they envied or resented as sell-outs. Most striking, resentment was vented against families who relied heavily on migrant labor for their incomes, indicating that land rights were becoming increasingly conflictual and the meaning of community membership increasingly contested within rural "communities." Indeed, Kriger documents cases where the lineage-based categories of insiders and outsiders that had become strained under the pressures of government policy became the focus of local political struggle, as "outsiders" used the war committees—set up in the villages to organize and coordinate support for the guerrillas—as a forum to challenge the political authority of the chiefly lineages.[43]

It is not easy to say how widespread such contests were. While they do contribute to a picture of flux in rural social and political relationships, associated with the onset of the war, such shifts and struggles did not add up to a significant realignment of power relations in the rural areas. One should not lose sight of the fact that the peasantry as a whole suffered intolerable hardships during the war. Many conceived an abhorrence for war, and blamed their difficulties sweepingly on the war itself—a pattern that reemerged in rural Matabeleland when the postindependence government ended its ethno-regional campaign of suppression in the late 1980s. But these disruptions of local power and authority relations did inject into community life an element of volatility that could either be a resource for the postindependence government, or a profound obstacle to the entrenchment of its own authority. Certainly, it posed the problem of how to institutionalize rural political authority in such a way that the state would be the final arbiter of these relationships.

Among all the ambiguities of local power, one fact stood

out clearly: the colonial state had forfeited all political authority in rural society. By the early 1970s, the contradictions of
rural social management were already developing into a political imperative for control. Paradoxically, as the state became
more coercive in its efforts to control the rural population and
to prosecute the war, its internal cohesion rapidly disintegrated. Principally, this was because the objectives of controlling the population and defeating the nationalists were inextricably connected, much as some administrators tried to keep
them separate. In 1971 and 1972 the government passed a
plethora of legislation to beef up central political control in
the African areas. Under the African Councils Amendment
Bill and the African Affairs Amendment Bill, considerable power
was ceded to Provincial Commissioners to prohibit public meetings, to appoint acting chiefs, and to regulate the mobility of
Africans within the tribal areas under their jurisdiction. The
government also amended the African Law and Tribal Courts
Act to allow a tribal court to remove a person from the area of
its jurisdiction without either providing alternative land or
paying compensation for improvements. The rationale of these
measures was clearly to exercise greater control over the countryside as the presence of guerrillas became increasingly apparent.

Paradoxically, the strengthening of Internal Affairs' powers accompanied a weakening of the ministry's position within
the state as the security forces became an increasingly significant part of the rural state apparatus. During the course of the
1970s, tensions deepened between Internal Affairs administrators, who regarded themselves as the Civil Authority and
still able to "retain or regain the vital support of the black
population groups," and the military authority who could not
abide "softness."[44] At the same time, however, the Internal Affairs apparatus itself became increasingly paramilitary. Much
of the tension was less about how to control the rural popula-

tion than about who would do it. Meanwhile, Head Office leadership in Internal Affairs had collapsed. DCs, given scant resources and the simple injunction to "keep administration going" felt increasingly isolated and embittered. In a plaintive and despairing voice remarkably reminiscent of the 1950s, one DC wrote:

District Commissioners have been the agents of political change since their formation. Also the link between the black/white. Never before has this role been more vital—yet never before has the District Commissioner been given such meagre support by Government. It is vital for the survival of this country as a civilised, democratic nation, that *every* effort be made for CABINET support at this time. So important is this that we feel a personal delegation by Intaf to the Prime Minister is required.

For these programmes to have a chance of success the current trend amongst Government Ministries to decry, hamper and discredit the position of the Ministry must be reversed. From the Secretary of Internal Affairs downwards the Ministry must be supported and assisted at all levels. This need is now recognised by Combined Operations Headquarters. The powers of District Commissioners to insist on support, co-operation and assistance must be recognised (they exist) NOT abrogated by other pressures. . . . At present their hands are tied and their activities hampered to an unacceptable degree. Too much emphasis is being placed on the purely Military. Instead of the Army being in support of the Civil Authority (Power) too often the reverse is actually the case.[45]

No more telling description could be offered of the crumbling of the Rhodesian state.

For the peasant population this crumbling was not immediately apparent. In a final spasm of coercion the state began in 1974 to move peasants in "hot" areas out of their homes into "protected villages" in order to separate them from the guerrillas. It was, as Coenraad Brand puts it, "an attempt to moderate an open conflict by reverting to modes of routinised control."[46] In 1973, under Emergency Powers Regulations, the government empowered provincial commissioners to impose collective fines on villages where they believed any inhabitant was supporting guerrillas.[47] These actions represent the final and utter refutation of the ideology of state retraction from civil society. The Ministry of Internal Affairs continued to instruct its national servicemen to support the chiefs and the tribal structure, and even to pursue community development projects in the PVs. But entrenched racial attitudes of young white trainees made even this a travesty. Ultimately, the state stood utterly exposed, its own ideological ramparts in shards, as the crude and unmediated broker of political oppression and coercion.

As subsequent political events showed, these measures were the vicious last throes of a dying power. Their failures, which culminated in the 1978 Internal Settlement and the 1979 Lancaster House independence negotiations, as well as the dreadful misery they visited upon the peasantry have been widely documented. But they are noteworthy here for their ambiguous political legacy. On the one hand, it was not difficult for ZANU(PF) to distance itself from the historical and political meanings of the colonial state and achieve a landslide victory in the independence elections of February 1980. Yet the critical state tasks of social management remained. The TTLs (henceforth known as communal lands) had been ravaged by the war. Conservation controls had fallen away completely, livestock diseases were out of control, agricultural infrastructure (such as dip tanks) had been destroyed. Rural poverty had increased massively, but so had economic stratification. Under the impact of the war, the rural population had become more fluid. Many had fled to the cities, many had broadened their geographical and experiential horizons through war activities. Hatred of the colonial regime was matched by expectations of the new government and suspicion of controls. Any vision of national development would require the new regime to bring rural society back within the ambit of comprehensive state authority. But it was clear that if the new government was to restructure and reestablish the authority of the state it would have a hard row to hoe.

Part Three

THE NATIONAL-POPULAR STATE

Collective action won the liberation war. . . . People working together and effective leadership is also the key to the second stage of the struggle: the economic independence of Zimbabwe. The challenge we face is how to transfer collective action from the battlefield to the productive sector. . . . Collective action is becoming a reality in another way with the formation of Village Development Committees (VIDCOs) and Ward Development Committees (WADCOs). The objective is to empower rural people to have a say in development planning. . . . this new initiative [is] an example of how policies and structures support a people-oriented Government.

—Teurai Ropa Nhongo, Minister of Community Development and Women's Affairs, editorial in *Community Action*

* *

Sir—As a communal farmer I must pose a question: has a communal farmer a place in the economy of this country?

Many people live in the communal lands. A communal farmer occupies only a fraction of the arable land yet about 45 percent of the maize is produced from this sector. Most of the cattle are said to be owned by the communal farmer yet he is not being given the same encouragement as the commercial farmer and the mining industry, etc.

The communal farmer is not being made to feel that the Government is a partner with him in his efforts to produce and share the good and the bad.

The present situation is unfair when, if the communal farmer smiles, the Government smiles with him, but if he (the communal farmer) weeps he is left to weep alone.

If the Government could be more involved and monitor the efforts of the communal farmer it would be found that he is far removed from being a parasite.

The doors of the "land bank" are closed to him. He does not qualify for a loan except from the AFC whose doors are not as wide open as they should be. All the research stations are found in the commercial farming areas, and most of the dams and boreholes for irigation are found in the commercial farming areas.

The roads on which the communal farmer transports his produce are neglected.

Soil erosion is worsening by the day and good schools are hard to come by for the communal farmer's child.

It is futile to think that if the communal farmer goes under the other sectors will survive.

—S. M. Mamfami, Chivhu:
Letter to the Editor, *The (Harare) Herald*

6

The Political Economy of Rural Control

Independence always brings new opportunities and constraints for political and economic development. During the colonial period it had become evident, for both political and economic reasons, that the economic structure demanded extensive state management. This was by no means at odds with the newly elected ZANU(PF) government's determination that the state should lead, guide, and regulate economic development. Despite important shifts in both the political character of the Zimbabwe state and the relationship of political power to economic power, however, the extent to which the postcolonial state was able to manage this development on its own terms was limited. The state's structural vulnerabilities remained, and the political-ideological traditions of social management that evolved under the colonial regime continued to inform the postcolonial regime's development strategies. These conditions severely compromised the government's efforts to distance the postcolonial state from its predecessor and to take up the challenges of national development and nation building. The consequence was a critical ambiguity in government attempts to recast and entrench state authority.

The following chapters examine these efforts. The continuities in development strategies are striking. The ZANU(PF) government drew heavily on institutional structures that the colonial government had begun to put in place as its capacity to regulate rural society dissipated in the 1970s. Like its late-colonial predecessor, the government sought to dispel local understandings of the state as overweening and domineering. But the logic of this objective had shifted significantly: whereas the RF government had aimed increasingly to extract the state from rural society, the postcolonial government set out to embed the state in rural society. This shift was contained most vividly in a generalized state effort to retain the idiom of self-reliance while transforming its popular meaning from one that stressed responsibility to one that stressed empowerment.

Against this background the hegemonic efforts of the state advanced through a complex but fractured set of political attempts to recast local concepts of Right, rights, and community membership. Once again, they rested on state efforts to define local conceptions of "community." Once again conservation and community development policies, which provided the main pillars of rural development strategies, constituted the chief conduits for these efforts. In combining the political problems of technical development and governance, they both addressed and exposed the vulnerabilities of the postcolonial state. On the one hand, they embodied the pursuit of control that is associated with both the partiality of the colonial state and the insecurity of emerging postcolonial elites. On the other hand, they embodied the pursuit of popular incorporation into the polity associated with the structurally vulnerable national-popular state. Moreover, in negotiating the terms of control and consent, they rested on a panoply of claims to knowledge of agrarian realities that were not always consistent, or consistently held by state agents.

This chapter sketches the political economy of rural development and rural control as it structured the regime's drive for national development and state building. It highlights the structural constraints on development policy and the shortcomings of populist strategies for the manipulation of the market as a way of "bringing in" the peasantry. The following chapter shows that, the government's commitment to land redistribution and resettlement notwithstanding, control of land remained both a nexus for managing rural society and an arena of rural struggle. The government's efforts to reorient social institutions for community resource management by linking the technical-managerial terms of conservation with the incorporative-cooperative terms of self-managed development provided an imaginative focus for constructing hegemony. But much depended on the sociocultural dimension of state making, couched in terms of community development. Chapter 8 shows that community development, as a state-directed attempt to combine market participation with self-reliance and limited proletarianization, remained a precarious co-optive strategy, partly because of the technocratic and managerial traditions of the state, partly because of interministerial insecurities reminiscent of the colonial era, and partly because of the enduring adversarial quality of state-peasant relations. Against this background, the hegemonic project of the state was faltering by the late 1980s. Struggling to bind a fragmented and fractious civil society, the state had by 1990 visibly slipped under the thrall of a small elite group, and the national-populist thrust of the regime's development strategy had become redefined in less inclusive ways. This shift was most clearly marked by the government's adoption of a World Bank–sponsored economic structural adjustment program that ushered in a new and as yet uncertain phase in Zimbabwean state construction. The 1990s have been marked by deepening elite corruption, increasingly authoritarian rule, and growing popular disaffection with an unsympathetic and capricious state.

State Power, Economic Development, and Peasant Agriculture

Political transitions are never smooth, and the Zimbabwean state's approach to development emitted mixed signals. It had inherited from the colonial state the problem of trying to establish some control over the labor market in the context of a destroyed rural economy, massive rural unemployment, and a number of social groups in the communal lands who were dependent on urban wages. As Gavin Williams notes, the new regime faced the challenge of "how to maintain the economic institutions which have proved able, in the past, to sustain a high rate of growth of industrial and agricultural output, while untying them from their moorings in a policy of racial exclusion, cheap labour, and the appropriation of fertile and irrigated land for capitalist farming."[1] This problem revealed the tension between the government's determination to manage the economy, and its reliance on private investment (at the level of both the national economy and local rural economies), which reflected its structural weaknesses.

As in other newly independent African states, the government announced a determination to extend its control over the economy in order to "lay the political, economic and social basis for transition to socialism."[2] Any state-directed form of transformation has to begin with the capacity of the state to exercise control over society, and any political group that has come to power through a bloody rural struggle is likely to have a healthy appreciation for the difficulties of establishing state dominance over rural society. Part of the socialist project, therefore, was to embark on a vigorous program of resettlement, reconstruction, and rehabilitation in the countryside. Notwithstanding a vigorous and sustained socialist rhetoric, the government did not, however, set out on a socialist development path. The party avoided class-based appeals and sought to present a broad national-populist front, a "collectivity of national will":

> Our concept of economic and social justice derives from the people we represent. These are the people who formed the coalition that fought for Zimbabwe's Independence. They are the poor peasants, the master farmers, the urban and rural wage workers, African traders and businessmen, intellectuals and professionals, in short, the great majority of the people of Zimbabwe.[3]

Populism thus expressed signaled the ambiguous class character of the party and the state, which was captured in the economic policy framework of Growth with Equity. While the policy had important redistributive components, and aimed to create jobs and expand the economic base, it did not assail the white-dominated private industrial and large-scale agricultural sectors, which were regarded as the motors of the economy.[4] In a 1982 interview, the Minister of Finance, Economic Planning and Development (FEPD), Bernard Chidzero, stressed that "the emphasis is on growth, with equity as the accompanying factor. It is not equity and then growth as a sideline—that is important."[5] The strategy welcomed private enterprise and foreign investment and, although the government was less sympathetic to capital in terms of wage and pricing policies, control and planning of the economy was no greater than under the Rhodesian Front. Indeed, in the first ten years of independence the state produced no clear investment or industrial development policy.

Thus, the new government confronted the problem of reconstructing the sociopolitical order under distinct constraints, especially in the countryside. The limits of transformation were demonstrated in the Communal Areas Act of 1982, which, following the requirements of the Lancaster House agreement, sustained the existing distinction between "freehold" and "communal" property regimes, and vested all communal land with the president, to be held in trust for the people. The act repealed the Tribal Trust Lands Act of 1979, which had vested all reserves with the president and had aimed to increase the powers of the Minister of Internal Affairs to intervene in matters of land management. Ab initio therefore, a separate sociolegal status for the communal lands was accepted, despite a development rhetoric that continued to bemoan the dual character of the economy. This separation rested on the different property regimes of the freehold and communal areas (and the different concepts of rights that accrued to those regimes) and thereby underwrote different conceptions of social being and citizenship. The distinction was most poignantly captured in the definition of voter eligibility laid down in the 1988 Rural Districts Councils Act, which took property as a yardstick in the noncommunal areas and residency as a yardstick in the communal areas. In noncommunal areas, farmworkers from outside the area but not owning or renting were not eligible to vote although alien property owners were. In the communal areas only the longest-standing wife of polygynously married men were eligible to vote.[6] In effect, dualism remained incorporated in the sociolegal order (as reflected in shifts over time in the official terminology for land occupied by African agrarian producers, from "reserves" to "tribal trust lands" to "communal areas").

This dualism was also marked by the generalized adoption, in both official and popular terminology, of *peasants* and the *peasant sector* to refer to communal area citizens as a social category. This terminology tended to minimize the fluidity of rural political economies shaped significantly by migrant labor, socioeconomic differentiation, and gendered power structures. It reflected not only the resilience of colonial conceptual categories (from "producer" to "tribesman" to "peasant") and the agrarian databases that the postindependence government had inherited from colonial bureaucracies, but also the new regime's national-populist development vision in which a stable, small-scale, and relatively homogeneous class of agrarian producers plays a distinctive national role. Indeed, the nationalist government viewed the tasks of developing, controlling, and securing the allegiance of rural populations as extremely urgent, for reasons not only of party support but also of managing society. In the first place, the government could only establish some control over the economy, let alone promote growth with equity, if the rural market base was expanded. Despite two boom years immediately after independence, the overall performance of the economy was dismal, with an annual average growth rate from 1980 through 1984 of less than one percent. With the country becoming once again a net agricultural importer, the government regarded self-sufficiency as a "matter of life or death" if it was to control its budgetary outlays, maintain an adequate level of investment and keep its urban constituencies reasonably happy. Moreover, the peasant sector provided a vital (though mainly potential) revenue base, not least to finance the new administrative and development structures in the rural areas. Finally, with a rapidly expanding rural population and a large number of ex-combatants to accommodate, the government sought to avoid the effects of a massive flood of job seekers into the urban areas. Yet, as we have seen, one of the legacies of colonial development was a severely debilitated agrarian economy in the communal farming areas.

Under these conditions, the Zimbabwe government finally took up seriously the arguments, advanced in the 1960s by the

Phillips Committee and the Sadie Commission, that the national economy depended on a revitalized peasant agricultural sector. It placed the incorporation of the peasantry, as well as the regulation of rural class formation, at the top of its political agenda. But managing development under conditions of unreconstructed colonial property structures, land pressure, and ecological decline, was a challenging political task. It demanded a sustained effort to root state hegemony in the countryside. The next two chapters analyze in detail how the government embarked on this project in the decade following independence. The remainder of this chapter sketches the structural constraints under which it proceeded.

Under the rubric of growth with equity, the government's agricultural policy aimed to create a fairer distribution of land access, to reduce poverty levels in rural areas, and to increase agricultural productivity.[7] While these objectives reflected the government's neopopulist development outlook, they also highlighted several powerful constraints on its approach to rural development. These included a perceived need to stabilize the labor force by limiting urban migration and absorbing the surplus population in the countryside, a perceived need to limit agrarian class formation while boosting productivity, and a perceived need to entrench the moral and political authority of the state in peasant communities.

Rural Stabilization

With a sluggish economy, and a population growth rate of well over 3 percent per annum, unemployment rose rapidly in the 1980s. The 1982 census estimated that 75 percent of the population lived in rural areas, and according to R. Whitlow population pressure in 1980 was nearly critical in almost 40 percent of the communal areas. On one estimate, the small size of the formal sector (employing 15% of the adult population in 1980) made it doubtful that it would import labor from the countryside for the next thirty years. At the same time, the 1982 census showed that the urban population more than doubled between 1969 and 1982, with the distribution heavily skewed toward the largest cities.[8] There was a massive shortage of urban housing and, under conditions of low urban job creation (and burgeoning government corruption), the low quality of life and the high cost of living in the high-density suburbs became an increasingly sensitive political issue.[9] Furthermore, given the close relationship between migrant remittances and expanded agricultural production, the slow growth of urban jobs resonated in the countryside, especially among young and poor households. Government policy formulators came to regard stabilization of the rural population as the basic requisite of all development strategies.[10] Not surprisingly, the government spurned institutionalized influx control measures such as the RF had employed, but without recourse to such measures stabilization was an extremely difficult—and politically delicate—maneuver to carry out.

Urban migration could perhaps be contained by keeping urban wages down and stimulating the rural economy. But keeping down wages required controls on consumer prices and this tended to bring the government into conflict with private capital interests, as happened when the government declared a price freeze in the mid-1980s. It also would reduce the size of urban remittances. If the government was to manage these conflicts effectively and not allow a severe rural-urban economic split to develop, it must stimulate the local consumption market, and this demanded that the peasant agricultural sector become a vigorous component of the national economy, not only in production but also in consumption. Moreover, there was an important link between controlling unemployment and controlling the unemployed. Given Zimbabweans' deep and tenacious rural roots, the government recognized the political danger of allowing the rural areas to become a reservoir of migrants and unemployed. Indeed, as Lionel Cliffe points out, constraints on land access made it unrealistic to think that the "excess" rural population could be siphoned off.[11]

The problem of rural stabilization thus created a powerful political tension in development policy. While policymakers recognized the increasing land pressure that must follow from a rapidly expanding rural population they also stressed the need to keep people on the land. It is in this context that the government rapidly adopted an ambitious land resettlement program after independence. It aimed to relieve land pressure among subsistence farmers and to increase productivity in the peasant sector, while also keeping the rural population on the land and supplementing the industrial and commercial sectors as a source of employment. Indeed, one of the conditions of settlement according to these schemes was that migrant labor among settlers was not allowed. But the land resettlement program was able to provide only a very limited response to this tension. Consequently, as one Provincial Development Plan acknowledged, "Strong control measures are necessary if the development of the Province is to achieve a balance between population and resources."[12] As we shall see, conservation and community development policies became the hegemonic conduits for such "strong measures."

Agricultural Productivity and Class Formation

Constrained by the survival of colonial land ownership structures, and eager to stabilize the labor force, the government was reluctant to boost rural productivity by creating a rural capitalist class and allowing a free rural proletariat to emerge. Apart from creating possible social instability, the emergence of such a proletariat would be costly to the government, either in terms of extending rural social welfare, or in terms of controlling urban consumer prices. To resolve the tension between boosting the material productive sector and keeping people on the land, therefore, development must take place under conditions in which economic stratification could be managed or controlled.

This imperative invoked an incipient conflict in agricultural development policy between the dual objectives of commercializing the communal farming sector and alleviating the lot of the rural poor. As Philip Raikes has shown, commercialization can exacerbate rather than ameliorate the lot of the rural poor since it tends to promote stratification, to bypass ecologically fragile areas, and to push goods toward markets rather than toward need.[13] To be sure, the market was already well entrenched in rural Zimbabwe. But the extent of participation in the market by households varied widely both across and within regions. Many households had scant contact with national markets and disbursed virtually their entire cash income on agricultural inputs. Many rural households continued to depend for a substantial proportion of their income on remittances from urban migrant labor. In the poorer and often more remote areas migrant labor was often the principal link between the local economy and the national economy.[14] The slow growth of the urban labor market thus exacerbated rural poverty even, in many cases, where families held sufficient land. J. C. Jackson and P. Collier, indeed, define the rural poor by a lack of direct access to wage incomes and a narrow agricultural base for their incomes. In a harsh and uncertain climate, large surpluses of marketed produce appeared alongside rural poverty and hunger.[15]

For the rural poor, security on the land was critically important. Rather than relinquish their land, poor families tended to rely on remittances from migrants—including males who possessed land rights—while migrants themselves would claim a piece of rural land for their family to occupy, sometimes being criticized by extension agents as "holiday farmers" or "weekend

farmers."[16] But for such people agricultural sufficiency was by
no means secure, especially if they held poor land. Where
male family members had to seek off-farm work on commercial farms or in the cities to earn cash for food or inputs, the
shortage of labor on their own holdings was aggravated unless they used remittances to hire local labor. The growth of
landlessness, especially in refugee-stricken areas such as the
Mozambique border, made cheap seasonal labor available to
those farmers who could afford to hire, but among poorer families group-based labor organization remained prominent.[17]
Labor demands on rural women grew, often exacerbating
strains on family relations. Households headed by women
tended to be among the poorest and their security of tenure
among the weakest, while younger siblings could look forward to allocations of smaller and less fertile pieces of land.
The result was a paradox of land shortage and underutilized
land. The Manicaland Provincial Development Plan complained
about "the wives or parents of urban migrants 'scratching'
land in order to retain their right to the land and not necessarily to earn a living as the case should be," though an Agritex study noted that underutilized land often belonged to
"better-off" landholders. Under conditions of land shortage,
some rural dwellers showed hostility and even physical violence towards migrants as local notions of rights and belonging came under increasing stress.[18]

Unwilling to subsidize the rural poor, the government was
eager both to keep these people on the land and to stimulate
their ability to generate rural cash incomes. To the extent that
existing conditions adversely affected productivity (or were
believed to have this effect) the situation raised the perpetual,
and always politically charged, question of land reform: Under
increasing land shortage, population pressure, and demands
for productivity, who should have access to land? And how can
such access be patrolled? There was also an ecological dimen-

sion to this question, for development agents saw land use patterns as linked to a serious ecological crisis. A World Bank land study summed up the problem:

> Between 1975 and 1984 . . . the cropped areas increased from 1.7 million ha to 2.3 million ha and the grazing areas correspondingly shrunk (from 11.6 million ha to 10.9 million ha) as more land was brought under cultivation at the expense of grazing land. The proportion of cropped land to total land rose to 14% in the Communal Areas, compared to only 4.0% in the Commercial Areas. Furthermore, the new land being brought under cultivation was more suited for grazing cattle than for growing crops, meaning that more land was now needed to produce the same quantity of grain as was previously produced on a smaller area. With the increase in population, the cattle herd had also increased, further intensifying the problem of a shrinking grazing resource. In some communal areas, stocking rates are more than three times above the recommended rate.

While the extent, nature, and impact of this ecological stress was a matter of some contention (and the debates were riddled with colonial conventional wisdoms), state technocrats believed that it demanded rapid and decisive action through conservation, control and incentive. Inevitably, there was ongoing debate, in both party and bureaucratic circles, on how the government should proceed, especially with regard to distribution of the land, forms of land tenure, and the control of common resources.[19] Thus the powerful legacy of state intervention in peasant patterns of land access, land tenure, and land use planning (particularly the management of grazing) became once again issues of potential state-peasant contention. This is the subject of chapter 7.

Accumulation, property rights, and public authority were all at stake. Despite its generally positive support for peasant production, the state retained its power to intervene, particularly by trying to take over land rights, in order to manage rural class formation and to establish a modicum of state control over the labor market. All the provincial development plans stressed the importance of developing skills, creating nonagricultural employment opportunities in the rural areas, and preventing the growth of a rural propertiless class. Policy was at once an attempt to mitigate the transforming effects on local social relations of an already incipient stratification in rural society, and an attempt to take over that transforming process under the government's own ambiguous, neopopulist, development vision. Like the Land Husbandry Act before it, such policy aimed to promote and support a middle peasantry. Also like the Land Husbandry Act, it placed at center stage the problem of land and rural property rights, for without control of land, class formation and rural struggles at the local level could not be controlled. At least within the communal areas, therefore, "growth with equity" should be viewed not as a trade-off but as a political necessity. But in the context of unstable agrarian environments, and rural citizens already under stress, it ran the risk of fragmenting local authority and activating the precarious strength of local notables and entrenched power holders against the state.

Authority and Hegemony

To develop the rural population as an economic resource, while managing class formation and the social tensions arising from changing agrarian structures, the government had to embed state authority securely in these areas. Fiscal imperatives intensified this requirement. Combined with the demands of postwar reconstruction, the goal of a more equitable distribution of economic resources, public expenditures, and infrastructural development placed an enormous burden on state coffers. The implementation of rural development programs therefore had to rely heavily on extensive input from local communities themselves. Initially, to emphasize the distinction between the new regime and its colonial predecessor, the government offered a poll tax reprieve to district councils. But when it restructured rural administration, it reintroduced the tax in order to fund the system through local revenues. This required that peasants be both able and willing to pay taxes. As in the colonial period, state reliance on community involvement in development gave communities significant bargaining power over the allocation and distribution of resources, a capacity that engaged community-level power structures and could push the government into unstable political alliances at the local level. Consequently, effective social management required that control be mitigated by a language of incorporation and cooperation. In the event, poll tax recoveries remained low, and for many district councils local revenues derived mainly from taxes on beer trading, the vehicle tax, and development levies.[20]

In addition, securing state authority in the countryside was linked to party patronage. As always, regime consolidation required that political alliances be forged in rural areas, either with existing elites or by fostering new elites. It also required that the government put in place apparatuses to suppress social conflicts, including class conflicts at the national level as well as localized conflicts over the quality of life—distribution of food, jobs, access to land, and so forth. Coming to power from an immediate history of violent conflict, not only between races but also between ZANU(PF), PF-ZAPU, and other smaller African parties, the new political leadership felt vulnerable and insecure. This sensibility was not assuaged by ZANU(PF)'s overwhelming electoral victory in 1980, and the party leaders rapidly showed themselves willing to use the coercive machinery of the state against political opponents. The government regularly renewed the state of emergency first imposed by Ian Smith in 1965 to cover acts of political violence. The most tragic example was the campaign of terror that the government unleashed on rural Matabeleland and Midlands between 1982 and 1987.[21]

Some scholars have suggested that this campaign reveals a critical ethnic fault line in Zimbabwean politics between the Shona majority that supported ZANU(PF) and the Ndebele minority that supported PF-ZAPU. Popular party support had in fact become substantially regionalized and ethnicized during the liberation war. Not only did ZAPU command almost exclusive support in the western provinces, but it had a much more effective grassroots intelligence apparatus than ZANU(PF). When several groups of ex-ZIPRA guerrillas decided to take up arms again in 1982, the ZANU(PF) leadership, recognizing that it simply did not know what was going on in the area, was seized by a fear that it might lose control of the west entirely. This fear was compounded by the fact that the state's intelligence agency (the CIO) remained riddled with ex-colonial operatives, many of whom were suspected of sympathy with South Africa's apartheid regime. South Africa, in turn, had set out to foment political chaos by infiltrating pseudodissidents into Matabeleland. The government responded by deploying its thuggish 5 Brigade, trained by North Koreans and composed of hand-picked Shona-speaking ZANLA cadres, to squash the dissidents—and ultimately ZAPU with them.

Seen in this light, the time of troubles in Matabeleland reflects less a resurgence of long-held ethnic sensibilities than the insecurities of an untried nationalist regime taking power in the context of a weak state and a fluid social base. The dissidents themselves—who never amounted to significant numbers—did not make ethnic claims, and very few had any connection to ZAPU. Many terrorized local populations, many were simply bandits, and only a few continued to argue that they were fighting for some vision of social transformation or land redistribution. Among the various state agencies engaged in the repression—the CIO, the police, 5 Brigade, and the party youth—only 5 Brigade systematically used ethnic factors to identify and terrorize their victims, attacking deep cultural precepts of local populations such as forcing people to transgress sexual taboos and forbidding mourning of the dead. But much of the terror involved crude tactics such as random torture or murder. The government and ruling party eschewed an ethnic discourse, instead using a rhetoric of "law and order" to advance the view that Zimbabwe's fragile nation-statehood was under attack from antinational dissidents. This rhetoric served as a pretext not only for attacking ZAPU party structures and persecuting party leaders but also for promoting the argument for a one-party state. Public conflicts between ZANU(PF) and PF-ZAPU over the steady erosion of ZAPU's rights and capacities were intense and vituperative, but they were notably free of ethnic arguments.

The Matabeleland security situation reveals a common sociological dimension of regime consolidation and state formation in newly independent African countries. As a systematic campaign of terror, it was rooted in the determination of the new regime to establish an effective hold on the national polity. During the 1980s regime consolidation rather than ethnic domination was at stake.[22] This view is supported by the widespread political violence that marred the 1985 and 1990 elections in which the ZANU(PF) youth league acquired a reputation for rather indiscriminate coercion against citizens. This violence stemmed, paradoxically, from Mugabe's determination to centralize regime power on the basis of "national unity" and a one-party state rather than on ethnic domination. Not only the dissidence in Matabeleland, but also the creation of a new populist party, the Zimbabwe Unity Movement, in Manicaland in October 1988, and the capacity of the voters of Gutu to throw out their MP—herself a Deputy Minister of Political Affairs—in 1988, indicate that the rural strength of the ruling party was patchy and fluid. In this situation, the ZANU(PF) government allowed its allies and supporters to intimidate and coerce the party's political foes relatively unconstrained. In 1990, Zimbabwean political scientist Lloyd Sachikonye noted that political violence had become "a sad and deplorable feature of recent Zimbabwean political culture."[23]

When the 1985 national election showed that the campaign of terror had not crushed rural support for ZAPU in Matabeleland, ZANU(PF) began to negotiate a Unity Accord with the ZAPU leadership. The accord was signed in 1987, unifying a new political leadership on both party and ethnic lines. Although it seemed to set the stage for consolidating a one-party state, it had the ironic effect of weakening elite cohesion by bringing opposing political visions within the party framework. The one-party blueprint was rapidly rejected by the party itself. Moreover, PF-ZAPU had been a fractious party with poor relations between its leaders and rank and file, so that capturing the leadership did not mean capturing the support base. A decade of authoritarian politics may therefore finally have created conditions conducive to democratic opening, though by the late 1990s Mugabe, increasingly isolated and embittered, was following the familiar postcolonial pattern of throwing up ramparts around his regime.[24] Although the Matabeleland campaign had not been intended as a campaign of systematic *cultural* terror, its effect was to lay down a sediment of ethnic sensibilities that will infuse the political cultures of Zimbabwe for generations to come and complicate the construction of working political coalitions on ethnic and regional lines.

More germane to our discussion here is that structures of political competition during a transition to independence (or democracy) establish very close links between regime consolidation and state construction that place a premium on securing popular allegiance to the new sociopolitical order. For insecure and resource-poor governments, this is a particularly difficult task that cannot be resolved by crushing or incorporating opposition parties. In the case of Zimbabwe, the regime's political insecurity, plus growing popular cynicism, along with emerging class interests of the party leadership and local struggles over power and patronage, made the consolidation of both the postcolonial regime and the postcolonial state a very uncertain business. Senior politicians and administrators rapidly showed a marked predilection for personal accumulation and corruption. As a group of land-owning Africans emerged, and politicians used the resources of the state to enrich themselves and their cronies (most notoriously in the 1988 "willowgate" vehicle importation scandal), state power and class power became increasingly congruent, and peasants increasingly dubious of the government's commitment to land reform. Establishing grounds for patronage was politically important for members of the party at all levels in order to develop the party base in the countryside. But using the party label was also a way for local notables or youths to develop their own semi-independent power base.[25] Moreover, given the petty bourgeois nature of the emerging party leadership, and the fact that the principal structures of the economy had been kept intact, it was unwilling to allow political rivals in a situation where it was not yet secure.[26] In short, popular support for the new regime could not be assumed.

Taken together, these conditions placed a further premium on establishing *state* authority in the countryside to manage social conflict. The government responded in part by massively expanding the provision of public goods to previously disadvantaged social groups. In particular, it launched impressive national education and health care programs in order to promote a new, congenial relationship between the state and society. This impulse, along with the revenue imperative and the impulse to social control, was also an impulse of *state* empowerment: it was part of the process of establishing the state as the overriding arbiter of social relations, and the organizing principle of the new incorporative public realm of the "national community." These impulses placed development strategies at the center of state construction for they governed the policy frameworks for economic development, social provision, and the distribution of public goods. If the state was to intrude upon the social organization of rural communities it must do so either by simply invoking its coercive power—an option that the government used in Matabeleland but could not generalize in areas that had supported ZANLA during the war—or in the name of some other appeal that peasant communities would understand and not associate unduly with state coercion or the whimsy of politicians.

The political tasks of building alliances and securing state authority, both essential to the state-making process, contained internal tensions: the less the state was able to bind and "bring in" fringe social groups of rural society the more it would have to rely on local alliances; the more it relied on such alliances the more difficult it would be to bring in rural society. In seeking to manage the labor force, the state looked to the countryside, for migrant workers maintained strong identification with the social relations of their "home communities." Chapters 7 and 8 show how this dilemma played a central role in the unfolding of rural development policies in the first decade of independence. The colonial regime had thrown up new social management institutions in the 1970s as its capacity to make or sustain political alliances fell apart. The postcolonial regime seized upon these institutional foundations to build the state in rural society in a context where it had no strong alliances to consolidate.

Administration, Governance, and Development

Local political relationships in rural Zimbabwe were shaped in important ways by the impact of the liberation war, resulting in considerable fluidity in relations between local communities, traditional leaders, local party organs, and local farmers' organizations.[27] These locally constituted relationships contested the overriding authority of the state, which was hampered by poor and unwieldy administrative organization and by interministerial struggles over areas of jurisdiction. The government believed that fluidity of state control and authority at the local level constituted a potential political threat. After independence, it therefore took a number of actions to entrench central government power and process in the countryside.

First, the party leadership moved rapidly to take control of local party groups and people's committees that had been created during the liberation war, and that in some cases not only enjoyed considerable legitimacy but had become a leading force in the community. Many of these committees had emerged spontaneously and organized around local grievances, especially questions of land distribution. Many were dominated by resident elders. The government was never sure that it would be able—for political, economic, or logistical reasons—to meet the demands they made and feared that they might continue to inspire political instability in the countryside.[28] Consequently, they were replaced with a new hierarchy of party organs.

Second, the government moved rapidly to curtail the status of traditional leaders. Under the Customary Law and Primary Courts Act of 1981 it replaced chiefs' jurisdiction in customary law with primary (community) courts, often under the jurisdiction of young ex-combatants, which were to bring the law enforcement machinery closer and more accessible to the ordinary person. Despite vigorous lobbying by chiefs, it also steadfastly denied any chiefly authority over land allocation. These efforts were an initial attempt to break down local power relations entrenched under the RF and to strengthen direct state access to rights of property and heritage that conditioned access to land. But this was an ambiguous initiative, reflecting both the insecurity of the party and debates within it. While party backbenchers argued that the conflict between chiefs and local officials made it inexpedient to restore chiefs' powers, the District Councils Act accorded chiefs and headmen ex officio positions on councils and assigned them specific policing duties. The government reinstated some chiefs, paid them an allowance, and maintained that it was "trying to do our best to graft the Chiefs into the whole system of administration in their areas so that they are not enunciators of tradition and custom, but leaders who participate in development programmes in their own areas."[29] Late in 1988 the government decided to restore to chiefs (though not to headmen) their legal powers because the community courts, poorly staffed with largely untrained personnel and lacking local authority in the application of Customary Law, had not been a success and were frequently bypassed. The Customary Law and Local Courts act of 1990 created a unitary court system—consisting of headmens' courts, chiefs' courts, magistrates' courts, the High Court, and the Supreme Court—in which civil and customary law cases may be heard at all levels of the judiciary. This relaxation of controls on chiefs represented an acceptance of chiefs' and headmen's powers of local control—as well as of patriarchal power structures—on a wider scale.

Third, and most broadly, the government promulgated a new system of rural administration to replace the African Council system with the object of introducing a standardized local government authority. The local authority was to be based on elected district councils, "large enough to be viable in terms of both human and material resources," but "free from the stigma of being the district commissioner's or chief's council."[30] The new structure would extend the electoral base of local government thereby allowing for the entrenchment of party organizations at the grassroots level, and it would drastically reduce the independent power of chiefs and traditional authorities. The structure provided for "locally and democratically elected bodies through which the communities would have a direct influence on development decision-making and implementation." Development priorities and objectives were to be set from the bottom up through a hierarchy of development institutions: Village Development Committees (VIDCOs), Ward Development Committees (WADCOs), District Councils, Provincial Councils. The stated role of VIDCOs was to help communities identify and articulate their needs, to coordinate and forward their proposals to the next tier, to improve communication, and to facilitate cooperation with government extension workers.[31] VIDCOs would comprise six locally elected members, including two chosen by village "mass organizations" to represent women and youths.

This framework, laid out in the prime minister's policy statement on Provincial Governorship and Decentralisation, 27 February 1984, and subsequently enshrined in the Provincial Councils and Administration Act, entailed a coordinated development strategy in which the government moved away from state direction, and presented decentralization and self-reliance as the key concepts of administration and development. The aim of the strategy was to forge hegemonic links between development, accountability, and state authority in rural development. The objectives of the decentralization policy, cast in terms of technical rationalization and efficiency, were to strengthen the link between development planning and implementation, and to broaden the base of accountability by bringing local authorities and communities into policy planning and implementation processes under the aegis of the national state. This initiative depended not only on the degree of government willingness to decentralize control over financial and humanpower resources to the local level but also the willingness of local people to cooperate in government structures.[32]

In fact this framework showed more continuity than change. First, it established the province as the level at which real political control over development would be situated. It created Provincial Councils to consider and approve Provincial Development Plans, chaired by politically appointed Provincial Governors. While governors would "have influence but not control" over provincial heads of ministries, their position was strengthened by their leading role in coordinating the production of provincial development plans, and their powerful party position.[33] In a limited sense, this strategy of situating government and party control at the provincial level resembled the RF government's strategy of provincialization—the buck of local self-determination would stop there. Second, the new government did not significantly dilute the powers of the colonial DC. In a formulation remarkably reminiscent of the prime minister's directive of 1965, the government designated the new District Administrators (DAs) "government's representatives at district level charged with the coordinative responsibility of ensuring that the policies of Government are executed efficiently in the districts. Accordingly, they have the right to seek information on the activities of any ministry in order that they may better discharge that special responsibility and their other co-ordinating functions."[34] DAs acted as Chief Executive of the council, chaired development committees, and provided the administrative link between the district council and the central government. These broad powers were replicated in resettlement areas by Resettlement Officers

(ROs), who coordinated all aspects of settlement (land use planning, land demarcation, land allocation, land tenure, communal activities such as dipping, grazing, woodlot use, etc.) and also had the power to evict settlers who failed to meet the program's requirements. Control of land occupation and use —including the power to control the type of crop grown, to demarcate lands for cropping and grazing, and to prescribe conservation measures—was vested in the district council.

Despite these initiatives, the capacity of the state to put its stamp on rural society remained tenuous. The immediate effect of the district council structure was to replace 242 African Councils with fifty-five district councils. In most areas, this meant that the district council was too distant from local communities to exercise effective authority or to dominate politics at the local level. Although the government threatened to prosecute any agent other than the district council who allocated land, and to remove any such land recipient, the district councils exercised little control, and became little more than rubber stamps for locally made decisions. These decisions themselves engaged local rivalries for power and authority. Moreover, DAs expended much energy in accounting to and seeking approval from Head Office through an onerous and time-consuming procedure of written reports. Peasants, finding colonial oppression replaced with "the oppression of the pen," were encouraged to look to other sources such as nongovernmental organizations (which do not demand taxes or allegiance in return for services) to promote and fund their development interests.[35] Conditions were little better in resettlement areas where overburdened ROs (government plans required one RO for 500 families) were given no clear definition of their role and no clear guidelines on how to proceed.[36] Most importantly, no fixed principle was laid down for the transmission of allocated plots of land, particularly on the demise of the original plot holder, although the control of land occupation was firmly vested in the RO. ROs made their own decisions on an ad hoc basis, and their reports to Head Office seldom evoked a response.

Like its late-colonial predecessor, the new regime set out to define the parameters of rural communities. Villages were to represent one hundred families (an estimated 1,000 people), and wards were to comprise a grouping of six villages (600 families; 6,000 people). But the delineation of villages and wards avoided the cultural intricacies of the 1960s delineation project that had tried to demarcate the lines of local political identities. Considerable flexibility was allowed in delineation, so that the size of villages and wards varied widely. Nevertheless, villages were delineated on lines that frequently had little local meaning, and some rural communities complained that the state was trying to press them into artificial social and political units. In some areas, VIDCOs could not be finalized because of boundary conflicts arising out of the land question.[37] Institutionally, this initiative recalls the Tribal Development Groups of the 1970s. Like the TDGs, VIDCOs were intended to refract political accountability at the local level. But the two initiatives reflected rather different interests. Whereas the colonial regime was intent on parceling local allegiances, the postcolonial regime sought to stress the permeability of the community and a wider public realm. TDGs, as we have seen, were intended to represent the retraction of an overweening state from rural society. VIDCOs, on the other hand, were part of an effort to *embed the state in* rural society. As Thomas Shopo puts it, they would lay the ideological foundation for "the new informal administrative logic of consultation and participation with the local community. . . . It is from the womb of these structures [of mass consultation at the level of both party and state] that an administrative logic for Zimbabwe's one party democracy will emerge."[38]

The essential aim of this structure was to make VIDCOs

and WADCOs the moral, political, and institutional core of community life. Not only would they provide a conduit for establishing the party's power base at the grassroots level, they would also provide the conduit for "incorporating the wishes of the affected" to enable "citizens individually and in groups as farmers, peasants, houseowners or businessmen to invest in development of their areas" and thereby "unleash local endeavour for genuine development."[39] In effect, these institutions would become incorporative mechanisms through which the state engineered and managed an extensive reorganization of productive, social, and physical life in the countryside. Thus, as grassroots participatory institutions, VIDCOs and the WADCOs were to become the nexus for control and consent between the state and peasant communities in the construction of a land-based yeoman democracy.

The following chapters examine the politics of this imaginative approach to postindependence statecraft. The discussion shows that, given the complex demands of state-making, agrarian strategy alone cannot sustain rural development. The chapters focus separately on "agrarian" strategies, which concern issues of land and agricultural productivity, and "nonagrarian" strategies, which concern sociocultural issues of social welfare and livelihood. Though the distinction is artificial, especially for rural citizens, it enables us to analyze different dimensions of the state's quest for hegemony, and to highlight common institutional and ideological themes as they are represented in the villagization program. It also exposes severe institutional and ideological faultlines within the state that undermine the coherence of the project. And it demonstrates that, in the context of state making, the state-society distinction is a process, always fragmented and contradictory. Indeed, it was against this background that "socialist development" in Zimbabwe rapidly became a strategy focused almost exclusively on the countryside, and aimed at managing rural political power as the new development policy sought to bring agricultural development and social control together under the aegis of state direction. It raised the political question of establishing the social legitimacy of state interventions in civil society and the market. Underlying the flux of class and state power at the level of the central political apparatus, therefore, was the political and economic imperative to incorporate the rural population into a new national political order as settled, productive, and self-reliant citizens. This was the crux of the quest for rural hegemony, which, as we shall see, linked the technical language of conservation and the sociocultural language of community development in independent Zimbabwe.

Peasants, Populism, and Markets

In the context of endemic government deficits, dismal economic performance, and escalating unemployment, the ZANU(PF) government faced the same overriding structural imperative that informed both the 1951 Land Husbandry Act and the RF's abortive policy of Community Development: to stabilize the labor force and the rural population, and to turn the peasant farming sector into a productive sector. As before, this imperative inspired a rural development vision that promoted neither large-scale industrialization nor urbanization, but rather the social and economic interests of the middle peasantry. This neopopulist vision was not simply a defense of a peasant mode of production, but of a small-scale, cooperative, and egalitarian productive order that evaded the inequalities of large-scale enterprise. It was a vision that contained a compromise with capitalism, and it illuminates the political-ideological importance of government attempts to distance the state from class interests, and to establish state dominance over society. The impetus for these attempts lay not only in the relationship of the state to the economy, but also in its structural *political* relationship with the rural population, in which the capacity of the state to implement its policies effectively was an urgent political issue. Yet, as Michael Drinkwater points out, the inherent weakness of such a strategy is that it may exacerbate rather than resolve major societal conflicts.[40]

While the new rulers in Zimbabwe enjoyed wide popular support at independence, they could not afford to interpret this support as "capturing" the peasantry. In the first heady days of independence a sense of oneness with the peasantry seems to have prevailed, marked by the solidarity of military-political victory and a magnificent bumper crop of peasant production in the 1980–81 season. But it was a fragile alliance, built partly on a massive commitment of agricultural inputs by the state that it could not afford to sustain and that was immediately tested by three consecutive years of crippling drought. The vast expansion of market participation by peasant farmers since independence has been widely noted and admired, but considerable evidence has also emerged that this great increase in peasant productivity was concentrated in a relatively small group of producers.[41] It was also partly a result of an increase in cropped lands by returning ex-combatants. With continued vulnerability to drought, food security remained a problem for large numbers of rural families, and state intervention in the management of land use and occupation remained a very sensitive political issue. Peasants—especially those who had supported PF-ZAPU or the UANC during the war—could be expected to wait and see what new benefits the new government would bring them—especially in terms of land, material benefits, and education.

The government rapidly demonstrated its commitment to developing and supporting communal farmers through supportive pricing policies that allowed the grain and cotton marketing boards to run at consistent losses, and through massively increasing the access of communal land farmers to credit and agricultural inputs. But the government also faced the same problem that had confronted the Rhodesian Front government in the late 1960s: promoting economic development by pricing and marketing incentives actually increased the sociopolitical strains in rural society. Furthermore, while the politics of development and state-peasant relations unfolded most intensely in local political struggles, the government had to respond to national-level structural and fiscal constraints. Inevitably, therefore, market manipulation provided an inadequate basis for a populist economic development strategy. The strategy was expensive and inefficient. With markets heavily conditioned by world prices, critical trade-offs had to be made between the differing interests of communal and commercial farmers, and between pricing supports for different crops, such as maize and sorghum. The Grain Marketing Board (GMB) and Cotton Marketing Board (CMB) suffered massive losses (in 1986-87, for instance, a combined loss of some Z$134 million), but when the government tried to reduce subsidies, communal land farmers were hit first and hardest because the factor cost of agricultural inputs is much higher for them than for commercial farmers.[42] Moreover, the massive increase in the availability of agricultural credit to the communal farming sector through the Agricultural Finance Corporation (AFC), and through the resettlement credit scheme, was enormously costly: in March 1988, the AFC declared that arrears in repayment had risen from 9 percent in 1983 to 35 percent, a total of Z$102 million.[43] By August the total had risen to Z$185 million, and the AFC had written off over Z$20 million as bad debts.[44]

While these enormous expenses raised serious questions about the sustainability of such strategies in a time of endemic economic vulnerability, local experiences of these policies were of more immediate importance in determining the tenor of state-peasant relations. Government loans were presented as a token of the government's commitment to and faith in the "people," in order to "revolutionise the entire peasant life . . . for the better."[45] But the state also had to keep loan money flowing in order to keep farmers on the land, even if this meant repeatedly rescheduling loans (Z$22 million in 1988). Nevertheless, market manipulating strategies did not reach deeply into rural society. They advantaged better-off and more successful peasant farmers, who were better able to respond to price incentives, better able to obtain and retain credit ratings, and better able to market their produce. Although by 1988, 90,000 loans were being made annually, they still only reached between 10 and 13 percent of communal area farmers and some 60 percent of resettlement farmers. Moreover, the rate of loan repayment was low, and peasants were showing reluctance to take loans.[46] Addressing a workshop in 1987 on the role of informal groups in the rural finance system, the then Minister of Lands Agriculture and Rural Resettlement, Moven Mahachi, stated, "Credit facilities by their very nature generally need to be targetted towards more commercially capable producers who have adequate access to land, draught power and extension services and who have a proven record of farming experience."[47] Those at the margins of the capitalist economy were least affected. A 1983 government survey of rural women noted that "lack of resources rather than sheer conservatism contributes to their inadequate agricultural productivity."[48] Short-term loans made in the form of an input package for cash crops (mainly cotton) excluded subsistence farmers from credit. Medium-term loans for farm equipment like scotch carts, plows, and fencing were frequently only available to master farmers or reputable AFC clients. Moreover, many peasants became chronically dependent on a vicious circle of loans. Thus, from the earliest days, agrarian strategy, which increasingly targeted the middle peasantry, was unable to adequately address the interests of substantial social groups, notably the rural poor and rural women.

In fact, market channels did not give the state much control over the peasant agricultural sector. The advantages of easier credit were severely vitiated by the incidence of chronic indebtedness, by peasants' vulnerability to drought, and by the poor quality of service delivered by rapidly expanding parastatals with inadequate resources—the AFC, the GMB, and the District Development Fund (DDF),which replaced the ADF. Farmers systematically avoided repaying AFC loans, often by side-marketing through unlicensed buyers. In many cases, side-marketing did not reflect merely an attempt to evade loan repayments. Processing of GMB cheques took so long that farmers needing immediate cash had to look elsewhere. As one woman explained, "I have no choice but to sell where I get cash. I need the money now and if the GMB can cash me, I would be glad to sell my maize to them."[49] Late GMB payments also forced farmers to buy their inputs late in the season when prices had risen, or they miss the rains and the peak planting periods. In many cases, therefore, particularly in areas more remote from GMB depots, peasant farmers did not seek out rural buyers but were dependent on them. Buyers took advantage of the situation by swindling their clients: overfilling and "skimming" bags, undergrading, and underpricing, sometimes in full view of their clients.[50] For many peasants, the specter of the old trader-producers refused to be laid to rest.

The vulnerability of communal area and resettlement area farmers to rural traders was compounded by their vulnerability to rural transport operators. The chronic shortage of transport in the rural areas enabled the small number of transporters to charge rates well above the government's recommended price. Occasionally, where local transport operators and traders were the same people, they forced farmers to sell them their grain at low prices by refusing to transport it. In mid-1988, the National Farmers' Association of Zimbabwe, the peasant farmers' organization, reported that 120,000 of its members in resettlement areas faced a crisis in getting their grain to depots because private transporters declared the roads unnavigable.[51] In the words of a NFAZ official, these conditions were "frustrating and demoralising." As a *Herald* editorial pointed out, "Transport is vital. It is no use producing a record harvest if you can't get it to the market." Some farmers argued that there was simply no point in "producing for transport."[52]

Thus, peasant market participation was constrained by factors that could not be addressed by straightforward manipulation of formal marketing channels. Many local notables had secured their economic and status positions by establishing transport and retailing businesses. This gave rise to localized conflicts and grievances over control of marketing outlets, transport facilities, and the deployment of labor. But such local conflicts were very difficult—and politically unattractive—for the state to regulate directly. The government and the AFC declined to take responsibility for rural transport, though it did deploy government vehicles in emergency situations. In general, the government confined its support role to expanding the network of GMB depots and funding the DDF to maintain and develop rural roads, a role severely limited by funding constraints. In 1988 it embarked on a campaign to encourage communal farmers to enter community-based group credit schemes and savings clubs to overcome obstacles to their market participation, thereby defining its own role in marketing and accumulation as decreasingly interventionist. In doing so, its supportive relationship with wealthier farmers strengthened as its relationship with poorer farmers weakened. This process increased the urgency for securing rural hegemony as it made it more difficult.

Conclusion

In the context of a resource-poor and politically insecure post-independence regime, the national-populist development vision associated with "growth with equity" contained within it political-ideological compromises and structural tensions that made the recasting of state-peasant relations, and the construction of state hegemony, a difficult political project. Certainly, a market-based development strategy provided a narrow and politically untrustworthy foundation for embedding state presence in rural social life. These conditions placed the control of land once again at the crux of state attempts to manage rural society, and reinvigorated conservation and community development as available idioms of accountability to forge the link between development, control, and consent. These idioms of control and accountability were cast in a specific institutional setting: new democratic, participatory, and cooperative grassroots development institutions at the community level—the Village Development Committees. VIDCOs would oversee and undertake conservation management and control, as well as promote community integration through "self-reliance," "participation," and "cooperation." They would instantiate a restitutive concept of *community* identity underwritten by the state within the rubric of the new nation. Thus, they would become the institutional nexus in which rural property rights and accumulation were regulated in a community context, and the intrusions of the state in rural society mediated. The next two chapters analyze the complex and symbiotic relations between control and conservation, community and cooperation, policy and people that link together the languages and institutions of state-peasant relations, and that forge the crucial political tie between the dual projects of rural development and state building.

7

The Quest for Hegemony

Land and Conservation

Very early on, the ZANU(PF) government declared its intention to take a highly interventionist part in structuring social and economic development in the communal areas. In language worth quoting, the Transitional National Development Plan made this intention clear:

> Government will investigate the legal, institutional, social and economic aspects of the traditional communal system with a view to its modification to achieve the following:
>
> (i) membership of a local community expressed principally in terms of management of common assets; the individual right to a share in the communal assets, separated from individual, group or communal exploitation of them;
>
> (ii) establishment of equal membership rights for men and women;
>
> (iii) a control system, overseen by Government but managed by the members, to prevent over-exploitation and misuse of natural assets; and
>
> (iv) realization of an agrarian system able to optimise land use patterns and maximise group and individual investment and effort.[1]

These objectives demonstrate the government's determination to extend and entrench state management of the social relations of property, power, and authority in the communal areas. Once again these efforts focused on rights of access to and use of land. In part this concern about land control was a response to the political problem of inherited colonial structures of land ownership and wartime promises to restore "lost lands." Yet the quest for control reached beyond lost lands into communal areas themselves. Explicitly, the first Five Year National Development Plan declared that the redistribution of land was inextricably linked to the reorganization of land use within the communal areas, with the resettlement program as a vanguard and model for a larger project in rural land control.[2] The government recognized, in short, that the land question had been recast but not resolved: it remained the pivot of rural politics and state construction because it provided the principal political nexus between development, governance, and party-political power.

For a still insecure ruling party and an uncertain officialdom, state control of land offered a vehicle for the exercise of patronage and largesse, for social management, and for rural empowerment; properly handled, it could be a powerful political resource. But for rural citizens, especially those who had not supported ZANU(PF) or occupied subordinate social positions, state control could be threatening and unsettling. Poorly handled, the land question could undermine the support base of the party and set the rural population against the state. The resettlement program could only extend to the beneficiaries of the program, and this raised the dilemma of selection and exclusion. Within the rubric of growth with equity, therefore, access to land remained a burning political question in postindependence Zimbabwe. To put its imprimatur on rural society the state had to put its imprimatur on rural land rights. But much depended on the capacity of the new government to establish the state as the final repository or arbiter of these rights. Given the political history of the land question, the government needed to devise authoritative institutional and discursive means of convincing rural dwellers that the state was not only the legitimate but indeed the appropriate agency to define and regulate rural land rights.

This task required the government to resolve the tensions between control and incorporation in establishing state authority and social management. It addressed this challenge by trying to reconcile a scientific-technical discourse focusing on conservation, management, and environmental protection with a democratic-cultural discourse focusing on grassroots participation and self-reliance. This chapter first sketches the government's interest in land control, and its articulation of that interest in technocratic terms. It then describes the obstacles and ambiguities of rural land control in terms of the resettlement program, the "squatter problem," and the fluidity of rural politics. The third section analyzes the state's focus on the social institutions of common resource management as a route to rural empowerment. Finally, the chapter shows how these institutions were designed to widen the realm of local political interaction with the state in a way that would create a close link between technical interests, management, and governance. But it was a fragile initiative. A decade after independence, the question of who controls the land in Zimbabwe—state or people, individual or community—remained complex, conflictual, and unresolved.

The Language of Land Policy: Management and Participation

Although the government moved to vest control of communal land in the state, district councils found it very difficult to impose a new, authoritative land regime. The political ambiguities of state presence in the countryside were deepened by the legacy of suspicion, hostility, and resistance left by colonial conservation efforts. In many areas, as a result of resistance, the breakdown of administration, and the ravages of the liberation war, land management appeared to state agents to be out of control. Old contours were not being maintained, steep slopes and natural drainage ways had been put under the plow, stream-bank cultivation was rife, and deforestation was widespread. On reduced grazing areas, just maintaining the size of herds meant increasingly severe overstocking. Farmers' financial and labor constraints reinforced resistance. Indeed, as Ken Wilson and Michael Drinkwater have pointed out, state agrarian policy frequently contradicted farmers' own understanding of their production needs.[3] In many areas the state lacked the resources to enforce conservation laws, and by the early 1980s the Natural Resources Protection Regulations and the legal powers of the Lands Inspectorate had fallen by and large into disuse. Legal enforcement had given way to persuasion, which was inhibited by the fact that farmers saw little change in the new era. Extension agents were still wielding colonial-era laws and techniques.[4]

Moreover, illegal "informal" land transfers continued, often through purchases of buildings or other permanent improvements. The prices paid for land were closely related to land potential and location, although land "purchases" did not necessarily mean that land was put to more productive or efficient use. Also, some farmers were able to extend their individual cropping areas into communal grazing areas, thereby reducing the communal capacity. Among those most able to use these channels for land acquisition were the relatively wealthy or powerful. Political patronage provided an important lever, and in some cases MPs and party elites became embroiled despite the ruling party's leadership code, which placed a limit on the amount of land party notables were allowed to own. Alienation of land outside of formal state regulation, therefore, was a central factor in growing economic stratification in the rural areas. It called into question security of tenure and raised the specter not only of a consolidation of land holdings by wealthier farmers but also increasing fragmentation of holdings.[5] This ran counter to all state land policy, from the Land Husbandry Act through the resettlement program. Not only was it anathema to the politics of "growth with equity" but, especially under conditions of severe land shortage, it had the capacity to further destabilize the rural population.

These rural conditions highlight the critical political links between technical development and governance, between land control and social control. If the government wanted to put the stamp of the state on rural land use, it needed to devise an authoritative institutional means of doing so that would mediate state impositions on rural society. It was against this background of tenuous state control and state authority that the government set out to devise hegemonic strategies that focused on management and participation.

Politicians and technocrats articulated land management interests first and foremost in ecological and technical terms that focused on the demands of productivity and the deepening ecological fragility of the communal areas arising out of overgrazing, deforestation, soil erosion, overpopulation and illegal occupation of land. Arguments over rural development retained the technocratic development ideology of the colonial period: belief in a principle of optimal land use in order to maximize marketing while obviating "costly ecological consequences." The 1982 Chavunduka Commission on agriculture rightly pointed out that "the nub of the problem is a physical one, namely the limited land area of Zimbabwe itself."[6] But the commission was wrong to imply that the problem was no longer a political one. For the technocratic approach that signaled a striking congruence between colonial and postcolonial development thinking also established a powerful political resonance between the National Land Use Strategy formally adopted in 1987 and the Land Husbandry Act of 1951.

Michael Drinkwater, analyzing agrarian policy at the level of implementation, has presented the continuity in technocratic thinking as the outcome of a purposive rationality associated with bureaucratic modernization.[7] This argument has particular merit for two reasons. First, it focuses attention on the nature of the data sources upon which claims to knowledge are made. Postindependence officials, for instance, had to rely heavily in the early years on preindependence research and technical data in devising their strategies and projects.[8] Because of the turpitude of the late-colonial government in pursuing rural development, the data base was small. The climatic volatility of rural Zimbabwe meant that little of it was reliable over time. Also, most development plans were devised in concert with external funding agencies, whose control of the purse strings influenced the construction of plans and made it imperative to keep *them* happy. Thus, policymakers had to work with development categories and data—both of which were frequently unreliable, sketchy, or inappropriate— that were handed to them by outside sources. It took time for more extensive data sources to be developed. Yet technical data provides the scientific-rational basis for development policy-making. Second, this approach draws attention to the state's desire to direct development activities, and the ensemble of institutions through which it sets out to do so. In effect these two factors established an alliance between state elites and external agencies against local populations for control of politically useful knowledge, notably in this case "science" and the "proper" modes of action that it calls for. However, to analyze the interplay between these factors they must be located within the nuanced historical-political processes of state making. The Land Use Strategy, like the other conservation measures analyzed in this book, was driven not just by a particular

bureaucratic rationality, but by the imperatives of constructing state authority. Technical order (the realm of scientific expertise) was intimately linked to political order (the realm of
state authority).

While the government's development vision was, as we
shall see, far more contested within the state than Drinkwater's account of a technocratic purposive rationality suggests,
it again adopted a policy language that linked calls for civic responsibility to the authority of science and rationalization. In
April 1980 the government adopted the World Conservation
Strategy sponsored by UNEP, UNESCO, and WWF as the
basis of its own national strategy for "[transforming] the
people and their resource base." Political leaders explicitly articulated a link between human and environmental transformation. On the one hand they stressed the need to develop social ethics, community codes, and cultural customs so that
"social conscience and social sanction [would] augment and
rapidly replace, in large measure, the need for coercive bureaucratic action."[9] On the other hand they ascribed extensive
land degradation to land use "malpractices" of peasant farmers (even presenting the effects of drought as "super-imposed
on decades of bad land-use and the resultant environmental
degradation"). Provincial and district development plans written under the auspices of the Ministry of Local Government,
Rural and Urban Development consistently described rural
society and the plights of peasants in terms of "poor husbandry methods and poor utilisation of farmland," "unplanned
settlement," and "poor land management," especially by en-
croachment of settlement and cropping into grazing areas.
The Manicaland Provincial Development Plan expressed the
interventionist logic of this view most starkly: "ensuring
man's responsibility for his environment will require substantial reform of land management techniques in communal
areas."[10] Meanwhile the government kept in place the colonial-

era conservation legislation and, in keeping with the spirit of this legislation, stressed the necessity of combating illegal settlement and removing squatters.

The interplay between these two themes, of environmental social ethics and agrarian practices, allowed the government to articulate solutions in the technical terms of designing land use and conservation strategies to redress the ecological degradation of the land. On these terms, the key solutions to rural depredation and instability could be found in "applying strict land management" or (more daringly) "land reorganization" and "rethinking the current land tenure system." All the rural development plans stressed the importance of resolving "conflicting land uses," and called for a systematic and controlled separation of grazing areas from arable land. Pursuing these objectives of land reform and rural control, the state devised an agrarian policy based on three types of state intervention in rural life. First, "proper" land use methods (safeguarding slope areas, containing and reclaiming gullies to curb erosion and siltation, protecting dam catchments, and preventing streambank cultivation) were to be inculcated, accompanied by intensive or "modern" methods of farming (crop rotation and cultivation of appropriate crops). Second, grazing areas were to be controlled by paddocking, fencing, and applying appropriate stocking rates. Third, scattered villages were to be consolidated into larger settlements through "villagization" in order to make more arable land available, to reduce the cost of providing infrastructure and transport access, and to allow the standards of rural housing to be improved. Thus, state incursions into rural society would go directly to the heart of local social organization—the relationship of communities and individuals to the land. They would entail "communal restructuring" and "village consolidation (rural reorganization)."[11]

This approach meant that the technical and political dimensions of development converged precisely on the nature of rural rights over land, labor, and accumulation. For land management involves not only implementing development initiatives such as reforestation, or increasing land fertility by using fertilizers, or promoting cooperatively organized irrigation schemes and market gardening projects (all of which feature prominently in the plans); it also involves telling people where and how they may use their land. Thus, if the government was to "accelerate the pace of scientific agriculture in the rural areas at the same time as we work to engender the spirit of cooperation," it would have to reorient local concepts of Right, rights, and community membership.[12] And it would have to proceed cautiously. It was to this end that the government set out to link its technocratic land management framework to the participatory developmental framework based on VIDCOs, WADCOs, and district councils. It hoped not only to harness local political will but to displace accountability for the state's managerial and coercive tendencies onto local institutions. In short, its strategy for securing the state as the final arbiter of social relations in the countryside, and for managing the tensions between social control and social consent, was to marry a scientific language of land management to a democratic language of public participation. But the state's capacity to cut through the tangle of power and authority relations at the local level and take control of land rights remained in question.

Struggles to Control Rural Land

The transmission of land rights and security of tenure in both the communal areas and the resettlement areas offers a picture of ambiguity and uncertainty in which the ability of the state to exercise comprehensive authority or control was seriously compromised. The government's efforts to place the imprimatur of the state on rural land rights had three dimensions: resettlement, eliminating "squatters," and controlling land allocation within the communal lands. Each case reflects the ambiguities of state power, and the tenuousness of state authority, in the countryside.

The Politics of Resettlement

ZANU(PF)'s land resettlement program had the political advantages of addressing the land question in a highly visible way and promoting the idea of a "socialist transformation of agriculture" and a "new social order" based on co-operative small-scale agrarian relations secured by the state.[13] But in its aim to establish a settled, contented, and productive yeoman class, the program reflected most strongly the political objectives of the 1951 Land Husbandry Act. Though a resettlement model of collective cooperatives (model B) was "conceived as the long term basis of the agricultural industry," over 80 percent of the program was settled on a model (model A) in which arable holdings were allocated to individual families on the basis of viability, and the government expected an increase in productivity.[14] This model strongly resembled the Land Husbandry Act. But there were two crucial differences. First, families were to be settled only after the demarcations had been made. This was to avoid the disruption of preexisting rights that had created massive resistance to the Land Husbandry Act. Second, where the Land Husbandry Act had looked to the ideological importance of individual freehold tenure rights to provide the guiding incentive for surplus production, land rights under the new policy remained strictly usufructuary and the right to allocate land remained firmly vested in the hands of the state, as embodied in the Resettlement Officer. It is worth remarking also that while both initiatives sought to stabilize rural populations, the LHA was devised in the context of a perceived shortage of urban labor, whereas the resettlement program responded to an escalating labor surplus.

The implementation of the policy rapidly fell far short of its projected goals, partly because the government faced political pressures in deciding who to resettle first in the wake of the war. It was also reluctant to start settling farmers before re-settlement areas had been fully surveyed and planned. In try-ing to exercise strict control, its implementation machinery became slow and ponderous. It also lacked funds and bureau-cratic capacity. By the end of the decade only 20 percent of the 75,000 families targeted in the first Five Year Development Plan (1985–1990) had been resettled and the resettlement rate was down to about 2,000 families a year.[15] Additionally, the ca-pacity of the resettlement program to provide a model for managing and stabilizing rural society rapidly came into doubt. The 1986 GOZ/UK Joint Review Mission acknowl-edged that the resettlement areas were becoming significantly stratified on lines of wealth, productive capacity, and gender. This increasing diversity of wealth and income generating ca-pacity reflected socioeconomic conditions similar to the com-munal lands. Those who owned the most cattle were the most productive, and able to make full use of their arable potential. Those who owned no cattle (25–30%) found it most difficult to realize the full potential of their holdings, and many found themselves in a "vicious cycle of poverty." The program ap-pears to have had very little impact on the poorest group of settlers, who had no direct access to draft power. After several years, they were no nearer to owning cattle, derived little eco-nomic advantage from their grazing rights, and were unable to maximize the use of their arable plots. Many sold their labor or exchanged it for the use of cattle.[16]

Thus the program had not succeeded markedly in bringing relief to the most disadvantaged rural sector and establishing a stable yeoman class, though it had provided vocational opportunities for thousands of Zimbabweans. Early on, the program was mainly redistributive, providing land to the landless and ex-combatants. But by the mid-1980s, seeking higher productivity levels as a mark of its success, the government had begun to target "better" farmers as the most appropriate settlers. The result, in many cases, was that successful farmers simply moved from the communal lands onto new land. In effect, the resettlement program mirrored the government's marketing and inputs policy, outlined in chapter 6, of shifting away from the rural poor to the middle and upper peasantry. Yet the program had not enabled the state to extend effective control and authority over this sector of the land market. Settlers frequently ignored cropping and grazing demarcations, so that destocking was necessary in some areas. ROs frequently lacked real control, sometimes allowing indiscriminate tree felling, game poaching, and stock grazing by adjoining communal area farmers. The program had not promoted equity with any marked success and it had not laid the groundwork for a new system of land use and control. In a mid-1990s survey, B. H. Kinsey found that resettlement farmers, like communal area farmers, still tend to rely on off-farm incomes for success. More surprisingly, he also found that despite a higher level of production in the resettlement areas, indications of long-term malnutrition are greater. This suggests that resettlement farmers lack the kin-based social security systems that persist in the communal areas, while they pour their resources into efforts to secure urban employment for family members.[17]

These trends indicate that the achievements of the resettlement program were ambiguous. The program enabled the government to show that it was tackling the land question seriously. Yet it had not lived up to the demands of "growth with equity," and the government had been unable to solve urgent questions about resource utilization, farming practices, and land conservation under conditions it had set up itself. The problem was not only one of land-use management, but one of the ruling party showing its ability to regulate national politics. And it was a problem of establishing clear local authority for the state. As the 1980s progressed the links between these questions became more manifest as the National Farmers' Association (NFAZ) and the media became increasingly vocal in their criticism of government's inability to overturn colonial structures.[18] This raised the premium on the government creating an authoritative link—under the aegis of the state—between the demands of conservation and control on the one hand, and accountability and cooperation on the other. The difficulty of this project was highlighted by the "squatter problem."

The "Squatter Problem"

As Jeffrey Herbst has shown, the control of land occupation rapidly broke down, and resettlement lands were from the early days overrun by informal occupation, or "squatting."[19] As disputes over land rights erupted, security on the land became a political issue, especially in some areas of Matabeleland and the Midlands, where dissidents took up squatter causes in the mid-1980s.[20] In some cases "squatters" claimed land on the argument that most of their ancestors were buried there. The Manicaland Provincial Development Plan estimated that there were some 37,000 people occupying land illegally in Manicaland. It noted that the insurgence of squatters had resulted in "a lack of security, administration and control over certain areas of land."[21] For the government, a situation of counterclaims and conflicts over land threatened its capacity to develop a system of land rights and land control to meet the objectives of productivity, stability, and rural hegemony. But the existing administration was unable to control the movement of people onto land. Squatting could provide land seekers with great leverage in negotiating for land. In Parliament, Edgar Tekere, a prominent party populist, argued furiously that the government was weaker than the Rhodesian Front, which had controlled land through a system of allocation by headmen; now, however, "Everybody is chaotic. . . . the Minister of Resettlement has got enough instruments, has he not got an instrument of enforcement of law? . . . let us not politic in chaos."[22] In this cry one detects an echo of the messy implementation of the Land Husbandry Act. But in order not to "politic in chaos" the government had to put the state's stamp on land redistribution procedures.

The government therefore embarked on a stringent antisquatting campaign that trumpeted the sanctity of property.[23] "Squatters" came to be defined as people who lived in areas not demarcated for settlement, or had not been allocated land in that particular area. Anybody who had not been expressly told that they might occupy a particular piece of land became a potential squatter. The police set up an antisquatter unit, and evictions were carried out with enthusiasm by both police and ministry officials.[24] In crusading against squatters the government was at pains to declare its support for those occupants of land who it regarded as legitimate. But it became increasingly unclear precisely who were squatters and who were not. Different groups appropriated the term *squatter* in order to legitimate acts of seizure, eviction, destruction of property, and even physical violence. At the same time, some of the more militant ZANU(PF) politicians themselves encouraged landless people to occupy land in the freehold sector.

Confusion and conflict ensued. Squatters who refused to be moved off commercial land they occupied on the claim that they were protecting their ancestors' graves were charged with hampering government's efforts to resettle people on arable land, but found this charge at odds with the party's promise to return lost lands. Squatters were frequently young or newly married couples unable to wait for a piece of land to become available while lineage elites allocated land to older families. Where outsiders desperate for a livelihood squatted on communal land, their plight made them both extremely resistant to expulsion and the foremost proponents of the popularly held right to farm for survival. The ideology of freedom farming developed during the war to counter colonial technocratic controls continued in some areas to provide a "moral right" to farmers to expand their individual holdings into common areas. The greatest culprits were wealthier farmers, for whom arable land was a severe production constraint. These farmers also tended to be important people in the area, many holding political office, and they were less subject to community sanction or eviction.[25]

By the mid-1980s, "legitimate" land rights were increasingly contestable. MPs complained that the government was unable to answer their constituents' requests for land allocation, "squatting" had become politicized, and the argument for "land hungry people" had become embattled.[26] While these struggles indicated increasing tensions in the ways in which rural people thought about their land, they also highlighted the tenuousness of the state's rural authority.

Local Politics, Power, and Authority

In a situation where no clear criteria for entitlement to land were established, rival land allocating "authorities" offered alternative "legitimacy" to rural claimants. In particular, chiefs and headmen reasserted their power to allocate land as a means to shoring up their political authority against the regime's onslaughts. They played a large role in the informal land market, frequently making allocations to "outsiders" in return for cash payment. In Goromonzi, the district council declared a "state of emergency on squatters" late in 1987, after allegations that traditional leaders were being bribed to allocate land to squatters. In October 1988 the Muzarabani district council, fearing serious overcrowding as a result of this practice, declared that all heads of villages who allocated land without the consent of the district council would be prosecuted. But the power of allocation remained mainly with local patrilineage structures, and headmen in particular continued on a wide scale to allocate land. There were even boundary disputes between local communities and the government's own resettlement areas. In some cases, control of land allocation was the focus of power struggles between rival chiefs, with the state on the sidelines. In Chiweshe, where the level of politicization during the liberation struggle was particularly high, control of land became the center of a power struggle between headmen and VIDCOs, which the state was unable to resolve. In Gutu communal land, one of the most densely populated areas in the country, rivalry and confusion between party structures, VIDCOs, and headmen over authority to allocate land was particularly marked and acerbic as these institutions jockeyed for power. In some cases, VIDCOs were successful because they are careful not to conflict with other established interests or authorities. Frequently they would ensure that village heads were involved in final decision making about land allocation.[27]

Against this political background, the state's ability to secure overriding authority over land rights was weak. Caught up in the uncertainty of land allocation structures, landless people—maturing children, urban dwellers casting around for rural security, or landless people from other communal areas —pursued whichever avenue seemed most likely to secure some title to land use and occupation. This issue became particularly acute in 1992, when the government began to designate farmland for expropriation under the 1990 Land Acquisition Act, and would-be farmers from all walks of life began to clamor for land with renewed hope. Disputes, sometimes violent, frequently erupted over such rights. Because struggles over land were integrally tied up with struggles over local economic power, district councilors frequently became directly embroiled in such struggles, creating political conflicts that were often impossible to resolve as rivals tried to force each other off the land. In one case in Wedza, migrant workers became afraid to return to their jobs in town lest the council evict their families in their absence. While there were often cross-cutting links, interests, and influences between contesting groups (e.g., a local headman might be chairman of the VIDCO) the lines of power, control, and authority were so tangled at the community level that the state often acted simply as a mediator between parties contending over land rather than the dispenser or arbiter of land rights. While rival claimants to chiefships were able to build strong support bases the state found itself in the unhappy and ironic position of vying with spirit mediums to legitimate particular candidates.[28]

This tangle of policy and power relations suggests strongly that government policy was shaped significantly in reaction to power struggles at the district level, rather than regulating those struggles. It also supports the view that the penetration of the rural areas by the central government through local party structures was not very deep. Indeed, it shows that there was a range of struggles within rural society over social and economic relationships on which state authority had scant purchase, despite the interventionist designs of the government. Such a state of affairs is not in principle undesirable—it may indeed provide fertile ground for democratic development—but it does help to explain the predilections of a nervous government for social control, and for securing viable political alliances in the countryside.

The indeterminacy of land control reveals the paradox of state weakness in which the state sets out to take command of local politics and to manage rural society on its own terms but is forced to defer to existing local concepts of right (themselves contested). State control strategies were themselves ambiguous, and the state had no comprehensive language of authority to offer. But if rights of land occupation and use were largely beyond state control, a second institutional focus for establishing an authoritative link between conservation-control and incorporation-cooperation could be pinpointed: local social institutions for managing communal resources. Such institutions provided a particularly attractive target because they allowed questions of access and local rights to be mediated through the community. Taking over or creating such institutions, therefore, provided the ground for reconfiguring local concepts of Right, rights, and community membership or citizenship. Two particular opportunities presented themselves. One was the management of common grazing resources (understood as a common access resource) through local grazing schemes underwritten by the VIDCO. The other was the management of wildlife resources (understood as an open access resource) under the aegis of the District council, designated as the "appropriate authority."

Building Local Power: Targeting the Commons

Under circumstances where the occupation of land is out of control, rights of tenure are in flux, and land grabbing frequently takes the form of "invasion of the commons," development agencies generally agree that clear lines of control over access to and use of public or common land are essential for increased productivity and sustainable land use. But any adjustment to current grazing and tenure arrangements involves an adjustment of individual peasants' land use rights, and that involves an intrusion into social and productive life. In Zimbabwe's rural development policy, this produced a profound tension between a perceived need to regulate livestock usage and inevitable intrusions into local cooperative and power structures. In the context of increasing land scarcity and population density, conservation-oriented policies of stock control and veld management took on a profound political significance, for they engaged the state's inability to control land transmission and tenure at the local level, as well as its interest in promoting agricultural productivity under conditions of managed stratification. Moreover, pricing policies to increase cattle off-take were not successful among peasants, who were concerned about the cost of cattle replacement and about local power relations that affected labor deployment and access to manure. The solution to the problem was therefore also necessarily political: how were stocking rates to be enforced without evoking resistance or exacerbating poverty and economic differentiation? Once again rights were at stake.

State officials tended to follow the colonial tradition of avoiding the appearance of political choice by considering the question in technocratic terms.[29] Agricultural economists, influenced by Garrett Hardin's paradigm of the "tragedy of the commons," argued that control could be exercised by opening up the land market for freehold tenure, or by individualizing grazing rights, so that stocking rates would be controlled by the farmers themselves through market-type mechanisms.[30] In 1984 senior officials in Agritex proposed a National Land Use Programme under which each member of a community would be allocated an equal grazing "share." Those with less cattle than represented in their share could either purchase animals to fill their quota or sell their grazing rights, on an annual basis, to other members of the community. The program was not confined to grazing land. The idea was that Communal Land Societies would be formed in each ward, village, or subward, with membership on the basis of equal voting rights and equal shares in all the common property controlled by the society. This system would provide the foundation for controlled land management through a localized market. The plan, however, raised political objections at the highest levels of policymaking, and was immediately rejected.[31] It would have been extremely difficult to administer in accordance with principles of equity, and would indeed have been likely to encourage a fairly rapid process of economic stratification. It would also have disrupted a wide-ranging and overlapping panoply of rights and powers already entrenched in the community. The government was quite aware that measures to regulate public resources from above could readily rekindle the tension between central and local control of land use, and between forced and voluntary change, that characterized the history of state-peasant relations in Zimbabwe. It seems likely that the precipitate dumping of the National Land Use Programme in 1984 reflected an appreciation within the government of the political dangers of tampering with people's stock rights.

The state thus faced the problem of changing farmers' rights to grazing while recognizing those rights as "most fundamental." It was a problem that demanded a convergence of political and technical thinking. In the mid-1980s agricultural research officers began to discard earlier conventional wisdoms of livestock control, and to focus closer attention on the local socioeconomic importance and role of stock holdings.[32] Here state officials recognized an opportunity to establish a foothold in local power structures. They devised a land use policy that called for stock control through community-based grazing schemes coordinated by VIDCOs.

Grazing schemes had already been implemented on a small scale during the colonial period as part of an effort to make farmers accept collective responsibility for the management of common land resources. The postcolonial state adopted this approach along with the idea that close cooperation between grazing schemes and VIDCOs would act as a vehicle for community integrity centered on the VIDCO. VIDCOs were to draw up and enforce local bylaws regulating community members' access to common resources. The policy therefore provided a way not only to regulate land and stock applications, but also a way to reorient the community. If the VIDCO could establish authority over those rights, it would be a first step to restructuring them. This was conceived as a symbiotic process, whereby the cooperative base of a grazing scheme provides the substantive roots for cohesion within a VIDCO, and the VIDCO takes responsibility for intervention, management, and control of land use patterns. Thus the National Conservation Strategy stressed that planning land use in the communal areas would "involve the active participation and commitment of the local communities and not be imposed upon them."[33] The VIDCO, as the controlling institution of grazing and land rights would establish an authoritative link between the demands of conservation and control on the one hand, and accountability and cooperation on the other. By becoming the source of legitimate control over land, the VIDCO would shift the focus of social organization in a "liberating" process whereby the central ideological allegiances of people would move from land and kinship to state and citizenship. As Ben Cousins put it, "Grazing schemes are at present a focus for an emerging redefinition of 'community identity' in the Communal Lands."[34] In this respect, control of stocking rates in fact became more than a concern with ecologically sustainable production. It became also a major conduit for state-community negotiations and social management. As a political initiative, in fact, it contained more than an echo of the Tribal Development Groups to which the increasingly demoralized Rhodesian state had turned in the 1970s.

A parallel initiative for institutionalizing and refracting state-community negotiations lay in the Communal Areas Management Programme for Indigenous Resources (CAMPFIRE), conceived in 1982, incorporated into the national conservation strategy in 1985, and implemented in 1989. It aimed to provide sustainable management of indigenous resources, such as woodlands and wildlife, that could be turned to economic advantage for communities in ecologically fragile areas where competition between animals and humans for resources was fiercest. It rested on an argument that in such areas the limitations of a strictly agrarian development strategy could be overcome by turning wildlife into an economic resource for the local community. Not only would it improve the local economy, it would be ecologically sustainable. Like the grazing schemes, CAMPFIRE had its roots in the death throes of the colonial regime. The 1975 Parks and Wild Life Act had designated landowners "appropriate authorities" over wildlife on their land and allowed them to use those resources "within the constraints of sound conservation practices." Its main object was to locate financial control of commercial safari operations in the hands of the District council as designated Appropriate Authority. In effect, the council was to take over both the accountability for resource management (animal control) and the authority for enforcement.[35]

Like grazing schemes, this program set out to link conservation and sociopolitical transformation. In the first place, it would distance the postcolonial state from its overweening predecessor, in whose hunting laws and wildlife control the value of wildlife not only loomed larger than human life but was determined by the sporting interests of white settlers or tourists rather than by local social needs or norms.[36] The state would establish this distance by decentralizing wildlife control and making it beneficial to local people, although the benefits would still derive from safari operations external to the community. The 1990 guide to CAMPFIRE rebuked the "paternalism and contempt" of colonial governments toward rural communities and praised "the innate ability of rural communities to identify their own needs and manage their own affairs"—though wildlife patrols sometimes maintained the colonial practices of threatening or beating villagers.[37] Under the program the spatial allocation of local wildlife areas and farming areas would be determined by local decision (ideally on a participatory basis) and the local use of wildlife would be patrolled by local institutions. Furthermore, any proceeds (such as the sale of hide or tusks) from wild animals killed by state officials for endangering the crops or lives of locals would be returned to the community. Thus, the program represented the friendly and supportive state.

In the second place, the strategy would put in place a common property regime that would be economically beneficial to community members. One critical feature of this regime was that the benefit would not derive from community use of the resource but from fees paid to the Appropriate Authority by external users (safari operators and their clients). Thus the conservation value of wildlife for the community would derive from its external market value; as one official put it, cash is the best extension worker.[38] One profound ramification of this arrangement was that communities would control and structure their own membership in accordance with the value of this external resource: only recognized community members would be eligible to receive the dividends of controlled hunting, and the community itself would prevent "squatters" from encroaching on wildlife areas. Thus this new common property regime would inculcate new social meanings of value, property, and community membership, which derived from a wider public realm (the market) underwritten by the state. This property regime established a clear connection between cash, conservation, and criminality (through "poaching land or wildlife") to be policed by the community. The concept was not abstract. Peterson superbly describes how the disbursement of Z\$60,000 (in Z\$20 notes) to the Chikwarakwara community by the district administrator was staged: "[The Council

Chairman] "ceremoniously carried in the cash (highly visible in a wire basket held high above his head). The scene was thus set to link cash (and the benefits it brought) to wildlife, and continued by placing the cash on the table in front of the speakers, giving the speeches real focus."[39]

In the third place, CAMPFIRE would put in place an institutional regime for development that would embody the virtues of "developing the communities" management capacity and institutional mechanisms to support and cause this betterment, educating people in the broadest sense, and decentralizing and democratizing decision-making on local issues."[40] This institution-building dimension was critical, for it established most boldly the links between environmental management and human development, participation and control, self-reliance and state construction that undergirded conservation and land policies.

It is in the light of these features that CAMPFIRE, like grazing schemes, should be understood as part of a wider state-building initiative. Both these sets of resource management institutions were designed to restructure local property regimes and were presented by the government as being inclusionary in two respects: they would be participatory, and they would link authority, responsibility and formal jurisdiction at the local level. In both respects, however, they would be embedded in a hierarchical structure of social management institutions underwritten by the state. Thus grazing control and wildlife management institutions had to be constructed in the context of state building. As such, these projects had three fundamental dimensions. First, grazing schemes and CAMPFIRE were ways of pushing the definition of local communities onto local populations through enhancing local responsibility. Second, by building upon the ideological-moral link between scientific conservation and civic responsibility, they would ensure that local definitions of community would be consonant with the local political economy, as community members perceived the clear link between their individual well-being and a sustainable agrarian order. Third, by establishing a close relationship between responsibility and accountability, these new definitions would be underwritten by the state through VIDCOs, District councils, and Appropriate Authorities.

It comes as no surprise to find strong echoes here of the crumbling colonial state's efforts to mitigate state presence in rural life without relinquishing the capacity for either social management or control. The critical difference was that the colonial state had sought to create a separate civic public realm in the countryside, whereas the postcolonial state sought to embed the state in that realm. Nevertheless, such continuity shows most poignantly that the problem of refracting accountability while underwriting the institutions through which it was refracted remained a difficult hegemonic project for the Zimbabwean state. Moreover, in approaching this project the political failure of the Land Husbandry Act loomed large. The LHA drew on the principle of individual ownership of land to underpin a sense of propriety and incentive among land users. As we have seen, the designers of the act seem to have believed that this would be sufficient to change the way people thought about their land. They were monumentally wrong. The postcolonial government, its political and structural vulnerabilities exposed by the "squatter problem" and recalcitrant headmen, sought a different basis for its ideological project of state construction. By focusing agrarian accountability on the VIDCO, it appealed to local traditions of agrarian cooperation while at the same time trying to refocus those traditions on a new, state-oriented institution. In short, the government set out to redefine the local community. These efforts are most clearly apparent in the connections between the technocratic control and management structures of the grazing scheme and CAMPFIRE strategies, the sociopolitical incorporation objectives of the VIDCO strategy, and the overall development vision of the village consolidation strategy commonly known as "villagization." In particular these strategies converged on an attempt to revise the relationship between private and public space in the community.

Such strategies were not novel in postcolonial Africa. They had been tried by neighbors, notably in Zambia's village regroupment program and Tanzania's *ujamaa* policy, whose failures had already been thoroughly documented.[41] The tendency to recapitulate what could be seen to be at best a very risky model of development, cast in the same development terminology, suggests that policymakers were trapped in a rigid and unimaginative development rationality. But it also signals the sociological importance of the task at hand—not only development, but a more far-reaching project of penetrating and shaping the rural social order. In this light, it is important not to gloss over the apparently familiar pattern of bungled development, but to reassess the Zimbabwe initiative carefully in its own historical context. The villagization strategy aimed to reorganize both the spatial arrangement of village life and the sociopolitical institutions of village authority. These policy components were ideologically linked, for the government expressly regarded the program as "a major vehicle through which rural society can be transformed."[42] The remainder of this chapter examines the role of spatial reorganization in state building. The next chapter examines the role of sociocultural policies that advanced the objectives of community development and self-reliance.

Most broadly, the village consolidation policy aimed to establish "a more equitable distribution of available land, to ensure proper land management and the intensive and efficient use of arable land leading to higher productivity," and to "foster a sense of community and co-operative development." It would also facilitate the economical provision of government services such as infrastructure (water, electricity, telephones, roads), housing, and community services (schools, clinics, play centers). This involved a massive incursion into the way that people conducted their lives, for the state took upon itself the task of determining and organizing basic institutions of daily life, including the spatial organization of community life itself. Land was to be reallocated into arable, grazing, residential, and woodlot areas. Villagers would have to give up redesignated areas and accept other land in return. For this incursion to be successful, individuals and communities must understand their land in a different way: "rural inhabitants [must] rededicate themselves to this new form and style of living through ideological reorientation."[43]

To understand the importance of this reorganization in shaping state-peasant relations, however, it is necessary to recognize that the relationship between the "new form and style of living" and the process of "ideological reorientation" was essentially symbiotic. By physically restructuring the settled social practices of everyday life the "new form and style of living" was also *part of* a process of "ideological reorientation" in which the state set out to build hegemony. Anthony Giddens has stressed the importance of spatial relations in the emergence of a geographically expanded public realm that goes with the modern nation-state. Deploying a concept of "time-space distanciation" to elucidate the cognitive ordering of social systems in which day-to-day discourses and conventions of action are institutionalized, Giddens argues that our perception of the social world is the product of particular processes of structuring; these processes "make" the world. They have a spatial dimension in the sense that space refers to the settings of interactions, and these settings "involve not just the 'distribution' of activities but their co-ordination with features of the locales within which these activities are carried out."[44] The restructuring of physical space in the village, along with the sociocultural rearrangements outlined in the next chapter, comprise such a process of "remaking" the world. It was already reflected in the centralization policies of the 1930s and 1940s in which "going into the lines" was part of an administrative attempt to structure and control rural society. The villagization program of the 1980s reflects the same principles. Like the centralizing project it takes place according to a given set of authoritative principles—rational, scientific planning and resource use—which imply not only transformation but also improvement and progress. As such, it is also part of an effort to repattern power, both allocative and symbolic, within the village.

This is not to argue that (standardized) space in any definitive way constitutes or determines social activity. Yet it does pattern and structure such activities. It underwrites a set of expectations and classifications that village dwellers bring to their physical environment in the everyday ordering of social activities. By demarcating territories according to legitimate usage (grazing, tillage, residence) the realms of public and private are realigned in relation to each other. This extends to concepts of property rights, especially that which is alienable and that which is not. In agrarian settings, it challenges cultural sensibilities in which land plays a pivotal role and the human and natural worlds are closely intertwined. In the name of progress, this intervention aims to introduce new authoritative epistemes patrolled by the legal institutions of the state (and it is in this respect that the party describes mediums as "atavistic"). Equally, it engages concepts of Right because "rational" use of space must be supervised, and the principles, organization, and legitimation of social supervision are the most important sociopolitical stakes of the villagization project. In short, the reordering of physical space also orders social relations according to a determinate social and political vision.

There is nothing mechanistically causal about such processes of structuration, for the ordering structures of social action are not immutable or historically determinate. They are processual—the stuff of tradition making and cultural struggles—and therefore ultimately uncertain. However, as I argue more expansively in chapter 8, if we understand social identities not as an expression of essence (as RF hardliners had insisted) but as generated in action or social practice, we can recognize the restructuring of village life as part of the purposive history of state making in Zimbabwe. For Zimbabwe's development planners, villagization would be attractive to people because it would offer improved services, just as CAMPFIRE would offer monetary returns for communally managed natural resources. It would also categorically change the classificatory schemes whereby people thought about their land and property. At the same time reorganization would boost the role of community institutions that would inculcate new patterns of social behavior and property use. These institutions, in turn, would both be participatory and implement technically sound policies drawing on state-supported scientific expertise. Once these institutions were in place their jurisdiction could be extended.[45] Thus the villagization plan and resource management strategies, as political initiatives, aimed to rearrange underlying patterns of local power and to reshape the concept of community as the guiding principle of social organization. It was self-consciously attached to the creation of a form of local democracy that would break down the distinction between local and national politics on the basis of people-driven development, would establish a close linkage between state and community at the grassroots level, and would lay the foundation for one-party democracy.[46]

In its communitarian appeals, this state project resonated with the characteristics of early agrarian capitalism elsewhere, and in particular with similar populist projects in other parts of Africa. In its objectives of promoting a stable and productive class of petty capitalist producers, it is most readily compared to the Land Husbandry Act. The vision of the LHA was that the people who use natural resources should also accept full responsibility and accountability for their conservation. This principle was retained under the postindependence land reorganization scheme. However, the emphasis on conservation by imposition, and on individual property rights was rejected. Under the postcolonial state conservation strategy, a collective community approach to the ownership and management of natural resources was strongly encouraged.[47] This approach acknowledged that not only the acquiescence of rural people but also their active cooperation and involvement was necessary for the success of rural reorganization.

Yet such transformations were uncertain, partly because their institutional and ideological foundations were insecure. To the extent that transformation rested on an appeal to science and technical expertise for authorization, both the supervising agency and the epistemes of authority lay outside of the community. Consequently, caught between a predilection for managing social change externally and a rhetoric of "community empowerment," the government was reluctant to allocate authority and control very precisely. It refused to take a clear position on the precise role of "public debate and community participation" in rejecting or revising existing concepts of land use.[48] Nevertheless, the rhetoric of popular participation, bottom-up development, and self-reliance was of central importance to the policy initiative. VIDCOs and WADCOs established a regular system of authority over land or resource use to which the state had direct access through its extension officers and advisors but which relieved the state of imposing its direct presence and control on local communities, especially in terms of unpopular measures such as denying land to aspirant farmers. The government was careful to publicly disavow the impression that the VIDCO was a state tool. Thus, accountability and enforcement were to be the province of the communities themselves through local organizations and authorities; state directiveness would be extensively mediated.

According to this vision, VIDCOs would provide an institutional forum for private citizens to congregate as a constituted public with membership rights in a community ultimately underwritten by the state. Yet it is important to bear in mind, as Giddens is at pains to point out, that attempts to shift underlying categories of social and political thought are both constraining and enabling. Thus, in a case where the sources of authority are up for grabs, they can intensify rather than mitigate social conflicts *within* the community. As we shall see further in chapter 8, the complex combination of external epistemological authority and internal tensions makes the process of dissolving the distinction between the village and a wider public realm a particularly difficult and nuanced one.

Dilemmas and Difficulties

The reliance placed by the government on establishing VIDCOs and WADCOs as the fundamental nexus of control and consent in "capturing" the countryside was more than a daring exercise in grassroots democracy. Its foundations lay in the relationship between an essentially coercive state attempt to reorganize rural society and the tenuousness of state hegemony in the countryside. Inevitably this was an extremely difficult relationship to negotiate.

VIDCOs and WADCOs were given a great deal of dirty work to do with respect to the implementation of land reform, including the demarcation and consolidation of land allocations and the centralization of villages. The government stressed that "the small man in the village is the key to the success of your development plan or projects. His willing participation in the identification and implementation of the projects in your development plan is the only guarantee to the success of your plan."[49] Yet the overall projects and incursions had already been identified from above in the context of national politics, the wider political economy and the structural imperatives of land reorganization. Policy statements emphasized the need for the state to retain ultimate control over decisions about carrying capacity and stocking rates as part of a *national* plan. In the case of CAMPFIRE, the participation of locals tended to be limited to receipt of a wildlife dividend that was much appreciated but that bore no immediate relation to the local value of wildlife. The willingness of the "small man" —and perhaps more significantly the "small woman"—to participate "responsibly" remained questionable, especially where VIDCOs continued to reflect local relations of patriarchal power. Moreover, the authority of the new social institutions for common property management was likely to remain tenuous unless illegal immigration ("squatting") could be controlled and the rural poor incorporated. Thus it remained to be seen whether the communitarian appeals of the strategy would be able to override existing stratification, especially on lines of wealth and gender. With the lines of local power and authority in flux, much would depend on who came to control the VIDCO and on whether the VIDCO was able to establish itself as the principal organization for cooperation in the community.

The grazing scheme strategy showed that this would not be easy or straightforward. Ambiguity persisted among allocating authorities, and neither government officials nor community agents had an overriding voice. The number of schemes remained small, the impetus for most grazing schemes originated in Agritex, and the bylaws that governed and enforced their operation also tended to originate outside of the community, either in the District council or in Agritex.[50] Yet, as Michael Drinkwater has shown, effective management of a fragile environment required considerable flexibility not only between localities but also between seasons. By long experience, farmers knew when and how to make best seasonal use of grasses, sponges, vleis, and watercourses located outside designated grazing areas.[51] But for Agritex officials it was difficult to sanction flexible usage systems of common resources because that hampered planning and control. Consequently, the dominant planning role played by Agritex frequently raised suspicion or anger where individuals' farming capabilities were compromised by conservation policies. In short, policy pulled in two different directions, which highlighted the tensions between coercion and incorporation in the state's quest for rural hegemony.[52]

Even within communities, the institutional flexibility necessary for effective management was somewhat at odds with state aims. The authority relationship between grazing scheme committees and VIDCOs and WADCOs was not well defined. According to Cousins, two-thirds of all schemes were either significantly smaller or significantly larger than VIDCOs in terms of households. Traditional leaders sat on the vast majority of committees, and many schemes that were established before independence showed a remarkable continuity of committee membership.[53] Grazing scheme committees were sometimes seen as a subcommittee of the VIDCO. In larger schemes, the VIDCO was represented on the committee, often by the chairman. In other cases, the two institutions seemed to operate in parallel, without clear delineation of their respective roles in land use planning or common property management. Such flexibility, although it may be locally desirable and enable broader participation, fragmented the hegemonic project of embedding the state in rural society. Indeed, grazing schemes created community-level conflicts where they tried to exclude nonmembers from traditional grazing areas, erected fences, or were dominated by master farmers with their own economic interests. Nonowners sometimes joined schemes because they were engaged in reciprocal arrangements.[54]

Conflicts consequently arose between farmers, groups of farmers, or communities *within* VIDCO areas, which complicated definitions of "community." Indeed, grazing schemes risked straining local community relations by reflecting lines of local socioeconomic stratification. Yet the success of grazing schemes depended heavily on community acceptance. Under such uncertain conditions, as Cousins points out, "the question of who has ultimate control over land use, state or community, will not be easily resolved."[55] The capacity to implement a grazing control program on a national basis remained questionable; yet a grazing control program that could not be implemented in a generally inclusive way was more likely to exacerbate than mitigate conflict. It was therefore essential for local groups to participate in the initiative, but to tailor their participation to local conditions. Although this approach became increasingly popular among researchers and agrarian technocrats, policymakers continued to regard it with suspicion and to cling to national administrative structures in planning. Theory and practice tended to diverge.

The problems outlined above are everyday development problems, well-known to developmentistas. But this should not obscure their profound political implications. The state promoted particular resource management regimes in order to take over and transfer the norms, conventions, and rules governing access to resources in specific ways. This project was understood to involve institution building for collective action (articulated as "self-management") within the rubric of the new state. On the ground, it raised the problem of how to take account of preexisting, locally well-understood, and effective institutions. The problem is nicely highlighted in the critiques of agrarian policies leveled by Drinkwater and James Murombedzi. Drinkwater argues that the technocratic purposive rationality of state policy precludes it, at least in practice, from taking account of local knowledge. Consequently, land use regulations are unable to embrace the intricacies of relations between ecology, resource use, and society at the local level. This critically undermines their capacity to build resource management institutions. Murombedzi criticizes the CAMPFIRE program because it embodies a clear distinction between resource-management (which falls to the community) and resource-use (which falls to outside hunters and safari operators). Because the ultimate orientation of this institutional regime is external (and is class- and market-based), it has tended to ignore local customs, ecological knowledge, and practice regarding natural resources. This has critically undermined its capacity to institutionalize an effective new common-property regime.[56]

Both these arguments, in accord with other studies, point out that local citizens have tended to remain unenthusiastic or suspicious of state initiatives.[57] Thus they question the extent to which institution building can be successful where the benefits to local communities are not readily identifiable by community members or, indeed, where the community is not readily identifiable to members. Such initiatives are confounded, as C. R. Cutshall puts it, by "the current pattern of residence and land-use, the spatial distribution of arable land, attitudes about land availability, future land requirements and expansion strategies, and indeed, the political-socioeconomic-ethnic cleavages which militate against any broad-based community consensus."[58] Thus, these authors point out the significance for the politics of development not only of local resistance to state initiatives, but of local definitions of the community itself. Bayart has pointed out that "it is important not to underestimate the capacity of the lineage to reappropriate the preserves of the contemporary state."[59] But in rural Zimbabwe, the problem has been a fragmentation rather than a reappropriation of social authority. Struggles for land politicized the question of community membership as they intensified competition between VIDCOs, chiefs, and headmen for allocating authority and consequently for broader social power and patronage. State efforts not only failed to transform local public institutions in order to bring local communities into a wider public realm, they disrupted local civic realms, thereby exacerbating the fragmentation of social authority.

This set of processes also illuminates a central conduit of state-building processes by drawing attention to the character of law and criminality—the realm of state supervision and sanction. Resource management bylaws are expected to be passed and enforced by district councils and their subordinate agencies. However, most of these laws originate outside of the local community, generally in Agritex or the Department of National Parks and Wildlife Management. Moreover, the colonial conservation laws governing land use and wildlife were retained more or less intact. Indeed, Sam Moyo and Tor Skalnes have noted that there remains considerable mistrust of peasant incorporation within the Ministry of Local Government, Rural and Urban Development, and that the bureaucracy tends to be divided into a technical wing with expertise in production processes, and a political wing overseeing land allocation.[60] Thus, the distance between the community and the law-imposing authority has not closed appreciably. This militates against the localized redefinition of communities, as is most readily apparent in the ways that local resource use becomes defined by state agencies as illegal through the use of the concept of "poaching"—either of wildlife, or of grazing resources, or of land itself. In a context of growing land pressure and competition over resources it is difficult indeed to transform concepts of value that accrue to animals. But without such transformation, poaching laws are likely to lack moral purchase at the local level, and antipoaching activity is likely to continue to generate resentment. As Donald Moore notes, Nyanga locals use a different term (*zvisikwa*, things created) to refer to the environment, rather than the "natural resources" stressed by state officials. This term takes its meanings from daily livelihood activities—hunting, fishing, pasturing, collecting firewood—that sometimes diverge from patterns of resource use recognized by the state as legitimate.[61] Thus a political tension is discernible between the definition of criminality and community "empowerment." This tension also fed into the fragmentation of authority as it became a focus for struggles between state judicial officers (Presiding Officers) and traditional authorities over legal jurisdiction. As we shall see in chapter 8, struggles over whose law held sway became particularly important to the state-building effort when men felt their patriarchal power threatened by state reforms of marriage, inheritance, and family laws.

One might suggest that the degree of local empowerment is reflected in the extent to which the legal regime is transformed. CAMPFIRE aims to locate definitions of poaching as antisocial behavior within the community on the grounds that poachers assail the well-being of the community in the marketplace. Clearly, under such conditions the social institutions that underwrite this system must be locally legitimated and representative. If these institutions appear to be politically partial they are more likely to intensify tensions within the community. Though local situations vary, the legal regime has not generally shifted much in Zimbabwe. Lacking significant input of local expertise it continues to place an external constraint on community empowerment.[62] This in turn makes it a continued focus of opposition, and constrains its capacity to regulate internal conflicts. Nevertheless, as we shall see in the next chapter, the law remains a central sociocultural arena for embedding the state in community structures.

On a more mundane level, the difficulties of incorporating the "small person" through development projects were clearly signaled by the villagization program. The progress of infrastructural development was very slow, most development depended on local labor inputs, and the Rural Housing Scheme increasingly depended on self-help and self-reliance, whereby people built their own houses with their own materials. Not surprisingly, the policy met with little popular enthusiasm despite a vigorous state "marketing campaign." Ironically, VIDCOs that tried to implement villagization found that it undermined their legitimacy. It was not easy to persuade people to abandon their homes and to rebuild their own dwellings elsewhere unless clear and reasonable incentives could be offered. Poorer villagers, who were often those most interested in villagization were frequently not able to afford the repayments on housing loans; indeed, the state struggled to secure repayment from participants in pilot schemes.[63] Wealthier villagers often already had decent homes, and did not relish the inconvenience and expense of hiring a local builder. Moreover, essential building materials promised by the ministry could not be relied on to arrive, and buildings were left half completed. In his analysis of village regrouping in Zambia, Michael Bratton has suggested that peasants will risk the disruptions associated with such intrusive policies as villagization if they rapidly see material benefits. But they will withdraw their support, and perhaps turn to political opposition, if the benefits do not materialize. These conditions pertained in Zimbabwe. As an editorial in the *Herald* warned, "Zimbabwe must get it right. Villagers asked to give up their traditional homes must be carefully educated to the point where they welcome the change. And promises must be kept."[64] Meanwhile, peasants would wait and see.

Sensitive to the failures of villagization programs elsewhere, the government was content to pursue the policy patiently through scattered pilot projects and education campaigns by MPs, District councils, state officials, and local party cadres. But it is clear that without the active support of legitimate organizations at the grass roots, persuasion would not be easy. As Jocelyn Alexander notes, educating villagers on the virtues of the program did not include consulting them on the planning of their new living spaces. In some cases, promises to provide services to villagers who moved shaded into threats to withhold them from villagers who did not.[65] District councilors, suspicious of the initiatives of central state experts, not only failed to "mobilize and educate" local citizens, but withheld council cooperation. The *Herald* of 22 May 1989 carried a story of opposition to a planned "model village" in Chikamba, in the Zvimba communal land. When the plan had been proposed in 1984, people had seemed to be willing to participate and residential stands had been pegged. Now, however, they were objecting; they wanted larger stands; they demanded that the graves of their ancestors not be disturbed; they demanded to be allowed to remain in their old homes. What better example that villagers had recognized this program as an arena for serious bargaining with the state? Most notably, the issues on which they sought to negotiate with the state were rooted solidly in questions of social identity—where they lived and who they were. In all these cases, rural citizens made it clear that an expansion of the public realm through a systematic reorientation of settled social practices depended not only on their cooperation and active participation, but indeed on a clearer definition of the state's own social responsibilities.

Conclusion

The picture sketched in this chapter shows that it is at the local level, in the structures and definitions of local communities, in local struggles and in control of local rights, that the prospects and politics of development are ultimately located. After a decade of independence, attempts by the postcolonial state to penetrate and define communities were still embryonic, and the authority of VIDCOs insecure. The language of conservation represented a key conduit for these attempts, underpinning both the resettlement program and the national land use strategy. It is here that the real piquancy of conservation as a political language is revealed. For conservation was not only a language of technical management, although management of resources and communities was its principal objective. It was also a language of legitimation whereby the government set out to lay the grounds for state incursions into the organization of rural society, in the absence of an already entrenched political language. It not only served as a substitute for such a language—drawing heavily on the understood terms of colonial technocratic control—but it also played a critical role in the attempts by the state to create one, by linking conservation management and control to new democratic, participatory, and cooperative grassroots development institutions at the community level. Ultimately, what is most politically intriguing about the language of conservation in independent Zimbabwe is the attempts of the state to route it through legitimate local organs of authority while at the same time using it to entrench that legitimacy and authority.

It is thus essential to recognize that the concept of "empowerment," offered to rural dwellers as the lodestar of development, applies implicitly to the state itself. In a narrow sense, the state sought to secure the economic incorporation and empowerment of rural dwellers. At the broadest level, it sought to inculcate an idea of citizenship, which entails the political empowerment of both individuals and the state. Land policy aimed not simply to remake rural property regimes but also to remake communities and citizens. Consequently state authority cannot be taken as a given in debates about appropriate property regimes. The quality of citizenship and the quality of stateness are two sides of the same coin, and both were integrally implicated in the construction of property regimes and appropriate authorities. This helps to explain the predilection of state agencies with national policies and their reluctance to bend to local epistemes. From this perspective there is a broader sociological process of state building at stake than is captured in arguments about the socialization of bureaucrats or their peculiar professional rationality.[66] It is in this broader processual context, in all its complex political manifestations, that state-peasant negotiations and rural social change must be understood.

From the discussion in this chapter we can cull several general conclusions, which I shall elaborate in the next chapter. First, the struggle for the definition of community was by no means resolved by state efforts to restructure rural property regimes. Second, the inseparability of popular empowerment and state empowerment shows that the state cannot be wished away in processes of social transformation. A strict distinction between the state on the one hand and the community or citizen on the other cannot be sustained in the construction of development strategies, for the state ultimately underwrites the wider public realm into which rural communities are incorporated. Thus a common institutional and discursive ground is essential for state construction. Finally, agrarian strategy alone could not provide a sufficient political-ideological basis for either rural development or state-building efforts. The relations between the state and peasant communities were more variegated than those specific relations that ran through the land. The inextricable links between economic development, social incorporation, political control, and social change demand that debates over appropriate property regimes can be sensibly conducted only in the context of "integrated" development strategies, both agrarian and nonagrarian; the predilection of states to separate these policy areas suggests that this point is not as obvious as it may appear. In this light we can now consider Zimbabwe's nonagrarian rural development strategies, which focused on community development articulated in a language of self-reliance and cooperation.

8

The Quest for Hegemony
Community Development and Self-Reliance

In its efforts to manage rural society and to embed state presence in the countryside, the Zimbabwe government went beyond agrarian strategies to policies that addressed the issue of
citizenship through local government and social development.
These efforts offer both intriguing parallels with agrarian policy and striking comparisons with the colonial regime's strategies of the 1960s and 1970s. They reveal the ambiguities of
state construction in the countryside arising out of the tensions between social control and social incorporation, the dependence of the government on the cooperation and participation of rural citizens, and its attempts to both secure the state
as the arbiter of social provision as well as to locate accountability elsewhere. Moreover, the state appealed once again to
concepts of community development, cooperation, and self-
reliance to moralize state-peasant relations and secure state
hegemony.

Social scientists studying the state have tended to give
ZANU(PF)'s community development rhetoric rather short
shrift, partly perhaps because the government itself appears to

have marginalized such policies in favor of more obvious service ministries, such as education and health. Yet this presents a puzzling paradox, for community development remains the central appeal of the government to rural citizens for structuring social provision and sociopolitical accountability. Even major education and health initiatives, such as adult literacy, preschools, and village health programs were incorporated into community development institutions. Indeed, these institutions provided the nexus for state-directed social provision and a society-based national culture. Though the government did pour an impressive amount of resources into education and health care to secure the state's role as preeminent provider of public goods, it could not build its relationship with rural citizens entirely on largesse, and it needed different resources to pursue its social management and rural development projects. Through community development initiatives cast in terms of self-reliance and cooperation the government sought to link its objectives of political and economic management with concepts of political inclusion and participation, and thereby to mold and structure relations between the state and rural communities. These initiatives played a crucial role in postindependence state making.

The postindependence government couched "self-reliance" and "community development" in a social-transformatory rhetoric that sought to both embed the state in rural localities and shift the responsibility for social provision onto local populations. Fundamentally, self-reliance policies were the response of a fiscally weak and politically insecure state to the social management imperatives sketched in chapter 6. With the economy in the doldrums, the government sought a development policy that would contain potential social conflicts. While locating the state at the crux of social development, it wanted also to reduce central state responsibility for financing and implementing development projects. Further, it needed to convince rural citizens that it represented a qualitatively different social order to its colonial predecessor, and a qualitatively different concept of citizenship (as well as secure the party's political base). Self-reliance provided the core of a political discourse through which it could link these tasks and negotiate control of social life with rural populations. But, as we shall see, this initiative was always fractured. On the ground, self-reliance strategies reflected the state's low capacity to manage economic development in the countryside. Within the state, the vision was fragmented by interministerial tensions over the control of development, and by party leaders' own preoccupations with accumulation, political support, and gendered politics. These conditions brought overwhelming cumulative pressures to bear on local institutions as vehicles for founding national identities, and severely undermined the state's quest for hegemony.

From the outset the government's ability to establish the state as the arbiter of social provision was tightly constrained. As it became increasingly clear that the unemployment rate was uncontrollable and that the state would have to extend its provisions to absorb the surplus population in the rural areas, the government sought a policy for generating a rural market base and stabilizing the rural population outside of agricultural employment. Its policy approach, based on rural growth points, was an almost exact replica of colonial policies of the 1970s. Together with the policies of cooperative development and resettlement, growth points would "facilitate in the creation and maintenance of high levels of productive employment in small- to medium-scale manufacturing and commercial establishments; thereby stemming rural-urban exodus of able-bodied manpower, and raise incomes and standards of living of rural people in line with the Government policy of 'Growth with Equity.'"[1] But returns on the policy were small. As before independence, private sector response was minimal without a preexisting rural consumer market, which private organizations thought it was up to state policy to generate. Yet the government lacked adequate financial and human power resources to plan and promote development investment in the rural areas. The Public Sector Investment Programme (PSIP), which was the main source of state funding, was chronically overstretched. The Small Enterprises Development Corporation—set up to promote and accelerate the development of commerce and industry in the rural areas and small towns by providing loan funding and business training—was understaffed, undercapitalized, and inefficient.[2] Under these circumstances, the state's ability to restructure national labor and consumer markets or to manage the economic and political development of rural society remained insecure.

In this context, the government turned to self-reliance as a stabilizing strategy, placing heavy dependence on the rural population to undertake and manage their own development. Self-reliance strategy had two aspects, both of which reflected a remarkable congruence with the objectives of colonial community development policy: (1) construction and development of infrastructure to improve the quality of rural life; and (2) generation of off-farm economic activity to stimulate local cash liquidity. Thus, state management of rural society and self-reliance were intimately connected.

But self-reliance was also presented as a core concept of social transformation. The 1982 annual report for the Ministry of Community Development and Women's Affairs (MCDWA) declared that

> Community Development in our context is directed at supporting democratic socioeconomic changes at the grass-roots because our national socialist goal demands this. Our special task has been the promotion of self-reliant projects through which the communities can develop and utilise local resources such as land, water and manpower to meet their needs.[3]

Thus understood, self-reliance had both an economic and a political meaning, for it tied the economic empowerment of rural dwellers intimately to their political incorporation. The ultimate aim of self-reliance policy was to promote economic activity, self-sufficiency, and stability in rural development, and at the same time to create a strong political base for the party state in rural areas.[4] These objectives depended on, aimed at, and created the need for cooperation and coordination between state agencies and local communities. The state needed to "bring in" rural communities, to establish some hold over local resources, and to involve the local population in the development process both materially and psychologically. Thus the ideas of citizenship and political empowerment of both individuals and the state were at stake.

Self-Reliance, Citizenship, and the Village

Following the government's emphasis that "the industrialisation strategy favours an approach which relies primarily on local financial resources and domestically produced raw materials," the Provincial Development Plans stressed the need to promote the concept of self-reliance in rural communities.[5] In general this objective took the form of encouraging local investment and training in small-scale industries and cooperatives. The keystone of this strategy was a cooperatives program that aimed to provide both the institutional and the normative core of managed rural development and "a vehicle for the promotion of the Government's socialist ideology and for the creation of an egalitarian society."[6] A Ministry of Cooperatives was created to promote cooperative ventures in both agricultural and nonagricultural production and retailing. The critical mobilizing idiom was self-reliance. In the words of one senior politician: "the government wants co-operatives to be formed in the spirit of self-reliance with help from elsewhere coming only in instances where it is very necessary and unavoidable."[7] There were two main advantages in linking cooperatives and self-reliance. First, cooperatives embodied the economic values of self-reliance that reduced the burden on state coffers. Second, cooperatives embodied the democratic and participatory values of self-reliance by "discouraging the individualistic set up" and vitiating the effects of the capitalist cash nexus at the periphery of the market—"co-operation," the government declared, "means self-reliance." The vehicle for this oft-stated vision, in which socioeconomic transformation and sociocultural transformation were inextricably intertwined, would be the Model B cooperative resettlement schemes. But, as we saw in chapter 7, these schemes never became a significant part of the resettlement program.[8]

The government also constructed links between the language of cooperatives and the language of community development in its approach to state building and social transformation. S. T. Agere, Under-Secretary for Community Development in MCDWA, argued:

> As a development strategy co-operatives are a form of "bottom-up" approach in which major initiatives, policy and decision-making and control of activities are undertaken by the members themselves, within the overall national development goals. . . . Through community development, co-operatives are a useful way of transforming people's minds in that they facilitate the altering of habits, morals and ways of thinking which have resulted from years of exploitation, oppression and social conditions favouring the desire for private enterprise.

Thus, community development "plays a crucial role in facilitating the social transformation of our society."[9] This "crucial role" was to provide a vehicle for the populist mediation of relations between local communities and the state, representing a constant presence and reminder of the state's concern for local development and transformation, and spearheading the hegemonic incorporation of the rural population in a state-led national-popular identity. Under the Unity government, the department of cooperatives (previously in the Ministry of Lands, Agriculture and Rural Resettlement) was incorporated into the Ministry of Community and Co-operative Development and Women's Affairs. The idea of "self-reliance" was intended to imply a new, progressive relationship between state and community, in which the tensions between antistatist development orientations and state direction were dissolved in the integration of state and society. As Mugabe put it, "to us, self-reliance is . . . an empty slogan unless it means hard work on the part of a people committed to a definite cause of national up-lift."[10] In a significant way, therefore, postcolonial community development, although institutionally very similar to its colonial predecessor, was ideologically its opposite. At the same time, we can discern the ethico- political connection between conservation and community development. For the politics of self-reliance, like the politics of conservation, had a basis in both political language and political institutions.

The main ideological thrust of community development was to create a sense of empowerment among rural citizens, as well as a sense of involvement in and solidarity with an organic-statist sociopolitical order. This aim was admirably conveyed by the Community Development Manual *Let's Build Zimbabwe Together:* "Development is not about projects, it is about building people, so that they can build a future for themselves."[11] In formulating this vision the manual set the thrust of postcolonial community development directly against its colonial precursor which, as we saw, stressed the importance of projects. Notably, the manual not only promoted participation but was itself the product of an extensively participatory production process, especially at the district level. In this vein, state ideology set out along two political trajectories to construct state

hegemony. First, it distanced itself from the predatory character of the colonial state. Second, it promoted specific social development strategies to enhance family and community life.
Together, these strands advanced a notion of citizenship as
embodied in participation in the community, and self-determination through the community.

In the first strand of the argument, the community development manual deployed a general critique of colonial political impositions on local communities:

> In Rhodesia, village people were held back because the govern-
> ment used top down, one way communication, and people were
> denied a voice in the running of the country. In Zimbabwe, the gov-
> ernment is trying to promote two-way communication through
> the development committees, as in order for development to take
> place, ideas and information should be continually exchanged.

The manual attempted not only to establish a clean break with
colonial times but to demonstrate that self-reliance and self-
control were the hallmarks of precolonial society and, in a
sense, the "natural order": "Before colonial times, this village
was large and self-reliant. People grew a lot of food and produced all the things that they needed. They had enough land
and made the most important decisions about their lives."
This state of affairs having been destroyed by colonialism, the
book set out to articulate a new mythology of regaining their
real history and heritage. This was a nuanced ideological project that was powerfully reminiscent of the ideas and concepts
of earlier theorists of African Socialism who had linked a regaining of history to the nationalizing of that heritage and to
the ruling group's ideology of transformation. In short, it involved making an appeal to traditions, while taking over and
transforming those traditions.[12]

The important point about this nationalizing ideological
project, however, is that the "rediscovery" of tradition was

aimed not at superseding local tradition and identity, but at linking local and national identity through the community. To entrench a sense of self-empowerment, to mobilize communities and to build the state into village life, the most serious institutional political focus was placed on the VIDCOs and WADCOs. The community development manual linked the concepts of self-reliance and self-control, to be coordinated by the VIDCO: "In the past, your village was forgotten. Everything important happened in the big towns. In the new Zimbabwe this is changing. Your VIDCO is becoming important, an essential part of a new nation."[13] Part of the Department of Culture's brief was to build a Culture House in each district to "serve as the focal point for the cultural activities of the district." These Culture Houses would place artifacts and objects of art and culture "within the reach of the people," provide a library and documentation center for local histories, and offer displays of cultural artifacts from other areas. Thus, the project involved expanding local knowledge and local histories to include new categories, and to transform the nature of existing imagined communities.

Carol Duncan has noted that, by appropriating and organizing cultural symbols in their displays, state museums can be used to demonstrate the civic virtue of the state.[14] The Culture Houses of Zimbabwe were intended to demonstrate to the local people that the state is at one with their symbols and values, as part of an effort to incorporate the locality into a larger public realm. Obversely, the broader public realm would become part of that which is culturally authentic. In this sense, cultural institutions were to become, in Dawson Munjeri's words, "the central artery of communication." By demonstrating the oneness of the state with local culture, these initiatives would set the postcolonial state directly in opposition to its predecessor.[15] The Department of Culture held that "there is . . . merit in devising a system which is capable of taking into account the important role played by the nation's cultural values and concepts in accordance with the socio-economic and political imperatives of our new socialist order." Its role, therefore, was to "foster the existence of a living cultural heritage through promotion, development and preservation of all aspects of visual, literary, and performing arts" by "implementing a programme of mass participation in a diversity of cultural activities in order to promote a national cultural identity."[16] This incorporative project included not only cultural education in traditional history, customs, folklore, and religion, but also the promotion of arts and crafts through the formation of arts and crafts cooperatives. Thus, it both appealed to tradition and preexisting community ties, and mobilized people into the marketplace, a linking of public realms that state rhetoric on national cultural development frequently stressed. This spirit was captured most powerfully in the presentation of the National Arts Council of Zimbabwe Bill (1985) which would, inter alia, promote

> the consolidation of the process of re-discovery of cultural identity by offering opportunities for the broad masses of the people to present and promote their own culture; the propagation of our national cultural heritage through the provision of funds for festivals and exhibitions at district, provincial and national levels; and the enhancement of self-identity of our people from the community to the national level and the promotion of community solidarity and national unity through the organisation of community and national arts festivals.

The first Culture House was opened in Wedza in 1986.

The second strand of the ideological project—social development strategies aimed at family and community life—set out to secure the state as the ideological focus of citizenship and community welfare, and as the final arbiter of the relationship between private and public. At the national level, education and health policies were of course mainstays of this project. But they were buttressed by the National Pre-Schools program, explicitly linked to a desire to free women "to participate more effectively in development activities," and the Adult Literacy Campaign, which promised to bring the benefits of modernity to a wider public.[17] Markedly more women participated in both these programs than men. At the local level, the grassroots cadres of MCDWA—community development workers and home economics demonstrators—represented the spearhead of state presence in family and community social life. They coordinated the activities of MCDWA in promoting income-generating initiatives as well as promoting community education in basic health practices, home economics, nutrition, child care, family planning, civic education, the philosophy of community development, and the like. The impulse behind the project was twofold: on the one hand, to improve the quality of life in the rural areas; on the other hand, "To develop among the communities a sense of citizenship, patriotism, collective participation, and an increased awareness of their democratic rights."[18] Most broadly, it would embed the state in local communities.

Community development workers, although full-time government employees, worked from their homes in or close to the village. Home economics demonstrators were locally selected women who had to be "a resident of the community to be served and be aware of the government development goals."[19] In 1984 village health workers, previously under the Ministry of Health and well regarded by the rural population, were brought under MCDWA and merged with home economics demonstrators to form a category of village community workers (VCWs) in order to consolidate and unify the community-oriented welfare role of the state.[20] Traditional midwives were brought into the primary health care program in order to "strike a balance" between traditional practice and modern medical practice. VCWs would also be trained to guide VIDCOs and WADCOs in the planning process. At the same time, "Under the villagisation programme, the VCW would become accountable to the community through the elected Village Development Committee."[21] In short, the government would have pulled off the delicate political maneuver of securing the state as the final arbiter of social provision while at the same time mediating social accountability through the local community.

Seen in this light, "community development" provided substantive political connections between the rural socioeconomic order and the sociocultural order, between commercialization and cooperation, between state and community, and between private and public spheres. In chapter 7 we saw the connection between conservation and villagization. The connection between community development and villagization can now be established. To engineer a broader political-ideological transformation, the villagization strategy set out to revise the relationship between private and public space in the community, and thereby to reshape the concept of the community as the guiding principle of social organization. A core component, as we have seen, was the penetration of social institutions that managed common resources. Additionally, within the villages the VIDCOs would expand the realm of public institutions and public discourse that underpins the quality of citizenship, while they also mitigated the appearance of urban domination from a distant seat of government. At the same time, they would establish an institutional-ideological forum for private citizens to congregate as a constituted public whose rights and membership in the community are underwritten by state-centered public authority.

This restructuring of the public realm also had a spatial dimension, on which I commented briefly in chapter 7. That discussion can be extended. Villagization would not only "rationalize" use of space in the village, it would reorient the settled social practices of villagers in such a way that institutional and ideological spaces underwritten by the *state* came to embody the public realm. One of the first community projects that MCDWA encouraged in rural villages (under the auspices of the VIDCO) was the construction of a community hall to house the VIDEC and to become the physical and institutional focal point of village life:

> Government plans that each VIDCO will eventually have a village development centre, VIDEC, to co-ordinate all village development. The VIDEC should be well situated, and the buildings should be multi-purpose. As a basis for village development the best use will be made of the land, and natural resources will be carefully managed. People will have full control over their own development, and development at different levels will be efficiently co-ordinated.[22]

Together with the Culture House, the community hall and VIDEC would take over the cultural and ritual spaces of the community. More than a social meeting place, it would also provide a venue for income-generating activities (craftwork, weaving, sewing, etc.) and community-level court proceedings. By becoming the locus of legal ritual, it would become the sociolegal hub of the village. This is significant not only because legal institutions provide essential conduits for defining social concepts of Right and rights of citizenship, but also because in times of social change such institutions become the focus for cultural struggles. As we shall see below, such cultural struggles did in fact erupt when, in an effort to inculcate a concept of citizenship that would both transcend and incorporate the community, the government declared its intention to reconstitute the differential holds of customary and statutory law over rural people's lives through legal reform of personal and family laws pertaining to gender, such as marriage, maintenance, and the age of majority.

It would be inaccurate to claim that the Zimbabwe government had set out to systematically and comprehensively overturn the worldview of rural villagers. But the vision propagated within the ministry was a radical one, which, as Bourdieu puts it, "provides the base for symbolic struggles for the power to produce and to impose a vision of the legitimate world."[23] The standardization of spacing arrangements (including the institutionalization of law and legal ritual, meetings, and even income generation schemes within the community hall) did aim at disrupting local patterns of arranging social space and transforming local concepts of property rights. The rearrangement of public life would give social activities a new focus and form. Public authority, underwritten by the state, would provide the basis for defining and securing a concept of membership (qua citizen) in the community. On this foundation the relationship between state and society could be reordered and the character of citizenship be reconceptualized. In this sense it was part of a state effort to secure authoritative schemes of classification for the social world.

The institutional conduit for this imaginative political-ideological project was to be the VIDCO. The administration, implementation, and coordination of the VIDCO and WADCO structures was entrusted to MCDWA, though district councils remained with the ministry of local government. Following the Prime Minister's Directive in February 1984, MCDWA was given the mandate to coordinate all development activities and government extension workers at the village and ward levels.[24] On paper, this gave the ministry considerable power to pursue its political-ideological tasks "to conscientise both men and women to the overall objectives of the new socialist order" and "to mobilise Zimbabweans to take charge of their own transformation at the grassroots level and to make the best use of assistance from Government."[25] This ministry became responsible for regulating almost all nonagrarian forms of penetration and contact between the state and rural communities at the grassroots level. Its mediating role gave MCDWA a base to expand its power.

Community development planners took their responsibilities very seriously. The community development manual *Let's Build Zimbabwe Together* stressed that the new development structures "enable people to take control of their own development" and "to learn self-management and self-government, while improving co-ordination." The gap between government and people, the manual argued, could be broken down through these structures and through decentralization: top-down control (the "overcentralization" often associated with improved technical programs) could be replaced with bottom-up control, so that people might feel that the power center was not so far away and that they were not necessarily at its mercy.[26] The driving principle of this vision was to move away from a "basic-needs" approach to development, and to politicize local communities by promoting a comprehensive notion of socialist development in which local communities would take power to themselves. In an interview, one planning official in the ministry remarked that the ministry recognized and promoted the idea that it was potentially the most subversive ministry because it recognized and promoted the power of the local community, even against the government. Thus conceived, the political-ideological thrust of self-reliance was to supersede the problem- and project-orientation of earlier community development and to present development as primarily a political process. On this account, the Zimbabwe revolution rested not with the Zimbabwe state but with the Zimbabwean people. As Robert Mugabe himself put it: "When we say the people are the makers of their own history we do not mean it only in a political sense. We also mean it in the sense in which the people are the active, indispensible, agents in the transformation of the material circumstances of life."[27]

However, this vision expressed the central conundrum of postcolonial state construction: the grounding of state authority in the countryside depended on the ability of state agents to create or to reorient social institutions to provide the framework for hegemonic strategies; but any attempt to rearrange the underlying structures of local power and combine local and national cultures engaged a range of economic, political, and cultural conflicts within communities to which the state enjoyed limited access. These social conflicts were rooted in stratification along lines of income, land access, gender, and generation. For two reasons, state hegemonic strategies had to address these conflicts. First, the politics of citizenship requires the state to control, and ultimately suppress, social conflicts in such a way that the state is secured as the arbiter of social provision in a national political community. Second, since some common understanding of social security is a core element of any political community's moral economy, these strategies had to take account of risk-ameliorating institutions, especially among the poor, at the local level. Thus, Zimbabwe's revolution could not ultimately rest with the state; but neither could it rest with the people.

The strategy of community development through self-reliance expressed the government's response to this conundrum, which also explains why that strategy came to focus on the task of "capturing" rural women and rural youths. As I noted in chapter 5, the coalescence of social change and political transition in the liberation war produced a fragmentation of social authority in rural Zimbabwe. These conditions impelled the postindependence regime to step in and stabilize and reorient social institutions within the village. In doing so, it was driven also by ZANU(PF)'s national-populist ideology that conflated social transformation and progress. This was reflected not only in the replacement of chiefs' judicial powers by community courts but also in legal reforms designed to address women's status under customary marriage and inheritance laws.

Rural women and youths were important social groups because they were preponderant in the countryside and because they were considered the "most disadvantaged Zimbabweans,'" at the margins of the national capitalist market and thus the most vulnerable to the breakdown of family-oriented and home-oriented production structures.[28] Both ZANU(PF) and PF-ZAPU saw them also as important political constituencies. Several scholars have noted that by the 1980s the rights of both women and youths to land were circumscribed, partly because of the inheritance structures and partly because of land shortages.[29] The stress on youths waiting for land to became available was exacerbated by the slow growth of employment opportunities. As education increasingly became a requisite for access to scarce jobs, the rural poor felt the rising costs of schooling very keenly. In hard times, young and female-headed households were most prone to a "reproduction squeeze." Yet, as social groups, rural women and youths had emerged from the liberation war with some political momentum. Under these conditions, while "capturing" rural youths and rural women were not the most prominent development projects of the postcolonial state, they were critical precisely because they operated at the fringes of agrarian development strategy. By targeting those social groups least addressed by agrarian strategies, and least involved in migrancy, the state could—at least potentially—exploit significant opportunities to penetrate rural society and at the same time extend sociopolitical stability in the countryside, along the same lines as its colonial predecessor. Marriage laws and inheritance laws, which regulated most intimately the local social relations of property, production, and authority, provided a specific nexus for the state to negotiate with rural citizens the legitimate and appropriate realms of state regulation. This was also the reason for designating one position on the VIDCO for each of these cohorts. The central point, however, was to mobilize these social constituencies into self-reliant development projects so that the state could shift the costs of providing social services onto rural citizens themselves, and define its own responsibilities for the supply of public goods quite narrowly.

Accordingly, government development strategies stressed the role of rural women and youths in "spearheading the socialist transformation." Notably, the Ministry of Community and Co-operative Development followed up the publication of the Community Development manual *Let's Build Zimbabwe Together* with a series of similar volumes titled *Building Whole Communities*. The purpose of these volumes was precisely to popularize the state's hegemonic project of reordering agrarian social relations so as to inculcate a concept of citizenship that would both transcend and incorporate the community,

Figure 1

Hegemonic Strategy in Rural Communities

| | | **State Action** | | |
		Ideological	**Procedural**	**Institutional**
Socio-Political Realm	**Property**	Conservation 'Progress' 'Science'	Re-Structuring Physical Space Local By-Laws	VIDCO Grazing Schemes CAMPFIRE
	Culture	Merging national & local cultures	Re-orienting village spaces (Community hall, etc)	VIDCO VIDEC
	Public goods & accountability	Community Development 'self-reliance' 'Empowerment'	Legal change Income-generation Literacy, etc.	VIDCO VCW

and root state authority in the countryside. We may now consider how this project fared on the ground.

Unmanaged Development:
Self-Reliance on the Ground

Stimulating rural economic growth and transforming citizenship while structuring and managing national consumer and labor markets was an imposing challenge for the insecure post-independence regime. As we have already noted, there is always a tension between a state's hegemonic objectives and its managerial objectives. Given the multiplicity of political tasks that the government needed to perform under severe fiscal constraints, it is not surprising that the realities of rural development did not conform to the transformative goals of community development and self-reliance. The government showed a consistent predilection for rural control. Rural development lagged, state presence in the countryside remained administrative and often subordinated to the party, and social authority continued to be fragmented. However, by examining the ways in which the realities of rural development became separated from the transformative project of self-reliance, we can illuminate both the character of the state and the politics of state construction in a neocolonial setting. Again, it is useful to focus on the policy arenas of income generation, rural stabilization, and local governance, which constitute the main nonagrarian conduits of state-peasant relations.

Cooperatives and the Informal Sector

The cooperative vision that drove state rhetoric bore little resemblance to the reality of self-help and self-reliance projects on the ground. Although the number of registered cooperatives rose from 370 in 1980 (all in the agricultural marketing and supply sector) to 1,832 in 1988, at the end of that period 34 percent were not functioning at all. As a senior official in the Department of Co-operatives pointed out: "In many cases, most of what are called co-ops are not. They are just groups of people with an income-generating project masquerading as co-operatives. This gives a bad name to the movement." The establishment of agricultural producer cooperatives proceeded slowly and inefficiently largely because of the absence of clear official policy, maladministration in the Ministry of Co-operatives (which led its incorporation in MCDWA in 1987), and the logistical burdens of planning and implementation.[30] Throughout the 1980s, the government based its policy on the 1956 Co-operatives Act, although NGOs called spiritedly for a national cooperatives plan "to spearhead the socialist trans-formation process." In 1989 the Minister of Co-operative and Community Development acknowledged that, given the mul-tifaceted problems facing cooperative groups, their employ-ment- and income-generating objectives appeared "remote, il-lusive and unattainable."[31]

To overcome these difficulties, the government shifted its attention to expanding and developing the already existing informal sector.[32] This sector was seen to have specific advan-tages, including the ease of entry, reliance on indigenous re-sources, family ownership of enterprises, small-scale operations, labor-intensive technology adapted to local conditions, skills acquired outside the formal schooling system, and unregulated and competitive markets. But for a government interested in managed economic development there were also disadvan-tages in depending on the informal sector. It is difficult to reg-ulate activities in that sector, either in terms of their role in a national market or in terms of their revenue-generating po-tential. Moreover, these activities are by their very nature lim-ited. Rural enterprises tended to operate intermittently and to find their markets locally among low-income groups. Thus, this approach did not generate a significant rural commodity market, nor did it advance the state's broad political concern to refashion rural production and land-holding patterns. Indeed, it highlighted the fact that the state could not build and regulate an economic and political order on an informal economy that remained substantially beyond its jurisdiction. These conditions emphasized the fragility of the rural economy, the tenuousness of the rural population's participation in formal economic structures, as well as the state's loose grip on those structures. Such fragility, endemic in African countries, could facilitate the disengagement of rural populations from public institutions. Furthermore, development officials regarded the existence of a well-serviced rural market in consumer goods as an important facet of attempts to modify the ways in which rural people think about their land, in order to establish new forms of petty capitalist production. It was therefore not insignificant that the principal targets for self-help and self-reliance programs and projects were the most marginalized constituencies: women and youths.

"Capturing" Rural Youths and Rural Women

State efforts to establish a hold on local social institutions through policies targeting rural youths and women followed the same logic as the RF government's initiatives. In the context of a rural strategy that neglected the rural poor, they aimed to mobilize youths into rural employment to keep them in the countryside, and to mobilize women into greater productivity to stimulate the rural cash economy. By encouraging self-reliance, they would also relieve the state from pouring resources into the rural areas. Under the guidance of the Ministry of Youth, Sport and Culture (MYSC) and MCDWA, they would bring sociocultural transformation together with self-reliant rural development. As Prime Minister Mugabe told the nation in 1982, these ministries were "charged with the task of organising our communities so they can be components of the machinery for consolidating the people's power through various communal activities, production and construction programmes, intellectual, physical, emotional and moral development. . . ."[33] But once again, these proved weak strategies for consolidating rural hegemony. Their failures are instructive because they hinged mainly on a political imperative to which the colonial administration had not been subject—the ruling party's need for electoral allies in the countryside. In different ways, these initiatives succumbed to the determination of a politically insecure ZANU leadership to place party political support above the interests of state hegemony.

The rapid increase in rural youth placed rural job creation high on the development agenda. The government accepted that job creation for youth "falls squarely and entirely on the shoulders of the government," and set out to "mobilise and organise youth into meaningful and manageable structures, and to establish self-reliance projects."[34] But its efforts were lackluster. MYSC's main task was to provide training in income-generating skills (such as agriculture, building, carpentry, home economics, book-keeping, office practice, typing, and physical education), but the ministry was characterized by inefficiency and maladministration, with hints of extensive corruption and self-aggrandizement by senior officials. It had a tiny staff, minuscule budget, and a limited operation. The main burden of funding and implementing the strategy fell to district and provincial development committees and to NGOs. The amount of funds either set aside for or invested by the state in schemes to generate youth employment was consequently small and created very few jobs.[35] In a passionate critique, the 1985 Nangati report on youth opportunities argued that the government's commitment to job creation for rural youths was undermined by its complicity with private sector interests in maintaining a handy reserve army of the unemployed. As a result, the training programs tended both to keep rural youths in the countryside and to maintain the "uneven development between urban and rural areas."[36]

But Nangati's radical political economy did not take account of the political role of this initiative. The principal mechanism for alleviating growing unemployment among youths was the Youth Brigade, a grass-roots organization with some half a million members that operated under the auspices of MYSC. The stated tasks of the organization were to instill discipline and responsibility among the youth, to inculcate loyalty and allegiance to the state of Zimbabwe, to impart skills, and to create jobs for youths through income-generating projects. Membership in the brigade was a requirement for admission to a youth training center. But the Youth Brigade's main activity was to promote the ZANU(PF) Youth Wing. According to reports, this interpenetration of state and party at the district and local levels mainly took the form of Youth Brigade members coercing citizens to buy ZANU(PF) party cards and to attend ZANU(PF) rallies.[37] These activities frequently reflected youths' use of the state and party names to pursue their own local interests rather than the will of the central party or government leadership. Rural youths experiencing the stress of long waits for land and narrowing employment opportunities became zealous party cadres in the hope of creating opportunities for themselves. The leadership allowed such local initiative free rein because it had neither the ability, under the circumstances, nor the political will to discipline youths. Despite its insistence that the Youth Brigade movement was "a national organisation, sponsored and promoted by the State of Zimbabwe for the benefit of all Zimbabwean youth," the government clearly saw the Youth Brigade's role in mobilizing the youth for national development as inseparable from the movement toward a one-party state. In some rural areas youths took on policing duties, providing a "vigilance" that was lauded by the ruling party but considered by some outside of the party as part of a "party onslaught." In areas where people lived in fear of being harassed by the Youth Brigades or the ZANU(PF) Youth Wing, or where youths ransacked and burned opposition party offices—especially in Matabeleland—there was considerable substance to this charge.[38]

Thus, the youth development strategy rapidly followed the familiar postcolonial pattern of bringing the party within the state rather than embedding a "universal" state in society. It was a bleak and somewhat paradoxical outcome. Both the severe shortage of training vacancies for youths and the limited number of job opportunities for graduates of training schools resulted in graduates "getting frustrated and drifting into antisocial activities."[39] The party used these conditions to build its own patronage base by shaping access to job opportunities. Thus, as an effort to penetrate and bind a civil society, based on economic and sociopolitical integration, youth policy did not offer an auspicious base for state building.

The strategy for rural self-reliance through income-generating schemes focused mainly on the participation of women. This concentration was not simply an outcome of the colonial legacy of support for women's groups and the politicizing role of women in the liberation war. Like its colonial predecessor, the government recognized that women play a pivotal role in the domestic and local economy. Their active participation in development initiatives was essential both to growth with equity and to strengthening the rural cash economy. Migrancy had an enormous impact on rural social relations, and female-headed households were frequently among the poorest. As elsewhere in rural Africa, women carried an enormous and varied labor burden, but occupied a subordinate and dependent position in controlling domestic accumulation and investment. Under patriarchal authority structures, their access to land was constrained, especially where land pressure was heavy. Their access to agricultural credit was restricted, and they tended to receive less extension services. A survey carried out in 1982 reported that many women resented their lack of control of production inputs and land, especially where men did not contribute to the generation of a surplus, and that this reduced their incentive for development work. These conditions led the government to establish an explicit link in state policy language between women's rights and women's productivity: to boost women's rights would also unleash great humanpower resources.[40]

As Sam Moyo has pointed out, the increasing number of landless and destitute rural men and women, "most of whom depended on the patriarchal benevolence of kin," and had little chance of finding wage employment, increased the opportunities for greater labor exploitation of the poor.[41] Income-generating schemes provided an avenue by which both the state and women themselves tried to alleviate that situation. On the state's side, the strategy was closely linked to a declared objective of eliminating practices and norms in customary law that discriminate against women, as part of transforming the polity. Rural women, for their part, were ready to undertake efforts to ameliorate their poor economic position within the household economy and the local economy. Most of the courses run at MCDWA's national training centers in project planning and management, marketing, credit, bookkeeping, and the like were for women, and the vast majority of projects were undertaken by rural women. A third of all nonagricultural enterprises in the communal areas involved clothing—tailoring, knitting, and crocheting—and 20 percent were primary processing and manufacturing operations like beer brewing, basket making, baking, grain milling, and leather tanning. The most popular schemes, by a considerable margin, were women's clubs and savings clubs, which helped women to overcome shortages of finance, equipment, and material. After independence, membership in such clubs grew rapidly under the auspices of the nongovernmental Savings Development Movement (with 5,700 clubs in 1983) and MCDWA (2,500 clubs). MCDWA encouraged these clubs partly because the ministry was itself severely hampered by financial constraints.[42] In fact the government looked upon savings clubs and informal credit as the essential financial underpinning of rural development initiatives.

Although it generated significant incomes for the families concerned, this approach severely limited self-reliance as a hegemonic strategy, partly for its reliance on women and the poor. It demonstrated that, while wealthier more productive peasant farmers had ready access to government credit, poorer farmers and rural people were required to generate their own. But in many communal areas where income-generating projects were viewed as a way to develop the agricultural base, the resource base for investing in such projects was poor due to a dwindling agricultural resource base. For poor women, liberation from intrahousehold dependency was tied in many cases to greater day-to-day drudgery. They participated for the support group, comradeship, and the opportunity to carve out at least some autonomy and control over their own lives. But it remained very difficult for development to achieve the community development bureaucracy's goal of transcending a basic-needs orientation of rural development as women's groups struggled to keep going in the face of debilitating shortages of finance, equipment, and expertise. Large numbers of projects failed because the government did not provide seed money. By the end of the decade "community development" contained a debilitating paradox in many areas: the rural poor had become marginal to "self-reliance" as understood in state policy; but self-help had become their most reliable strategy for survival. Meanwhile, the government tried to restrict its own responsibilities by appealing to self-help, informal credit, and local participation.[43] In short, the self-reliance strategy on the ground provided neither a conduit for rural citizens to secure resources from the government nor to negotiate the definition of *public* goods in the new social order.

In the absence of a clear and coordinated state commitment to the improvement of rural livelihoods, basic-needs projects remained the cornerstone of rural development work. This situation was very reminiscent of community development under the colonial regime: if rural communities were to enjoy the benefits of development, they should also bear the burdens of development and state responsibility should be mitigated. Yet this approach depended ultimately on the cooperation and energy of rural communities themselves. Despite a significant expansion of infrastructure,[44] it was an unpromising strategy for rural development and state construction, especially as the shrinking fiscal resources of the state, the slow progress of the resettlement program, and the effects of drought increased pressure on the regime to secure political allies in the countryside. Women and youths offered ready social cohorts for stabilizing rural society, but—beyond the crude coercive utility of the party youth—they did not offer useful political alliances.

In such circumstances, it became almost inevitable that the government's commitment to women's rights, always ambiguous, would dissipate. Just as it responded to agrarian pressure by shifting its economic resources away from the rural poor and toward wealthier peasants, it shifted its political resources away from women to men. Shaken by sustained and vociferous male opposition to proposed marriage, maintenance, and inheritance laws that would benefit women, the government clung to its male and patriarchal support base. It moved very gingerly in pressing through reforms, and by the end of the decade gender issues were being edged off the public agenda of transformation. Indeed, the ability of the state to implement family- and gender-based laws in a systematic fashion was always circumscribed. On the ground, as Donna Pankhurst notes, the letter of the law was not as important as its implementation, which was frequently circumvented by village or lineage leaders, or depended on court officers who were themselves chiefs or headmen. Many rural women, in fact, remained unaware of changes in their rights.[45] Despite criticism, customary courts continued to rule on rape cases, over which they had no jurisdiction. Consequently, the application of customary law and statutory law in the regulation of rural life remained a muddled affair. By the end of the decade much of the confidence expressed by rural women in the Zimbabwe Women's Bureau's 1981 report had ebbed away. The 1992 follow-up report suggested that a significant number of women understood their plight not in terms of government policy and male domination (as they had at the end of the colonial period), but in terms of cultural transgressions against ancestors or against traditional ways and beliefs, often inspired by the new laws. By the end of the decade, women's participation in income-generating schemes was declining.[46]

This was not an auspicious basis for state-building, for it left social authority at the local level fragmented and vulnerable to aggrandizement by local "big men." By leaving in place gendered patriarchal power relations but targeting women to undertake developmental collective action through self-reliance, the state failed to address the disjuncture between those who had local power and those to whom the tasks of empowerment fell. In effect, it expanded women's responsibilities for social reproduction but allowed their citizenship rights to lag behind. Women remained marginal in local political activity and development decision making. Many migrant workers forbade their wives from attending public development meetings as a way of maintaining household control. For female-headed households meetings were sometimes a prohibitive time investment. Women's labor often provided men with the opportunity to attend meetings and participate in discussions. Women who did attend meetings tended to be quiet as men argued the issues. Many women had to vote their husband's choice.[47] At the same time, much of the income-generating and savings work of women aimed at providing some discretionary income outside state and patrilineal control. Though women often put this income to household purposes, such as children's school fees or clothes, it was neither a household nor a community resource. In this sense, local self-reliance was not "community" development.

This outcome is not insignificant. Indeed, it illuminates a paradox of the Zimbabwean state construction project, during both the late colonial and the postcolonial periods. As I have noted, it is in the context of scarce resources that the government turned to women to refract accountability for social provision and thereby restructure state-society relations; but the context of scarce resources made such an effort politically unfeasible. As Susan Jacobs has noted, women in Zimbabwe have been treated as "class competitors" with men when it comes to access to resources.[48] As a result, postcolonial strategy was no more successful than colonial strategy, though for different reasons. Patriarchy and electoral politics went hand in hand. Self-reliance strategy in rural Zimbabwe did not mobilize a broadly based movement, as Kenya's Harambee did, through which local-level resources could be distributed under the umbrella of a national program, nor did it institutionalize a significant conduit through which rural citizens could bargain with the state for resource transfers. Rather, it left the principles of power and authority at the local level substantially intact, with the state continuing to play an external and unpredictable role.

With respect to the sociocultural role of law in state making, we can discern parallel tensions in agrarian-based and non-agrarian-based hegemonic strategies, which made it difficult to secure the overriding authority of the law at the local level. In agrarian strategies, as we saw, where the state targeted common property institutions, locals were expected to formulate bylaws whose epistemic weight was determined outside the community and which often conflicted with local cultural perceptions of nature and resources. In nonagrarian strategies, transforming the legal status of women in order to reorient rural society antagonized men. In a striking revisitation of arguments made by patriarchal authorities in the 1930s, this "problem" too was articulated in a normative public discourse that focused on the personal morals of "liberated" women. It was expressed most dramatically in regular, heavy-handed, and arbitrary antiprostitution campaigns by the Zimbabwe Republican Police. The 1986 Manicaland Provincial Development Plan spoke darkly, though unspecifically, about "attitudinal problems" among rural women, and a prominent female ZANU(PF) politician exhorted Zimbabwean women to "shun laziness, gossiping and drunkenness and devote their time to improving their living standards."[49] Thus, neither set of strategies was able to effectively reorient community identities and social relations in ways that would effectively place the "universalized" state at the center of public authority and social order.

In short, as a strategy for pursuing the multiple objectives of stabilizing rural society, incorporating the rural poor, and securing the state as the arbiter of social provision while also refracting the responsibility for expanding social services, "self-reliance" on the ground faced a daunting array of political obstacles and weaknesses. To the extent that state construction involves the definition of claims that citizens can make against the state, it showed little advance on its colonial predecessor. As a normative appeal for remoralizing state-peasant relations by empowering rural citizens to take control of their own destinies, self-reliance in practice had little to recommend it to resource-poor peasants. Yet the effect of this appeal depended very much on the ways in which it was deployed or mediated by local institutions of resource allocation and governance.

Revenue Generation and Institutional Development

The success of the government's hegemonic project depended on the ability of the regime to put in place the institutional framework capable of promoting socioeconomic and sociopolitical development. According to the postcolonial system of decentralized local government, administration and political representation and participation were intended to mesh most comprehensively at the level of the district council. As Robert Mugabe put it: "the local authorities in a lot of countries are the organs of power closest to the people. The paramount concern of these authorities we believe is the provision of essential services to the people. . . . to undertake their tasks effectively, local authorities must be based on, and fully reflect, the will of the people."[50] As in the colonial period, however, these intentions were inhibited by a weak institutional base. Rural citizens displayed a generalized apathy that politicians, officials and scholars have described as a "syndrome of dependency" whereby they expect government to do everything for them; "self-reliance" and "self-management" should aim to break this syndrome.[51] But it is a complex problem. As we have seen, the "apathy" that is its hallmark has a long history, rooted not in dependence but in anger and suspicion as well as a popular conviction that the state should live up to its responsibilities. Moreover, dependency is Janus-faced: it constrains the state just as it does rural citizens. Thus the "syndrome of dependency" must be understood in a broader processual and sociological sense of rural state building.

The capacity of councils to effectively promote local initiatives and proposals was constrained by the fact that final authority for planning lay with the central government. In many instances councils simply rubber-stamped proposals that had been prepared outside the council (frequently in technical departments such as Agritex) in order to pass them on to a higher government authority for acceptance. Many Local Government Promotion Officers (LGPOs) were ex-combatants with poor skills in managing committees, generating consensus, and cooperating with the local representatives of other ministries. Nevertheless, as Drinkwater points out, they were able to advance their own agendas by their capacity to write and submit proposals, call and control meetings, and the like.[52] The relationship of councils to local communities tended to be one more of development control than of representation, and they were agencies of administration rather than participation and integration. Councils controlled greater political and economic resources than VIDCOs and were generally dominated by local notables who used their influence to determine the distribution of public goods, such as the siting of schools. With a few noteworthy exceptions, even those councils implementing CAMPFIRE balked at allowing communities themselves to decide how funds generated from local wildlife management should be deployed. In the main, councils allocated such funds toward basic-needs projects devised for rather than by rural communities, although CAMPFIRE's goal was to provide disposable income to households. Councils were not known for genuine popular participation.[53]

As institutional nodes for self-reliant development, then, the councils were essentially ambiguous. Like their colonial predecessors, they were dependent on the state and unable to regulate the allocation of land effectively. In many cases, they were captured by the party and became vehicles for party patronage. This situation was exacerbated by the 1988 Rural Districts Councils Act, which expanded the range of ministerial patronage by providing for appointed councilors.[54] In short, the councils often lacked accountability. In 1986, for instance, the government dismissed all twelve councilors in the Wedza Council (although some were party officials) for insubordination, which included "openly dining and wining with an enemy of the Party."[55] Yet popular acceptance of the councils was crucial because they relied heavily on local sources of revenue. The less service councils provided the less people liked to pay up; the less they paid up, the smaller the capacity of the council to provide services and the greater the dependence of councilors on patronage to deliver their own largesse. Drinkwater states the dilemma well:

> Both [the political commissar] and the councillor, in order to sustain their positions, have to balance conflicting demands. Their authority, for external agents, depends on their capacity to deliver the compliance of the ward population with government and party initiatives. For the ward population it is their capacity to deliver greater access to production resources that is valued.[56]

This institutional dilemma was deepened by funding difficulties. Government allocations, which came mainly from recurrent expenditure, grants, and the PSIP, were unreliable because they were allocated according to national rather than provincial priorities. Nonstate funding provided by NGOs and foreign aid for development projects was frequently tied to particular uses, and was frequently allocated for construction but not for maintenance of infrastructure. Councils thus had to operate on very shaky fiscal foundations.

The government stressed the need for local authorities to generate their own revenues and infrastructure. Income generation, as Mugabe put it, would not only "contribute . . . increased revenues for the local authorities concerned, but also place the people in their proper role as their own liberators from the shackles of poverty and underdevelopment."[57] District councils were empowered to collect rates, charge fees, and impose levies, but they were fiscally weak. They tended to raise their revenues from economic taxes such as business licenses and fees and beer levies, and from such income-generating sources as the sale of liquor, but these sources were meager. Some councils implemented development fees but these were a unit tax not unlike the colonial poll tax, and had low recovery rates.[58] Chronically poor, most district councils were not able to institute their own projects. The incentive structure favored those already better-off. Thus councils remained externally dependent for both expertise and finance, which not only curtailed their capacity for independent decisions but made them vulnerable to political manipulation.

Two common instances demonstrate this vulnerability. One was the Food for Work program, first implemented in 1984 as a direct response to the trauma of drought. Under this program the rural poor were employed at a wage of Z$2.00 a day to work on infrastructural development projects, building bridges, dams, roads, schools, and clinics. This proved to be a cheap way of developing infrastructure (in some cases workers received handouts of maize because funds were not available to pay them), and it was implemented on a wide scale, including in relatively wealthy areas. The provincial governor of Manicaland was so pleased with the program that he called drought a "blessing in disguise" since it had necessitated rapid development. In Mutoko the success of the scheme led the district council to try to keep people on the program even in good seasons to "ensure continuity." Presented as a way to preempt the "dependency syndrome" among rural dwellers, food-for-work thus offered a safety net to the rural poor and laid the same claims to *virtue* as arguments for self-management.[59] But the rural poor were not always the chief beneficiaries of the program. Food-for-work recipients worked on agricultural projects to which they were not connected. In some cases, local politicians interfered, pressuring district administrators either to employ more people per project than planned for or to employ their own candidates, thereby using the program as a base to build local power and patronage. By using their positions to influence the distribution of food they were able to influence both the kinds of community development projects undertaken, and their beneficiaries.[60] In June 1988 the Food for Work program was suspended because of "problems of a political and technical nature," but was rapidly reinstituted to meet important needs. Widespread abuses continued.

The other source of dissatisfaction was the development of the rural road system, which was critical to the expansion and integration of the rural agrarian market. After independence, this task was performed mainly by the District Development Fund, now funded entirely from central sources. The DDF was consistently underfunded in budgetary allocations and road construction in the communal areas tended to be neglected. This had two political effects. First, it raised local questions about the state's commitment to rural development. Second, it set up competition within councils for scarce resources. Repair of access roads to dip tanks, clinics, and schools tended to depend on the capacity of individual district councilors to put pressure on the council and local DDF officials.[61] These political effects were directly related to the "problems of a political and technical nature" that had led to the suspension of the Food for Work program in 1988. They resulted in political conflict within councils over the distribution of government services, and exacerbated social tensions within rural communities over access to resources.

Neither food-for-work nor the road construction program were bad programs. They provided valuable services. But they illuminate the invidious position in which district councils found themselves. They were vulnerable to political manipulation, and they were dependent from both above and below. They depended on some degree of local consensus, but they were not consensual institutions. In many areas, locals felt themselves remote from the government and from government decisions, and councils often failed to draw great allegiance from the local people. In the words of one villager, "The council has done absolutely nothing for us here. No boreholes, no help in the transportation of our crop harvests. We don't know why we have a council."[62] Another called the council "a thief": "It takes our revenues away from us with one hand and offers nothing but food-for-work drought relief handouts with the other."[63] And in some cases councils themselves defied the desires of government. Under these conditions, it was very difficult to ground state demands on a hegemonic rural presence, or indeed to create such a presence. This situation also brought the central paradox of postcolonial development into relief: part of the state's political viability depends on its ability to distribute goods; and part of its ability to distribute goods depends on its political viability. Thus, the Zimbabwe government faced the same political dilemma as other newly independent African states: to take command of rural society to pursue its own political and ideological objectives, or to risk losing control of the national polity.

Conflicts within the State

Self-reliance, as we have seen, rapidly came to reflect not a cooperative initiative in social and economic transformation but an inchoate panoply of survival strategies open to political manipulation. The incoherence of development visions within the state and the preoccupations of the party with political control left nonagrarian socioeconomic policies in disarray. But this situation was not merely the outcome of rural encounters between state agents and peasants. Ideological and power struggles within the state also undermined the hegemonic development strategy. Partly this was a result of poor coordination of development tasks between (and within) ministries, which the decentralization program of 1984 was intended to resolve.[64] Partly it was a result of interministerial rivalry for funding from the ministry of finance, which guarded its control of funding jealously. Partly it arose from the different epistemic claims upon which the ministries based their programmatic objectives. Peter de Valk has referred to a "border conflict" between the Ministry of Local Government, Rural and Urban Development (MLGRUD) and MCDWA, with the first subjecting participatory structures to stringent rules related to administrative and technical extension functions, and the latter trying to mitigate and control top-down impositions in order to strengthen bottom-up involvement in planning. This situation, de Valk implies, reflected an interministerial struggle to increase respective domains of responsibility and authority.[65] It was also a struggle for better budget allocations.

The influence of these ministries varied dramatically. At local and provincial levels, MLGRUD exercised wide influence through the offices of the Department of Physical Planning, the Department of Rural Development, and the District Development Fund, and through its powerful presence in the district administrative apparatus, especially in the persons of DAs and LGPOs. Not unlike Internal Affairs in the colonial era, the ministry provided the dominant arm of the administration and was able to exercise a high level of control over the councils themselves.[66] Agritex, which oversaw agricultural development, also had considerable influence at this level but the sociocultural ministries such as MCDWA and MYSC were much weaker than the ministries with technical or administrative interests, especially since their sphere of influence was at the very local (VIDCO) level.

MCDWA occupied an anomalous political position within the state apparatus. It was entrusted with a wide range of functions aimed at improving social provision and the quality of citizenship, including elementary hygiene, adult literacy, child care, preschools, and income generation.[67] The ministry's main role was to coordinate the efforts of communities, the state, NGOs and development aid agencies to promote socio-economic development and governance. Thus, it had a central place in the politics of state building. But this multisectoral approach, devised before the strengthening of "civil society" became a core tenet of development discourses, was not well understood in either the state administration or in Parliament. The ministry had to struggle against a general indifference to its goals and was overwhelmed by more "mainstream" ministries, such as Education or Health, with which it had to liaise. It was desperately underfunded and understaffed at both head office and field levels. This situation not only reflected its poor status, but also prevented it from carrying out many of its projected activities. Very few of the plans made at Head Office reached the rural areas, and fieldworkers got on with it as best they could. Ministry officials' concern about top-down domination was thus somewhat misplaced: rural people complained rather that the ministry did nothing for them. Indeed the ministry was not very visible in the countryside. It lacked qualified personnel, funding, and technical resources. In the field, it relied on NGOs to fill many of the gaps left by its limitations, and its role of coordinating technical and service inputs of other ministries was also undermined by their frequent failure to respond to requests.[68]

Not only did MCDWA occupy a weak position within the central state, its role, along with that of other sociocultural ministries, was poorly understood within the Provincial Development Committees, which were dominated by administrators and technocrats. These ministries featured peripherally in the provincial development plans, their role described in very general terms and their resources in many cases not coherently deployed. VCWs complained that they were overworked, spent too much time writing reports, and were accountable to too many ministries. In the context of weak state institutions, poor infrastructure, and low investment resources, material resource development was the first priority of social management. Agrarian strategies promoted by Agritex enjoyed pride of place in the rural development apparatus of the state, and peasants' main interactions with the state continued to be with extension officers. In a telling comment, one MP declared that "the Ministry is trying to do its best, but because it bears the name 'woman' it is at a disadvantage. . . ."[69]

Within the state apparatus, then, the postcolonial vision of community development enjoyed a rather ironic resonance with its colonial predecessor: in both cases it suffered from a lack of interest and understanding by officials with other technical, administrative, or political preoccupations, who were more deeply concerned with the demands of social management. But, as with the colonial period, it would be wrong to think of MCDWA as merely a much misunderstood and maligned poor cousin of more powerful technical ministries. The ministry itself, especially in its early years, lacked coherence of vision, policy objectives, direction at the level of policy implementation, and administrative leadership. There were several reasons for this situation. The creation of the ministry represented in part a gesture toward the political rhetoric of the war and a politically inspired response to the objectives of the UN Decade for Women. In this respect, it followed the example of many other African countries that at independence had embarked upon transformatory political projects, usually in service of national unity or socialist ideology. Consequently, the rhetoric tended to define the goals rather than the other way around. On the ground, the ministry's terms of reference

were vague, and this led personnel to rely heavily on definitions of the ministry's role that were already available in preexisting community development structures.

Thus, the ministry's weaknesses were partly internal. This
hampered its struggle for rural legitimacy and support. At the
local level, there was a low acceptance rate. In some cases,
people who had been linked with colonial community development policies had to be expressly excluded because of their
lack of legitimacy. This caused a shortage of humanpower.
Where experienced workers had retained their legitimacy, the
only community development strategies that they knew and
understood were those of the colonial state. For newcomers, it
took time to build either community ties or an authoritative
position in the community, especially since the state provided
scant infrastructural support. Rural women had a long history
of defining and pursuing their own agendas, and using the
state along the way. Thus, political and ideological limitations
were imposed on the ministry by its own weaknesses. On one
hand, a basic-needs orientation continued to find expression
in the ministry's self-description; on the other hand, the ministry's operation was severely constrained by its own basic logistical shortcomings. Community development policy, in
short, remained largely in the mold of the colonial system.

There were also tensions between party leaders' interests
in pleasing their largely male support base and the commitment of senior ministry officials to the tasks of rural social development that focused on women. In 1989–90 the government brought women and youth, as political categories, into
the Ministry of Political Affairs and more directly under the
control of the party. Early in 1990 president Mugabe's wife,
Sally, entered the politiburo, unelected by women's associations, to take over the secretariat of Women's Affairs. The centralization and politicization of the ministry most committed
to local self-determination and empowerment did not bode

well for the prospect of establishing institutions of local self-determination and empowerment as the nexus of state authority. Indeed, these shifts seemed to vindicate the accusations that had long been made by opposition politicians that the ministry was a waste of money and a source of patronage for ZANU(PF) women.[70]

These conditions do not invalidate the ideological-political project of the state, which, as an attempt to embed the state in rural social life, was the opposite of its colonial predecessor. Indeed, they offer a fresh perspective on important features of the postcolonial state. First, the state was not ideologically monolithic in a strictly political sense. Second, no cohesive or integral bureaucratic ideology had emerged to replace the colonial administrative ideology. Third, an institutionally weak state in a poor and resource-dependent rural economy was particularly vulnerable to political manipulation. Fourth, social authority in rural locales had become fragmented rather than secured or consolidated. This situation, similar to postindependence conditions elsewhere in Africa, had important political implications. Within the state bureaucracy, they created space for the emergence of alternative procedures of decision making and service allocation. Elsewhere in Africa this space has been seized to entrench forms of personal patronage and bureaucratic corruption. By 1990, Zimbabwe was moving in the same direction as political elites struggled for influence and wealth. If these conditions prevailed, rural people already only peripherally engaged in the polity might simply decide that this government (like its colonial successor) had nothing to offer them. By 1996, massive voter indifference, as well as ZANU's efforts to mollify disaffected peasants through offers of expropriated land, showed that this was indeed happening.

In addition, the political-ideological project of the state, *on the ground*, was fragmented and compromised. The Midlands Provincial Development Plan noted delicately that

Community Development and Organisation as a means of uplifting standards of living of people by enlisting their support and cooperation has been found to be simple in concept but complex in practice. It has been observed that the capacity of organisations and individuals to perform the task of choice allocation, distribution, mobilisation and productive use of resources is not yet well developed, eg. VIDCOs and WADCOs. It is observed that none of the agencies involved in community development is co-ordinated enough to achieve such mobilisation. There is criss-crossing and uncertainty between the roles of different levels of these organisations and between community workers and extension workers.[71]

These factors conspired to compromise the credibility of incorporative strategies at the local level and to perpetuate a rural development approach remarkably reminiscent of the technocratic colonial model. It was, of course, precisely this outcome that incorporative strategies and the VIDCO policy were supposed to circumvent. Yet the persistent low political status of the sociocultural ministries, as well as the ruling party's proclivity for using violence against its opponents, questioned the government's commitment to the initiative and set the political status of VIDCOs on rather tenuous foundations. These weaknesses had deep political implications for the development potential of the VIDCO-WADCO system and the construction of state authority.

VIDCOs and the Politics of Identity

As the institutional conduit for self-reliance and community development, VIDCOs were designed to perform a crucial mediating role in relations of control and accountability between the state and rural communities. In this respect, they strongly resembled the Tribal Development Groups of the colonial period, and the colonial concept of "self-responsibility." We have seen that the state's capacity to manage rural socioeconomic development was shaky. An important role of the VIDCO, therefore, was to mediate political responsibility, to bridge informal and formal forms of economic activity, to play an informal but central role in the allocation of local labor supplies by coordinating local off-farm economic activities and cooperatives, and to manage local economic relations by such means as coordinating group credit facilities. In some areas, selection of candidates for resettlement took place through the VIDCO. To reiterate a point made earlier, VIDCOs were given a great deal of dirty work to do.

The state-building objectives of VIDCOs could best succeed if VIDCOs actually promoted local participation. But it was, paradoxically, their role in mediating political responsibility that made the VIDCOs subject to a range of rural suspicions, from those who felt their local power threatened to those who saw VIDCOs as yet another form of arbitrary control over their lives. By the early 1990s, the VIDCO system had not been in existence long enough to become fully understood, accepted, and operational, but two trends were discernible. VIDCOs were founded on locally specific patterns of compromise between (and within) rural communities and the state. Thus one trend was a high degree of fluidity between social and institutional sources of authority in which the state was not clearly the keystone. Second, VIDCOs were founded from the top down on shifting patterns of compromise within the state determined partly by a still scientistic and technocratic development approach. The result was a predilection within the state for political and administrative control.

As in the colonial period, agricultural extension officers tended to regard them as essentially a policy implementing vehicle, a situation exacerbated in those provinces where designation of VIDCOs was entrusted to Agritex. Although development projects were encouraged, and frequently required, to work through the VIDCOs the aims of citizen participation and utilization of local knowledge were not met. Coenraad Brand notes that locals remained "'clients,' recipients of benefits, or users of services."[72] These trends hampered VIDCOs' prospects of becoming the political and moral focus of village life and state-community relations. Indeed, the Minister of Local Government lamented in 1989 that rural people were "not being effectively mobilised to actively participate in development committees in order for them to identify, prepare and plan their development needs. The tendency is for them to say 'leave [it] to the chefs or politicians.'"[73] As a vehicle for bringing local populations into a wider public sphere, therefore, VIDCOs got off to a shaky start.

But the directive attitudes of state agents was not the only difficulty that VIDCOs faced. Their local identity was frequently obscure or suspect to villagers, partly because it was a multidimensional identity, embracing geographical, social, political, and functional features that did not always correspond. As a geographical unit created by government delineation, VIDCOs incorporated a number of village settlements, which peasants sometimes resented as arbitrary. In some cases, development projects were unequally divided between settlements within the VIDCO, reflecting local patterns of economic and political power. Such internal tensions compromised the corporate geographical and social integrity of the VIDCO. The problem was exacerbated where extension officers focused their efforts on better-off areas and better-off farmers. Moreover, as a planning unit, the VIDCO was external to already existing local systems of cooperation and action, which were frequently less formal, more fluid, and more intimate than the operation of the VIDCO allowed.[74] On the other hand, the VIDCO was subordinate to the council, which had bureaucratic clout. This made it extremely difficult for VIDCOs to assume a unified social corporate identity, and easy for villages to fall back into old patterns of control by patriarchal authorities, now running councils and committees.

The political impediments to VIDCOs establishing their authority at the grassroots level were severe. They were subject to power struggles between party, VIDCO, and traditional leaders; they communicated poorly with extension officers, the district council, and the community; and they were heavily dependent on outside help from government or NGOs. Participation in VIDCOs was dominated not only by men but by local notables with particular interests—those who derived their social position from agricultural achievements (master farmers), from local off-farm enterprise (shop owners, transport operators), or from literacy skills and service positions (schoolteachers). In particular, the role of women in local decision making remained very circumscribed. Sam Moyo has pointed out that because women had the weakest claims on land, issues of land allocation, government services, and material inputs remained in the power frame of elders, master farmers, and influential lineage groups—who also provided the vehicle for mobilizing local electoral support. In 1990 only 10 percent of councilors were women.[75]

This low level of participation fits the pattern, described by Jane Parpart and Kathleen Staudt, in which an emphasis on savings clubs and women's clubs can have the effect of gendering political participation in such a way that women remain marginal in local politics.[76] The Ministry of Community Development and Women's Affairs was too institutionally weak to bridge the distinction between agrarian and nonagrarian initiatives and promote integrated rural development. The VIDCO was thus not only a conduit for community organization and participation, and a mediator of state services and impositions, but also a forum for local political conflicts and a conduit for political patronage in which the interests of subordinate groups, or of the community as a whole, were often not advanced. The effect was to inhibit the capacity of VIDCOs to reorient local social institutions. Coenraad Brand has noted that the gravest danger facing VIDCOs is that they might "serve mainly as instruments of an alliance between the bureaucracy and technical staff on the one hand, and those rural elites who stand to gain most from sponsored development, on the other. In this form, VIDCOs would readily develop into nodes of local patronage."[77] Where this happens they will, ironically, realize a variant of the community development vision espoused by W. H. H. Nicolle in the 1960s and 1970s.

As a mechanism for promoting community integrity, and as a vehicle for mediating political responsibility and accountability, therefore, VIDCOs were deeply problematic. In particular, their capacity to build a coherent concept of national citizenship by bridging local identities and understandings of the national state remained questionable. I have suggested throughout this volume that the nature of rural politics is defined by local conflicts and struggles in which the state is inextricably implicated. It is therefore important to build these structures both out of and into existing systems, structures, and organizations—to transform, as it were, already imagined communities. VIDCOs had to take their identity from the ground up. But the state showed little willingness to let this happen. National politics remained remote in the lives of rural Zimbabweans while the administrative presence of the state remained extensive and immediate. There was little evidence that VIDCOs were becoming the focal point of a reoriented community life providing a linchpin for integration into the national polity.

Conclusion

This chapter has sketched a picture of a largely unsuccessful hegemonic project in which the Zimbabwean state used a normative discourse of self-reliance to rearrange patterns of social management and social authority in the countryside. Students of Harambee in Kenya have suggested that self-reliance can be an effective strategy for distributing local-level resources as well as for shaping state-society relations in rural areas. Indeed, Frank Holmquist has suggested that it contains the kernel of a political theory on which an agrarian social order can be constructed.[78] But it also contains the risk of increasing inequalities—and perhaps conflicts—across regional, class, ethnic, or gender lines as those with access to the state or organizational capabilities are able to capitalize on these resources. Self-reliance can also become a strategy for cheaply stabilizing poor and demoralized populations on the fringes of the polity. This was the tendency in Zimbabwe by the early 1990s.

There is a paradox to the failure of self-help as a hegemonic strategy. It was grounded not in the power of peasant resistance against state predations, but in the character of the state itself. In a sense, the state undermined its own objectives. The centrally controlled finance ministry guarded its resources jealously, so that self-reliance strategies never became an arena for state-citizen partnership or bargaining over social services within a wider public realm. Development ministries were divided not only along lines of agrarian and nonagrarian functions, but also along lines of gender that critically undermined the local politics of citizenship. There is a significant literature on African development that elucidates the deleterious effects of state policies on women. By contrast, we have seen here how the rural politics of gender can significantly undermine rural state construction. The concentration of community development and self-reliance policies on rural women had been inherited from the colonial government. But it also had sound structural foundations and had been validated by international political movements in the 1980s. However, in the context of scarce resources, a migrant economy, and an insecure regime, the policy clashed head-on with electoral and patronage politics. As a result, strategies that targeted youths and women foundered on the political rocks of party and patriarchy.

At the level of electoral politics, this failure was reflected in Mugabe's increasing intolerance for political opposition and his invigorated promises to secure peasant political support through land expropriation. Though the stridency of these promises intensified through the 1990s and seriously threatened white farmers, their sincerity, for peasants, was undermined by the tendency for large farms acquired for resettlement to find their way into the hands of high-level government officials, politicians, and their wealthy allies. Especially after the government adopted the economic structural adjustment program in 1990, peasants—and especially the rural poor—had little reason to view the state as their friend; as Ian Scoones notes, a popular rural wordplay on the acronym for the structural adjustment program is *satan ari pano* (Satan is here), and peasants blame the government.[79]

Yet the weaknesses of the state's hegemonic project do not render it insignificant in the development history of Zimbabwe. The central argument of this book has been that such a project, however compromised, is integral to the process of state building in agrarian settings, and that analysis of such a project illuminates the contours of state power. The discussion in this chapter exposes the political and ideological faultlines within the state that determined how the state pursued its goals of social management within the parameters of a neocolonial capitalist economy. It reveals the ever-present tension in state making between securing the authority of the state and entrenching the power of the party among poor and marginal peasant populations, and it shows how the quest for consent easily succumbs to a predilection for control. It demonstrates that the discursive and institutional arenas in which state agents and rural citizens can negotiate the control of rural social life take a limited number of forms, and that local government institutions are the most important. Most important, however, this analysis shows that the predilection for authoritarian political domination is not a straightforward or self-evident feature of postcolonial regimes. Within the Zimbabwean state, there were officials, bureaucrats, and even politicians who actively pursued the goal of remoralizing state-peasant relations in order to improve the quality of rural citizenship. While it is clear that state agents cannot unilaterally decide the terms on which rural life will be negotiated, these efforts demonstrate that the political, ideological, and institutional resources exist within the state to establish a common ground of political argument with the rural citizenry. This can perhaps provide a source of hope for rural Zimbabweans, and the basis for the "especially creative statecraft" that Zimbabwe, like other African countries, requires to secure a more effective postcolonial state.

Conclusions

The process of state formation in Zimbabwe has been a messy, though not incoherent, political business. Indeed, it is the historical coherence of the process that allows us to reflect upon both the past and the future. From the 1950s to the present, agrarian development strategies focused on the promotion of a stable, productive middle peasantry. Such an agrarian strategy demands a significant level of supervision and management of rural society, which was articulated in the technical-managerial terms of conservation. Nonagrarian development strategy, cast in a political-incorporative idiom of self-management, self-reliance, and cooperation, entailed sustained efforts to stabilize the rural population. Taken together, these strategies established the institutional and discursive terrain on which state agencies and peasants negotiated authoritative definitions of the social good, rights, and citizenship. But the efforts of successive governments to root state authority in the countryside remained constrained, fractured, and compromised.

At the level of central state policy formulation, state-peasant negotiations were constrained by entrenched economic structures, the class interests and political fears of the party leadership, and the divergent institutional interests of development ministries. Consequently, the construction of state authority and legitimation strategies were deeply ambiguous, and ultimately contradictory. Not only was the state unable to dominate the terrains of argument upon which it encountered rural populations, but the cognitive and ideological underpinnings of state practice were never homogeneous. State agents, in acting as the state, did invoke the peculiar purposive presuppositions of state power and state authority: rule-governed social management, institutionalized community membership, political domination. But these presuppositions themselves contained deep political tensions that bubbled to the surface in the context of state building. Within state apparatuses, different interests—and at time different authoritative epistemes—subverted the emergence of a common understanding of the meaning of community membership or citizenship. Preoccupations with control and strategies for legitimation repeatedly conflicted. Thus, at the national level, visions of sociopolitical development and transformation within the state were fragmented and frequently incompatible.

At the local level, the ability of state agents to regulate social tensions within the peasantry was always tenuous and sporadic. Indeed, state interventions were more likely to exacerbate than regulate intracommunity tensions. This is most broadly shown in their efforts to target rural youths and women as points of access to rural society. These groups had an essential role in any strategy of managed development. They were also responsive, recognizing opportunities to improve their conditions of life. But in targeting such weak rural social groups to penetrate rural society, the state challenged other community groups, especially elders, men, and migrants. This strategy thus highlighted a contradiction between the desires of patriarchs to maintain discipline over subordinates —notably youths and women—and the desires of state agents to reorient social authority through those very groups. This was a particularly important constraint for the postindependence government because, unlike its colonial predecessor, it depended on the political mobilization of a popular base. As we saw, it prompted the government, under pressure from males, to turn to a kind of gendered hegemony that undermined the state's strategy of self-reliance. In short, both the late-colonial regime and the as-yet insecure postcolonial regime found it difficult to penetrate and stabilize rural society, while also securing reliable political allies in the countryside. The result was a consistent predilection for control that inhibited the restructuring of local, colonially entrenched power structures and the dissemination of new national conceptions of citizenship.

In pursuing political and economic goals that reflected the close relationship between the political agendas of dominant groups and shifting ideas of the national interest, successive regimes thus encountered the most difficult problem of social management: restructuring political authority and extending state hegemony. The history I have recounted shows repeated attempts by the regimes to remoralize relations of control and consent between the state and the peasantry. From the 1950s on, state policies built upon, and sought to entrench, specific definitions of local "community," generated by central state officials for particular political purposes. But it proved impossible either to define the state clearly outside of communities under the RF, or to place the state at the center of communities under ZANU(PF). Control of rural social life was hotly contested from the early days of colonialism, and state power in the countryside was always fragmented. A critical tension in successive regime strategies, both colonial and postcolonial, was that agrarian strategies had no rural roots; they always presupposed peasant backwardness. Nonagrarian strategies, on the other hand, appealed directly to the power of tradition. This tension made it extremely difficult for the regime of the day to establish a common ground of political argument with rural citizens especially as successive regimes, for their own political and fiscal reasons, sought to define the state's social responsibilities narrowly.

Colonial governments used the control of land and land rights under the Land Husbandry Act to try to regulate the mobility and supply of African laborers to white employers and to constrain the development of African agrarian capitalism. But there was no common ideological ground between administrators' thoroughgoing faith in the progressive character of individual property rights and peasants' senses of community relationships in the face of a state-created land shortage. Similarly, when the Rhodesian Front implemented community development to preside over the decline of the Tribal Trust Lands, it did so not merely out of state incapacity or indifference. Community development was a policy of *actively* narrowing the realm of state activity in rural society as part of a process of shifting the burdens of accountability back onto traditional authorities. Turning to "tradition" to substantiate legitimate public authority, the colonial regime aimed to restore authoritative traditions in order to obscure state domination of society. Since these traditions were already distorted by the effects of colonialism, as well as poorly understood, or even created, by government leaders, this project proved contradictory and impossible. But it also shows that the principles of customary power entrenched by the colonial power did not conform to a single unifying logic of "tradition" that was promoted throughout the colonial period. In returning to tradition, the late colonial government promoted the fragmentation of social authority beyond what Mamdani presents as a straightforward bifurcation between rural customary power (decentralized despotism) and urban (rights-based) civic power.

Postindependence community development, on the other hand, aimed to distance the state from its overweening colonial predecessor, and to dissolve the separation between state and society in forging a new national identity. Consequently, the regime aimed to transform traditions of community life in order to promote an ideological unity of state and community (an effort that resonated powerfully at the level of political institutions with the regime's determination to establish a one-party state). Yet the sustained separation of agrarian and non-agrarian state-building strategies in institutional, ideological, political, and gender terms, as well as the government's inability to materially underwrite this hegemonic strategy, compromised the strategy deeply. As colonial community development strategies had shown, where development policy is unable to transcend a basic-needs approach, the sociocultural aspects of the hegemonic project are likely to collapse. "Integrated development" rapidly devolved into a politically more conservative technocratic managerialism. VIDCOs were not merely organs of political-ideological incorporation; they were also, crucially, conduits of control. On the ground, community development offered little more than a panoply of survival tactics.

Ultimately, then, the presence of the state in rural society remained paradoxical. Riven by internal tensions and contradictions, successive regimes were unable to establish local governance institutions that could address the social conflicts arising from changing agrarian relations. The state continued to loom over communities, directive and managerial, but its access to local power relations remained tenuous and sporadic. As we have seen, such conditions provide very shaky foundations for a rural state-building project. Not least, they are sociologically reminiscent of the 1950s, and the shift in state discourse from the "responsibility" of subjects stressed by the colonial state to the "empowerment" of citizens asserted by the postcolonial state was not signally borne out in the experience of rural citizens. Indeed, taking these two points—managerial intentions and tenuous control—together as defining the ethico-political terrain of state building, it is easier to see the central ambiguity in the political process of state construction. In the context of a precarious postcolonial state, empowerment of rural citizens—the lodestar of rural development—not only presupposed an empowered state but was also a vehicle for state empowerment. This ambiguity explains the complementary character of community development and conservation as political languages of legitimation and control. Both provided the terms in which the state laid the ground for negotiating incursions into the organization of rural society. But it also explains the ultimate impulse toward social management and control. By the end of the decade the populist agrarian policy outlined in chapter 6 was the basis for state-building in the rural areas; everything else was tacked on. "Socialist development" had become a meaningless notion and the legacy of the colonial state loomed large still, managerially present in rural life but shallowly embedded in rural society.

At the end of the 1980s, the government abandoned socialist development and adopted an economic structural adjustment program (ESAP) underwritten by the World Bank. The move toward the ESAP shifted the politics of state building significantly. Predicated, like other structural adjustment programs, on both political and economic liberalization, the ESAP raised two political concerns for the ruling party that focused attention on social control. On the one hand, even vestigial support for the one-party state principle had to be abandoned, thereby opening the space for political competition. On the other hand, the regime realized that, as elsewhere, economic liberalization would hit the poor the hardest, thereby opening the space for disenchantment. The government reacted to these pressures first by bringing the Department of Co-operatives into the Ministry of Community Development, thereby implicitly recognizing that the essential role of the ministry was to offer a rather minimal safety net for the poor and marginal. Second, in 1989 the government removed the Department of Youth from MYSC and Women's Affairs from MCDWA, placing both in the Ministry of Political Affairs, which, from the early days of independence, had been mainly concerned with sustaining the power base of ZANU(PF). This shift was facilitated by the 1987 unity pact between ZANU and ZAPU. The adoption of the ESAP ushered in a new phase in Zimbabwe's development history that cannot yet be fully evaluated. Yet the state has continued to be administrative, managerial, and at once distant and overweening in the lives of rural citizens. The tendency for structural adjustment to increase the precariousness of many rural livelihoods, and to exacerbate inequalities, makes it more likely to entrench than to reform the organizing principles of power in rural Zimbabwe.

State Construction and the Problem of Authority

"Today," wrote Weber, "the relation between the state and violence is an especially intimate one." Yet few regimes sustain themselves on appeals to coercive power alone.[1] State formation and the construction of state authority is a deeply textured political and historical process whose prospects rest on the existence or establishment of a common ground of political argument. This is the sphere of ethico-political relations and it explains the political appeals and political uses of tradition in the formation and transformation of state authority.

In demonstrating the fragmentary character of state authority in the countryside, an analysis of state efforts to expand that authority also illuminates the character of state power. The extension of state authority by both colonial and postcolonial regimes in an African country is revealed as an extraordinarily difficult process. Struggles over control and legitimation in Zimbabwe were struggles over what realms of rural social life would be appropriate realms for state intervention, and what forms such interventions might (legiti-

mately) take. Strategies of legitimation (and state power itself)
were always fragmented, compromised, and contested. Yet they
demonstrated that, while the broad objectives of social management strategies were determined at the level of national
political economy, the form and prospects of such strategies
were laid down on common institutional and ideological terrains of political argument where realms of legitimate state intervention were negotiated. Thus we saw how the Zimbabwe
government set out after independence to reconstruct conservation and community development as traditions of social
management to converge on the establishment of VIDCOs
and villagization in order to reorientate the politics of rural
communities and to mediate state-peasant relations. Significantly, the postcolonial government's project of creating grassroots participatory organs in the countryside was founded on
institutions thrown up by an increasingly desperate colonial
state to mediate and mitigate state domination in the countryside. A processual analysis of state formation thus brought us
ultimately to focus on a rather intimate institutional nexus in
which the control and legitimation aspects of social management were to be realized: local institutions for human and resource management at the community level. Through these
institutions the dominant presence of the state in the lives of
rural people would be mediated and mitigated. Here, the ideologues of postcolonial transformation argued, lay the nexus of
the national democratic revolution.

This end point, however, is in important ways a starting
point. The uncertainties of Zimbabwe's political prospects emphasize the broader processes of political transition in Africa
today. The processes of state construction I have described indicate that political transition is a long-term project—definitions of community and languages of authority cannot be laid
down overnight—and it is a local project, whose prospects lie
not principally at the level of central state institutions. This is

not to neglect the importance of central state institutions in the making of these processes; indeed, the central theme of this book is to demonstrate that the viability of those institutions themselves is at stake. But it is to indicate that the conception of social transformation, so prized by Third World radicals in the 1960s and 1970s, whereby local peasant struggles are appropriated and led by urban social groups, is not compelling in agrarian settings. No more persuasive are the contending arguments that development demands either a strong independent bourgeoisie that can keep the state honest, or a strong autonomous—and perhaps authoritarian—state that can keep the bourgeoisie honest.[2] The prospects and politics of political development in the agrarian societies of Africa lie ultimately at the local level—in the structures and definitions of local communities, in local struggles over conceptions and control of local rights, and in local struggles over sources of authority in rural social life. For it is here that the construction of state legitimacy (and indeed of a democratic political culture) must begin. And it is in unpacking these struggles that analysis of postcolonial states must start, the contours of state power be traced, and the degree of stateness be determined.

The point is demonstrated by the efforts of both the late colonial and postcolonial governments to stabilize rural society by recognizing the pivotal role of women in the agrarian political economy, and linking gender and productivity in their development policies. These strategies reveal the realization by state officials that the principles of state power are profoundly rooted in the political economy of agrarian production. But they also demonstrate how the weak hold of state authority on the social cleavages generated by that political economy undermined those very strategies and intensified policy contradictions. The late colonial regime attached its gendered appeals for self-reliance to government-sponsored

tradition, and hoped that the resulting tensions could be locally mediated by tribal development groups. The effect was
to fracture social authority and social allegiance more direly.
The postcolonial regime found its gendered self-reliance strategy at odds with its desires to entrench party and state patronage networks, and hoped that VIDCOs would paper over
the contradictions. But in a context of scarce resources, power
and development diverged, the government became increasingly authoritarian, and the languages of state increasingly
contradictory. We can draw two important general points from
these processes. First, in the agrarian political economies of
contemporary Africa, issues of gender and generation create
crucial faultlines in the consolidation of public authority. While
these faultines may be traced to long-established patterns of
social hierarchy, their current forms are a product of modern
political interactions and shaped in response to socioeconomic
change. Second, if we are to understand the trajectory of politics in Africa—and most especially the prospects for democratization—we must address the question of what local communities make of the languages of the state, and we must ask
whether they have some part in the construction of such languages.[3]

Such an understanding of state politics challenges "relative
autonomy" conceptions of African states by suggesting that
they underestimate the significance of political authority as a
critical dimension of state power. The state (qua state) is more
than a mechanism for articulating discrete and rational political interests. States are constructed in historical processes of
contestation and struggle and their relative autonomy from
social and economic demands is reined in by their structural
relationship to national modes of production and accumulation.
But it is also reined in by the nature of the terrains of political
argument and contestation—that is, not only by a state's separation from but also by its links to society. State development

in Zimbabwe entails a succession of efforts to establish a common ground of political argument underwritten by the state. In this respect, the determinants of state formation and state power are greater than the institutions or the incumbents of state apparatuses. They lie in fact at several historical planes that Bourdieu might call the "logic of practice"—indeterminate, fragmented, and driven by considerations of power:

1. The particular objectives of political domination, incorporation and transformation held by dominant political groups at particular times.

2. The political economy (national and international) which structures a particular state's efforts to manage the social relationships between classes (and incipient classes) in which the character of the social formation is revealed.

3. The historically constructed traditions of social management in which state-society relations are structured over time.

4. The generalized assumptions of state sovereignty which underlie state claims to authority.

The first two planes establish the links between the state and modes of accumulation. Thus, we saw how from the early days colonial governments set out to promote a peculiar form of racial capitalism, using the control of land as a mechanism to regulate the supply of African labor to white employers, to manage the participation of rural Africans in national commodity markets (as producers and as consumers), and to constrain the development of African agrarian capitalism. The latter two planes establish the links between state and society. Thus, we saw how colonial governments set out to manage rural African society by advancing arguments for resource management, by partially incorporating African authorities into the polity through the local councils, and by manipulating concepts of property rights. The planes interact at the level of hegemony. Thus, we saw how the adversarial and fractious interests of the state and the peasantry both developed from and resulted in intense struggles over control of rural social life that were by no means settled a decade after independence.

These two sets of factors together define the moral economy of the state. While the state does, as Jeffrey Herbst points out, have "a degree of freedom to act in response to its environment,"[4] its character is critically dependent on historically constructed ideological and political traditions that determine not only what the relationship of the state to its environment is but how it is socially understood. States do promote the interests of discrete political groups (the colonial history that we have analyzed at length demonstrates this) and they do allocate and distribute social goods on their own recognizance. But their capacity to do both (or indeed either) effectively on a national basis depends over time on the general acceptance of their sovereignty. The point is nicely made by John Dunn, writing in a different context: "Rational cooperation between citizens and government will necessarily depend upon how cogently [a government's understanding of social causality] meshes with and modifies the amateur social theories of the citizens at large. Political authority can certainly be heuristic. But it cannot appropriately and in general be didactic, because there is nothing determinate for it to teach."[5] Political sovereignty, as we have seen, is not unproblematic in the transition from colonialism. Most particularly, the authority of the state has not been secured as the final arbiter of property rights that profoundly affect the lives and opportunities of rural citizens.

This understanding of African state formation thus also challenges conceptions of neocolonialism. Neocolonialism is more than persistent economic orientations determined by the structures of the colonial economy and the demands of capitalist world markets—although these structures do severely constrain macroeconomic choices for postcolonial states. It is also more than persistent traditions of political domination and social control laid down by colonial state structures—although these traditions do inform the principal institutional conduits for state-society relations (bureaucracies, school curricula, codes of law, and the like). Neocolonialism also entails the persistence of a peculiarly narrow common ground for political argument. The partiality of the colonial state has been destroyed; the impartiality of the postcolonial state has been extraordinarily difficult to construct. This fact underpins the preoccupations of such disparate liberationist thinkers as Julius Nyerere and Steven Biko with concepts of "Africanness." It fuels the broad national populist and organic-statist ideologies of much transformatory socialist rhetoric in Africa. And it provides a starting point for analyzing the importance and character of ethnicity in much African national political life. Ethnicity provides a readily accessible ground of common political argument. But as the terrible destruction and violence undertaken in the name of ethnicity across much of contemporary Africa demonstrates, appeals to tradition can be made easily and effectively. In a neocolonial world it is a far harder task to transform traditions in the name of nation and state building.

This understanding exposes the fundamental political tension in the national development strategies of "weak" African states. Lacking a formidable state presence in rural society, they depend on the cooperation and incorporation of rural people, but they also feel compelled to take command of rural society in pursuit of their own political objectives, and to embed state presence on their own terms (or to risk losing control of the national polity). Where social change or political transition involve a fragmentation of social authority, as happened in decolonizing and postcolonial Africa, states step in to stabilize social institutions. They do so within the parameters of the national political economy, and proceed either by reinforcing existing institutions, taking them over, or creating new social management institutions. States that try to stabilize existing social institutions, such as customary courts or property relations, are vulnerable to manipulation by agents (such as chiefs) who have power within those institutions. Thus, the central paradox of postcolonial development is that part of the state's political viability depends on its ability to distribute goods; and part of its ability to distribute goods depends on its political viability. This paradox is the root of extraordinarily severe structural constraints on African states.[6] It also has a corollary: the more limited their capacity to exercise social management, the greater the predilection for control exhibited by African regimes. Authoritarian politics both arises from and sustains the instability created by fragmented social authority. It produces a spiral that undermines the possibility of negotiating a moral economy that might anchor a new, stable, public authority of the state.

This analysis suggests that when postcolonial African states slide under the thrall of small and unstable elites—a common enough political feature—it is less an indication of the power wielded by those elites or indeed of the power still held by partially unincorporated classes than of the peculiar and constrained contours of state power in African countries. A narrow terrain of political argument does not indicate that weak states confront strong societies, secure in their own (perhaps ethnic) moral economies and able to resist new normative languages of state. Rather, the fragmentation of social authority that we have revealed helps to prevent rural citizens from claiming citizenship rights (partly because it constrains sustained collective action), and no one is able to dictate the terms of debate. Yet this weakness raises the political stakes attached to the tension between social control and social incorporation in strategies of managed development. The process of state formation in rural Zimbabwe shows that where massive coercive capacity (or will) is absent and the transformation or regulation of social relations is the goal the establishment of common ethico-political ground is essential. The story presented here is one of ongoing and successive struggles by regimes to contain the fragmentation of state power in the countryside.

In this light, to think of African politics as a peculiar mode of regulation implies a coherence to the state, and indeed to the popular cultural responses that it evokes, that are not readily discernible in agrarian locales. Further, it suggests that when political elites narrow the social range within which they seek to exercise dominance it is not because their interests are limited but because their capacity for control is poor. African states have struggled to direct social change not despite their capacity to penetrate society, as various scholars maintain, but because of their incapacity to do so effectively as states. This trend is discernible in Zimbabwe, where the government's declared intention to undertake large-scale land expropriation has become increasingly strident in recent years as peasant cynicism has escalated. It is in this light that the 1990 Land Acquisition Act, which expanded the state's right to acquire white-owned land, should be understood, rather than as an attack on an alien capitalist class. Ironically, the adoption of ESAP fueled, rather than attenuated, the importance of controlling access to state resources as the cost of living soared. Mugabe's authoritarianism and ZANU's political and electoral caprice have traveled in step. In many rural locales, the party's popular base has weakened over time but no effective political opposition has been able to organize because the fragmentation of social authority that inhibits state construction also inhibits rural citizens from mobilizing collectively to claim citizenship rights. In late 1996 the prominent Zimbabwean scholar Masipula Sithole suggested that Zimbabwe's authoritarianism was eroding because elite cohesion was cracking and urban movements of students, intellectuals, and workers becoming more vocal.[7] It is certainly noteworthy that when

a new party, the Movement of Independent Electoral Candidates, finally emerged in late 1997 to demand democratic opening, its leading political light was a woman, Margaret Dongo,
who loudly assailed not only the corruption of the regime but
also its betrayal of the women who had played a pivotal role in
the liberation struggle. From the perspective of the countryside, however, these shifts did not address the localized forms
of authoritarianism that characterized the regime, and that
were deeply rooted in the long historical patterns of institutional flexibility detailed in this essay. Unless those forms of
authoritarianism, and the social memories of coercion and constraint that they sustain among rural citizens are transformed,
it seems premature to talk of significant changes in the nature
of the polity.

Finally, this understanding challenges prevalent models for
political development. Statist theories of development that
maintain that states should regulate the process of national construction carefully are now generally rejected. Such arguments,
advanced by some modernization theorists and by African
regimes who appealed to Marxism-Leninism for a normative
political foundation, proved a recipe for Jacobinism and political disaster in postcolonial Africa. More prevalent today are
theories of development that maintain that the tasks of the
state should be to structure property rights and to allow market institutions to dictate the contours of society relatively
unconstrained. But as this analysis of state formation in Zimbabwe has shown, the capacity of the state to structure property rights and social institutions is not so much the solution
as part of the problem of state authority. Indeed, by the mid-
1990s, some political economists had begun to point out that
neither an emphasis on policy nor the state-market distinction
provided very helpful starting points for understanding the
malaise of African development. Some noted that it is not reduced states that Africa needs as much as more effective states.

But in most accounts state "effectiveness" translates into some scale of "managerial efficiency."[8] Even the World Bank has begun to take states more seriously, recognizing that, at the very least, state policies and institutions set the parameters for development initiatives. As the Bank's 1994 *World Development Report* puts it:

> In addition to taking steps to improve the performance of infrastructure provision under their direct control, governments are responsible for creating policy and regulatory frameworks that safeguard the interests of the poor, improve environmental conditions, and coordinate cross-sectoral interactions—whether services are produced by public or private providers. Governments also are responsible for developing legal and regulatory frameworks to support private involvement in the provision of infrastructure services.

In this framework theory of government, the principal role of the state is to depoliticize and legitimate the sociopolitical order; effective states are those that provide a congenial environment for the operation of private economic and social interests.

Yet, as we have seen, legitimation is a complex political process, inseparable from the demands of political domination and social accumulation, whose dynamics change over time according to the shifting imperatives of state hegemony. Colonial and postcolonial states have faced the prior problem of *constructing* state authority. If, as Marx argued, class struggles are political struggles, so too are struggles to embed the overriding authority of the state within a recalcitrant rural society. In developed societies the former frequently appears more visible than the latter, which appears to provide a backdrop to political struggles. In the postcolonial context, however, the latter is more visible for it does not take place within the rubric of accepted and understood institutions; nor is it about the shape of those institutions. It is about which institutions ought to underwrite citizenship. In that sense, it is a more radical political struggle, as indeed the history of postcolonial Africa demonstrates. Any conception of state effectiveness must take historical account of this struggle that has produced the peculiarly fragmented patterns of public authority that characterize contemporary African polities.

It is clear, moreover, that such institutions cannot ignore the state. If relations between peasants and states have been, as Sara Berry puts it, "inconclusive encounters," these encounters must be understood not only from the point of view of local farmers, or of powerful interest groups, but also from the point of view of state logics and imperatives. Arguments that advocate disengagement from the state, or strengthening the institutions of civil society against the state, must thus be treated with caution. Recent academic writing and policy prescription in Africa concerned with strengthening civil society has urged a reduction in such responsibilities by allowing private-sector or nongovernmental organizations to play a larger role in social management activities. Norman Uphoff, for instance, has defined NGOs as part of a collective action sector distinct from the public and the private sectors.[9] Yet, however attractive this scenario is, it curtails the state's ability to manage the distribution of public goods, and thus makes the incumbents of an insecure state nervous. As Paul Wapner notes, "empowering local communities diminishes state authority by reinforcing local loyalties at the expense of national identity."[10] Strategies to curtail the role of the state have, in fact, tended to generate political tensions on the ground between state agencies and NGOs over the management of resources. For state agencies, it is often important to bear ultimate authority, not only for reasons of patronage but also for reasons of hegemony.

The analysis offered here has indicated that it is important to "take the state back out"; not out of development analysis or policy prescription, but out into the countryside. Underlying both agrarian and nonagrarian development is the quality of citizenship, and organizing development cannot be seriously thought about outside of that context. The fragmented lines of power and authority in rural society are deeply implicated by state power. In Scott's moral economy of the peasantry, conditions of scarcity provide the social and ecological environment in which the claims that community members can legitimately make on each other are negotiated. Similarly, in postcolonial Africa conditions of scarcity provide the environment in which regimes try both to secure the state as the final arbiter of social order and the public good and to delimit the claims that citizens can legitimately make on the state. Where the state takes over or reorients social institutions, it also disrupts existing conceptions of public goods, social security, and welfare. As recent political history shows, African regimes have found it difficult to mediate between securing the state and negotiating citizens' claims. In Africa, the regional unevenness of development has been linked with ethnic favoritism, but it is also closely linked to considerations of class, gender, and ecology. However, this creates a dilemma for governments. While controlling the management of services enables a government to determine the distribution of public goods, it also embroils the state in expensive responsibilities to maintain social stability in nonfavored areas, or to prevent the influx of a volatile population into urban areas. Such measures include food relief, basic incomes for the rural poor, and rudimentary health-care provision, which, as we have noted, are also a policy component of the revenue imperative. Consequently, national development plans fall less between the stools of state and market, as much recent development literature has proposed, than between the regime's interests in managing the national political economy and its need to take account of risk-mitigating institutions among local communities. In this light, the moral economy of the state must be understood as a process in which social management is constantly negotiated in terms of the rights of citizens to make claims on the state and the appropriate realms of state intervention in the social organization of citizens' lives.

Partly for this reason, the syndrome of dependency that state officials decry in peasants must be recast, for it reflects less the abjection of rural people than their determination to negotiate legitimate claims on the state and to insist that the state meet its responsibilities. "Self-help" and "self-reliance" are meaningless if they imply, as some scholars suggest, a reduction in state authority and state responsibility; communities will not exist outside of the state. As we saw in chapter 8, cultural production without service delivery cannot sustain a state-making project. Therefore, the state must engage with local citizens in civic responsibility. Patterns of extraction and distribution are inextricably linked to a legitimating moral economy, and the moral economy of the state is rooted in local debates over public authority. This places local government institutions at the epicenter of state construction. Further, since the agrarian populations at the fringes of African states are frequently poor, and social security is a central element in the makeup of political communities, the construction of state authority must take account of risk and of local institutions that mitigate risk. In this context, the moral economy of the state is neither the moral economy of the peasant writ large (a national rather than a local *mentalité*), nor its mirror image (a *mentalité* of state agents); it moves between the imperatives of national political economy and the political economy of peasant production, and between national discourses of development and local struggles over the supply and definitions of public goods, taking account of both. It is a moral economy which, in E. P. Thompson's terms, arises from historical and political needs to remodel popular cultural conceptions of need and expectation.[11] Recent shifts in the global economy, as well as the heightened awareness of ecological fragilities manifested in the growth of global and local ecological social movements, have added urgency to these pressures. This analysis suggests that effective development requires both the real participation of rural inhabitants and the construction of participatory public institutions.

This means that it is impossible to keep separate the technical and social realms of development, either in state policy approaches or in its legitimating languages. Many development policy prescriptions in the 1980s suggested that African countries cannot afford social policies. Yet the dilemma of state construction is that African countries cannot afford to be without such policies. Indeed, the state's responsibilities should be expanded, for the institutions of community development have to be politically and materially underwritten by the state. The capacity of the state to manage society does matter. It matters to governments whose hold on political power or on the economy is threatened; and it matters to people who are concerned about the quality of life and citizenship in Africa today. One must, ultimately, take seriously Samuel Huntington's argument that "authority must exist before it can be limited."[12] But authority cannot, as Huntington implies, be created unilaterally by the state. If political authority is to reconcile the tension between control and incorporation that lies at its core, it must draw upon the "amateur social theories of the citizens at large," and it must be limited as it is created. Our extended discussion of control and legitimation strategies in Zimbabwe showed that, in contemporary Africa, this is an intricate political and historical problem. But it is also the starting point for creative statecraft in fin de siècle agrarian settings.

Notes

Introduction

1. Quoted in G. Collier, *Basta! Land and the Zapatista Rebellion in Chiapas* (Oakland, Calif.: Institute for Food and Development Policy, 1994), p. 15. See also J. Gould, *To Lead as Equals: Rural Protest and Political Consciousness in Chinandega, Nicaragua, 1912–1979* (Chapel Hill: University of North Carolina Press, 1990). On India, see T. Brass, ed., *New Farmers' Movements in India* (London: Frank Cass, 1995). The reference to an infantilizing state is especially noteworthy. M. C. Young notes that colonial rulers in Africa resorted to a tactic of systematically infantilizing African subjects; *The African Colonial State in Comparative Perspective* (New Haven: Yale University Press, 1994), p. 224. See also M. Mamdani, *Citizen and Subject: Contemporary Africa and the Legacy of Late Colonialism* (Princeton: Princeton University Press, 1996), pp. 1–2.

2. T. Callaghy, "State, Choice and Context: Comparative Reflections on Reform and Intractability," in *Political Development and the New Realism in Sub-Saharan Africa*, ed. D. Apter and C. G. Rosberg (Charlottesville: University Press of Virginia, 1994), p. 204; C. Ake, *Democracy and Development in Africa* (Washington, D.C.: Smithsonian Institution Press, 1996).

3. P. Evans, "The State as Problem and Solution: Predation, Embedded Autonomy, and Structural Change," in *The Politics of Economic Adjustment: International Constraints, Distributive Conflicts, and the State*, ed. S. Haggard and R. Kaufman (Princeton: Princeton University Press, 1992). The idea of a state "floating above society" is from G. Hyden, *No Shortcuts to Progress: African Development Management in Perspective* (Berkeley: University of California Press, 1983), p.

19, who describes the state as having no structural roots in society, "as a balloon suspended in mid-air." The term "lame leviathan" belongs to Thomas Callaghy.

4. A. Gramsci, *Selections from the Prison Notebooks*, ed. and tr. Q. Hoare and G. K. Smith (New York: International Publishers, 1971), p. 167, and pp. 158–68 more generally.

5. See J. Ferguson, *The Anti-Politics Machine: Development, Depoliticization and Bureaucratic Power in Lesotho* (Minneapolis: University of Minnesota Press, 1994); A. Escobar, *Encountering Development: The Making and Unmaking of the Third World* (Princeton: Princeton University Press, 1995); J Crush, ed., *Power of Development* (London: Routledge, 1995).

6. It is important to note that legitimation strategies were also reflexive—aimed not only at peasants but also at other social groups and, indeed, at state agents themselves.

7. E. P. Thompson, *Customs in Common: Studies in Traditional Popular Culture* (New York: Free Press, 1991), p. 2, chap. 3, and passim; J. Scott, *The Moral Economy of the Peasant: Subsistence and Rebellion in Southeast Asia* (New Haven: Yale University Press, 1976).

8. For seminal contributions see R. Guha, ed., S*ubaltern Studies: Writings on South Asian History and Society*, 4 vols. (New Delhi: Oxford University Press, 1982–1985); J. Scott, *Weapons of the Weak: Everyday Forms of Peasant Resistance* (New Haven: Yale University Press, 1985). See also G. Joseph and D. Nugent, eds., *Everyday Forms of State Formation* (Durham, N.C.: Duke University Press, 1994); F. Mallon, *Peasant and Nation: The Making of Postcolonial Mexico and Peru* (Berkeley: University of California Press, 1995).

9. L. Hunt, *Politics, Culture and Class in the French Revolution* (Berkeley: University of California Press, 1984), p. 54.

10. D. Held, *Political Theory and the Modern State* (Stanford: Stanford University Press, 1989), p. 199.

11. The concepts of consent and social control—and in particular the nature and role of ideology—are, of course, highly contested in social and political theory (perhaps the suspicion of many scholars arises out of the difficulty of measuring the forms and extent of such control). It is sufficient, for the time being, to note that it is an acceptable enough practice to define and describe states in terms of the ways in which they regulate people's lives, and that, while domination is never entirely uncontested, the ground rules for social and

political contestation require some (and various) forms of consent that are at least in part ideological.

12. See A. De Janvry, E. Sadoulet, and L. Wilcox Young, "Land and Labour in Latin American Agriculture from the 1950s to the 1980s," *Journal of Peasant Studies* 16, no. 3 (1989); T. Barry, *Zapata's Revenge: Free Trade and the Farm Crisis in Mexico* (Boston: South End Press, 1995).

13. For comments on this resonance, see R. Bush and L. Cliffe, "Agrarian Policy in Migrant Labour Societies: Reform or Transformation in Zimbabwe?" *Review of African Political Economy* 29 (July 1984); M. Drinkwater, *The State and Agrarian Change in Zimbabwe's Communal Areas* (New York: St. Martins Press, 1991); J. Alexander, "State, Peasantry and Resettlement in Zimbabwe," *Review of African Political Economy* 21, no. 61 (1994). See also W. Beinart, "Soil Erosion, Conservation and Ideas about Development: A Southern African Exploration 1900–1960," *Journal of Southern African Studies* 11 (1984).

14. For various perspectives, see J-F. Bayart, *The State in Africa: The Politics of the Belly*, tr. Mary Harper, Christopher Harrison, and Elizabeth Harrison (London: Longman, 1993); Young, *African Colonial State*; Mamdani, *Citizen and Subject*; A. Mbembe, "The State, Violence and Accumulation: The Case of Sub-Saharan Africa," Centre of Non-Western Studies, University of Leiden, 1989.

15. P. Kaarsholm, "The Past as Battlefield in Rhodesia and Zimbabwe: The Struggle of Competing Nationalisms over History from Colonization to Independence," *Culture and History* 6 (1989), p. 104.

16. The original research design for this study included ethnographic fieldwork in the Zimuto communal area of Masvingo province. When research clearance for this component was not granted, my direct and detailed access to some local sources, and in particular rural voices, was curtailed. As a result, rural voices are less prominent in this account, which addresses national-level processes and is cast at the level of the state. However, I have traced them in a growing number of ethnographic studies, in a wide variety of popular sources, and in conversations with Zimbabwean citizens who regularly move back and forth between rural and urban domains. To incorporate these voices more centrally into the story would add a desirable vitality and texture, but would have made this volume impossibly long.

17. On agrarian change, see Drinkwater, *State and Agrarian Change*; N. Amin, "State and Peasantry in Zimbabwe since Independence," *European Journal of Development Research* 4, no. 1 (June 1992); M. Masst, "Exploring Differentiation among the Zimbabwean Peasantry," University of Zimbabwe Centre for Applied Social Sciences Occasional Paper, June 1994; D. Pankhurst, "The Dynamics of Social Relations of Production and Reproduction in Zimbabwe's Communal Areas" (Ph.D. thesis, Southampton University, 1988); B. Cousins, D. Weiner, and N. Amin, "The Dynamics of Social Differentiation in Communal Lands in Zimbabwe," University of Zimbabwe, Centre for Applied Social Sciences Occasional Paper—NRM Series, 1990; M. van den Pool, C. Jackson, R. Mula. M. Ning, O. P'Obwoya, and H. Thompson, *Changing Farming Systems in a Migrant Labour Economy: Masvingo South Communal Area, Masvingo Province, Zimbabwe*, ICRA Working Document no. 9, June 1989; B. Cousins, "Power and Property in Zimbabwe's Communal Lands: Implications for Agrarian Reform in the 1990s," University of Zimbabwe, Centre for Applied Social Sciences Occasional Paper—NRM Series, 1993. On state politics, see J. I. Herbst, *State Politics in Zimbabwe* (Harare: University of Zimbabwe Publications, 1990). On the party, see M. Bratton, "The Comrades and the Countryside: The Politics of Agricultural Policy in Zimbabwe," *World Politics* 49 (1987); Alexander, "State, Peasantry and Resettlement."

Chapter One

1. G. Poggi, *The Development of the Modern State: A Sociological Introduction* (Stanford: Stanford University Press, 1978), p. 95.

2. On citizenship as a feature of modernity, see A. Giddens, *The Nation-State and Violence* (Berkeley: University of California Press, 1987), especially chap. 8; Held, *Political Theory*, chap. 7.

3. For classical discussions, see M. Weber, "Politics as a Vocation," in *From Max Weber: Essays in Sociology*, tr. and ed. H. H. Gerth and C. Wright Mills (New York: Oxford University Press, 1946), p. 78; K. Marx, *The Eighteenth Brumaire of Louis Bonaparte* (New York: International Publishers, 1963). See also B. Jessop, "Capitalism and Democracy: The Best Political Shell?" in *Power and the State*, ed. G. Littlejohn (New York: St. Martin's Press, 1978), p. 11.

4. Held, *Political Theory*, especially chap. 1. On Africa, see M. C.

Young, "Patterns of Social Conflict: State, Class and Ethnicity," *Daedalus* 111 (1982). On nationalism as the taken-for-granted basis of development thinking, see G. Kitching, *Development and Underdevelopment in Historical Perspective* (London: Routledge, 1989), p. 4.

5. For a provocative marxist perspective, see E. M. Wood, "The Uses and Abuses of Civil Society." in *Socialist Register*, ed. R. Miliband and L. Panitch (London: Merlin Press1990); for a liberal point of view, see J. Keane, *Civil Society and the State* (London: Verso, 1988), chap. 2.

6. See G. F. W. Hegel, *Hegel's Philosophy of Right*, tr. T. M. Knox (London: Oxford University Press, 1952), especially pp. 122–60. The importance of Hegel's concept of state universality lies in the argument that the link between the universality of the state and the particularity of civil society is law, which establishes the "right as law" (see esp. pp. 134–39). See also J. Habermas, *Legitimation Crisis*, tr. T. McCarthy (London: Heinemann, 1976), part 1.

7. The most dramatic example of such a compromise is the comprehensive systemic crisis of sociopolitical systems in the Soviet Union and eastern Europe. Such crises demonstrate the intimate yet complex relationships between the social allocations demanded by the organization of material production and distribution in society and the social allocations demanded by sociopolitical organization and distribution. This is the burden of Habermas's "legitimation crisis."

8. J. Bayart, "Civil Society in Africa," in *Political Domination in Africa: The Limits of State Power*, ed. P. Chabal (Cambridge: Cambridge University Press, 1986), pp. 117–20. Though Bayart no longer uses the term "civil society," this discussion is illuminating.

9. S. N. Sangpam, "The Overpoliticized State and Democratization: A Theoretical Model," *Comparative Politics* 24, no. 4 (1992), pp. 401–17; Sangpam, "The Overpoliticised State and International Politics: Nicaragua, Haiti, Cambodia and Togo," *Third World Quarterly* 16, no. 4 (1995), pp. 607–29; Mbembe, "State, Violence and Accumulation."

10. See C. B. MacPherson, *The Political Theory of Possessive Individualism: Hobbes to Locke* (London: Oxford University Press, 1962); J. Habermas, *Communication and the Evolution of Society*, tr. T. McCarthy (Boston: Beacon Press, 1979), chaps. 3 and 5. On Africa, see A. Hughes, "The Nation-State in Black Africa," in *The Nation-State: The Formation of Modern Politics*, ed. L. Tivey (New York: St. Martin's Press, 1981); Young, *African Colonial State.*

11. J. Lonsdale, "Political Accountability in African History," in

Political Domination in Africa: The Limits of State Power, ed. P. Chabal (Cambridge: Cambridge University Press, 1986), p. 128; Lonsdale, "States and Social Processes in Africa," *African Studies Review* 24, nos. 2/3 (1981), p. 204. H. Howe and M. Ottoway distinguish usefully between a secure regime and a weak state; "State Power Consolidation in Mozambique," in *Afro-Marxist Regimes*, ed. E. J. Keller and D. Rothchild (Boulder: Lynne Rienner, 1987).

12. W. M. Adams, *Green Development: Environment and Sustainability in the Third World* (London: Routledge, 1990); D. Anderson and R. Grove, eds., *Conservation in Africa: People, Policies and Practice* (Cambridge: Cambridge University Press, 1987).

13. J. S. Migdal, *Strong Societies and Weak States: State-Society Relations and State Capabilities in the Third World* (Princeton: Princeton University Press, 1988), pp. 10–15; M. C. Young, *Ideology and Development in Africa* (New Haven: Yale University Press, 1982); R. H. Bates, *Beyond the Miracle of the Market: The Political Economy of Agrarian Development in Kenya* (Cambridge: Cambridge University Press, 1989), p. 3; J. Breman and S. Mundle, eds., *Rural Transformation in Asia* (Oxford: Oxford University Press, 1991), pp. xi–xii; D. B. Cruise O'Brien, J. Dunn, and R. Rathbone, eds., *Contemporary West African States* (Cambridge: Cambridge University Press, 1989), p. 3.

14. See especially A. Stepan, *The State and Society: Peru in Comparative Perspective* (Princeton: Princeton University Press, 1978); T. Skocpol, *States and Social Revolutions: A Comparative Analysis of France, Russia and China* (Cambridge: Cambridge University Press, 1979); P. Evans, D. Rueschemeyer, and T. Skocpol, eds., *Bringing the State Back In* (Cambridge: Cambridge University Press, 1985).

15. Migdal, *Strong Societies and Weak States*; Herbst, *State Politics in Zimbabwe*. For more normative arguments on the importance of state autonomy and state capacity as measures of stateness, see T. Callaghy and J. Ravenhill, "Lessons and Prospects of Africa's Responses to Decline," in *Hemmed In: Responses to Africa's Economic Decline*, ed. T. Callaghy and J. Ravenhill (New York: Columbia University Press, 1993).

16. T. M. Callaghy, *The State-Society Struggle: Zaire in Comparative Perspective* (New York: Columbia University Press, 1984).

17. See, for instance, C. Boone, *Merchant Capital and the Roots of State Power in Senegal, 1930–1985* (Cambridge: Cambridge University Press, 1992); W. Reno, "Who Really Rules Sierra Leone? Infor-

mal Markets and the Ironies of Reform" (Ph.D. dissertation, University of Wisconsin, Madison, 1992).

18. T. Mitchell, "The Return of the State," paper presented to conference on "Power," University of Michigan, Ann Arbor, 1992, p. 18.

19. B. Jessop, *State Theory: Putting Capitalist States in Their Place* (University Park: Pennsylvania State University Press, 1990), p. 360.

20. Quoted in R. Jeffries, "Ghana: The Political Economy of Personal Rule," in *Contemporary West African States,* ed. D. Cruise O'Brien, J. Dunn, and R. Rathbone (Cambridge: Cambridge University Press, 1989), p. 87.

21. M. Mann, *The Sources of Social Power* (Cambridge: Cambridge University Press, 1993) vol. 2, chap. 3.

22. Even in cases where citizenship is not formally extended to all, it is the social position of those to whom citizenship is extended that defines the public realm. See J. Habermas, *The Structural Transformation of the Public Sphere* (Cambridge, Mass.: MIT Press, 1989), chap. 1.

23. Here I differ specifically with Skocpol, who views the state as "a set of administrative, policing, and military organisations headed by an executive authority" that "extracts resources from society and deploys these to create and support coercive and administrative organisations" (*States and Social Revolutions,* p. 29). For Skocpol, the administrative and coercive organizations are the basis for state power. This institutional conception of the state is partial; there is ultimately a difference between the form of state power, and the nature of state power.

24. P. Corrigan and D. Sayer, *The Great Arch: English State Formation as Cultural Revolution* (Cambridge Mass.: Blackwell, 1985); D. Hay, P. Linebaugh and E. P. Thompson, *Albion's Fatal Tree: Crime and Society in Eighteenth-Century England* (New York: Pantheon Books, 1975); also Thompson, *Customs in Common.* As C. B MacPherson argues, this process also drove trends in political philosophy which made Locke the doyen of the "Political Theory of Possessive Individualism."

25. Bayart, *State in Africa,* pp. ix, 249.

26. M. Levi, *Of Rule and Revenue* (Berkeley: University of California Press, 1988), chaps. 1 and 3.

27. On the peasantry, see especially G. Hyden, *Beyond Ujamaa in Tanzania: Underdevelopment and an Uncaptured Peasantry* (Berkeley:

University of California Press, 1980); on markets, see especially J. MacGaffey, *The Real Economy of Zaire: The Contribution of Smuggling and Other Unofficial Activities to National Wealth* (London: James Currey, 1991); on the irrelevant state, see J. Ihonvbere, "The 'Irrelevant' State: Ethnicity and the Quest for Nationhood in Africa," *Ethnic and Racial Studies* 17, no. 1 (1994); also M. C. Young, "Zaire: Is There a State?" *Canadian Journal of African Studies* 18, no. 1 (1984).

28. P. Evans, "Predatory, Developmental and Other Apparatuses: A Comparative Analysis of the Third World State," ms., 1989, p. 2. Evans implicitly accepts the juxtaposition of state and market by equating developmentalism with economic transformation.

29. On China, see E. Friedman, P. G. Pickowicz and M. Selden, *Chinese Village, Socialist State* (New Haven: Yale University Press, 1991), pp. 228–34, 245–52. On Africa, see P. Raikes, *Modernising Hunger: Famine, Food Surplus and Farm Policy in the EEC and Africa* (London: James Currey, 1988); R. E. Downs, D. Kerner, and S. P. Reyna, eds., *The Political Economy of African Famine* (Langhorne Pa.: Gordon and Breach, 1991).

30. M. Mann, *Sources of Social Power*, p. 59. Such an approach also provides a better conceptual framework for measuring rent seeking.

31. Keane, *Civil Society*, pp. 7–13.

32. Young, *African Colonial State*, pp. 279–80, 211–13.

33. P. Richards, *Fighting for the Rain Forest: War, Youth and Resources in Sierra Leone* (Oxford: James Currey, 1996), p. xiv, note 5.

34. G. Williams, "Taking the Part of Peasants: Rural Development in Nigeria and Tanzania," in *The Political Economy of Contemporary Africa*, ed. P. Gutkind and I. Wallerstein (Beverly Hills, Calif.: Sage Publications, 1985).

35. For an optimistic reading of Harambee, see J. Barkan and F. Holmquist, "Peasant-State Relations and the Social Base of Self-Help in Kenya," *World Politics* (1989); F. Holmquist, "Self-Help: The State and Peasant Leverage in Kenya," *Africa* 54, no. 3 (1984). For a more cautious view, see B. Thomas, "Development through Harambee: Who Wins and Who Loses? Rural Self-Help Projects in Kenya," *World Development* 15, no. 4 (1987).

36. For a useful, if broad, typology, see S. Amin, "Dependency and Underdevelopment in Africa: Origins and Contemporary Forms," *Journal of Modern African Studies* 10, no. 4 (1972). See also A. Phillips, *The Enigma of Colonialism: British Policy in West Africa* (London: James Currey, 1989); Young, *African Colonial State*; R. H. Bates,

Markets and States in Tropical Africa: The Political Bases of Agricultural Policies (Berkeley: University of California Press, 1981).

37. G. Arrighi, "Labour Supplies in Historical Perspective: A Study of the Proletarianisation of the African Peasantry in Rhodesia," *Journal of Development Studies* 6 (1970), p. 214; C. Bundy, *The Rise and Fall of the South African Peasantry* (Berkeley: University of California Press, 1979); R. Palmer and N. Parsons, eds., *The Roots of Rural Poverty in Central and Southern Africa* (London: Heinemann, 1977); K. Hart, *The Political Economy of West African Agriculture* (Cambridge: Cambridge University Press, 1982); K. Mann and R. Roberts, eds., *Law in Colonial Africa* (London: James Currey, 1991); Phillips, *Enigma of Colonialism.*

38. Mamdani, *Citizen and Subject*; Young, *African Colonial State*, especially chaps. 1 and 9; Bayart, *State in Africa*, pp. 70–73; Mbembe, "State, Violence and Accumulation."

39. See, for instance, M. Foucault, "The Subject and Power," in *Michel Foucault: Beyond Structuralism and Hermeneutics*, ed. H. Dreyfus and P. Rabinow (Chicago: University of Chicago Press 1982), pp. 208–25.

40. D. Harvey, *The Condition of Postmodernity* (Cambridge Mass.: Blackwell, 1990); A. Giddens, *The Constitution of Society* (Berkeley: University of California Press, 1984). On education, see P. Bourdieu, "Cultural Reproduction and Social Reproduction," in *Knowledge, Education, and Cultural Change*, ed. Richard Brown (London: Tavistock, 1973).

41. On colonial education as a part of a struggle over cultural meanings, see Young, *African Colonial State*, p. 280. Bayart argues in *The State in Africa* (pp. 75, 155–57) that education policy has been a central element in the extraversion principle of African politics. Richards argues in *Fighting for the Rainforest* that Sierra Leoneians view education as the hallmark of modernity.

42. For excellent examples, see P. Chatterjee, "Development Planning and the Indian State," in *The State and Development Planning in India*, ed. T. Byres (Delhi: Oxford University Press, 1994), pp. 51–72; R. Menchu, *I, Rigoberta Menchu: An Indian Woman in Guatemala* (London: Verso, 1984), pp. 103–4.

43. P. Duara, "State Involution in Comparative Perspective," in *Rural Transformation in Asia*, ed. J. Breman and S. Mundle (Oxford: Oxford University Press, 1991).

44. Levi, *Of Rule and Revenue*, pp. 18–19; Bates, *Miracle of the Mar-*

ket, p. 28; also K. Firmin-Sellers, "The Politics of Property Rights," *American Political Science Review* 89, no. 4 (December 1995), 867–79.

45. See especially E. Wolf, *Peasant Wars of the Twentieth Century* (New York: Harper and Row, 1969); J. Paige, *Agrarian Revolution: Social Movements and Export Agriculture in the Underdeveloped World* (New York: Free Press, 1975); A. de Janvry, *The Agrarian Question and Reformism in Latin America* (Baltimore: Johns Hopkins University Press, 1981).

46. See, for instance, D. Brautigam, "What Can Africa Learn from Taiwan? Political Economy, Industrial Policy and Adjustment," *Journal of Modern African Studies* 32, no. 1 (March 1994); P. Dorner, *Latin American Land Reforms in Theory and Practice: A Retrospective Analysis* (Madison: University of Wisconsin Press, 1992).

47. Scott, *Moral Economy of the Peasant,* p. 3; Scott, *Weapons of the Weak;* A. Isaacman, "Peasants and Rural Social Protest in Africa," in *Confronting Historical Paradigms: Peasants, Labor, and the Capitalist World System in Africa and Latin America,* ed. F. Cooper et al. (Madison: University of Wisconsin Press, 1993).

48. S. Marks and A. Atmore, eds., *Economy and Society in Pre-Industrial South Africa* (London: Longman, 1980); T. Ranger, *Peasant Consciousness and Guerrilla War in Zimbabwe: A Comparative Study* (London: James Currey, 1985); B. Berman and J. Lonsdale, *Unhappy Valley;* W. Beinart and C. Bundy, *Hidden Struggles in Rural South Africa: Politics and Popular Movements in the Transkei and Eastern Cape 1890–1930* (Johannesburg: Ravan Press, 1987).

49. The term *partiality* refers to more than simply the political base of the state. It entails also the consistent bias of the state toward particular social groups. See S. B. Greenberg, *Legitimating the Illegitimate: State, Markets and Resistance in South Africa* (Berkeley: University of California Press, 1987), chap. 2.

50. Callaghy, *State-Society Struggle,* pp. 31–32. See also J. Saul, "The State in Post-Colonial Societies: Tanzania," *Socialist Register* (1974); R. Higgot, "The State in Africa," in *Africa Projected: From Recession to Renaissance by the Year 2000?* ed. T. Shaw and O. Aluko (London: Macmillan, 1985); J. Barkan and J. Okumu, eds., *Politics and Public Policy in Kenya and Tanzania* (New York: Praeger, 1979).

51. K. Polanyi, *The Great Transformation: The Political and Economic Origins of Our Time* (Boston: Beacon Press, 1944), p. 140; K. Marx, *Capital: A Critique of Political Economy,* tr. Ben Fowkes (New York: Vintage Books, 1977), 1:885.

52. D. Zweig, "Struggling over Land in China: Peasant Resistance after Collectivization, 1966–1986," in *Everyday Forms of Peasant Resistance*, ed. F. Colburn (Armonk, N.Y.: M. E. Sharpe, 1989), p. 170.

53. For excellent discussions, see R. E. Downs and S. P. Reyna, eds., *Land and Society in Contemporary Africa* (Hanover N.H.: University Press of New England, 1988); T. Bassett and D. Crummey, eds., *Land in African Agrarian Systems* (Madison: University of Wisconsin Press, 1994); S. Berry, *No Condition Is Permanent: The Social Dynamics of Agrarian Change in Sub-Saharan Africa* (Madison: University of Wisconsin Press, 1993).

54. J. Plamenatz, "Two Types of Nationalism," in *Nationalism: The Nature and Evolution of an Idea*, ed. E. Kamenka (Canberra: Australian National University Press, 1973), especially pp. 34–36.

55. For a theoretical discussion of organic-statism, see Callaghy, *State-Society Struggle*, pp. 14–17. On African populism, see G. Arrighi and J. Saul, *Essays on the Political Economy of Africa* (New York: Monthly Review Press, 1973); and Kitching, *Development and Underdevelopment*. On one-party statism see A. Zolberg, *Creating Political Order: The Party-States of West Africa* (Chicago: Rand McNally, 1966).

56. R. Oyatek, "Burkina Faso: Between Feeble State and Total State, the Swing Continues," in *Contemporary West African States*, ed. D. Cruise O'Brien, J. Dunn, and R. Rathbone (Cambridge: Cambridge University Press, 1989), p. 14.

57. E. S. Atieno Odhiambo, "Democracy and the Ideology of Order in Kenya," in *Democratic Theory and Practice in Africa*, ed. W. Oyugi et al. (London: James Currey, 1988), pp. 116–17; also Zolberg, *Creating Political Order*, p. 75.

58. See E. Mandala, *Work and Control in a Peasant Economy* (Madison: University of Wisconsin Press, 1990); J. Carney and M. Watts, "Manufacturing Dissent: Work, Gender and the Politics of Meaning in a Peasant Society," *Africa* 60, no. 2 (1990).

59. Lonsdale, "States and Social Processes," p. 195.

60. Hyden, *Beyond Ujamaa in Tanzania*.

61. S. Feierman, *Peasant Intellectuals: Anthropology and History in Tanzania* (Madison: University of Wisconsin Press, 1990); P. Shipton, *Bitter Money: The Classification of Forbidden Commodities among the Luo of Kenya* (Washington, D.C.: American Ethnological Society, 1989).

62. Lonsdale, "States and Social Processes," p. 179.

63. For a striking example, see Greenberg's discussion of South Africa in *Legitimating the Illegitimate*.

64. Gramsci, *Prison Notebooks*, p. 168.

65. As Bourdieu points out, social actions occur according to social rules because they are only intelligible to the participants within the context of those rules, but they cannot be determined by those rules because there are invariably more ways than one to respond to a proposition; *Outline of a Theory of Practice* (Cambridge: Cambridge University Press, 1977), pp. 29–30.

66. C. Tilly, *From Mobilization to Revolution* (Reading, Mass.: Addison-Wesley, 1978), pp. 133–38.

67. See S. Tarrow, *Power in Movement: Social Movements, Collective Action and Politics* (Cambridge: Cambridge University Press, 1994).

68. Bourdieu, *Theory of Practice*, pp. 29–30.

69. Greenberg, *Legitimating the Illegitimate*, p. 149.

70. J. Wunsch and D. Olowu, eds., *The Failure of the Centralized State: Institutions and Self-Governance in Africa* (Boulder: Westview Press, 1990).

71. Here I draw on Alasdair MacIntyre's notion of "narrative histories," that people and communities understand and constitute themselves as parts of socially local histories and traditions; *After Virtue: A Study in Moral Theory* (Notre Dame, Ind.: University of Notre Dame Press, 1981), pp. 119, 122, 142–53.

72. B. Anderson, *Imagined Communities: Reflections on the Origins and Spread of Nationalism* (London: Verso, 1989).

73. I. Shapiro, "Realism in the Study of the History of Ideas," *History of Political Thought* 3, no. 3 (Winter 1982), p. 554.

74. Gramsci, *Prison Notebooks*, pp. 167–68.

75. Zolberg, *Creating Political Order*, p. 44; A. Ashforth, "Reckoning Schemes of Legitimation: On Commissions of Inquiry as Power/Knowledge Forms," *Journal of Historical Sociology* 3, no. 1 (March 1990).

Chapter Two

1. G. Arrighi, "Labour Supplies"; R. H. Palmer, *Land and Racial Domination in Rhodesia* (London: Heinemann, 1977); Palmer and Parsons, *Rural Poverty;* C. Van Onselen, *Chibaro: African Mine Labour in Southern Rhodesia, 1900–1933* (London: Pluto, 1976); I. Phimister, *An Economic and Social History of Zimbabwe 1890–1948: Capital Accumulation and Class Struggle* (London: Longman, 1988).

2. See Palmer, *Land and Racial Domination*, pp. 132–34; L. Gann and M. Gelfand, *Huggins of Rhodesia: The Man and His Country* (London: Allen and Unwin, 1964), p. 58; C. Coggin, "'Don't Worry Headquarters!'," *NADA* 11, no. 2 (1975).

3. A. Wright, *Valley of the Ironwoods* (Cape Town: Bulpin, 1972), p. 5; C. L. Carbutt, "Reminiscences of a Native Commissioner," *NADA*, no. 2 (1924); Carbutt, "Some More Reminiscences of a Native Commissioner," *NADA*, no. 4 (1926).

4. J. MacLean, *The Guardians* (Bulawayo: Books of Rhodesia, 1974), pp. 175–76.

5. N. A. Hunt, interviewed by I. J. Johnstone, 27 November 1983, NAZ Oral/240; F. A. Staunton, interviewed by I. J. Johnstone, 1986, NAZ Oral/256.

6. For a crisp representation, see ex-CNC Stanley Morris's foreword to Joy MacLean's memoir, *The Guardians:* "For what were the Native Commissioners and their wives but guardians—"fathers and mothers" of the African people, from infancy to maturity—indeed, from 'cradle to coffin'?"

7. Palmer, *Land and Racial Domination*, p. 144.

8. S. Dubow, "Race, Civilisation and Culture: The Elaboration of Segregationist Discourse in the Inter-War Years," in *The Politics of Race, Class and Nationalism in Twentieth-Century South Africa*, ed. S. Marks and S. Trapido (London: Longman, 1987); Phillips, *Enigma of Colonialism;* L. H. Gann, *A History of Southern Rhodesia: Early Days to 1934* (London: Chatto and Windus, 1965), pp. 183–88. Palmer, *Land and Racial Domination*, pp. 136–37, 140–41.

9. H. R. G. Howman, interviewed by M. C. Steele, 10 and 26 August 1971, NAZ Oral/HO3, p. 33. For additional portraits, see NAZ interviews; Wright, *Valley of the Ironwoods;* MacLean, *Guardians;* J. F. Holleman, *African Interlude* (Cape Town: Nasionale Boekhandel, 1958); *Mangwende Commission Report.*

10. Wright, *Valley of the Ironwoods*, p. 204.

11. Department of Native Affairs. *Annual Report of the Chief Native Commissioner* (*CNC Annual Report*), 1954, p. 17.

12. R. Blake, *A History of Rhodesia* (London: Eyre Methuen, 1977), p. 164.; Howman interview, p. 49 [NAZ].

13. H. Child, *The History and Extent of Recognition of Tribal Law in Rhodesia* (Rhodesia Government: Ministry of Internal Affairs, 1965), pp. 9–12.

14. Quoted by P. Mason, "Land Policy," in R. Gray, *The Two*

Nations: Aspects of the Development of Race Relations in the Rhodesias and Nyasaland (Oxford: Oxford University Press, 1960), p. 61.

15. N. H. Wilson, "The Development of Native Reserves: One Phase of Native Policy for Southern Rhodesia," *NADA*, no. 1 (1923), p. 87.

16. H. S. Keigwin, "Native Development," *NADA*, no. 1 (1923), p. 12.

17. MacLean, *Guardians*, pp. 23–24; my emphasis.

18. For a fascinating, though self-serving, account of Alvord's Gospel of the Plough, see his autobiographical account of agricultural development in Southern Rhodesia, "Development of Native Agriculture and Land Tenure in Southern Rhodesia," (typescript, Waddilove, 1956 [?]), esp. pp. 4–12. In 1961 the term *producers* was replaced in official language by the term *tribesmen;* see chaps. 4 and 5. For the urban concentration of arguments about African "advancement," see Gray, *Two Nations;* and H. Holderness, *Lost Chance: Southern Rhodesia 1945–58* (Harare: Zimbabwe Publishing House, 1985).

19. F. Mackenzie, "Selective Silence: A Feminist Encounter with Environmental Discourse in Colonial Africa," in *Power of Development*, ed. J. Crush (London: Routledge, 1995), p. 101 (Mackenzie is paraphrasing Mudimbe). On scientific development, see M. Yudelman, "Imperialism and the Transfer of Agricultural Techniques," in *Colonialism in Africa 1870–1960*, ed. J. Duignan and L.Gann (Stanford: Hoover Institution Press, 1975), pp. 339–40. For the notion of ecological managerialism, see Adams, *Green Development*, pp. 23–27.

20. For illustrations of Alvord's crusading zeal, see Alvord, "Development of Native Agriculture;" Alvord, "the Great Hunger," *NADA*, no. 6 (1928). See also Gann and Gelfand, *Huggins of Rhodesia*, pp. 129–30.

21. I. Scoones and K. Wilson, "Households, Lineage Groups and Ecological Dynamics: Issues for Livestock Development in Zimbabwe's Communal Lands," in *People, Land and Livestock*, ed. B. Cousins (Harare: University of Zimbabwe Centre for Applied Social Sciences, 1989), pp. 15–16; Drinkwater, *State and Agrarian Change*, pp. 55–57; L. L. Bessant, "Coercive Development: Peasant Economy, Politics and Land in the Chiweshe Reserve, Colonial Zimbabwe, 1940–1966" (Ph.D. dissertation, Yale University, 1987), pp. 75–77.

22. R. W. M. Johnson, *The Labour Economy of the Reserves*, Department of Economics, Occasional Paper no. 4 (Salisbury: University College of Rhodesia and Nyasaland, 1964), pp. 20, 38–42.

23. Quoted in Phimister, *History of Zimbabwe*, p. 278.

24. K. B. Wilson, "Trees in Fields in Southern Zimbabwe," *Journal of Southern African Studies* 15, no. 2 (1989), p. 373.

25. Quoted in G. Passmore, *The National Policy of Community Development in Rhodesia*, Department of Political Science Source Books Series, no. 5 (Salisbury: University of Rhodesia, 1972), p. 50.

26. Ranger, *Peasant Consciousness*, pp. 60–65. B. N. Floyd, *Changing Patterns of African Land Use in Southern Rhodesia* (Lusaka: Rhodesia-Livingstone Institute, [1959]), pp. 118–21.; M. A. Stocking, "The Relationship of Agricultural History and Settlement to Severe Soil Erosion in Rhodesia," *Zambezia* 6, no. 2 (1978), pp. 134–35. See also L. Bessant and E. Muringai, "Peasants, Businessmen, and Moral Economy in the Chiweshe Reserve, North-Central Zimbabwe, 1940–1968," mimeographed (1990), pp. 5–7, 12–14; Phimister, *History of Zimbabwe*, p. 279; M. Yudelman, *Africans on the Land: Economic Problems of Agricultural Development in Southern, Central and East Africa, with Special Reference to Southern Rhodesia* (Cambridge, Mass.: Harvard University Press, 1964), pp. 141–42; T. W. F. Jordan, "The Victoria Master Farmers' Association," *NADA* 11, no. 5 (1978); A. Cheater, *Idioms of Accumulation: Rural Development and Class Formation among Freeholders in Zimbabwe* (Gweru: Mambo Press, 1984), p. 5.

27. Quoted in Ranger, *Peasant Consciousness*, p. 71. See also the assistant agriculturist, Chiweshe's 1938 report, quoted in Bessant, *Coercive Development*, p. 68.

28. *CNC Annual Report*, 1949, p. 12; also *Chief Agriculturists' Report*, 1934, p. 18.

29. Bessant and Muringai, "Peasants, Businessmen, and Moral Economy," p. 11; also *Report of the Native Production and Marketing Branch*, 1948, p. 98; W. Dopke, "State and Peasants in Mazoe District in the 1930s," University of Zimbabwe, Henderson Seminar, 1985, pp. 12–13; Johnson, *Labour Economy*, pp. 35–38; van den Pool et al., *Farming Systems*, p. 52.

30. A. K. H. Weinrich, *African Farmers in Rhodesia: Old and New Peasant Communities in Karangaland* (London: Oxford University Press, 1975), p. 63. See also Johnson, *Labour Economy*, pp. 35–49; J. D. Jordan, "Zimutu Reserve: A Land-Use Appreciation," *Rhodes-Livingstone Journal*, no. 36 (n.d.), pp. 67, 74–75; Yudelman, *Africans on the Land*, pp. 130–40.

31. *CNC Annual Report*, 1957, p. 7.

32. Bessant, *Coercive Development*, pp. 25–26. Bessant and Muringai

remark that Chiweshe peasants remember the 1940s as marking the emergence of "jealousy" among young men—jealousy being marked partly by the unwillingness of sons to turn their entire pay packet over to fathers ("Peasants, Businessmen, and Moral Economy," p. 14).

33. Motion by Joseph Gusha to Native Board, Chiweshe Reserve, April 1931, quoted in Dopke, "State and Peasants," p. 19. See also S. Ranchod-Nilsson, "'Educating Eve': The Women's Club Movement and Political Consciousness among African Women in Southern Rhodesia," mimeographed (n.d.), pp. 7–8; E. Schmidt, *Peasants, Traders and Wives: Shona Women in the History of Zimbabwe, 1870–1939* (London: James Currey, 1992), chap. 4; Pankhurst, *Dynamics of Social Relations,* chap. 5.

34. Yudelman, *Africans on the Land,* p. 238; also citations in Pankhurst, *Dynamics of Social Relations,* pp. 153–54.

35. *CNC Annual Report,* 1949, p. 23.

36. See Department of Statistics. *Statistical Handbook of Southern Rhodesia, 1945.* 26/10/45, p. 112; *Phillips Committee Report,* p. 158.

37. Quoted in Bessant, *Coercive Development,* p. 68.

38. J. C. Barratt, "An Economic Model of Animal Draught Power in Agropastoral Farming Systems in Zimbabwe," paper presented to workshop on A Systems Approach to the Analysis and Planning of Communal Resource Management, University of Zimbabwe, 1989, pp. 2–3; Barratt, "Valuing Animal Draught in Agropastoral Farming Systems in Zimbabwe," paper presented at workshop on Tillage: Past and Future, CIMMYT FSR Networkshop Report no. 22, March 1991, p. 28; R. M. G. Mtetwa, "Myth or Reality: The 'Cattle Complex' in South East Africa, with Special Reference to Rhodesia," *Zambezia* 6, no. 1 (1978), pp. 32–33; M. C. Steele, "The Economic Function of African-Owned Cattle in Rhodesia," *Zambezia* 9, no. 2 (1981), p. 30.

39. L. Cliffe, *Policy Options for Agrarian Reform in Zimbabwe: A Technical Appraisal,* FAO Report to the Government of Zimbabwe, 1986, pp. 25–29; van den Pool et al., *Farming Systems,* pp. 42–48. Estimates of stock ownership and stock holding have varied quite widely, and it is likely that different surveys use different measures (and therefore measure different things). Agritex's Wedza baseline study, for instance, places the figure at 58 percent. However, all studies agree that the pattern of ownership is heavily skewed.

40. See, variously, MLARR, Department of Veterinary Services,

Monthly Reports, July and August 1988; M. Bratton, "Farmer Organizations and Food Production in Zimbabwe," *World Development* 14, no. 3 (March 1986); interviews, Chinamora communal area October 1988; Drinkwater, *State and Agrarian Change* pp. 170–72, 179, 226–227; Zimbabwe Women's Bureau, *We Carry a Heavy Load: Rural Women in Zimbabwe Speak Out*, report of a survey (Harare, 1981), p. 24; Scoones and Wilson, "Households," p. 29.

41. Agritex, *Wedza Baseline Study: Summary and Analysis*, pp. 3–4; Agritex report on Shurugwi; Ministry of Lands, Agriculture and Rural Resettlement (MLARR), *First Annual Report of Farm Management Data for Communal Area Farm Units*, 1988/89 farming season, p. 22. Also E. M. Jassat and B. Chakaodza, *Socio-Economic Baseline Study of Rushinga District (Mashonaland Central Province)*, Consultancy Paper prepared for the FAO (Harare: Zimbabwe Institute for Development Studies, July 1986), pp. 53–55; I. Staunton, *Mothers of the Revolution* (London: James Currey, 1991), pp. 5–6.

42. Cliffe, *Agrarian Reform*, p. 23; *Hansard* 15, no. 29, 14 September 1988.

43. Phimister, *History of Zimbabwe*, p. 186; Pankhurst, *Dynamics of Social Relations*, p. 266; N. Amin, "State and Peasantry."

44. Phimister, *History of Zimbabwe*, pp. 171–82; P. Mosley, *The Settler Economies: Studies in the History of Kenya and Southern Rhodesia 1900–1963* (Cambridge: Cambridge University Press, 1983), pp. 178–80; C. F. Keyter, *Maize Control in Southern Rhodesia, 1931–1941: The African Contribution to White Survival*, Central African Historical Association, Local Series no. 34 (1978); Dopke, "State and Peasants," p. 14; Bessant, *Coercive Development*, p. 66. Not all districts were controlled; the drier areas of Matabeleland and Nyanga were excluded from control.

45. Quoted in Keyter, *Maize Control*, p. 22.

46. Quoted in Palmer, *Land and Racial Domination*, p. 220.

47. Witness to the Godlonton Commission, quoted in J. F. Holleman, *Chief, Council and Commissioner: Some Problems of Government in Rhodesia* (Assen, Netherlands: Royal VanGorcum, 1968), p. 48. See also Palmer, *Land and Racial Domination*, p. 219.

48. MacLean, *Guardians*, p. 205.

49. Department of Veterinary Services, *Annual Report*, 1988, Masvingo Province, p. 3. See also *Monthly Reports* from Masvingo and Matabeleland South provinces.

50. There is an extensive and contentious literature on this issue.

My discussion here draws mainly on D. Lan, *Guns and Rain: Guerrillas and Spirit Mediums in Zimbabwe* (Harare: Zimbabwe Publishing House, 1985), especially pp. 19–26, 113–17; C. J. K. Latham, "Mwari and the Divine Heroes: Guardians of the Shona" (M.A. thesis, Rhodes University 1986), pp. 11–13, 26–28, 66–75, 118–31, and passim; F. W. T. Posselt, *Fact and Fiction: A Short Account of the Natives of Southern Rhodesia* (1935; Bulawayo: Books of Rhodesia, 1978), pp. 43–95, 100–104. Also of interest are J. M. Schoffeelers, ed., *Guardians of the Land* (Gweru: Mambo Press, 1979) and the large number of lay interpretations of African chiefdoms, spirits and mediums in the pages of *NADA*.

51. J. Holleman maintains that the ward is the most important social unit, being both permanent and small enough to provide a sense of community. Recent technical appraisals seem to challenge this view, and suggest that the real focus of community is a smaller unit at the village level; *Shona Customary Law* (Manchester: Manchester University Press, 1969), pp. 7–8. For exploratory discussions, see B. Cousins, ed., *People, Land and Livestock: Proceedings of a Workshop on the Socio-Economic Dimensions of Livestock Production in the Communal Lands of Zimbabwe* (Harare: University of Zimbabwe, Centre for Applied Social Sciences, 1989).

52. Lan, *Guns and Rain*, pp. 115, 25; there is some dispute over whether the social distinction between "royal" and "stranger" lineages is socially significant. Lan suggests that it is not, as do Kuper, Hughes, and van Velsen. J. G. Mutambara, however, argues that "royals" rank above "strangers" whether they hold office or not, and that this distinction is realized in the size and quality of land holdings allocated; "Africans and Land Policies: British Colonial Policy in Zimbabwe, 1890–1965" (Ph.D. dissertation, University of Cincinnati, 1981), p. 113.

53. Witchcraft was outlawed by the Suppression of Witchcraft Act of 1899. But it has played an extensive role in the regulation of community relations. See G. L. Chavunduka, "Witchcraft and the Law in Zimbabwe," *Zambezia* 8, no. 2 (1980), p. 133; I. Scoones et al., *Hazards and Opportunities: Farming Livelihoods in Dryland Africa: Lessons from Zimbabwe* (London: Zed Books, 1996), pp. 158–59. Among rural administrators, see Posselt, *Fact and Fiction*, pp. 54–56; Wright, *Valley of the Ironwoods*, p. 217; Latham, *Mwari*, pp. 65–66.

54. Cousins et al., "Dynamics of Social Differentiation."

55. I. Phimister, "Zimbabwe: The Path of Capitalist Develop-

ment," in *History of Central Africa*, vol. 2, ed. D. Birmingham and P. Martin (London: Longman, 1983), p. 285.

56. C. Thompson and H. Woodruff, *Economic Development in Rhodesia and Nyasaland* (London: Dennis Dobson, 1954); *Report of Industries Branch of Treasury*, 20 February 1962.

57. See A. Astrow, *Zimbabwe: A Revolution That Lost Its Way?* (London: Zed Press, 1983); C. Stoneman, ed., *Zimbabwe's Inheritance* (London: Macmillan, 1981); A. M. Hawkins, *Economic Growth, Structural Change and Economic Policy in Rhodesia 1965–1975* (Salisbury: Whitsun Foundation, June 1976).

58. Phimister, "Zimbabwe," pp. 286–89.

59. *Hansard* 30/2, 1949, col. 2483. See also Minute from Agricultural Marketing Officer to SNA, 20 February 1948, S482/145/17/48.

60. *Hansard* 30/2, 1949, col. 2662; *Rhodesia Herald*, 3 February 1951; *Hansard* 31/2, 1951, cols. 3587–90; Reports of Commissioner of Native Labour for 1948 (p. 53) and 1953 (p. 20).

61. Minister of Native Affairs, *Hansard* 32/1, 1951, cols. 625–26.

62. *CNC Annual Reports* for 1948 (pp. 1, 3, 19) and 1949 (pp. 7, 26).

63. *Report of the Native Production and Marketing Branch*, 1948, p. 98; *Report of the Maize and Small Grains Commission, 1962/63*, pp. 60–61; *What the Native Land Husbandry Act Means to the Rural African and to Southern Rhodesia: A Five Year Plan That Will Revolutionise African Agriculture*, 1955, p. 12 (hereafter, *What the NLHA Means*); Mosley, *Settler Economies*, pp. 91–92; *Hansard* 30/2, 1949, col. 2483.

64. *Report of the Native Economics and Marketing Department*, 1956, p. 2; *CNC Annual Report*, 1949, p. 12.

65. Natural Resources Board (NRB), *Notes on Conservation Policy*, 20 September 1944, p. 21; *Hansard* 30/2, 1949, col. 2488.

66. H. R. G. Howman, "The Native Affairs Department and the Native," *NADA* 31 (1954), p. 48; Holleman, *Chief, Council and Commissioner*, p. 47.

67. The policy was described in these terms in the *CNC Annual Report*, 1961, pp. 25–27.

68. Beinart, "Soil Erosion, Conservation and Ideas about Development." *Report of the Agriculturist, Native Development*, 1934, p. 18. Alvord, "Development of Native Agriculture," pp. 26–30.

69. By 1959 the government viewed the growth of African nationalism as such a threat that it declared a state of emergency and banned the African political groups. See T. Ranger, "African Politics in Twen-

tieth Century Rhodesia," in *Aspects of Central African History,* ed. T. Ranger (Evanston: Northwestern University Press, 1968).

70. *Report of Native Production and Marketing Branch,* 1951, pp. 115, 117; *Report of the Maize and Small Grains Commission, 1962/63,* pp. 76.

71. *Report of Production and Marketing Branch,* 1948, p. 99; idem, 1952, p. 113.

72. Secretary of Internal Affairs [hereafter, SIA], *Annual Report,* 1962, p. 18; *CNC Annual Report,* 1953, p. 118; idem, 1952, p. 112; *Report of Native Economic and Marketing Branch,* 1956, p. 5.

73. *Report of Production and Marketing Branch,* 1952, pp. 110, 113; idem 1953, p. 115.

74. Quoted in *CNC Annual Report,* 1952, p. 17.

75. Director of Native Agriculture, *NADA,* 1960, p. 33; *Report of the Commission of Enquiry into Certain Sales of Native Cattle in Areas Occupied by Natives,* 1939, paras.12–20, 87, 88, 147–54, 165–87; *Hansard* 30/2 1949, col. 2490. Yudelman, *Africans on the Land,* pp. 190–91; H. Dunlop, *The Development of European Agriculture in Rhodesia, 1945–1965,* Department of Economics Occasional Paper no. 5 (Salisbury: University of Rhodesia, 1971), pp. 29–31; Phimister, *History of Zimbabwe,* pp. 184–85.

76. Wright, *Valley of the Ironwoods,* pp. 232, 238–41; *Robinson Commission Report,* p. 20.

77. The discussion draws mainly on the Ministry of Internal Affairs Monthly Summary of Cattle Sales, 1960–1979. See also Mosley, *Settler Economies,* pp. 104–5; Mtetwa, "Myth or Reality."

78. Quoted in Passmore, *Community Development,* pp. 37–38.

79. See, for instance, NRB, *Notes on Conservation Policy,* 20 September 1944; NRB, *Memorandum on the Conservation of Natural Resources on the Land Occupied by Natives,* 14 January 1943.

Chapter Three

1. R. Werbner, *Tears of the Dead: The Social Biography of an African Family* (Harare: Baobab Books, 1991), especially chap. 1.

2. *CNC Annual Report,* 1951, pp. 3–4; emphasis in original For the political rationale of the act, see also *Hansard* 32/1, 1951, col. 88.

3. Ferguson, *Anti-Politics Machine.*

4. *CNC Annual Report,* 1951, p. 115; R. M. Davies, interviewed by I. J. Johnstone, 17 November 1983, NAZ Oral/241.

5. *Report of the Interdepartmental Working Party to Consider Social Security for the Urban African,* December 1956, pp. 1–3; *What the NLHA Means,* pp. 4, 5; *Hansard* 32/1, 1951, col. 38.

6. D. A. Robinson, "Soil Conservation and Implications of the Land Husbandry Act," *NADA* 37 (1960), p. 33. For the urban preoccupations of the act, see the *Report of the Interdepartmental Working Party,* 1956; the United Party never lost this urban bias.

7. H. R. G. Howman, *NADA,* 1954, pp. 43–44; *Hansard* 32/1, 1951, cols. 76–79.

8. See *Report of the Commission of Inquiry into Alleged Discontent In the Mangwende Reserve [Mangwende Commission Report]* 1961; Holleman, *Chief, Council and Commissioner,* p. 66; interviews with Nicolle [Durban, 18 September 1987]; N. A. Hunt [NAZ]; Davies [NAZ]; Staunton [NAZ].

9. *Hansard* 32/1, 1951, cols. 38, 103–4; *Hansard* 30/2, 1949, cols. 2683–90; NAD statement in *NADA,* 1958, p. 46.

10. *CNC Annual Report,* 1954, p. 15; *What the NLHA Means,* p. 5; also Mason, "Land Policy," p. 61.

11. *CNC Annual Report,* 1961, extracted in *NADA,* 1963, p. 94; also *What the NLHA Means,* p. 14; *Hansard* 30/2, 1949, cols. 2683–90, 2701–2.

12. *CNC Annual Report,* 1952, p. 32.

13. For expanded discussions, see Werbner, *Tears of the Dead,* pp. 19–21; W. Duggan, "The Native Land Husbandry Act of 1951 and the Rural African Middle Class of Southern Rhodesia," *African Affairs* 79, no. 315 (April 1980), p. 232; Holleman, *Chief, Council and Commissioner,* p. 64; Johnson, *Labour Economy,* p. 9; A. K H. Weinrich, *African Farmers in Rhodesia,* p. 63; also N. A. Hunt, "Age and Land in a Native Reserve," *NADA* 40 (1963); *What the NLHA Means,* pp. 5–6.

14. *What the NLHA Means,* p. 12; *CNC Annual Report,* 1959, p. 11.

15. *Hansard* 32/1, 1951, col. 46.

16. The quotation is from *CNC Annual Report,* 1951, p. 4.

17. *What the NLHA Means,* p13; see also p. 2.

18. Holleman, *Chief, Council and Commissioner,* pp. 62–63.

19. Werbner, *Tears of the Dead,* especially chap. 1; Schmidt, *Peasants, Traders and Wives,* pp. 44–53, 104–10.

20. Floyd, *African Land Use,* p. 126; Robinson, *NADA,* 1960, p. 33; *What the NLHA Means,* p. 5.

21. Weinrich, *African Farmers in Rhodesia,* p. 63; Werbner, *Tears of the Dead,* p. 26. Holleman, *Chief, Council and Commissioner,* p. 65; Bes-

sant and Muringai, "Peasants, Businessmen, and Moral Economy," pp. 27–28.

22. Minister of Native Affairs, *Hansard* 32/1, 1951, cols. 1073, 1063; *CNC Annual Report*, 1952, p. 4.

23. *Report of Land Board*, 1952, p. 39; I. Cormack, *Towards Self-Reliance: Urban Social Development in Zimbabwe* (Gweru: Mambo Press, 1983), pp. 87–89; Gray, *Two Nations*; J. Barber, *Rhodesia: The Road to Rebellion* (London: Oxford University Press, 1967), p. 116.

24. *Report of Land Board*, 1956, p. 8; Robinson, *NADA*, 1960, p. 31.

25. 1959/60 CSO [Central Statistical Office], *Sample Survey of African Agriculture.*

26. See variously *Mangwende Commission Report*; interviews with R. M. Davies, Staunton, N. A. Hunt [NAZ]; for an excellent discussion of implementation in Chiweshe, see Bessant, *Coercive Development*, pp. 206–16.

27. From a vast literature on these traumas, see *Mangwende Commission Report*, p. 172; H. J. Quinton, interviewed by E. G. Gibbons, May 1977–May 1978, NAZ Oral/Qu2; *CNC Annual Report*, 1956, pp. 3, 11; Bessant, *Coercive Development*, pp. 93–104; Werbner, *Tears of the Dead*; R. Loewenson and M. Gelfand, "Customary Law Cases in Two Shona Chieftainships," *NADA* 12, no. 2 (1980).

28. *CNC Annual Report*, 1956, p. 25; Passmore, *Community Development*, p. 30.

29. *CNC Annual Report*, 1957, p. 32.

30. On the role of nationalists see *Mangwende Commission Report*, p. 172; also the dissenting minority report by the Reverend J. A. C. Shaw, who was one of the commissioners [*Shaw Minority Report*, 1960] pp. 12–13; Ranger, "African Politics," p. 238; also H. R. G. Howman, *NADA*, 1956.

31. SIA, *Annual Report*, 1964, p. 10.

32. Quoted in Gray, *Two Nations*, p. 299.

33. Holleman, *Chief, Council and Commissioner*, p. 61.

34. Numerous cases are cited in the NAD's community delineation reports of 1962–65; see also Holleman, *African Interlude* (Cape Town: Nasionale Boekhandel, 1958), pp. 240–48.

35. Child, *Tribal Law in Rhodesia*, p. 15.

36. See *Mangwende Commission Report* and *Shaw Minority Report*; Weinrich, *African Farmers in Rhodesia*, pp. 69–70; *CNC Annual Report*, 1948, p. 18; idem, 1956, p. 27.

37. *Mangwende Commission Report*; Wright, *Valley of the Ironwoods*, pp. 201–3; Holleman, *African Interlude*, p. 251.

38. See *Mangwende Commission Report* and *Shaw Minority Report*. For an explicit connection between a chief's opposition to the NLHA and his opposition to threats from local elites, see Ministry of Internal Affairs, *Community Delineation Reports*, Gwanda District. See also Wright, *Valley of the Ironwoods*, pp. 197–98.

39. Werbner, *Tears of the Dead*, p. 43.

40. *CNC Annual Report*, 1961, pp. 2–3, 9. On economic decline, see R. A. Griffith, "The Part Played by Government in the Development of Agriculture in Tribal Trust Lands," paper presented at NRB Conference on the Tribal Trust Lands, University College of Rhodesia, 2–3 February 1966.

41. *Robinson Commission Report*, p. 48.

42. *Hansard* 49, 16 November 1961, col. 101; SIA, *Annual Report*, 1963, p. 8; idem, 1964, p. 10. Secretary of Internal Affairs Nicolle was a significant exception to the general view that the LHA had failed.

43. Quoted in A. J. B. Hughes, *Development in Rhodesian Tribal Areas: An Overview* (Salisbury: Tribal Areas of Rhodesia Research Foundation, 1974), p. 148; emphasis in original.

44. *Hansard* 49, 14 November 1961, cols. 7–8; D. G. Clarke, *The Unemployment Crisis* (Gweru: Mambo Press, 1978), p. 6.

45. The relevant commissions were the 1958 Plewman Commission, the 1961 Robinson Commission, the 1962 Phillips Committee's report on economic development. See also M. Hirsch, *A Decade of Crisis: Ten Years of Rhodesian Front Rule* (Salisbury: Peter Dearlove, 1973), p. 116.

46. Quoted in Barber, *Rhodesia*, p. 118; Joint Committee on Technical Education, *Confidential Report on The African School-Leaver*, 1962, p. 4.

47. *Report of Joint Committee on Technical Education*, pp. 1–2; see also Judges Commission on Education, quoted in Hirsch, *Decade of Crisis*, p. 113.

48. Quoted in Hughes, *Development in Tribal Areas*, p. 78.

49. *Hansard* 50, col. 154, 26 June 1962; Clarke, *Unemployment Crisis*, p. 7.; also D. Caute, *Under the Skin: The Death of White Rhodesia* (Harmondsworth: Penguin, 1983), pp. 91–92.

50. For a revealing discussion, see Holderness, *Lost Chance*, 1945–58.

51. Quoted in *Hansard* 53, 22 August 1963, col. 1878; see also *Hansard* 50, 28 June 1962, cols. 262–65.

52. *CNC Annual Report, 1955,* pp. 28–29.

53. Ibid., 1952, p. 32.

54. Wright, *Valley of the Ironwoods,* p. 214; *Mangwende Commission Report.*

55. *Robinson Commission Report,* pp. 21–22; H. R. G. Howman, *NADA,* 1954, pp. 46–48.

56. Howman, *NADA,* 1954, p. 43.

57. *Report of the Native Councils Board,* 1958, p. 133.

58. *Robinson Commission Report,* p. 30.

59. See especially Howman, *NADA,* 1956, pp. 13, 20; idem, "The Community Board," in *Rhodesian Community Development Review,* 1, no. 2 (1966), p. 7; idem, "Changing Social Structure and Land Tenure," paper delivered to Symposium on Drought and Development, Bulawayo, 1968; personal interview with Howman, 9 August 1989; Passmore, *Community Development,* p. 53.

60. *CNC Annual Report,* 1961, pp. 9, 26, 27.

61. Quoted in L. Holdcroft, "The Rise and Fall of Community Development in Developing Countries," Rural Development Paper no. 2 (East Lansing: Michigan State University, 1978). See also G. Passmore, "Historical Rationale of the Policy of Community Development in the African Rural Areas of Rhodesia," *Zambezia* 2, no. 1 (1971), pp. 8–10.

62. *Report on African Development and Local Government in Southern Rhodesia,* by J. Green, September 1962, part 1; Working Party "A" Report, p. 16; *CNC Annual Report,* 1961, p. 1.

63. *Report of the Commission on Urban African Affairs (Plewman Commission),* 1958, pp. 108–109.

64. *Report of Native Councils Board,* 1961, pp. 16, 97, 149; Working Party "A" Report, 1961, p. 10.

65. *Hansard* 48, 24 August, 1961, cols. 477–95.

66. *Hansard* 49, 21 November 1961, cols. 161–62.

67. For discussion of the campaign, see N. Shamuyarira, *Crisis in Rhodesia* (London: André Deutsch, 1965), pp. 42–43, 48.

68. *CNC Annual Report,* 1955, p. 8.

69. Ibid., 1961, p. 4.

70. MacLean, *Guardians,* p. 226.

71. SIA, *Annual Report,* 1962, p. 2. The staffing problem was so

great that all leave was canceled in 1963. To remedy the problem the ministry began in the following year to recruit in boys' high schools.

Chapter Four

1. H. R. G Howman, "Economic Growth and Community Development in African Areas," *NADA*, 10, no. 1, 1969.
2. See Working Party "A" Report, p. 17; Working Party "B" (Agriculture) Report, pp. 12, 18.
3. M. Murphree, "A Village School and Community Development in a Rhodesian Tribal Trust Land," *Zambezia* 1, no. 2 (1970); Bessant, *Coercive Development*; D. Mungazi, *Education and Government Control in Zimbabwe; A Study of the Commissions of Inquiry, 1908–1974* (New York: Praeger, 1990).
4. *Robinson Commission Report*, p. 48.
5. *National Development Plan*, 1965, p. 1; Rhodesian Front, *Principles of the Rhodesian Front*, 1969; see also Whitsun Foundation, *Agriculture in Rhodesia* (Salisbury: Whitsun Foundation, 1977); interviews with F. A. Staunton, N. A. Hunt, J. Howman [NAZ], and S. E. Morris [Durban, 10 March 1988]; Working Party "B" Report.
6. A. F. Hunt, "The Economic Position of the Tribal Trust Land in Relation to Agriculture," paper presented at NRB Conference on the Tribal Trust Land, University College of Rhodesia (2<3> February1966); See also R. Riddell, *The Land Question*, From Rhodesia to Zimbabwe, vol. 2 (Gwelo: Mambo Press, 1978), pp. 7–8; M. Blackie, "The Elusive Peasant: Zimbabwe Agriculture Policy, 1965–1986," in *Food Security for Southern Africa*, ed. M. Rukuni and C. Eicher (Harare: University of Zimbabwe, Department of Agricultural Economics and Extension, UZ/MSU Food Security Project, 1987). On white business, see articles by J. G. Hillis, *NADA*, 1971–1973; I. Hancock, *White Liberals, Moderates and Radicals in Rhodesia* (London: Croom Helm, 1984). See Hughes, *Development in Tribal Areas*, p. 27.
7. C. S. Davies, "Tribalism and Economic Development," *NADA* 10, no. 2 (1970), p. 82.
8. Cheater, *Idioms of Accumulation*, p. 171; A. M. Hawkins, "African Unemployment in Rhodesia," *Rhodesia Science News* 8, no. 7 (July 1974); Cormack, *Towards Self-Reliance*, pp. 99–100.
9. D. Martin and P. Johnson, *The Struggle for Zimbabwe: The*

Chimurenga War (Johannesburg: Ravan Press, 1981); K. Flower, *Serving Secretly: Rhodesia's CIO Chief on Record* (Alberton, S.A.: Galago, 1987).

10. *Report by J. L. Sadie on Planning for the Economic Development of Rhodesia*, 1967 [CSR 35-1967], pp. 7, 19–23, 46–48.

11. The series was reprinted in a Ministry of Information, Immigration and Tourism booklet, *The Border Lands*, by J. A. Hughes. See also J. J. Wrathall, "Developing the Tribal Trust Lands," *Rhodesian Journal of Economics* 2, no. 4 (December 1968). The arguments were repeated, almost verbatim, in a prize-winning essay in a schools' essay competition that year.

12. See Smith's statement the "Independence" debate: *Hansard* 55, 26 November 1963, cols. 194–95.

13. R. C. Haw (Ministry of Information), *Land Apportionment in Rhodesia*, January 1965, p. 14; emphasis in original.

14. Interview with former Provincial Commissioner, Harare, 1987; J. Howman interview [NAZ].

15. W. H. H. Nicolle, "The Legal and Social Status of the Tribal Trust Lands in Rhodesia," paper presented at NRB Conference on the Tribal Trust Lands, University College of Rhodesia, 2–3 February 1966, pp. 1–2.

16. This point was made by a number of interviewees. It was sometimes accompanied by the argument that Africans would readily maximize their profits if they could get around this millstone; no interviewees explained the relationship between the individual's communal self-understanding and the desire to escape the claims of family in terms of their capacity to accumulate. See especially letter from Nicolle to St. Quintin, lodged in St. Quintin Papers; Nicolle interview, Durban 1987; interview with F. A. Staunton [NAZ].

17. W. H. H. Nicolle, "The Development of the Tribal Trust Lands of Rhodesia," paper presented at NRB Conference on the Tribal Trust Lands, University College of Rhodesia, 2–3 February 1966, p. 11; *Hansard* 68, 20 July 1967, col. 31. See also Hughes, *Development in Tribal Areas*; Wrathall, *NADA*, 1968, p. xi.

18. SIA, *Annual Report*, 1965, p. 7.

19. *CNC Annual Report*, 1961, p. 9.

20. Wrathall, "Developing the Tribal Trust Lands," p. 54.

21. Quoted in SIA, *Annual Report*, 1972, p. 17. In most TTLs, transportation facilities were scant and markets distant; quoted in D.

K. Davies, *Race Relations in Rhodesia: A Survey for 1972–73* (London: Rex Collings, 1975), p. 277.

22. A. J. B. Hughes, "The Inter-Relation of Social Structure, Land Tenure, and Land Use," paper delivered to Symposium on Drought and Development, Bulawayo, May 1967, p. 9.

23. Nicolle, "Legal and Social Status," pp. 1–2.

24. As Hughes concluded, "it would seem reasonable to argue that there are, in effect, 252 separate land communities in the TTLs" (*Development in Tribal Areas*, p. 46).

25. Ibid., p. 47.

26. *Hansard* 54, 29 August 1963, col. 185.

27. Child, *Tribal Law in Rhodesia*, p. 15.

28. N. D. Mutizwa-Mangiza notes that only voluntary resettlement was undertaken after 1964; *Community Development in Pre-Independence Zimbabwe*, supplement to *Zambezia* (Harare: University of Zimbabwe, 1985), p. 18. See also Hughes, *Border Lands*, p. 2.

29. This paragraph is based on the Internal Affairs Community Delineation Reports from Umvuma and Gokwe districts, 1963–64. See also SIA, *Annual Report*, 1970, p. 20.

30. SIA, *Annual Report*, 1970, p. 31. For a detailed discussion of the Tangwena struggle see H. Moyana, *The Political Economy of Land in Zimbabwe* (Gweru: Mambo Press, 1984), chap. 6. On current politics, see D. Moore, "Contesting Terrain in Zimbabwe's Eastern Highlands: Political Ecology, Ethnography, and Peasant Resource Struggles," *Economic Geography* 19, no. 4 (1993).

31. Hughes, *Development in Tribal Areas*, pp. 58–64. SIA, *Annual Report*, 1972, p. 13. Griffith, "Development of Agriculture," p. 6.

32. T. A. Murton, "Land-Use Planning in Tribal Areas in Rhodesia," *Rhodesian Agricultural Journal* 68, no. 1 (1971), pp. 6–7; emphasis in original.

33. Hughes, *Development in Tribal Areas*, pp. 150–55; SIA, *Annual Report*, 1968, p. 3; Murton, "Land-Use Planning," p. 7; Loewenson and Gelfand, *NADA*, 1980.

34. Many people refer to Nicolle's influence; one interviewee referred to him as the "thirteenth cabinet member," another simply as "the government." On community development, one ex-DC remarked, "One had the impression that he was luke-warm at best, and suspicious." See also Blake, *History of Rhodesia*, pp. 400–401; Barber, *Rhodesia*; Flower, *Serving Secretly*, pp. 87–88, 294–98.

35. SIA, *Annual Report*, 1966, p. 9.

36. Nicolle, "Development of the Tribal Trust Lands," p. 2.

37. SIA, *Annual Report*, 1969, p. 1.

38. Statement of Policy and Directive by the Prime Minister, 1965, para. This directive was also unique in being the first directive issued to all ministries.

39. See, for instance, Community Development and Local Government Co-Ordinating Committee, *Memo on Local Government and Community Development Policy*, 1972, pp. 5, 2–4; interview with ex-DC Mount Darwin.

40. Community Development and Local Government Co-Ordinating Committee, *Memo on Local Government and Community Development Policy*, 1971, p. 1; my emphasis; Passmore, *Community Development*, pp. 221–29.

41. Cormack, *Towards Self-Reliance*, p. 177.

42. K. Bloore, "A Condensation of the Batten Report," *Community Development Review*, p. 1.

43. A. Hunt, "Economic Position," pp. 3–4.

44. See especially SIA, *Annual Report*, 1973, p. 14.

45. Murton, "Land-Use Planning," p. 8; *Hansard* 68, 20 July 1967, col. 31; *Hansard* 78, 8 September 1970, cols. 570–71.

46. This was the thrust of the magazine *Projects and People* that the Branch of Community Development Training began publishing in 1971.

47. *Prime Minister's Directive*, paras. 30, 33.

48. R. C. Woollacott, "Community Boards," in *Community Development and Local Government Bulletin*, no. 6 (May 1966), pp. 11–13.

49. Passmore, *Community Development*, p. 250; SIA, *Annual Reports*, 1966, p. 8; 1968, pp. 7–8.

50. Ministry of Internal Affairs, *Community Delineation Reports*, Gwanda, 23 July 1964; SIA, *Annual Report*, 1966, p. 8; Passmore, *Community Development*, pp. 250–56.

51. M. Bratton, *Beyond Community Development: The Political Economy of Rural Administration in Zimbabwe* (Gwelo: Mambo Press, 1978), p. 23; also Passmore, *Community Development*, pp. 256–57.

52. Working Party "B" Report, p. 22; SIA, *Annual Report*, 1962, p. 17. See also *Hansard* 54, 28 August 1963, cols. 97–105; Whitsun Foundation, *Agriculture in Rhodesia*, p. 11.

53. Ministry of Internal Affairs, *Community Delineation Report*, Gwanda district, 8 May 1964; interview with ex-DC Binga.

54. Ministry of Internal Affairs, *Community Delineation Report,* Zaka district, 28 September 1964. See also the *Community Delineation Reports* for Umvuma, Gutu, and Gokwe districts; Barber, *Rhodesia,* pp. 228–29.

55. SIA, *Annual Report,* 1968, p. 14.

56. Ministry of Internal Affairs, *Projects and People,* no. 2 (1971), and no. 3 (December 1972); SIA, *Annual Reports,* 1969, p. 19; 1970, pp. 1–2; Weinrich, *Chiefs and Councils,* p. 168; *X-Ray,* August 1970; Murphree, "Village School."

57. Quoted in *X-Ray,* September 1972.

58. See Ministry of Internal Affairs, *Projects and People,* no. 2 (1972), p. 5.

59. SIA, *Annual Report,* 1970, p. 49.

60. Quoted in Bessant, *Coercive Development,* p. 17; Rapoko is finger millet, Ministry of Internal Affairs. *Community Delineation Report,* Filabusi district; Weinrich, *Chiefs and Councils,* p. 168; Ministry of Internal Affairs, *Internal Affairs National Serviceman's Handbook,* section on teachers.

61. Murton, "Land-Use Planning," p. 8; emphasis in original. *Hansard* 54, 28 August 1963, cols. 98–100; R. Griffith, "Development of Agriculture."

62. SIA, *Annual Report,* 1973, p. 10; T. W. F. Jordan, *NADA,* 1978, pp. 517–18.

63. SIA, *Annual Report,* 1970, p. 24; B. Elkington and R. Woollacott, "The Role of Education and Communication in Community Development in African Rural Areas," *Rhodesia Science News* 6, no. 2 (February 1972), p. 60.

64. Elkington and Woollacott, "Role of Education," pp. 57–61. Elkington was Director, Community Development Training, and Woollacott was Provincial Commissioner.

65. "Building Communities of the Future—DEEDS not WORDS," *Projects and People,* no. 3 (December 1972), supplement on Young Farmers and Natural Resources Clubs. This paragraph draws heavily on this publication.

66. SIA, *Annual Reports,* 1972, p. 13; 1973, pp. 10–11. Hughes, *Development in Tribal Areas,* p. 117.

67. SIA, *Annual Report,* 1971, p. 22; Elkington and Woollacott, "Role of Education," p. 58; G. M. Masterson, "Memories of a Native Commissioner's Wife," *NADA* 11, no. 4 (1977), p. 399.

68. Ministry of Internal Affairs, *A Decade of Challenge and Achieve-*

ment: The Story behind the Community Development Section (Women) of the Ministry of Internal Affairs of Rhodesia, 1976.

69. Ibid., p. 22. In the original, this passage appeared in bold capital letters.

70. G. A. Smith, "A Strategy for Rural Development: Savings Clubs and Package Programmes," University of Rhodesia, Institute of Adult Education, June 1974, pp. 2, 7.

71. Ministry of Internal Affairs, *Decade of Challenge*, p. 31.

72. Ranchod-Nilsson, "Educating Eve," pp. 28–34.

73. Ministry of Internal Affairs, *Government Grants to African Councils from 1 July 1970*.

74. See Bratton, *Beyond Community Development*, p. 23.

75. See *Community Delineation Reports* from Darwin, Filabusi, Gwanda, Hartley, Gutu districts.

76. See especially *Community Delineation Reports*, introduction, Gutu, Darwin districts.

77. *Hansard* 80, cols. 582–85, 633–34, 3 and 7 September 1971.

78. Quoted in Blake, *History of Rhodesia*, p. 405.

79. Howman, "Changing Social Structure," p. 11. Notably, however, Howman proceeds to endorse the government's policy of bolstering tribal authorities wholeheartedly.

Chapter Five

1. See variously, Agricultural Development Authority (ADA), *Annual Report* for year ending 30 June 1976, pp. 6–7; *Hansard* 82, 6 September 1972, cols. 1201–2; 15 November 1972, cols. 1528–29; A. Astrow, *Zimbabwe*, pp. 59, 150; *Rhodesia Herald*, 9 May 1974, 11 May 1974; Hawkins, "African Unemployment."

2. RF Policy Statement, n.d.

3. *Rhodesia Herald*, 27 May 1972; *Rhodesian Forum*, July 1972.

4. SIA, *Annual Report*, 1973, p. 1; Davies, *Race Relations in Rhodesia*, p. 107; *Rhodesian Forum*, August 1972.

5. See TILCOR, *National Development: Proposals for the Under Developed Parts of the Country*, December 1976, p. 8.

6. See R. C. Plowden, "The Modern Role of Rhodesia's Chiefs," in *Rhodesia Calls*, January/February 1977.

7. *Rhodesian Forum*, August 1972.

8. Ibid., November 1972.

9. Ibid., August 1972 and November 1972.

10. See Minister of Local Government and Housing's address to annual conference of the Local Government Association, 1972; *Hansard* 82, col. 486, 29 November 1972; Davies, *Race Relations in Rhodesia*, pp. 277, 313.

11. TILCOR, *Urban Development at TILCOR Growth Points*, 25 June 1976, NAZ Gen/Tri-p, p. 1; idem, "Tilcor's Growth Point Policy," 22 June 1977, NAZ Gen/Tri-p.

12. D. Seager, "A Salisbury Squatter Settlement: The Struggle for Shelter in an Urban Environment," *South African Labour Bulletin* 3, no. 6 (May 1977).

13. *Policy on Decentralization*, Cmd.R.R.31—1974, p. 7; Hawkins, *Economic Growth*, p. 31. The Select Committee was not permitted to visit any Tribal Trust Land; *Hansard* 82, 7 September 1972, cols. 1328, 1339.

14. *Policy on Decentralization*, pp. 6–8; interview with former Provincial Commissioner; J. Hillis, *NADA*, 1972, pp. 110–11; idem, *NADA*, 1973, especially pp. 14–15, 36; Ministry of Internal Affairs, "Business and Trading Functions of Sites Leased in the Tribal Trust Lands: May 1978" by F. H. Dodd (June 1978), p. 10.

15. *Hansard* 82, 5 September 1972, cols. 1181–82.

16. Minister of Local Government and Housing, quoted in Davies, *Race Relations in Rhodesia*, pp. 305–6.

17. *Hansard* 82, 29 November 1972, col. 493.

18. *Rhodesia Herald*, 4 December 1972.

19. Minute to Minister of Internal Affairs, on RF Papers on Constitution, 26 August 1968, reproduced in G. Passmore, ed., *H. R. G. Howman on Provincialisation in Rhodesia 1968–1969; and Rational and Irrational Elements* (Cambridge: Cambridge African Occasional Papers no. 4, n.d.), pp. 43–48. See also Minute on Provincial Councils (2 September 1968) and Minute on Provincialisation (11 March 1969), also reproduced here.

20. ADA, *Annual Report* for year ending June 1978, p. 5; address by Director of Whitsun Foundation to National Affairs Association of Rhodesia, 30 January 1976; director's address to Geographical Association, p. 17.

21. For a characterization of state-business relations in market-oriented societies as "close but uneasy" see C. Lindblom, *Politics and Markets: The World's Political-Economic Systems* (New York: Basic Books, 1977), pp. 170–85.

22. Ministry of Finance, *Integrated Plan for Rural Development, July 1978*, pp. 3, 12, 14, 23, 29.

23. C. J. K. Latham, "Some Notes on the Tribes in the Mount Darwin, Rushinga and Centenary Districts," *NADA* 11, no. 2 (1975), p. 96.

24. R. Riddell, *Land Question.*

25. See T. Ranger, "Tradition and Travesty: Chiefs and the Administration in Makoni District, Zimbabwe, 1960–1980," *Africa* 52 (1982); Latham, *Mwari*, pp. 72–75.

26. A. J. B. Hughes, *Development in Tribal Areas*, p. 160; emphasis in original. Internal Affairs Circular 205 of 1973.

27. A. J. B. Hughes, *Development in Tribal Areas*, p. 181.

28. Ranger, "Tradition and Travesty," p. 32.

29. A. K. H. Weinrich, *Black and White Elites in Rural Rhodesia* (Manchester: Manchester University Press, 1973), pp. 200–202; A. Elliott, "Witchcraft in the Lowveld." *NADA* 9, no. 3, 1966, pp. 5–9; Latham, *Mwari*, pp. 72–74.

30. Lan, *Guns and Rain*, pp. 35–39, 142; Scoones et al. *Hazards and Opportunities.*

31. Werbner, *Tears of the Dead*, pp. 149–51; Lan, *Guns and Rain*, pp. 167–70; Ranger, "Tradition and Travesty," pp. 27–28.

32. Interview with ex-DC Mount Darwin; Martin and Johnson, *Struggle for Zimbabwe*, pp. 73–92. For growing interest in the role and power of the spirit mediums, see *NADA* articles by Gelfand and Gelfand, Bourdillon, Woollacott, Kaschula, Latham.

33. Latham, *Mwari*, pp. 156, 5; Ministry of Internal Affairs, *Serviceman's Handbook*, section 35.

34. Latham, *NADA*, 1975, p. 172.

35. For the political manipulations of the struggle, and its effects on people's lives (and deaths), see Latham, *Mwari*, pp. 150–211; M. F. C. Bourdillon, "Spirit Mediums in Shona Belief and Practice," *NADA* 11, no. 1 (1974); M. Raeburn, *Black Fire! Accounts of the Guerilla in Rhodesia* (London: Julian Friedmann, 1978), pp. 216–22.

36. Lan, *Guns and Rain*, pp. 136–53, 164, 167, 220–21; Ranger, *Peasant Consciousness*, pp. 291–98.

37. See P. Chabal, "People's War, State Formation, and Revolution in Africa: A Comparative Analysis of Mozambique, Guinea-Bissau, and Angola," in *State and Class in Africa*, ed. N. Kasfir (London: Frank Cass, 1984), especially pp. 119–25.

38. On cultural nationalism in rural appeals, see Wright, *Valley of the Ironwoods*; J. Frederikse, *None But Ourselves: Masses vs. Media in the Making of Zimbabwe* (Johannesburg: Ravan Press, 1982); R. Mugabe, *Our War of Liberation: Speeches, Articles, Interviews 1976–1979* (Harare: Mambo Press, 1983), pp. 48–58, 121–37, 153–60, and passim.

39. N. Kriger, *Zimbabwe's Guerrilla War: Peasant Voices* (Cambridge: Cambridge University Press, 1992); Ranchod-Nilsson, "'Educating Eve.'"

40. The following paragraphs draw mainly on Kriger, *Zimbabwe's Guerrilla War*, pp. 176–211, and passim.

41. T. Ranger, "Bandits and Guerrillas: The Case of Zimbabwe," in *Banditry, Rebellion and Social Protest*, ed. D. Crummey (London: James Currey, 1986); Werbner, *Tears of the Dead*, p. 150.

42. Zimbabwe Women's Bureau, *We Carry a Heavy Load*; interview with MCDWA official; Frederikse, *None But Ourselves*, pp. 339, 346; I. Staunton, *Mothers of the Revolution*; Ranchod-Nilsson, "'Educating Eve.'"

43. Kriger, *Zimbabwe's Guerrilla War*, pp. 187–89, 196–205.

44. For hints at this tension, see especially the Ministry of Internal Affairs, *Serviceman's Handbook*, section 58; *Operation Hurricane: Civil and Military*, memorandum, DC Mount Darwin, 1 October 1975; interviews with DC Mount Darwin, DC Nuanetsi. For the dislocation felt by DCs under the new regime, see also A. R. Fynn, "The New Administration." *NADA* 11, no. 5 (1978).

45. *The Role of Internal Affairs and the Future of Rhodesia*, secret memorandum, DC Mount Darwin, 26 May 1977; emphasis in original. Interviews with DC Mount Darwin, DC Nuanetsi.

46. C. Brand, "From Compound to Keep: On the Nature of Settler Control in Southern Rhodesia," paper read at a session of the Research Committee on Ethnic, Race, and Minority Relations, 9th World Congress of Sociology, Uppsala, Sweden, August 1978; A. K. H. Weinrich, "Strategic Resettlement in Rhodesia," *Journal of Southern African Studies* 3, no. 2 (April 1977); Internal Affairs, *List of Protected Sub-Offices; Protected Villages; Unprotected Sub-Offices*, April 1978; Ministry of Internal Affairs, *Serviceman's Handbook*; Astrow, *Zimbabwe*, p. 64.

47. See *Hansard* 86, 28 March 1974, col. 443; see also 20 March 1974, col. 69, and 30 March 1974, col. 1174.

Chapter Six

1. G. Williams, "Growth, Equity and the State," *Africa* 52, no. 3 (1982), p. 114.

2. ZANU(PF), *Zimbabwe at Five Years of Independence: Achievements, Problems and Prospects* (Harare: Nehanda Publishers, 1985), p. ix.

3. Robert Mugabe, addressing the Justice and Peace Commission, Gweru, 6 February 1982; ZANU(PF), *Zimbabwe at Five Years*, introduction.

4. Ministry of Finance, Economic Planning and Development (MFEPD),, *Growth with Equity: An Economic Policy Statement*, Cmd. R.Z.4-1981, February 1981; MFEPD, *First Five Year National Development Plan, 1986–1990*, vol. 1, April 1986, pp. 10, 12; see also pp. 2–3, and passim.

5. *Africa Report*, May-June 1982, p. 10.

6. *Hansard* 14, no. 55, 10 March 1988, cols. 2977–88.

7. GOZ, *Growth with Equity*, p. 4–5.

8. CSO, *1982 Population Census*; CSO, *Main Demographic Features of the Population of Zimbabwe*, 1982 Population Census, June 1985, pp. 9–13, 27–30, 53–57; R. Whitlow, "Environmental Constraints and Population Pressures in the Tribal Areas of Zimbabwe," *Zimbabwe Agricultural Journal* 77, no. 4 (1980); Dr. Norman Reynolds, Symposium on the Promotion of Small-Scale Entrepreneurs, October 1988, cited in *Financial Gazette*, 4 November 1988; Ministry of Natural Resources and Tourism, *The National Conservation Strategy: Zimbabwe's Road to Survival*, April 1987, p. 8.

9. D. Patel, "Urbanisation, Population and Development," paper presented to Seminar on Population in Development Planning, Harare, 28–30 October, 1987.

10. See, for instance, Ministry of Local Government, Rural and Urban Development (MLGRUD), *Manicaland Provincial Development Plan*, July 1986, p. 518.

11. L. Cliffe, *Agrarian Reform*, p. 55.

12. MLGRUD, *Matabeleland North Provincial Development Plan*, 1986, vol. 2, p. 50.

13. Raikes, *Modernising Hunger*, pp. 79, 84.

14. J. Stanning, "Household Grain Storage and Marketing in Surplus and Deficit Communal Farming Areas in Zimbabwe: Preliminary Findings," in *Food Security for Southern Africa*, ed. M. Rukuni and C. Eicher Cliffe, *Agrarian Reform*, pp. 35–36; N. Amin, "State and

Peasantry"; *Report of the Commission of Inquiry into the Agricultural Industry* (Chavunduka Commission Report), June 1982, p. 3; M. Bratton "Financing Smallholder Production: A Comparison of Individual and Group Credit Schemes in Zimbabwe," University of Zimbabwe, Department of Land Management Working Paper 2/5, February 1987, p. 7; Drinkwater, *State and Agrarian Change*, chap. 5; van den Pool et al. "Farming Systems."

15. J. Jackson and P. Collier, "Incomes, Poverty and Food Security in the Communal Lands of Zimbabwe," Department of Rural and Urban Planning Occasional Paper no. 11 (Harare: University of Zimbabwe, 1988), pp. 1–2, 30, 38; Agritex, *Wedza Baseline Study*, pp. 2, 12.

16. C. Mutambirwa, "Population and Migration," paper presented to Seminar on Population in Development Planning, Harare, 1987, pp. 13–14; M. Mukundu, "Factors Limiting Increased Crop Production in Tribal Trust Lands as an Extension Worker Sees Them," *Rhodesia Science News* 10, no. 10 (October 1976).

17. Agritex, *Report on Training and Visiting System in Midlands Province*, June 1985, p. 4; W. Zehender et al., *Options for Regional Development in the Pfura and Rushinga Districts, Zimbabwe* (Berlin: German Development Institute, 1984), p. 32.

18. *Manicaland Provincial Development Plan*, p. 273; Agritex, *Wedza Baseline Study*, p. 10; see also Agritex, *Training and Visiting System in Midlands Province*, June 1985, p. 3; Ranger, *Peasant Consciousness*, pp. 286–87.

19. World Bank, *Zimbabwe: Land Subsector Study*, report no. 5878-ZIM (Washington, D.C.: World Bank, 1986), pp. 15–17; B. Cousins, *A Survey of Current Grazing Schemes in the Communal Lands of Zimbabwe* (Harare: University of Zimbabwe, Centre for Applied Social Sciences, September 1987), pp. 69–76; Cliffe, *Agrarian Reform*, appendix 4.

20. Minister of Local Government, address to Association of Rural Councils, 5 April 1989; A. H. J. Helmsing et al., *Limits to Decentralisation in Zimbabwe* (Harare: University of Zimbabwe, Press 1991); U. Otzen et al., *Development Management from Below: The Potential Contribution of Co- Operatives and Village Development Committees to Self-Management and Decentralised Development in Zimbabwe* (Berlin: German Development Institute, 1988), p. 65.

21. The following paragraphs draw mainly on Lawyers Committee for Human Rights, *Zimbabwe: Wages of War: A Report on Human*

Rights (New York: Lawyers Committee for Human Rights, 1986); Catholic Commission for Justice and Peace in Zimbabwe, *Report on the Disturbances in Matabeleland and the Midlands (1983–1987)* (March 1997); Werbner, *Tears of the Dead*, 161–73. See also T. Ranger, "Matabeleland since the Amnesty," *African Affairs* 88, no. 351 (April 1989); Kaarsholm, "Past as Battlefield."

22. J. Moyo argues persuasively that ethnic tensions, to the extent that they existed, operated within each party and not between them; *Voting for Democracy: A Study of Electoral Politics in Zimbabwe* (Harare: University of Zimbabwe Press, 1992), pp. 22–31. For contending views see M. Sithole, "Zimbabwe: In Search of a Stable Democracy," in *Democracy in Developing Countries*, vol. 2: *Africa*, ed. Larry Diamond, J. Linz, and S, Lipset (Boulder: Lynne Rienner, 1989); Herbst, *State Politics in Zimbabwe*, pp. 168–72.

23. L. Sachikonye, "The 1990 Zimbabwe Elections: A Post-Mortem," *Review of African Political Economy*, no. 48 (1990), p. 96; idem, "The Debate on Democracy in Contemporary Zimbabwe," *Review of African Political Economy*, nos. 45–46 (1989), p. 117; C. Sylvester, "Unities and Disunities in Zimbabwe's 1990 Elections," *Journal of Modern African Studies* 28, no. 3 (1990).

24. C. Sylvester, *Zimbabwe: The Terrain of Contradictory Development* (Boulder: Westview Press, 1991), chap. 3; M. Sithole, "Zimbabwe's Eroding Authoritarianism," *Journal of Democracy*, 8, no. 1 (1997).

25. *Hansard* 10, no. 28, 5 September 1984, especially cols. 1619–1625. Ben Cousins, personal communication on Zimuto and Mhondoro; Lawyers Committee for Human Rights, *Zimbabwe*, pp. 54–56.

26. I. Mandaza, ed., *Zimbabwe: The Political Economy of Transition, 1980–1986* (Dakar: CODESRIA, 1986), p. 53; A. Sibanda, "The Political Situation," in *Zimbabwe's Prospects: Issues of Race, Class, State and Capital in Southern Africa*, ed. C. Stoneman (London: MacMillan, 1988), pp. 264–68. This characterization indicates the fluid character of the elite. The rural strength of the party is a matter for argument. There are wide regional differences, and there is evidence that the party label is used by local notables or youths to carve out local domains of power, rather than the other way around. See also Ranger's concluding argument in *Peasant Consciousness and Guerilla War in Zimbabwe* and Norma Kriger's reply in "The Zimbabwean War of Liberation: Struggles within the Struggle," *Journal of Southern African Studies* 14, no. 2 (January 1988). See also Ranger, "Matabeleland since the Amnesty."

27. Scoones and Wilson, "Households"; Pankhurst, *Dynamics of Social Relations;* S. Moyo, "Zimbabwe's Agrarian Reform Process: Lessons or Domino Strategies?" Zimbabwe Institute of Development Studies Discussion Paper no. 12 (1991). I am grateful to Ben Cousins for discussions on the party and the state in Zimuto, Mhondoro, and Mwenezi. See also M. Bratton, "Comrades and the Countryside"; Herbst, *State Politics in Zimbabwe*, chap. 4.

28. Ranger, *Peasant Consciousness*, pp. 291–97; Lan, *Guns and Rain*, pp. 217–22; R. Murapa, *Rural and District Administrative Reform in Zimbabwe* (Bordeaux: Centre d'Etude a'Afrique Noire, 1986), pp. 32–33; Pankhurst, *Dynamics of Social Relations;* C. Brand, "Will Decentralization Enhance Participation?" in Helmsing et al. *Limits to Decentralization in Zimbabwe*, pp. 89–90.

29. *Hansard* vol. 11, no. 2, 12 September 1984, cols. 135–36; see also vol. 11, no. 3, col. 204; Murapa, *Administrative Reform*, p. 25.

30. Murapa, *Administrative Reform*, p. 21.

31. Ministry of Local Government and Town Planning, *Delineation of VIDCOs and WADCOs*, p. 2; Ministry of Community Development and Women's Affairs (MCDWA), *Annual Report*, 1983, p. 9; MCDWA, *Let's Build Zimbabwe Together*, pp. 34–35.

32. GOZ, "Provincial Councils and Administration in Zimbabwe: A Statement of Policy and a Directive by the Honourable Robert Gabriel Mugabe, M.P., Prime Minister, Government of the Republic of Zimbabwe," pp. 7–13; MPDC, *Midlands Provincial Development Plan*, 1986, p. 3; D. Conyers, "Decentralization and Development Planning: A Comparative Perspective," paper presented to Workshop on the Planning System in Zimbabwe, University of Zimbabwe Department of Rural and Urban Planning (4–7 February 1986), p. 21.

33. GOZ, "Provincial Councils and Administration," p. 3; P. de Valk, "An Analysis of Planning Policy in Zimbabwe," paper presented to Workshop on the Planning System in Zimbabwe, University of Zimbabwe, Department of Rural and Urban Planning (4–7 February 1986), p. 14; *Moto*, 27 September 1984, p. 6.

34. GOZ, "Provincial Councils and Administration," pp. 14–15.

35. This phrase, used by a rural citizen, was quoted to me by Coenraad Brand; see also S. Nyoni, "Indigenous NGOs: Liberation, Self-Reliance and Development," *World Development* 15, supplement (1987); M. Bratton, "Non-Governmental Organizations in Africa: Can They Influence Public Policy?" *Development and Change* 21, no. 1 (1990), especially pp. 88–89.

36. MLARR, Monitoring and Evaluation Unit, *Resettlement Report*, 1986, p. 69.

37. MCDWA, *Let's Build Zimbabwe Together*, pp. 34–35; Brand, "Will Decentralization Enhance Participation?" pp. 85–86; van den Pool et al., *Farming Systems*, p. 7.

38. T. Shopo, "Some Perspectives on Administrative Accountability for Nation Building and Development," paper read to University of Zimbabwe Department of Rural and Urban Planning Workshop on Planning, February 1986, p. 22.

39. Minister of Local Government, Rural and Urban Development, Enos Chikowore, addressing the inaugural meeting of the Matabeleland South Provincial Council at Gwanda, 7 March 1986, reported in *Zimbabwe News* 17, no. 4 (April 1986), p. 13; Brand, "Will Decentralization Enhance Participation?" p. 91.

40. Drinkwater, *State and Agrarian Change*, p. 97.

41. D. Rohrbach, "A Preliminary Assessment of Factors Underlying the Growth of Communal Maize Production in Zimbabwe," in *Food Security for Southern Africa*, ed. M. Rukuni and C. Eicher, pp. 145–48; Stanning, "Household Grain Storage"; H. Coudere and S. Marijsse, "'Rich' and 'Poor' in Mutoko," *Zimbabwe Journal of Economics* 2, no. 1 (1988); J. Adams "Wage Labour in Muturikwi Communal Land, Masvingo," University of Zimbabwe, Centre for Applied Social Sciences seminar paper, 10 June 1987; Drinkwater, *State and Agrarian Change*, chap. 5; N. Amin, "State and Peasantry."

42. AMA Quarterly Bulletin, July-September, 1989; Minister of Finance's Budget Statement 1984; *Hansard* 10. no. 27, 4 September 1984, cols. 1468–73.

43. *Herald*, 1 March 1988, 23 March 1988.

44. MLARR, draft *Resettlement Report*, 1987, p. 50; *Financial Gazette*, 2 December 1988.

45. *Herald*, 5 December 1985.

46. MLARR, draft *Resettlement Report*, 1987, p. 50; *Financial Gazette*, 23 September 1988, 14 October 1988; *Herald*, 4 December 1987, 7 July 1988.

47. Quoted in the *Herald*, 13 October 1987.

48. Ministry of Community Development and Women's Affairs, *Report on the Situation of Women in Zimbabwe*, February 1982, p. 27.

49. Quoted in the *Herald*, 25 June 1988; also *Zimbabwe News* 17, no. 4 (April 1986), p. 35.

50. MLARR, draft *Resettlement Report*, 1986, pp. 53–55; 1987, pp.

16, 50; *Herald,* 29 November 1985, 18 November 1985, 12 February 1988, 7 November 1985; *Financial Gazette,* 2 December 1988; *Herald,* 25 June 1988; *Hansard* 13, no. 27, 11 September 1986, col. 1185.

51. *Sunday Mail,* 8 May 1988, 29 May 1988.

52. *Sunday Mail,* 24 July 1988; *Herald,* 1 September 1988.

Chapter 7

1. Ministry of Finance, Economic Planning and Development (MFEPD), *Transitional National Development Plan, 1982/83–1984/85,* vol. 1, November 1982, p. 66.

2. MFEPD, *First Five-Year National Development Plan, 1986–1990,* vol. 1, April 1986, p. 28; statement by Minister of Lands Agriculture and Rural Resettlement, 22 February 1989 [61/89/SM/SK/EMM]; MLGRUD, *Manicaland Provincial Development Plan,* p. 292.

3. Drinkwater, *State and Agrarian Change,* especially pp. 115–32; K. Wilson, "Research on Trees in the Mazvihwa and Surrounding Areas." (Mimeograph, ENDA-Zimbabwe, 1987).

4. *Hansard* 10, no. 23, 23 August, col. 1191; MLGRUD, *Manicaland Provincial Development Plan,* pp. 122–23; Gesellschaft für Agrarprojekte in Übersee M.B.H. (GFA), *Study on the Economic and Social Determinants of Livestock Production in the Communal Areas—Zimbabwe: Final Report* (Hamburg, March 1987), p. 26.

5. World Bank, *Land Subsector Study,* p. 29; MLGRUD, *Matabeleland North Provincial Development Plan,* vol. 1, p. 63; *Herald,* 10 April 1989.

6. *Chavunduka Commission Report,* pp. 35, 4.

7. Drinkwater, *State and Agrarian Change,* esp. chaps. 1, 2 and 8.

8. This is particularly true of the early commissions, such as the Riddell Commission and the Chavunduka Commission. For a good example of this tendency, see also MLGRUD, *Matabeleland North Provincial Development Plan.*

9. See, for instance, speeches by President Banana, opening Mukuvisi Woodland, 4 July 1984 [456/84/SC/DB]; Prime Minister Mugabe, address to the nation, 17 April 1981; idem, address to conference on Zimbabwe's National Conservation Strategy, 4 November 1985 [555/85/BCC/GR]; Victoria Chitepo, Minister of Natural Resources and Tourism, addressing same meeting, 8 November 1985. See also B. Child and J. H. Peterson, "Campfire in Rural Develop-

ment: The Beitbridge Experience," University of Zimbabwe, Centre for Applied Social Sciences, 1991, mimeographed.

10. MLGRUD, *Manicaland Provincial Development Plan*, pp. 521, 334; see also Chitepo: address to the governing council of the United Nations Environmental Program (UNEP), 22 May 1984 [365/84/BPF/SC]; 568/85/ME/SM; R. Herring, *Land to the Tiller: The Political Economy of Agrarian Reform in South Asia* (New Haven: Yale University Press, 1983), p. 46.

11. Mashonaland Central Provincial Development Plan, pp. 43, 45.

12. Mugabe, address to the nation, 17 April 1981.

13. S. Geza, "The Role of Resettlement in Social Development in Africa," *Journal of Social Development in Africa* 1, no. 1 (1986).

14. MFEPD, *Socio-Economic Review of Zimbabwe, 1980–1985*, pp. 125–26; MLARR, *Resettlement Report*, 1987, p. 4.

15. Ministerial Statement, 22 February 1989; MLARR, *Resettlement Reports* 1986, 1987; B. H. Kinsey, "Forever Gained: Resettlement and Land Policy in the Context of National Development in Zimbabwe," *Africa* vol. 52, no. 3, 1982, pp. 286–87; Herbst, *State Politics in Zimbabwe*, pp. 45–49, 71.

16. MLARR, *Resettlement Report*, 1986, pp. 8–9, 58–60; draft *Resettlement Report*, 1987, pp. 36, 45; *Hansard* 14, no. 48, 3 February 1988, cols. 2697–2710.

17. Department of Veterinary Services, *Monthly Report*, August, 1988; MLARR, *Resettlement Report*, 1986, p. 64; MLARR, draft *Resettlement Report*, 1987, p. 35, 55; *Hansard* 14, no. 48, 3 February 1988, cols. 2697–2710. B. H. Kinsey, "Household-Level Outcomes of Land Reform in Post-Conflict Societies: The Case of Zimbabwe," Paper presented at 40th Annual Meeting of the African Studies Association, Columbus OH, 15 November 1997.

18. See, for instance, *Herald*, 14 May 1989; *Sunday Mail*, 16 April 1989.

19. Herbst, *State Politics in Zimbabwe*, pp. 65–75, 77–80; MFEPD, *Socio-Economic Review*, p. 126.

20. *Hansard* 10, no. 15, 25 July 1984, cols. 708–9; MLGRUD, *Matabeleland North Annual Provincial Development Plan*, 1987/88, p. 32; Ranger, "Matabeleland since the Amnesty."

21. MLGRUD, *Manicaland Provincial Development Plan*, pp. 65–66, 93; *Herald*, 22 November 1985.

22. MLGRUD, *Matabeleland North Annual Provincial Development Plan*, 1987/88, p. 31; Agritex, *Aspects of Resettlement*, pp. 18–19; Herbst, *State Politics in Zimbabwe*, chap. 4; *Hansard* 10 no. 15, 25/7/1984, cols. 708–9.

23. See *Herald*, 16 December 1985 (headline, p. 1).

24. See, for instance, *Hansard* 7, no. 16, 21 July 1983, cols. 680–81; *Hansard* 15, no. 28, 13 September 1988, col. 1517; *Herald*, November 1985, 22 November 1985, 1 September 1992.

25. Scoones and Wilson, "Households," pp. 32–33; *Herald*, 16 December 1985; *Sunday Mail*, 5 March 1989, 30 August 1992.

26. See, for example, *Hansard* 15, no. 28, 13 September 1988, col. 1516; *Moto* 80 (September 1989), p. 23; Zimbabwe Women's Bureau, *We Carry A Heavy Load: Rural Women in Zimbabwe Speak Out*, part 2, 1981–1991, summary of report on the Follow-Up Survey (Harare, 1992), p. 24.

27. For cases, see R. B. Gaidzanwa, "Women's Land Rights in Zimbabwe: An Overview," Department of Rural and Urban Planning, Occasional Paper no. 13 (Harare: University of Zimbabwe, 1988); interview, former Secretary of Internal Affairs; J. Murombedzi, "Decentralization or Recentralization? Implementing CAMPFIRE in the Omay Communal Lands of the Nyaminyami District," University of Zimbabwe, Centre for Applied Social Sciences, 1992, mimeographed, p. 57; *Herald*, 19 November 1987, 28 December 1987, 1 November 1988; Scoones and Wilson, "Households," pp. 31–32; interview, Ben Cousins; Pankhurst, *Dynamics of Social Relations*, p. 265; S. Moyo, "Zimbabwe's Agrarian Reform Process," p. 18; *Herald*, 29 November 1985; *Sunday Mail*, 24 July 1988, 22 January 1989, 16 April 1989; *Herald*, 28 December 1987, 7 March 1989; *Sunday Mail*, 30 August 1992; Brand, "Will Decentralization Enhance Participation?" pp. 92–93; *Herald*, 29 November 1985; Otzen et al., *Development Management from Below*, p. 121. V. Dzingirai, "Politics and Ideology in Human Settlement: Getting Settled in the Sikomena Area of Chief Dobola." University of Zimbabwe, Centre for Applied Social Sciences. Occasional Paper-NRM Series, 1994, p. 2 and *passim*.

28. Scoones et al., *Hazards and Opportunities*, pp. 35–37; *Sunday Mail*, 22 January 1989, 16 April 1989; *Herald*, 20 February 1989, 10 December 1985, 6 March 1989; see also the review of Lan's book in the party organ *Zimbabwe News* (vol. 17, no. 5, May 1986) for a view of mediums as "atavistic" and the "institutional basis for tribalism."

29. See, for example, *Chavunduka Commission Report,* pp. 49–50; MLGRUD, *Manicaland Provincial Development Report,* p. 74.

30. World Bank, *Land Subsector Study,* p. 30; Cousins, *Current Grazing Schemes,* pp. 76–84.

31. Cousins, *Current Grazing Schemes,* pp. 23–24.

32. See especially Cousins, *People, Land and Livestock*; GFA, *Economic and Social Determinants.*

33. Ministry of Natural Resources and Tourism, *National Conservation Strategy,* p. 23

34. Cousins, *People, Land and Livestock,* p. 365.

35. S. Metcalfe, "'Empowerment' versus 'Participation' in Natural Resource Management in the Masoka Community," Harare, Zimbabwe Trust, 1990, mimeographed; M. Murphree, "Communities as Institutions for Resource Management," paper presented to the National Conference on Environment and Development, Maputo, Mozambique, 7–11 October, 1991; C. Roberts, "Environmental Ethics and Wildlife Policy in Zimbabwe" (B.A. thesis, Department of Religious Studies and Studies in the Environment Program, Yale University, 1991).

36. See J. M. MacKenzie, "The Natural World and the Popular Consciousness in Southern Africa: The European Appropriation of Nature," in *Cultural Struggle and Development in Southern Africa,* ed. P. Kaarsholm (London: James Currey, 1991); Ranger, "Matabeleland since the Amnesty."

37. Quoted in Roberts, "Environmental Ethics," p. 53.

38. Child and Peterson, "Campfire in Rural Development," p. 39; Murphree, "Communities as Institutions."

39. Child and Peterson, "CAMPFIRE in Rural Development," pp. 38–41, 70–73.

40. Child, in "Campfire in Rural Development," p. 9.

41. On Zambia, see M. Bratton, *The Local Politics of Rural Development: Peasant and Party- State in Zambia* (Hanover, N.H.: University Press of New England, 1980). On Tanzania, See Hyden, *Beyond Ujamaa in Tanzania;* M. von Freyhold, *Ujamaa Villages in Tanzania: Analysis of a Social Experiment* (New York: Monthly Review Press, 1979).

42. Minister of LGRUD, Enos Chikowore, reported in *Zimbabwe News,* 17, no. 4, April 1986.

43. Ibid.

44. A. Giddens, *Social Theory and Modern Sociology* (Stanford: Stanford University Press, 1987), especially pp. 144, 196–98; idem,

Constitution of Society; P. Bourdieu, *In Other Words: Essays Towards a Reflexive Sociology* (Stanford: Stanford University Press, 1990).

45. This point is made in CASS/WWF/ZimTrust (1989), pp. 1–3.

46. MCDWA, *Let's Build Zimbabwe Together,* p. 174; Shopo, "Administrative Accountability."

47. MFEPD, *Transitional National Development Plan,* p. 66; MLGRUD, *Manicaland Provincial Development Plan,* pp. 291–92.

48. For such equivocation, see Ministry of Natural Resources and Tourism, *National Conservation Strategy,* 1987, p. 23.

49. Minister of LGRUD, Enos Chikowore, reported in *Zimbabwe News,* 17, no. 4, p. 14.

50. Statement by the Minister of Lands Agriculture and Rural Resettlement, 22 February 1989.

51. Drinkwater, *State and Agrarian Change,* pp. 132–40.

52. Cousins, *Current Grazing Schemes,* p. 68.

53. Ibid., pp. 49–52.

54. World Bank, *Land Subsector Study,* p. 31; Cousins, *People, Land and Livestock,* p. 363; Otzen et al., *Development Management from Below,* 106.

55. Cousins, *Current Grazing Schemes,* p. 83; idem., People, Land and Livestock, pp. 421–23; Otzen et al., *Development Management from Below,* p. 119; World Bank, *Land Subsector Study,* p. 31.

56. Drinkwater, *State and Agrarian Change;* Murombedzi, "Decentralization or Recentralization?" especially pp. 40–50; Metcalfe, "'Empowerment' versus 'Participation,'" p. 7.

57. See especially Cutshall, "Kanyemba/Chapoto Ward," pp. 63–69; Child and Peterson, "Campfire in Rural Development"; Thomas, "Dualism and Decision-Making, p. 11; Roberts, "Environmental Ethics," pp. 57–58; Adams and McShane, *Myth of Wild Africa,* pp. 179–81.

58. Cutshall, "Kanyemba/Chapoto Ward," p. 67; also Robins, "Close Encounters at the 'Development' Interface: Local Resistance, State Power and the Politics of Land-Use Planning in Matabeleland, Zimbabwe" (Ph.D. dissertation, Columbia University, 1995), pp. 159–61.

59. Bayart, *State in Africa,* p. 138.

60. S. Moyo and T. Skalnes, *Zimbabwe's Land Reform and Development Strategy: State Autonomy, Class Bias and Economic Rationality,* Zimbabwe Institute of Development Studies Research Paper no. 3 (1990), p. 13.

61. Moore, "Contesting Terrain," pp. 39–40.

62. For a useful overview, see Thomas, "Dualism and Decision-Making."

63. MLGRUD, *Manicaland Provincial Development Plan*, pp. 164, 441–42; *Herald*, 22 September 1987, 17 February 1988, 23 February 1988; M. Chenga, "Rural Housing Programmes in Zimbabwe: A Contribution to Social Development," *Journal of Social Development in Africa* 1, no. 1 (1986), p. 44.

64. Bratton, *Local Politics of Rural Development*, pp. 154–57; *Herald*, 23 September 1987.

65. Alexander, "State, Peasantry and Resettlement," p. 340.

66. See especially "Murphree's Law": that "there is an inbuilt tendency at any level in bureaucratic hierarchies to seek increased authority from levels above and resist its devolution to levels below," in Murphree, "Communities as Institutions"; also Drinkwater, *State and Agrarian Change*.

Chapter Eight

1. Addresses to ZIDS seminar by Minister of Manpower Development and Planning and Minister of Local Government and Town Planning, Harare, May 1983; *Hansard* 10, no. 18, cols. 877–78.

2. *Hansard* vo.10, no. 1815 August 1984; MLGRUD, *Matabeleland North Annual Development Plan*, 1987/88, pp. 22–23; MFEPD, *First Five Year Development Plan*, p. 2; *Financial Gazette*, 4 November 1988; Minister of FEPD, *Budget Statement 1985*, p. 45.

3. MCDWA, *Annual Report*, 1982, p. 7.

4. For the emphasis on the role of the party, see MFEPD, *First Five Year Development Plan*, p. 2.

5. Ibid., p. 13; MLGRUD, *Matabeleland North Provincial Development Plan*, vol. 1(a), p. 49.

6. ZANU(PF), *Zimbabwe at Five Years*, p. 11.

7. Mark Dube, Deputy Minister of Lands, Resettlement and Rural Development, 28 September 1983. See also PS 632/83/RC/DB, 29 August 1983.

8. Minister of Co-operative Development, Maurice Nyagumbo, cited in *Herald*, 25 September 1986; speech by Minister of Lands, Resettlement and Rural Development, Moven Mahachi, 6 December

1984; speech by Mark Dube, 29 August 1983; speech by Moven Mahachi, 19 August 1983; MFEPD, *Socio-Economic Review*, p. 103; see also Minister of Co-operative and Community Development and Women's Affairs, Joyce Mujuru, cited in *Herald*, 29 March 1988; Press Statement 805/84/AM/EM (6 December 1984); MLARR, *Model B Co-Operative Resettlement Schemes: Policy Objectives and Achievements*, November 1988 (draft); also MLARR, *Base Line Survey and Technical Appraisal of Model B Co-Operative Resettlement Schemes*, November 1988 (draft).

9. S. T. Agere, "Towards Public Enterprise: The Role of Community Development in the Promotion of Co-Operatives," *Zambezia* 11, no. 2 (1983), pp. 106–7.

10. Address to International Conference of Local Authorities, 6 March 1984.

11. MCDWA, *Let's Build Zimbabwe Together*, p. 19.

12. Ibid., pp. 84–85, 15. Though lack of space prohibits discussion here, the project can be traced elsewhere, especially in the orientations of the departments of Youth Services and Culture in the Ministry of Youth, Sport and Culture. For a revealing discussion see the interview with the minister, "Towards a National Culture" in *Moto* 21 (March 1984), especially pp. 10–11.

13. MCDWA, *Let's Build Zimbabwe Together*, p. 7.

14. C. Duncan, "Art Museums and the Ritual of Citizenship," in *Exhibiting Cultures: The Poetics and Politics of Museum Display*, ed. I. Karp and S. Lavine (Washington, D.C.: Smithsonian Institution Press, 1991), p. 93.

15. D. Munjeri, "Refocusing or Reorientation? The Exhibition of the Populace: Zimbabwe on the Threshold," in *Exhibiting Cultures*, p. 454. For Munjeri, who was associate director of Zimbabwe's national museums, these tasks are precisely the mission of the national museums.

16. MLGRUD, *Matabeleland North Provincial Development Plan*, vol. 2, p. 160; Munjeri, "Refocusing or Reorientation?"; Ministry of Co-operative and Community Development (MCCD), *Building Whole Communities*, vol. 4, pp. 110–14. This project was mirrored in the National Arts Council of Zimbabwe Bill (1985), which created the National Arts Council (*Hansard* 12, no. 22, 9 November 1985, col. 930).

17. MCDWA, *Policy Statement*, n.d., p. 3; MCDWA, *Community Action*, no. 2, 1984, p. 9.

18. MCDWA, *Policy Statement*, n.d., p. 5.

19. MCDWA, *Report on Extension Work in Zimbabwe: A Prelimi-nary Survey*, April 1983, pp. 19–20. MCCD, *Building Whole Communities*, vol. 3, p. 53.

20. Training of Village Health Workers began in 1980 as a party initiative, in which VHWs served their communities on a part-time and unpaid basis. They were brought under the state umbrella in late 1981.

21. See MCDWA, *Field Survey of Community Development Workers*, 1984; MCCD, *Building Whole Communities*, vol. 4; Deputy Minister of Agriculture, address to graduating class of traditional health workers and farm health workers, 27 June 1984 [PS 430/84/EM].

22. MCDWA, *Let's Build Zimbabwe Together*, p. 174. This vision contrasts dramatically with the colonial vision of W. H. H. Nicolle, quoted above, p. 167.

23. Bourdieu, *In Other Words*, pp. 133–34.

24. MCDWA, *Community Development Workers*, 1984. In 1983 the proposals for the formation of VIDCOs and WADCOs were drawn up as a combined project of the Ministry of Local Government and Town Planning, and the Research, Planning and Projects section of MCDWA.

25. MCDWA, *Policy Statement*, n.d., p. 1; MCDWA, *Community Action*, no. 2, 1984, p. 9.

26. MCDWA, *Let's Build Zimbabwe Together*, p. 29.

27. Mugabe, address to International Conference of Local Authorities, 6 March 1984.

28. See MCDWA, *Community Action*, no. 2, 1984, p. 14

29. S. Moyo, "Zimbabwe's Agrarian Reform Process"; Masst, "Differentiation among the Zimbabwean Peasantry"; Pankhurst, *Dynamics of Social Relations*.

30. Under-Secretary for Co-operative Education and Training, quoted in *Herald*, 18 November 1988; C. Mumbengegwi, "Agricultural Producer Co-Operatives and Agrarian Transformation in Zimbabwe: Policy, Strategy and Implementation," *Zimbabwe Journal of Economics* 1, no. 1 (July 1984); *Hansard* 15 August 1989, col. 940; MLARR, draft *Resettlement Report*, 1987, p. 50.

31. *Hansard* 15 August 1989, col. 940.

32. MFEPD, *Growth with Equity*; MFEPD, *First Five Year Development Plan*, pp. 12–13, 18; *Hansard* 10, no. 28, 24 August 1984, col.

1277. See also Zehender et al., *Options for Regional Development*; ML-GRUD, *Provincial Development Plans* for Mashonaland East (p. 38), Mashonaland Central (pp. 47–48), Manicaland (pp. 466, 469). Several plans recommended that established urban-based companies should be prohibited from entering markets that could be serviced by the informal sector.

33. Prime minister addresses the nation, New Year's Eve 1982.

34. Ministry of Natural Resources and Tourism, *National Conservation Strategy*, p. 24; MLGRUD, *Matabeleland North Provincial Development Plan*, vol. 2, pp. 157–58; see also MLGRUD, *Manicaland Provincial Development Plan*, p. 474; *Herald*, 11 December 1985, 12 December 1985.

35. *Hansard* 10, no. 6, 10 July 1984, cols. 219–21; *Herald*, 12 December 1985; *Moto* 24 (June 1984); MLGRUD, *Manicaland Provincial Development Plan*, pp. 234, 509–10; MLGRUD, *Matabeleland North Provincial Development Plan*, 1986, vol. 2; MLGRUD, *Matabeleland North Annual Provincial Development Plan*, 1987/88, p. 54.

36. Ministry of Youth, Sport and Culture (MYSC), *Study of the Needs of Rural Youths and Prospects of Their Integration into the Zimbabwean Economy*, by F. Nangati (Ministry of Youth, Sport and Culture in collaboration with UNICEF- Zimbabwe, December 1985), p. 5.

37. *Hansard* 5, no. 19, 15 July 1982, col. 791; *Herald*, 11 December 1985; *Hansard* 10, no. 28, 5 September 1984, cols. 1657, 1659–60, 1669; *Moto* 24 (June 1984), pp. 9–10; Lawyers Committee for Human Rights, *Zimbabwe*, pp. 54–57; Minister of YSC, press statement, 11 January 1988 [12/88/SG/ME].

38. Minister of YSC, address to University of Zimbabwe students, 30 April 1984; *Zimbabwe News* 17, no. 2 (February 1986); *Moto* 24 (June 1984); *Hansard* 23, August 1989, cols. 1304–5. See also ZANU(PF), *Zimbabwe at Five Years*, p. 256; Catholic Commission, *Disturbances in Matabeleland*.

39. MLGRUD, Manicaland Provincial Development Plan, p. 234.

40. O. Muchena, "The Changing Position of African Women in Rural Zimbabwe," *Zimbabwe Journal of Economics* 1, no. 1 (March 1979); International Union for the Conservation of Nature and Natural Resources (IUCN), *The Nature of Zimbabwe: A Guide to Conservation and Development* (Harare: IUCN, 1988), p. 78; Sylvester, *Zimbabwe*, pp. 143–52; Zimbabwe Women's Bureau, *We Carry a Heavy*

Load, parts 1 and 2; Gaidzanwa, "Women's Land Rights," pp. 3–4; Pankhurst, *Dynamics of Social Relations,* p. 237; interview, extension officer, Chinamora CA; Masst, "Differentiation among the Zimbabwean Peasantry," pp. 56–57; MCDWA, *Situation of Women,* pp. 28–29; MCDWA, *Extension Workers,* 1983; MCCD, *Building Whole Communities,* vol. 3, p. 26; MCDWA, *Policy Statement,* n.d., p. 1; MCDWA, *The Zimbabwe Report on the United Nations Decade for Women,* esp. p. 25.

41. S. Moyo, "Zimbabwe's Agrarian Reform Process," p. 16.

42. MCDWA, *Report of DANIDA/GOZ Mission on Zimbabwe National Training Centre for Women: Jamaica Inn,* September, 1985; MCDWA, *Community Action,* no. 2, 1984, p. 11; MCDWA, *Annual Report,* 1983; A. Helmsing, "Non-Agricultural Enterprise in the Communal Lands of Zimbabwe: Preliminary Results of a Survey," University of Zimbabwe, Department of Urban and Rural Planning, Occasional Paper no. 10, 1987; R. Chimedza, *Savings Clubs: The Mobilization of Rural Finances in Zimbabwe* (draft ILO Report, February 1984), pp. 28–29.

43. MCDWA, *Community Development Workers,* 1984, p. 5; T. Mulders, "Report on the Survey on Income Generating Projects, That are Assisted by the Ministry of Community Development and Women's Affairs," mimeographed, 1986; Zimbabwe Women's Bureau, We Carry a Heavy Load, Part II; MCDWA (CD Section), "The 'Integrated Approach' to Rural Development," n.d.; *Moto,* "Basic Needs Equals Socialism," November 1984.

44. Between 1984 and 1989, 4,796 boreholes, 12,837 wells, and 30,000 Blair toilets were constructed each year under the National Water and Sanitation Programme, involving community participation supported by interagency collaboration; MCCD, *Building Whole Communities,* vol. 3, pp. 34–35.

45. Pankhurst, *Dynamics of Social Relations,* pp. 269, 282–83; J. May, *Changing People, Changing Laws* (Gweru: Mambo Press, 1987), passim; also S. Moyo, "Zimbabwe's Agrarian Reform Process," p. 18.

46. Zimbabwe Women's Bureau, *We Carry a Heavy Load,* part 2, especially pp. 19–21; *Hansard* 23, August 1989.

47. For close studies, see Moore, "Contesting Terrain"; Robins, "Close Encounters," chapters 3–5.

48. S. Jacobs, "Zimbabwe: State, Class, and Gendered Models of Land Resettlement," in *Women and the State in Africa,* ed. J. Parpart and K. Staudt (Boulder: Lynne Rienner, 1989), p. 179.

49. MLGRUD, *Manicaland Provincial Development Plan*, p. 252. Deputy Minister of State (Political Affairs), Shuvai Mahofa, cited in *Herald*, 9 February 1988. In 1990, Mahofa was placed in charge of Women's Affairs.

50. Address to first African regional congress of the International Union of Local Authorities, Harare, 6 March 1984.

51. See M. Murphree and D. H. M. Cumming, "Savanna Land Use: Policy and Practice in Zimbabwe," University of Zimbabwe, Centre for Applied Social Sciences, 1991, mimeographed, pp. 12–13, 18; Child and Peterson, "CAMPFIRE in Rural Development"; Adams and McShane, *Myth of Wild Africa*, p. 178.

52. Drinkwater, *State and Agrarian Change*, pp. 141–42; also Minister of Education, address to Association of District Councils, 10 April 1984; *Hansard* 15, no. 28, col. 1516, 13 September 1988; MCDWA, *Extension Workers*.

53. de Valk, "Planning Policy in Zimbabwe," pp. 26, 29–30; Murombedzi, "Decentralization or Recentralization?" pp. 19–20; Child and Peterson, "CAMPFIRE in Rural Development"; Murphree, "Communities as Institutions"; Metcalfe, "'Empowerment' versus 'Participation'"; *Sunday Mail*, 7 May 1989.

54. *Hansard* 14, no. 53, 8 March 1988, cols. 2875, 2968–76; speech by Minister of Local Government and Town Planning to Senior Executives of Councils, 28 October 1983; Helmsing (1991), p. 5; Murombedzi, "Decentralization or Recentralization?", p. 17.

55. *Zimbabwe News* 17, no. 7 (July 1986).

56. Drinkwater, *State and Agrarian Change*, p. 143.

57. Address to International Conference of Local Authorities, 6 March 1984.

58. A. H. J. Helmsing and K. Wekwete, "Financing District Councils: Local Taxes and Central Allocations," Department of Rural and Urban Planning Occasional Paper no. 9 (Harare: University of Zimbabwe, 1987), p. 13; Otzen et al., *Development Management from Below*, p. 65; *Hansard* 11, no. 3, 13 September 1984, col. 201; Minister of LGRUD, address to Association of Rural Councils, 5 April 1989.

59. *Herald*, 22 January 1988; Murombedzi, "Decentralization or Recentralization?" p. 50.

60. See *Hansard* 13, nos.13 and 14, 14–15 April 1987; vol. 14, no. 41, 13 November 1987; *Herald*, 31 August 1992; MLARR, Department of Veterinary Services, *Monthly Reports*, Masvingo, May, June 1988; *Herald*, 31 August 1992.

61. See MLARR, Department of Veterinary Services, *Monthly Report* for Masvingo, July 1988. This also explains in part the pressures placed by politicians on the food-for-work program.

62. *Sunday Mail*, 26 August 1984; I am grateful to Leslie Bessant for information on Chiweshe.

63. Quoted in Adams and McShane, *Myth of Wild Africa*, p. 180.

64. See MLGRUD, *Mashonaland East Provincial Development Plan*, p. vii; MLGRUD, *Mashonaland Central Provincial Development Plan*, p. 11; de Valk, "Planning Policy in Zimbabwe;" GOZ, "Provincial Councils and Administration," pp. 7–13.

65. de Valk, "Planning Policy in Zimbabwe," p. 25.

66. N. D. Mutizwa-Mangiza, "Decentralization in Zimbabwe: Problems of Planning at the District Level," University of Zimbabwe, Department of Rural and Urban Planning. Occasional Paper no. 16, January 1989.

67. See *Hansard 5*, no. 21, 21 July 1982, col. 849. For a comprehensive list of MCDWA tasks, see K. Jirira, "The Position of Women in Employment with Specific Reference to the Public Sector," Zimbabwe Institute of Development Studies Consultancy Report 23, 1991.

68. MCDWA, *Annual Report*, 1982, pp. 9–11; MCDWA, *Annual Report*, 1983, pp. 2, 19; Minister of CDWA, press statement, 30 July 1988 [325/88/54/SB/BJ]; MCDWA, *Plan of Action, January- December 1986: Review of Progress*, n.d.; *Hansard* 10, no. 28, 5 September 1984, cols. 1619–20; *Hansard* 10, no. 28, 5 September 1984, col. 1925; *Sunday Mail*, 22 January 1989; Zimbabwe Women's Bureau, *We Carry a Heavy Load*, part 2, pp. 34, 41; MLGRUD, *Manicaland Provincial Development Plan*, pp. 116, 242–43; MLGRUD, *Matabeleland Annual Provincial Development Plan*, 1987/88, p. 54; de Valk, "Planning Policy in Zimbabwe," pp. 10–12. In a television interview in March 1989, the minister, Joyce Mujuru, complained that the ministry's budget was too small to help cooperatives despite the crucial importance of the department of cooperatives in development and job creation, that the government did not seem to take it seriously, and that the department could not be run on "peanuts."

69. *Hansard* 7, no. 9, 7 July 1983, col. 281–82; see also Brand, "Will Decentralization Enhance Participation?" p. 89.

70. *Hansard* 5, no. 21, 20 July 1983, cols. 1333–37; vol. 7, no. 17, 22 July 1983, cols. 738–39; vol. 10, no. 28, 5 September 1984, especially col. 1625.

71. MLGRUD, *Midlands Provincial Development Plan*, p. 58.

72. Brand, "Will Decentralization Enhance Participation?" p. 82. For further discussions of VIDCOs, see MCDWA, *Let's Build Zimbabwe Together*; Otzen et al., *Development Management from Below*; de Valk, "Planning Policy in Zimbabwe"; Murombedzi, "Decentralization or Recentralization?"

73. Minister of LGRUD, addressing Association of District Councils, 8 February 1989.

74. Otzen et al., *Development Management from Below*, p. 124, refer to this as a "planning paradox."

75. MCDWA, *Let's Build Zimbabwe Together*, pp. 46–51; MCCD, *Building Whole Communities*, vol. 5, pp. 59, 82–96; S. Moyo, "Zimbabwe's Agrarian Reform Process," p. 18.

76. J. Parpart, J. and K. Staudt, eds., *Women and the State in Africa* (Boulder: Lynne Rienner, 1989), pp. 11–13.

77. Brand, "Will Decentralization Enhance Participation?" p. 93.

78. Holmquist, "Self-Help"; Barkan and Holmquist, "Peasant-State Relations"; Thomas, "Development through Harambee."

79. Scoones et al., *Hazards and Opportunities*, pp. 159–61.

Conclusions

1. Weber, "Politics as a Vocation," p. 78.

2. For the first position, see C. Leys, "What We Learned from the Kenya Debate," in *Political Development and the new Realism in Sub-Saharan Africa*, ed. D. Apter and C. Rosberg (Charlottesville: University Press of Virginia, 1994). For the latter position, see T. Callaghy, "Political Passions and Economic Interests: Economic Reform and Political Structure in Africa," in *Hemmed In: Responses to Africa's Economic Decline*, in *Hemmed In: Responses to Africa's Economic Decline*, ed. T. M. Callaghy and J. Ravenhill (New York: Columbia University Press, 1993); M. Mugyenyi, "Development First, Democracy Second," in *Democratic Theory and Practice in Africa*, ed. W. Oyugi et al. (London: James Currey, 1988).

3. For a provocative exploration of public debates over authoritative meanings in discourses of state power, see D. W. Cohen and E. S. Atieno Odhiambo, *Burying SM: The Politics of Knowledge and the Sociology of Power in Africa* (London: James Currey, 1992).

4. Herbst, *State Politics in Zimbabwe*, p. 261, and chap. 11 generally.

5. J. Dunn, *Rethinking Modern Political Theory* (Cambridge: Cambridge University Press, 1985), pp. 137–38.

6. For the impact of this paradox on individual investment decisions of rural citizens, see S. Berry, "Concentration without Privatization? Some Consequences of Changing Patterns of Rural Land Control in Africa," in *Land and Society in Contemporary Africa*, ed. R. Downs and S. Reyna (Hanover, N.H.: University Press of New England, 1988).

7. Sithole, "Zimbabwe's Eroding Authoritarianism."

8. See J. Rapley, "New Directions in the Political Economy of Development," *Review of African Political Economy* 62 (1994); S. Bromley, "Making Sense of Structural Adjustment," *Review of African Political Economy* 65 (September 1995); H. Stein, ed., *Asian Industrialization and Africa: Studies in Policy Alternatives to Structural Adjustment* (London: MacMillan, 1995); Callaghy and Ravenhill, *Hemmed In.*

9. N. Uphoff, "Grassroots Organizations and NGOs in Rural Development: Opportunities with Diminishing States and Expanding Markets," *World Development* 21, no. 4 (April 1993); A. Fowler, "Non-Governmental Organisations in Africa: Achieving Comparative Advantage in Relief and Micro-Development," IDS Discussion Paper no. 249.

10. P. Wapner, "Politics beyond the State: Environmental Activism and World Civic Politics," *World Politics* 47, no. 3 (April 1995), p. 335; M. Bratton, "Non-governmental Organizations in Africa."

11. Thompson, *Customs in Common*, p. 14.

12. S. Huntington, *Political Order in Changing Societies* (New Haven: Yale University Press, 1968), p. 8.

Bibliography

Documentary Sources

Government of (Southern) Rhodesia

Agricultural Development Authority. *Annual Reports.* Years ending 30 June 1976 and 30 June 1977.

Department of Native Affairs. *Annual Report of the Chief Native Commissioner* (CNC), 1949–1961/2.

Department of Statistics. *Statistical Handbook of Southern Rhodesia, 1945.* 26/10/45.

Joint Committee on Technical Education. *The African School-Leaver.* N.d. [1966].

Legislative Assembly Debates, various volumes. Cited throughout as *Hansard.*

Local Government and Community Development: The Role of Ministries and Co-Ordination. [Prime Minister's Directive] Statement of Policy and Directive by the Prime Minister, 1965.

Local Government and Community Development Policy: The Role of Ministries and Co-Ordination. Memorandum by the Community Development and Local Government Co-Ordinating Committee issued by direction of the prime minister, 1971.

Ministry of Finance. *Integrated Plan for Rural Development, July 1978.* 1979.

Ministry of Information, Immigration and Tourism. *The Border Lands,* by J. A. Hughes. November 1968.

_____. *Land Apportionment in Rhodesia,* by R. C. Haw. January 1965.

Ministry of Internal Affairs. *Annual Report of the Secretary of Internal Affairs (SIA)*, 1963/4–1973.

————. "Business and Trading Functions of Sites Leased in Tribal Trust Lands: May 1978." by F. H. Dodd, June 1978. NAZ Gen/ Dod-p.

————. *A Decade of Challenge and Achievement: The Story behind the Community Development Section (Women) of the Ministry of Internal Affairs of Rhodesia.* May 1976.

————. *Delineation Reports. Delineation Exercise, 1963–1965.* [NAZ— Microfilm.]

————. *Government Grants to African Councils from 1 July 1970.*

————. *Internal Affairs National Serviceman's Handbook.* April 1978.

————. *Projects and People.* Irregular Periodical.

————. *Rhodesian Community Development Review.* Periodical.

Operation Hurricane: Civil and Military. Memorandum, DC Mount Darwin, 1 October 1975.

Policy on Decentralization. Cmd.R.R.31—1974.

Report by J. L. Sadie on Planning for the Economic Development of Rhodesia. 1967 [CSR 35-1967].

Report of the Advisory Committee on the Development of the Economic Resources of Southern Rhodesia with Particular Reference to the Role of African Agriculture [Phillips Committee Report]. 1962 [CSR 15-1962].

Report of the Commission Appointed to Inquire into and Report on the Administrative and Judicial Functions in the Native Affairs and District Courts Departments [Robinson Commission Report]. 1962.

Report of the Commission of Enquiry into Certain Sales of Native Cattle in Areas Occupied by Natives. 1939.

Report of the Commission of Inquiry into Alleged Discontent in the Mangwende Reserve [Mangwende Commission Report]. 1961. See also the *Minority Report* submitted in protest by Rev. J. A. C. Shaw [Shaw Minority Report]. 1960.

Report of the Commission on Urban African Affairs [Plewman Commission]. 1958.

Report of the Interdepartmental Working Party to Consider Social Security for the Urban African. December 1956.

Report of the Maize and Small Grains Commission, 1962/3. 1963.

Report on African Development and Local Government in Southern Rhodesia, by James W. Green, Community Development Advisor to the Southern Rhodesian Government. 24 September 1962.

The Role of Internal Affairs and the Future of Rhodesia. Secret Memorandum, DC Mount Darwin, 26 May 1977.

Report of Working Committee 'A' on the Robinson Commission. 1961.

Report of Working Committee 'B' on the Robinson Commission. 1961.

What the Native Land Husbandry Act Means to the Rural African and to Southern Rhodesia: a Five Year Plan That Will Revolutionise African Agriculture. 1955.

Government of Zimbabwe

Agricultural Marketing Authority. *Economic Review of the Agricultural Industry.*

Agritex. *Aspects of Resettlement* 1986.

_____. *Report on the Training and Visiting System in Midlands Province.* June *1985.*

_____. *Wedza Baseline Study: Summary and Analysis* n.d.

Central Statistical Office. *Main Demographic Features of the Population of Zimbabwe.* 1882 Population census, 1882. June 1985.

Ministry of Community Development and Women's Affairs (MCDWA). *Annual Reports,* 1982, 1983.

_____. *Community Action.* First half 1984, no. 2.

_____. *Field Survey of Community Development Workers.* 1984.

_____. *The "Integrated Approach" to Rural Development.* N.d.

_____. *Let's Build Zimbabwe Together: A Community Development Manual.* 1987.

_____. *Plan of Action, January-December 1986: Review of Progress.* N.d.

_____. *Report of DANIDA/GOZ Mission on Zimbabwe National Training Centre for Women: Jamaica Inn.* September 1985.

_____. *Report on Extension Work in Zimbabwe: A Preliminary Survey.* April 1983.

_____. *Report on the Situation of Women in Zimbabwe.* February 1982.

_____. *The Zimbabwe Report on the United Nations Decade for Women.* July 1985.

Ministry of Co-Operative and Community Development (MCCD). *Building Whole Communities.* 7 vols., 1991–1992.

Ministry of Finance, Economic Planning and Development (MFEPD). *First Five-Year National Development Plan, 1986–1990.* Vol. 1, April 1986.

_____. *Growth with Equity: An Economic Policy Statement.* Cmd. R.Z.4-1981. February 1981.

_____. *Socio-Economic Review of Zimbabwe, 1980–1985.* 1986.

_____. *Transitional National Development Plan, 1982/3–1984/5.* 2 vols. (November 1982, May 1983).

Ministry of Lands, Agriculture and Rural Resettlement (MLARR). *Base Line Survey and Technical Appraisal of Model B Co-Operative Resettlement Schemes.* (Draft) November 1988.

_____. Department of Veterinary Services. *Monthly Reports,* various months.

_____. *First Annual Survey of Settler Households in Normal Intensive Model A Resettlement Schemes: Main Report.* September 1986.

_____. *Intensive Resettlement Schemes (Model A): Annual Household Survey 1985/86.* (Draft) September 1987.

_____. *Model B Co-Operative Resettlement Schemes: Policy Objectives and Achievements.* (Draft) November 1988.

Ministry of Local Government and Town Planning. *The Delineation of Village and Ward Development Committee Areas in District Council Areas of Zimbabwe, 1984.* [NAZ Gen/Del] May 1985.

Ministry of Local Government, Rural and Urban Development (MLGRUD). Department of Physical Planning (Provincial Development Committees). *Manicaland Provincial Development Plan.* July 1986.

_____. *Mashonaland Central Provincial Development Plan.*

_____. *Mashonaland East Provincial Development Plan.* August 1986.

_____. *Mashonaland West Provincial Development Plan.* July 1986.

_____. *Matabeleland North Provincial Development Plan.* 2 vols.

_____. *Midlands Provincial Development Plan.* April 1986.

Ministry of Natural Resources and Tourism. *The National Conservation Strategy: Zimbabwe's Road to Survival.* April 1987.

Ministry of Youth, Sport and Culture. *Study of the Needs of Rural Youths and Prospects of Their Integration into the Zimbabwean Economy* (in collaboration with UNICEF-Zimbabwe, December 1985). By F. Nangati.

Parliamentary Debates, various dates. Cited throughout as *Hansard*.

"Provincial Councils and Administration in Zimbabwe: A Statement of Policy and a Directive by the Honorable Robert Gabriel Mugabe, M.P., Prime Minister, Government of the Republic of Zimbabwe."

Report of the Commission of Inquiry into the Agricultural Industry [Chavunduka Commission Report]. June 1982.

Interview Transcripts, National Archives of Zimbabwe (NAZ)

Davies, R. M. Interview by I. J. Johnstone. NAZ Oral/241. 17 November 1983.

Howman, H. R. G. Interview by M. C. Steele. NAZ Oral/HO3. 10, 26 August 1971.

Howman, J. H. Interview by I. J. Johnstone. NAZ Oral/238. 7, 13, 23, 27 June 1983.

Hunt, N. A. Interview by I. J. Johnstone. NAZ Oral/240. 27 November 1983.

Quinton, H. J. Interview by E. G. Gibbons. NAZ Oral/Qu2. May 1977–May 1978.

Robinson, D. A. Tape recording. NAZ Oral/230. 1979–1984.

Staunton, F. A. Interview by I. J. Johnstone. NAZ Oral/256. 1986.

Native Affairs Department Annual (NADA)

Alvord, E. D. "The Great Hunger." *NADA*, no. 6 (1928).

Bourdillon, M. F. C. "Spirit Mediums in Shona Belief and Practice." *NADA* 11, no. 1 (1974).

Carbutt, C. L. "Reminiscences of a Native Commissioner." *NADA*, no. 2 (1924).

_____. "Some More Reminiscences of a Native Commissioner." *NADA*, no. 4 (1926).

Davies, C. S. "Tribalism and Economic Development." *NADA* 10, no. 2 (1970).

Elliott, A. D. "Witchcraft in the Lowveld." *NADA* 9, no. 3 (1966).

Fynn, A. R. "The New Administration." *NADA* 11, no. 5 (1978).

Gelfand, M. "The Great Muzukuru: His Role in the Shona Clan." *NADA* 9, no. 3 (1966).

————. "the Mhondoro Cult among the Manyika Peoples of the Eastern Region of Mashonaland." *NADA* 11, no. 1 (1974).

Gelfand, M., and J. Henry. "The Chiota Dynasty." *NADA* 12, no. 1 (1979).

Hillis, J. G. "An Account of a Market Research in a Tribal Trust Area." *NADA* 10, no. 3 (1971).

————. "Commerce and the Tribal Trust Lands." *NADA* 10, no. 5 (1973).

————. "Marketing in the Tribal Trust lands." *NADA* 10, no. 4 (1972).

Howman, H. R. G. "African Leadership in Transition." *NADA* 33 (1956).

————. "Economic Growth and Community Development in African Areas.: *NADA* 10, no. 5 (1969).

————. "The Native Affairs Department and the Native." *NADA* 31 (1954).

Hunt, N. "Age and Land in a Native Reserve." *NADA* 40 (1963).

Jordan, T. W. F. "The Victoria Master Farmers' Association." *NADA* 11, no. 5 (1978).

Kaschula, T. D. "The Selection and Installation of Chief Mola." *NADA* 11, no. 3 (1976).

Keigwin, H. S. "Native Development." *NADA*, no. 1 (1923).

Latham, C. J. K. "The Social Organisation of the Mashona." *NADA* 12, no. 1 (1979).

————. "Some Notes on the Tribes in the Mount Darwin, Rushinga and Centenary Districts." *NADA* 11, no. 2 (1975).

Loewenson, R., and M. Gelfand. "Customary Law Cases in Two Shona Chieftainships." *NADA* 12, no. 2 (1980).

Masterson, G. M. "Memories of a Native Commissioner's Wife." *NADA* 11, no. 4 (1977).

Robinson, D. A. "Soil Conservation and Implications of the Land Husbandry Act." *NADA* 37 (1960).

Wilson, N. H. "The Development of Native Reserves: One Phase of Native Policy for Southern Rhodesia." *NADA*, no. 1 (1923).

Woollacott, R. C. "Pasapamire—Spirit Medium of Chaminuka, the 'Wizard' of Chitungwiza." *NADA* 11, no. 2 (1975).

Wrathall, J. J. "Foreword." *NADA* 9, no. 5 (1968).

————. "The Tribal Trust Land: Their Need for Development." *NADA* 10, no. 1 (1969).

Newspapers and Periodicals

Africa Report. various dates.

Financial Gazette. Harare: various dates.

The Herald. Harare: various dates.

Moto. Harare: various dates.

Review of the Press. UK: Britain-Zimbabwe Society, various dates.

Rhodesia Herald. Salisbury (Harare): various dates.

The Sunday Mail. Harare: various dates.

X-Ray: Current Affairs in Southern Africa. London: Africa Bureau, vol. 1, no. 1 July (1970–November/December 1983).

Zimbabwe News. Harare: ZANU(PF), various dates.

Miscellaneous Documents

Rhodesian Front. *Policy Statement* [1969].

————. *Rhodesian Forum.* various dates.

Books, Articles, Papers, and Dissertations

Adams, J. "Wage Labour in Muturikwi Communal land, Masvingo." University of Zimbabwe, Centre for Applied Social Science seminar paper, 10 June 1987.

Adams, J. S., and T. O. McShane. *The Myth of Wild Africa: Conservation without Illusion.* London: Norton, 1992.

Adams, W. M. *Green Development: Environment and Sustainability in the Third World.* London: Routledge, 1990.

Agere, S. T. "Towards Public Enterprise: The Role of Community

Development in the Promotion of Co-Operatives." *Zambezia* 11, no. 2 (1983).

Ake, C. *Democracy and Development in Africa.* Washington, D.C.: Smithsonian Institution Press, 1996.

Alexander, J. "State, Peasantry and Resettlement in Zimbabwe." *Review of African Political Economy* 21, no. 61 (1994).

Amin, N. "State and Peasantry in Zimbabwe since Independence," *The European Journal of Development Research* 4, no. 1 (1992).

Alvord, E. D. "Development of Native Agriculture and Land Tenure in Southern Rhodesia." Typescript, Waddilove, 1956[?]

Amin, S. "Dependency and Underdevelopment in Africa: Origins and Contemporary Forms." *Journal of Modern African Studies* 10, no. 4 (1972).

Anderson, B. *Imagined Communities: Reflections on the Origins and Spread of Nationalism.* London: Verso, 1989.

Anderson, D., and R. Grove, eds. *Conservation in Africa: People, Policies and Practice.* Cambridge: Cambridge University Press, 1987.

Arrighi, G. "Labour Supplies in Historical Perspective: A Study of the Proletarianisation of the African Peasantry in Rhodesia." *Journal of Development Studies* 6 (1970).

Arrighi, G., and J. S. Saul. *Essays on the Political Economy of Africa.* New York: Monthly Review Press, 1973.

Ashforth, A. "Reckoning Schemes of Legitimation: On Commissions of Inquiry as Power/Knowledge Forms." *Journal of Historical Sociology* 3, no. 1 (March 1990).

Astrow, A. *Zimbabwe: A Revolution That Lost Its Way?* London: Zed Press, 1983.

Atieno Odhiambo, E. S. "Democracy and the Ideology of Order in Kenya." In *Democratic Theory and Practice in Africa,* ed. W. Oyugi et al. London: James Currey, 1988.

Barber, J. *Rhodesia: The Road to Rebellion.* London: Oxford University Press, 1967.

Barkan, J., and F. Holmquist. "Peasant-State Relations and the Social Base of Self-Help in Kenya." *World Politics* (1989).

Barkan, J., and J. Okumu, eds. *Politics and Public Policy in Kenya and Tanzania.* New York: Praeger, 1979.

Barratt, J. C. "An Economic Model of Animal Draught Power in Agropastoral Farming Systems in Zimbabwe." Paper presented to workshop on "A Systems Approach to the Analysis and Planning of Communal Resource Management," University of Zimbabwe, 8 August 1989.

————. "Valuing Animal Draught in Agropastoral Farming Systems in Zimbabwe." Paper presented at workshop on "Tillage: Past and Future." CIMMYT FSR Networkshop Report no. 2, March 1991.

Barry, T. *Zapata's Revenge: Free Trade and the Farm Crisis in Mexico.* Boston: South End Press, 1995.

Bassett, T., and D. Crummey, eds. *Land in African Agrarian Systems.* Madison: University of Wisconsin Press, 1994.

Bates, R. H. *Beyond the Miracle of the Market: The Political Economy of Agrarian Development in Kenya.* Cambridge: Cambridge University Press, 1989.

————. *Markets and States in Tropical Africa: The Political Basis of Agricultural Policies.* Berkeley: University of California Press, 1981.

Bayart, J. "Civil Society in Africa." In *Political Domination in Africa: The Limits of State Power,* ed. P. Chabal. Cambridge: Cambridge University Press, 1986.

————. *The State in Africa: The Politics of the Belly.* Tr. Mary Harper, Christopher Harrison, and Elizabeth Harrison. London: Longman, 1993.

Beinart, W. "Soil Erosion, Conservation and Ideas about Development: A Southern African Exploration 1900–1960." *Journal of Southern African Studies* 11 (1984).

Beinart, W., and C. Bundy. *Hidden Struggles in Rural South Africa: Politics and Popular Movements in the Transkei and Eastern Cape 1890–1930.* Johannesburg: Ravan Press, 1987.

Berman, B. and J. Lonsdale. *Unhappy Valley: Conflict in Kenya and Africa* 2 vols. London: James Currey, 1992.

Berry, S. "Concentration without Privatization? Some Consequences of Changing Patterns of Rural Land Control in Africa." In *Land and Society in Contemporary Africa,* ed. R. E. Downs and S. P. Reyna, Hanover, N.H.: University Press of New England, 1988.

_____. *No Condition Is Permanent: The Social Dynamics of Agrarian Change in Sub-Saharan Africa.* Madison: University of Wisconsin Press, 1993.

Bessant, L. L. "Coercive Development: Peasant Economy, Politics and Land in the Chiweshe Reserve, Colonial Zimbabwe, 1940–1966." Ph.D. dissertation, Yale University, 1987.

Bessant, L. L., and E. Muringai. "Peasants, Businessmen, and Moral Economy in the Chiweshe Reserve, North-Central Zimbabwe 1940–1968." December 1990. Mimeographed.

Blackie, Malcolm J. "The Elusive Peasant: Zimbabwe Agriculture Policy, 1965–1986." In *Food Security for Southern Africa*, ed. M. Rukuni and C. K. Eicher. Harare:University of Zimbabwe, UZ/MSU Food Security Project, 1987.

Blake, R. *A History of Rhodesia.* London: Eyre Methuen, 1977.

Bloore, K. "A Condensation of the Batten Report." *Community Development Review.*

Boone, C. *Merchant Capital and the Roots of State Power in Senegal, 1930–1985.* Cambridge: Cambridge University Press, 1992.

Bourdieu, P. "Cultural Reproduction and Social Reproduction." In *Knowledge, Education, and Cultural Change*, ed. R. Brown. London: Tavistock, 1973.

_____. *In Other Words: Essays Towards a Reflexive Sociology.* Stanford: Stanford University Press, 1990.

_____. *Outline of a Theory of Practice.* Cambridge: Cambridge University Press, 1977.

Brand, C. "From Compound to Keep: On the Nature of Settler Control in Southern Rhodesia." Paper read at a session of the Research Committee on Ethnic, Race, and Minority Relations, 9th World Congress of Sociology, Uppsala, Sweden, August 1978.

_____. "Will Decentralization Enhance Participation?" In *Limits to Decentralization in Zimbabwe*, ed. A. H. J. Helmsing et al. Harare: University of Zimbabwe, 1991.

Brass, T. *New Farmers' Movements in India.* London: Frank Cass, 1995.

Bratton, M. *Beyond Community Development: The Political Economy of Rural Administration in Zimbabwe.* From Rhodesia to Zimbabwe, vol. 6. Gwelo: Mambo Press, 1978.

_____. "The Comrades and the Countryside: The Politics of Agricultural Policy in Zimbabwe." *World Politics* 49 (1987).

_____. "Farmer Organizations and Food Production in Zimbabwe." *World Development* 14, no. 3 (March 1986).

_____. "Financing Smallholder Production: A Comparison of Individual and Group Credit Schemes in Zimbabwe." University of Zimbabwe, Department of Land Management Working Paper 2/5, February 1987.

_____. *The Local Politics of Rural Development: Peasant and Party-State in Zambia.* Hanover, N.H.: University Press of New England, 1980.

_____. "Non-Governmental Organizations in Africa: Can They Influence Public Policy?" *Development and Change* 21, no. 1 (January 1990).

Brautigam, D. "What Can Africa Learn from Taiwan? Political Economy, Industrial Policy and Adjustment." *Journal of Modern African Studies* 32, no. 1 (March 1994).

Breman, J., and S. Mundle, eds. *Rural Transformation in Asia.* Oxford: Oxford University Press, 1991.

Bromley, S. "Making Sense of Structural Adjustment." *Review of African Political Economy* 65 (September 1995).

Brown, R., ed. *Knowledge, Education and Social Change.* London: Tavistock, 1973.

Bundy, C. *The Rise and Fall of the South African Peasantry.* Berkeley: University of California Press, 1979.

Bush, R., and L. Cliffe. "Agrarian Policy in Migrant Labour Societies: Reform or Transformation in Zimbabwe?" *Review of African Political Economy* 29 (July 1984).

Callaghy, T. M. "Political Passions and Economic Interests: Economic Reform and Political Structure in Africa." In *Hemmed In: Responses to Africa's Economic Decline*, ed. T. M. Callaghy and J. Ravenhill. New York: Columbia University Press, 1993.

_____. "Politics and Vision in Africa: The Interplay of Domination, Equality and Liberty." In *Political Domination in Africa: The Limits of State Power*, ed. P. Chabal. Cambridge: Cambridge University Press, 1986.

_____. "State, Choice and Context: Comparative Reflections on

Reform and Intractability." In *Political Development and the New Realism in Sub-Saharan Africa*, ed. D. Apter and C. Rosberg. Charlottesville: University Press of Virginia, 1994.

————. *The State-Society Struggle: Zaire in Comparative Perspective.* New York: Columbia University Press, 1984.

Callaghy, T. M., and J. Ravenhill. *Hemmed In: Responses to Africa's Economic Decline.* New York: Columbia University Press, 1993.

Carney, J., and M. Watts. "Manufacturing Dissent: Work, Gender and the Politics of Meaning in a Peasant Society." *Africa* 60, no. 2 (1990).

Catholic Commission for Justice and Peace in Zimbabwe. *Report on the Disturbances in Matabeleland and the Midlands (1983–1987).* March 1997.

Caute, D. *Under the Skin: The Death of White Rhodesia.* Harmondsworth: Penguin, 1983.

Chabal, P. "People's War, State Formation and Revolution in Africa: A Comparative Analysis of Mozambique, Guinea-Bissau, and Angola." In *State and Class in Africa*, ed. N. Kasfir. London: Frank Cass, 1984.

Chatterjee, P. "Development Planning and the Indian State," In *The State and Development Planning in India*, ed. T. Byres. Delhi: Oxford University Press, 1994.

Chavunduka, G. L. "Witchcraft and the Law in Zimbabwe." *Zambezia* 8, no. 2 (1980).

Cheater, A. P. *Idioms of Accumulation: Rural Development and Class Formation among Freeholders in Zimbabwe.* Gweru: Mambo Press, 1984.

Chenga, M. "Rural Housing Programmes in Zimbabwe: A Contribution to Social Development." *Journal of Social Development in Africa* 1, no. 1 (1986).

Child, B., and J. H. Peterson. "CAMPFIRE in Rural Development: The Beitbridge Experience." University of Zimbabwe, Centre for Applied Social Sciences. 1991. Mimeographed.

Child, H. *The History and Extent of Recognition of Tribal Law in Rhodesia.* Rhodesia Government: Ministry of Internal Affairs, 1965.

Chimedza, R. *Savings Clubs: The Mobilization of Rural Finances in Zimbabwe.* Draft ILO Report, February 1984.

Clarke, D. G. "Settler Ideology and African Underdevelopment in Postwar Rhodesia." *Rhodesian Journal of Economics* 8, no. 1 (March 1974).

_____. *The Unemployment Crisis.* Gweru: Mambo Press, 1978.

Cliffe, L. *Policy Options for Agrarian Reform in Zimbabwe: A Technical Appraisal.* FAO Report to the government of Zimbabwe, February 1986.

Cohen, D., and E. S. Atieno Odhiambo. *Burying SM: The Politics of Knowledge and the Sociology of Power in Africa.* London: James Currey, 1992.

Collier, G. *Basta! Land and the Zapatista Rebellion in Chiapas.* Oakland, Calif.: Institute for Food Development Policy, 1994.

Conyers, D. "Decentralization and Development Planning: A Comparative Perspective." Paper presented to Workshop on The Planning System in Zimbabwe, University of Zimbabwe Department of Rural and Urban Planning, 4–7 February 1986.

Cooper, F., A. Isaacman, F. Mallon, W. Roseberry, and S. Stern. *Confronting Historical Paradigms: Peasants, Labor, and the Capitalist World System in Africa and Latin America.* Madison: University of Wisconsin Press, 1993.

Cormack, I. *Towards Self-Reliance: Urban Social Development in Zimbabwe.* Gweru: Mambo Press, 1983.

Corrigan, P., and D. Sayer. *The Great Arch: English State Formation as Cultural Revolution.* Cambridge, Mass.: Blackwell, 1985.

Coudere, H. and S. Marijsse. "'Rich' and 'Poor' in Mutoko." *Zimbabwe Journal of Economics* 2, no. 1 (January 1988).

Cousins, B. "Power and Property in Zimbabwe's Communal Lands: Implications for Agrarian Reform in the 1990s." University of Zimbabwe, Centre for Applied Social Sciences. Occasional Paper —NRM Series, 1993.

_____. *A Survey of Current Grazing Schemes in the Communal Lands of Zimbabwe.* Harare: University of Zimbabwe, Centre for Applied Social Sciences, September 1987.

Cousins, B., ed. *People, Land and Livestock.* Proceedings of a Workshop on the Socio-Economic Dimensions of Livestock Production in the Communal Lands of Zimbabwe, 12–14 September 1988. Harare: University of Zimbabwe, Centre for Applied Social Sciences, 1989.

Cousins, B., D. Weiner, and N. Amin, "The Dynamics of Social Differentiation in Communal Lands of Zimbabwe." University of Zimbabwe, Centre for Applied Social Sciences. Occasional Paper —NRM Series, 1990.

Cruise O'Brien, D. B., J. Dunn, and R. Rathbone, eds. *Contemporary West African States*. Cambridge: Cambridge University Press, 1989.

Crush, J., ed. *Power of Development*. London: Routledge, 1995.

Cutshall, C. R. "Kanyemba/Chapoto Ward: A Socio-Economic Survey of Community Households." University of Zimbabwe, Centre for Applied Social Sciences. 1990. Mimeographed.

Davies, D. K. *Race Relations in Rhodesia: A Survey for 1972–73*. London: Rex Collings, 1975.

De Janvry, A. *The Agrarian Question and Reformism in Latin America*. Baltimore: Johns Hopkins University Press, 1981.

De Janvry, A., E. Sadoulet, and L. Wilcox Young. "Land and Labour in Latin American Agriculture from the 1950s to the 1980s." *Journal of Peasant Studies* 16, no. 3 (1989).

de Valk, P. "An Analysis of Planning Policy in Zimbabwe." Paper presented to Workshop on the Planning System in Zimbabwe, University of Zimbabwe, Department of Rural and Urban Planning, 4–7 February 1986.

Dopke, W. "State and Peasants in Mazoe District in the 1930s." University of Zimbabwe, Henderson Seminar, 1985.

Dorner, P. *Latin American Land Reforms in Theory and Practice: A Retrospective Analysis*. Madison: University of Wisconsin Press, 1992.

Downs, R. E., D. Kerner, and S. P. Reyna, eds. *The Political Economy of African Famine*. Langhorne, Pa.: Gordon and Breach, 1991.

Downs, R. E., and S. P. Reyna, eds. *Land and Society in Contemporary Africa*. Hanover, N.H.: University Press of New England, 1988.

Drinkwater, M. *The State and Agrarian Change in Zimbabwe's Communal Areas*. New York: St. Martins Press, 1991.

Duara, P. "State Involution in Comparative Perspective." In *Rural Transformation in Asia*, ed. J. Breman and S. Mundle. Oxford: Oxford University Press, 1991.

Dubow, S. "Race, Civilisation and Culture: The Elaboration of Segregationist Discourse in the Inter-War Years." In *The Politics of*

Race, Class and Nationalism in Twentieth-Century South Africa, ed. S. Marks and S. Trapido. London: Longman, 1987.

Duggan, W. R. "The Native Land Husbandry Act of 1951 and the Rural African Middle Class of Southern Rhodesia." *African Affairs* 79, no. 315 (April 1980).

Duncan, C. "Art Museums and the Ritual of Citizenship." In *Exhibiting Cultures: The Poetics and Politics of Museum Display,* ed. I. Karp and S. Lavine. Washington, D.C.: Smithsonian Institution Press, 1991.

Dunlop, H. *The Development of European Agriculture in Rhodesia, 1945–1965.* Department of Economics, Occasional Paper no. 5. Salisbury: University of Rhodesia, 1971.

Dunn, J. *Rethinking Modern Political Theory.* Cambridge: Cambridge University Press, 1985.

Dzingirai, V. "Politics and Ideology in Human Settlement: Getting Settled in the Sikomena Area of Chief Dobola." University of Zimbabwe, Centre for Applied Social Sciences. Occasional Papers—NRM Series, 1994.

Elkington, B. D., and R. C. Woollacott. "The Role of Education and Communication in Community Development in African Rural Areas." *Rhodesia Science News* 6, no. 2 (February 1972).

Escobar, A. *Encountering Development: The Making and Unmaking of the Third World.* Princeton: Princeton University Press, 1995.

Evans, P. "Predatory, Developmental and Other Apparatuses: A Comparative Analysis of the Third World State." Ms., 1989.

―――. "The State as Problem and Solution: Predation, Embedded Autonomy, and Structural Change." In *The Politics of Economic Adjustment: International Constraints, Distributive Conflicts, and the State,* ed. S. Haggard and R. Kaufman. Princeton: Princeton University Press, 1992 .

Evans, P., D. Rueschemeyer, and T. Skocpol, eds. *Bringing the State Back In.* Cambridge: Cambridge University Press, 1985.

Feierman, S. *Peasant Intellectuals: Anthropology and History in Tanzania.* Madison: University of Wisconsin Press, 1990.

Ferguson, J. *The Anti-Politics Machine: "Development," Depoliticization, and Bureaucratic Power in Lesotho.* Minneapolis: University of Minnesota Press, 1994.

Firmin-Sellers, K. "The Politics of Property Rights." *American Political Science Review* 89, no. 4 (December 1995).

Flower, K. *Serving Secretly: Rhodesia's CIO Chief on Record.* Alberton, S.A.: Galago, 1987.

Floyd, B. N. *Changing Patterns of African Land Use in Southern Rhodesia.* Lusaka, Zambia: Rhodes-Livingstone Institute, [1959].

Foucault, M. "The Subject and Power." In *Michel Foucault: Beyond Structuralism and Hermeneutics,*ed. H. Dreyfus and P. Rabinow. Chicago: University of Chicago Press, 1982.

Fowler, A. "Non-Governmental Organisations in Africa: Achieving Comparative Advantage in Relief and Micro-Development." IDS Discussion Paper no. 249.

Frederikse, J. *None But Ourselves: Masses vs. Media in the Making of Zimbabwe.* Johannesburg: Ravan Press, 1982.

Friedman, E., P. Pickowicz, and M. Selden. *Chinese Village, Socialist State.* New Haven: Yale University Press, 1991.

Gaidzanwa, R. B. "Women's Land Rights in Zimbabwe: An Overview." Department of Rural and Urban Planning, Occasional Paper no. 13. Harare: University of Zimbabwe, August 1988.

Gann, L. H. *A History of Southern Rhodesia: Early Days to 1934.* London: Chatto and Windus, 1965.

Gann, L. H., and M.Gelfand. *Huggins of Rhodesia: The Man and His Country.* London: Allen and Unwin, 1964.

Gesellschaft für Agrarprojekte in Übersee M.B.H. (GFA). *Study on the Economic and Social Determinants of Livestock Production in the Communal Areas—Zimbabwe: Final Report.* Hamburg, March 1987.

Geza, S. "The Role of Resettlement in Social Development in Africa." *Journal of Social Development in Africa* 1, no. 1 (1986).

Giddens, A. *The Constitution of Society.* Berkeley: University of California Press, 1984.

————. *The Nation-State and Violence.* Berkeley: University of California Press, 1987.

————. *Social Theory and Modern Sociology.* Stanford: Stanford University Press, 1987.

Gould, J. *To Lead as Equals: Rural Protest and Political Consciousness in Chinandega, Nicaragua, 1912–1979.* Chapel Hill: University of North Carolina Press, 1990.

Gramsci, A. *Selections from the Prison Notebooks.* Ed. and tr. Q. Hoare and G. K. Smith. New York: International Publishers, 1971.

Gray, R. *The Two Nations: Aspects of the Development of Race Relations in the Rhodesias and Nyasaland.* Oxford: Oxford University Press, 1960.

Greenberg, S. B. *Legitimating the Illegitimate: State, Markets, and Resistance in South Africa.* Berkeley: University of California Press, 1987.

Griffith, R. A. "The Part Played by Government in the Development of Agriculture in the Tribal Trust Lands." Paper presented at NRB Conference on the Tribal Trust Lands, University College of Rhodesia, 2–3 February 1966.

Guha, R., ed. *Subaltern Studies: Writings on South Asian History and Society.* 4 vols. New Delhi: Oxford University Press, 1982–1985.

Habermas, J. *Communication and the Evolution of Society.* Tr. T. McCarthy. Boston: Beacon Press, 1979.

_____. *Legitimation Crisis.* Tr. Thomas McCarthy. London: Heinemann, 1976.

_____. *The Structural Transformation of the Public Sphere.* Cambridge, Mass.: MIT Press, 1989.

Hancock, I. *White Liberals, Moderates and Radicals in Rhodesia.* London: Croom Helm, 1984.

Hart, K. *The Political Economy of West African Agriculture.* Cambridge: Cambridge University Press, 1982.

Harvey, D. *The Condition of Postmodernity.* Cambridge, Mass.: Blackwell, 1990.

Hawkins, A. M. "African Unemployment in Rhodesia." *The Rhodesia Science News* 8, no. 7 (July 1974).

_____. *Economic Growth, Structural Change and Economic Policy in Rhodesia 1965–1975.* Salisbury: Whitsun Foundation, June 1976.

Hay, D., P. Linebaugh, and E. P. Thompson. *Albion's Fatal Tree: Crime and Society in Eighteenth-Century England.* New York: Pantheon Books, 1975.

Hegel, G. F. W. *Hegel's Philosophy of Right.* Tr. T. M. Knox. London: Oxford University Press, 1952.

Held, D. *Political Theory and the Modern State.* Stanford: Stanford University Press, 1989.

Helmsing, A. H. J. "Non-Agricultural Enterprise in the Communal Lands of Zimbabwe: Preliminary Results of a Survey." Department of Rural and Urban Planning, Occasional Paper no. 10. Harare: University of Zimbabwe, September 1987.

Helmsing, A. H. J. et al. *Limits to Decentralization in Zimbabwe Essays on the Decentralization of Government and Planning in the 1980s.* Harare: University of Zimbabwe, 1991.

Helmsing, A. H. J., and K. Wekwete. "Financing District Councils: Local Taxes and Central Allocations." Department of Rural and Urban Planning, Occasional Paper no. 9. Harare: University of Zimbabwe, June 1987.

Herbst, J. I. *State Politics in Zimbabwe.* Harare: University of Zimbabwe Publications, 1990.

Herring, R. *Land to the Tiller: The Political Economy of Agrarian Reform in South Asia.* New Haven: Yale University Press, 1983.

Higgott, R. "The State in Africa." In *Africa Projected: From Recession to Renaissance by the Year 2000?* ed. T. Shaw and O. Aluko. London: MacMillan, 1985.

Hirsch, M. I. *A Decade of Crisis: Ten Years of Rhodesian Front Rule.* Salisbury: Peter Dearlove, 1973.

Holdcroft, L. E. "The Rise and Fall of Community Development in Developing Countries." Rural Development Paper no. 2. East Lansing: Michigan State University, 1978.

Holderness, H.. *Lost Chance: Southern Rhodesia, 1945–58.* Harare: Zimbabwe Publishing House, 1985.

Holleman, J. F. *African Interlude.* Cape Town: Nasionale Boekhandel, 1958.

———. *Chief, Council and Commissioner: Some Problems of Government in Rhodesia.* Assen, Netherlands: Royal VanGorcum, 1968.

———. *Shona Customary Law.* Manchester: Manchester University Press, 1969.

Holmquist, F. "Self-Help: The State and Peasant Leverage in Kenya." *Africa* 54, no. 3 (1984).

Howe, H., and M. Ottoway. "State Power Consolidation in Mozambique." In *Afro-Marxist Regimes* ed. E. J. Keller and D. Rothchild. Boulder: Lynne Rienner, 1987.

Howman, H. R. G. "Changing Social Structure and Land Tenure."

Paper presented to Symposium on Drought and Development, Bulawayo, May 1967.

————. "The Community Board." *Rhodesian Community Development Review* 1, no. 2 (1966).

————. "Economic Growth and Community Development." *Rhodesian Journal of Economics* 2, no. 3 (November 1968).

Hughes, A. "The Nation-State in Black Africa." In *The Nation-State: The Formation of Modern Politics*, ed. L. Tivey. New York: St. Martins Press, 1981.

Hughes, A. J. B. *Development in Rhodesian Tribal Areas: An Overview.* Salisbury: Tribal Areas of Rhodesia Research Foundation, 1974.

————. "The Inter-Relation of Social Structure, Land Tenure, and Land Use." Paper presented to Symposium on Drought and Development, Bulawayo, May 1967.

Hughes, J. A. *The Border Lands.* Harare: Ministry of Information, 1968.

Hunt, A. F. "The Economic Position of the Tribal Trust Land in Relation to Agriculture." Paper presented at NRB Conference on the Tribal Trust Land, University College of Rhodesia, 2–3 February 1966.

Hunt, L. *Politics, Culture, and Class in the French Revolution.* Berkeley: University of California Press, 1984.

Huntington, S. *Political Order in Changing Societies.* New Haven: Yale University Press, 1968.

Hyden, G. *Beyond Ujamaa in Tanzania: Underdevelopment and an Uncaptured Peasantry.* Berkeley, University of California Press, 1980.

————. *No Shortcuts to Progress: African Development Management in Perspective.* Berkeley: University of California Press, 1983.

Ihonvbere, J. "The 'Irrelevant' State: Ethnicity and the Quest for Nationhood in Africa." *Ethnic and Racial Studies* 17, no. 1 (1994).

International Union for the Conservation of Nature and Natural Resources (IUCN). *The Nature of Zimbabwe. A Guide to Conservation and Development.* Harare: IUCN, 1988.

Isaacman, A. "Peasants and Rural Social Protest in Africa." In *Confronting Historical Paradigms: Peasants, Labor, and the Capitalist World System in Africa and Latin America*, ed. F. Cooper et al. Madison: University of Wisconsin Press, 1993.

Jackson, J. C., and P. Collier. "Incomes, Poverty and Food Security in the Communal lands of Zimbabwe." Department of Rural and Urban Planning, Occasional Paper no. 11. Harare: University of Zimbabwe, May 1988.

Jacobs, S. "Zimbabwe: State, Class and Gendered Models of Land Resettlement." In *Women and the State in Africa*, ed. J. Parpart and K. Staudt. Boulder: Lynne Rienner, 1989.

Jassat, E. M., and B. Chakaodza. *Socio-Economic Baseline Study of Rushinga District (Mashonaland Central Province)*. Consultancy Paper prepared for the FAO. Harare: Zimbabwe Institute for Development Studies, July 1986.

Jeffries, R. "Ghana: The Political Economy of Personal Rule." In *Contemporary West African States*, ed. D. Cruise O'Brien, J. Dunn, and R. Rathbone. Cambridge: Cambridge University Press, 1989.

Jessop, B. "Capitalism and Democracy: The Best Political Shell?" In *Power and the State*, ed. G. Littlejohn. New York: St. Martins Press, 1978.

_____. *State Theory: Putting Capitalist States in Their Place*. University Park: Pennsylvania State University Press, 1990.

Jirira, K. "The Position of Women in Employment with Specific Reference to the Public Sector." Zimbabwe Institute of Development Studies Consultancy Report no. 23, 1991.

Johnson, R. W. M. *The Labour Economy of the Reserves*. Department of Economics, Occasional Paper no. 4. Salisbury: University College of Rhodesia and Nyasaland, 1964.

Jones, G. S. *Languages of Class: Studies in English Working Class History, 1832–1982*. Cambridge: Cambridge University Press, 1983.

Jordan, J. D. "Zimutu Reserve: A Land-Use Appreciation." *The Rhodes-Livingstone Journal*, no. 36 (n.d).

Joseph, G., and D. Nugent, eds. *Everyday Forms of State Formation*. Durham, N.C.: Duke University Press, 1994.

Kaarsholm, P. "The Past as Battlefield in Rhodesia and Zimbabwe: The Struggle of Competing Nationalisms over History from Colonization to Independence." *Culture and History* 6 (1989).

_____, ed. *Cultural Struggle and Development in Southern Africa*. London: James Currey, 1991.

Keane, J. *Civil Society and the State*. London: Verso, 1988.

Keyter, C. F. *Maize Control in Southern Rhodesia, 1931–1941: The African Contribution to White Survival.* Central African Historical Association, Local Series no. 34, 1978.

Kinsey, B. H. "Forever Gained: Resettlement and Land Policy in the Context of National Development in Zimbabwe." *Africa* 52, no. 3 (1982).

————. "Household-Level Outcomes of Land Reform in Post-Conflict Societies: The Case of Zimbabwe." Paper presented at the 40th Annual Meeting of the Association of African Studies, Columbus OH, 15 November 1997.

Kitching, G. *Development and Underdevelopment in Historical Perspective.* London: Routledge, 1982.

Kriger, N. J. "The Zimbabwean War of Liberation: Struggles within the Struggle." *Journal of Southern African Studies* 14, no. 2 (January 1988).

————. *Zimbabwe's Guerrilla War: Peasant Voices.* Cambridge: Cambridge University Press, 1992.

Lan, D. *Guns and Rain: Guerrillas and Spirit Mediums in Zimbabwe.* Harare: Zimbabwe Publishing House, 1985.

Latham, C. J. K. "Mwari and the Divine Heroes: Guardians of the Shona." M.A. thesis, Rhodes University 1986.

Lawyers Committee for Human Rights. *Zimbabwe: Wages of War: A Report on Human Rights.* New York: Lawyers Committee for Human Rights, 1986.

Levi, M. *Of Rule and Revenue.* Berkeley: University of California Press, 1988.

Leys, C. "What We Learned from the Kenya Debate." In *Political Development and the New Realism in Sub-Saharan Africa,* ed. D Apter and C. Rosberg. Charlottesville: University Press of Virginia, 1994.

Lindblom, C. E. *Politics and Markets: The World's Political-Economic Systems.* New York: Basic Books, 1977.

Lonsdale, J. "Political Accountability in African History." In *Political Domination in Africa: The Limits of State Power,* ed. P. Chabal. Cambridge: Cambridge University Press, 1986.

————. "States and Social Processes in Africa." *African Studies Review* 24, nos. 2/3 (1981).

MacGaffey, J. *The Real Economy of Zaire: The Contribution of Smuggling and Other Unofficial Activities to National Wealth.* London: James Currey, 1991.

MacIntyre, A. *After Virtue: A Study in Moral Theory.* Notre Dame, Ind.: University of Notre Dame Press, 1981.

MacKenzie, F. "Selective Silence: A Feminist Encounter with Environmental Discourse in Colonial Africa." In *Power of Development*, ed. J. Crush. London: Routledge, 1995.

MacKenzie, J. M. "The Natural World and the Popular Consciousness in Southern Africa: The European Appropriation of Nature." In *Cultural Struggle and Development in Southern Africa*, ed. P. Kaarsholm. London: James Currey, 1991.

MacLean, J. *The Guardians.* Bulawayo: Books of Rhodesia, 1974.

MacPherson, C. B. *The Political Theory of Possessive Individualism: Hobbes to Locke.* London: Oxford University Press, 1962.

Mallon, F. *Peasant and Nation: The Making of Postcolonial Mexico and Peru.* Berkeley: University of California Press, 1995.

Mamdani, M. *Citizen and Subject: Contemporary Africa and the Legacy of Late Colonialism.* Princeton: Princeton University Press, 1996.

Mandala, E. *Work and Control in a Peasant Economy.* Madison: University of Wisconsin Press, 1990.

Mandaza, I., ed. *Zimbabwe: The Political Economy of Transition, 1980–1986.* Dakar: CODESRIA, 1986.

Mann, M. *The Sources of Social Power.* Cambridge: Cambridge University Press, 1993.

Mann, K., and R. Roberts, eds. *Law in Colonial Africa.* London: James Currey, 1991.

Marks, S., and A. Atmore, eds. *Economy and Society in Pre-Industrial South Africa.* London: Longman, 1980.

Martin, D., and P. Johnson. *The Struggle for Zimbabwe: The Chimurenga War.* Johannesburg: Ravan Press, 1981.

Marx, K. *Capital: A Critique of Political Economy.* Vol. 1. Tr. Ben Fowkes. New York: Vintage Books, 1977.

————. *The Eighteenth Brumaire of Louis Bonaparte.* New York: International Publishers, 1963.

Mason, P. "Land Policy." In *The Two Nations: Aspects of the Develop-*

ment of Race Relations in the Rhodesias and Nyasaland, ed. R. Gray. Oxford: Oxford University Press, 1960.

Masst, M. "Exploring Differentiation among the Zimbabwean Peasantry." Centre for Applied Social Sciences Occasional Paper. Salisbury: University of Zimbabwe, June 1994.

May, J. *Changing People, Changing Laws.* Gweru: Mambo Press, 1987.

Mbembe, A. "The State, Violence and Accumulation: The Case of Sub-Saharan Africa." [Centre of Non-Western Studies, University of Leiden, 1989].

Menchu, R. *I, Rigoberta Menchu: An Indian Woman in Guatemala.* London: Verso, 1984.

Metcalfe, S. "'Empowerment' versus 'Participation' in Natural Resource Management in the Masoka Community." Harare: Zimbabwe Trust, 1990. Mimeographed.

Migdal, J. S. *Strong Societies and Weak States: State-Society Relations and State Capabilities in the Third World.* Princeton: Princeton University Press, 1988.

Mitchell, T. "The Return of the State." Paper presented to conference on Power, University of Michigan, Ann Arbor, 1992.

Moore, D. "Contesting Terrain in Zimbabwe's Eastern Highlands: Political Ecology, Ethnography, and Peasant Resource Struggles." *Economic Geography* 19, no. 4 (1993).

Mosley, P. *The Settler Economies: Studies in the Economic History of Kenya and Southern Rhodesia 1900–1963.* Cambridge: Cambridge University Press, 1983.

Moyana, H. V. *The Political Economy of Land in Zimbabwe.* Gweru: Mambo Press, 1984.

Moyo, J. *Voting for Democracy: A Study of Electoral Politics in Zimbabwe.* Harare: University of Zimbabwe, 1992.

Moyo, S. "Zimbabwe's Agrarian Reform Process: Lessons or Domino Strategies?" Zimbabwe Institute of Development Studies Discussion Paper no. 12, 1991.

Moyo, S., and T. Skalnes. *Zimbabwe's Land Reform and Development Strategy: State Autonomy, Class Bias and Economic Rationality.* Zimbabwe Institute of Development Studies Research Paper no. 3, 1990.

Mtetwa, R. M. G. "Myth or Reality: The 'Cattle Complex' in South East Africa, with Special Reference to Rhodesia." *Zambezia* 6, no. 1 (1978).

Muchena, O. "The Changing Position of African Women in Rural Zimbabwe." *Zimbabwe Journal of Economics* 1, no. 1 (March 1979).

Mugabe, R. G. *Our War of Liberation: Speeches, Articles, Interviews, 1976–1979.* Harare: Mambo Press, 1983.

Mugyenyi, M. "Development First, Democracy Second." In *Democratic Theory and Practice in Africa*, ed. W. Oyugi et al. London: James Currey, 1988.

Mukundu, M. Z. "Factors Limiting Increased Crop Production in Tribal Trust Lands as an Extension Worker Sees Them." *Rhodesia Science News* 10, no. 10 (October 1976).

Mulders, T. *Report on the Survey on Income Generating Projects, That are Assisted by the Ministry of Community Development and Women's Affairs.* 1986. Mimeographed.

Mumbengegwi, C. "Agricultural Producer Co-Operatives and Agrarian Transformation in Zimbabwe: Policy, Strategy and Implementation." *Zimbabwe Journal of Economics* 1, no. 1 (July 1984).

Mungazi, D. A. *Education and Government Control in Zimbabwe: A Study of the Commissions of Inquiry, 1908–1974.* New York: Praeger, 1990.

Munjeri, D. "Refocusing or Reorientation? The Exhibition of the Populace: Zimbabwe on the Threshold." In *Exhibiting Cultures: The Poetics and Politics of Museum Display*, ed. I. Karp and S. Lavine. Washington, D.C.: Smithsonian Institution Press, 1991.

Murapa, R. *Rural and District Administrative Reform in Zimbabwe.* Bordeaux: Centre D'Etude A'Afrique Noire, 1986.

Murombedzi, J. "Decentralization or Recentralization? Implementing CAMPFIRE in the Omay Communal Lands of the Nyaminyami District." University of Zimbabwe Centre for Applied Social Sciences. 1992. Mimeographed.

Murphree, M. "Communities as Institutions for Resource Management." Paper presented to the National Conference on Environment and Development, Maputo, Mozambique, 7–11 October 1991.

————. "A Village School and Community Development in a Rhodesian Tribal Trust Land." *Zambezia* 1, no. 2 (1970).

Murphree, M., and D. H. M. Cumming. "Savanna Land Use: Policy and Practice in Zimbabwe." University of Zimbabwe Centre for Applied Social Sciences. 1991. Mimeographed.

Murton, T. A. "Land-Use Planning in Tribal Areas in Rhodesia." *Rhodesian Agricultural Journal* 68, no. 1 (1971).

Mutambara, J. G. "Africans and Land Policies: British Colonial Policy in Zimbabwe, 1890–1965." Ph.D. dissertation, University of Cincinnati, 1981.

Mutambirwa, C. C. "Population and Migration." Paper presented to Seminar on Population in Development Planning, Harare, 28–30 October 1987.

Mutizwa-Mangiza, N. D. *Community Development in Pre-Independence Zimbabwe.* Supplement to *Zambezia.* Harare: University of Zimbabwe, 1985.

_____. "Decentralization in Zimbabwe: Problems of Planning at the District Level," University of Zimbabwe, Department of Rural and Urban Planning. Occasional Paper no. 16, January 1989.

Nicolle, W. H. M. "The Development of the Tribal Trust Lands of Rhodesia." Paper presented at NRB Conference on the Tribal Trust Lands, University College of Rhodesia, 2–3 February 1966.

_____. "The Legal and Social Status of the Tribal Trust Lands in Rhodesia." Paper presented at NRB Conference on the Tribal Trust Lands, University College of Rhodesia, 2–3 February 1966.

Nyoni, S. "Indigenous NGOs: Liberation, Self-Reliance and Development." *World Development* 15 (1987), supplement.

Otzen, U., T. Feige, H-J. Friedrich, B. Martin, D. Scheidel, and S. Wille. *Development Management from Below: The Potential Contribution of Co-Operatives and Village Development Committees to Self-Management and Decentralised Development in Zimbabwe.* Berlin: German Development Institute, September 1988.

Oyatek, R. "Burkina Faso: Between Feeble State and Total State, the Swing Continues." In *Contemporary West African States*, eds., D. Cruise O'Brien, J. Dunn, and R. Rathbone. Cambridge: Cambridge University Press, 1989.

Paige, J. *Agrarian Revolution: Social Movements and Export Agriculture in the Underdeveloped World.* New York: Free Press, 1975.

Palmer, R. H. *Land and Racial Domination in Rhodesia.* London: Heinemann, 1977.

Palmer, R. H., and N. Parsons, eds. *The Roots of Rural Poverty in Central and Southern Africa*. London: Heinemann, 1977.

Pankhurst, D. "The Dynamics of Social Relations of Production and Reproduction in Zimbabwe's Communal Areas." Ph.D. thesis, Southampton University, 1988.

Parpart, J., and K. Staudt, eds. *Women and the State in Africa*. Boulder: Lynne Rienner, 1989.

Passmore, G. "Historical Rationale of the Policy of Community Development in the African Rural Areas of Rhodesia." *Zambezia 2*, no. 1 (1971).

_____. *The National Policy of Community Development in Rhodesia*. Department of Political Science Source Book Series, no. 5. Salisbury: University of Rhodesia, 1972.

_____, ed. *H. R. G. Howman on Provincialisation in Rhodesia 1968–1969; and Rational and Irrational Elements*. Cambridge: Cambridge African Occasional Papers no. 4, n.d.

Patel, D. "Urbanisation, Population and Development." Paper presented to Seminar on Population in Development Planning, Harare, 28–30 October 1987.

Phillips, A. *The Enigma of Colonialism: British Policy in West Africa*. London: James Currey, 1989.

Phimister, I. *An Economic and Social History of Zimbabwe 1890–1948: Capital Accumulation and Class Struggle*. London: Longman, 1988.

_____. "Zimbabwe: The Path of Capitalist Development." In *History of Central Africa*, ed. D. Birmingham and P. M. Martin. Vol 2. London: Longman, 1983.

Plamenatz, J. "Two Types of Nationalism." In *Nationalism: The Nature and Evolution of an Idea*, ed. E. Kamenka. Canberra: Australian National University Press, 1973.

Plowden, R. C. "The Modern Role of Rhodesia's Chiefs." *Rhodesia Calls*, January/February 1977.

Poggi, G. *The Development of the Modern State: A Sociological Introduction*. Stanford: Stanford University Press, 1978.

Polanyi, K. *The Great Transformation: The Political and Economic Origins of Our Time*. Boston: Beacon Press, 1944.

Posselt, F. W. T. *Fact and Fiction: A Short Account of the Natives of Southern Rhodesia*. 1935; Bulawayo: Books of Rhodesia, 1978.

Raeburn, M. *Black Fire! Accounts of the Guerrilla War in Rhodesia.* London: Julian Friedmann, 1978.

Raikes, P. *Modernising Hunger: Famine, Food Surplus and Farm Policy in the EEC and Africa.* London: James Currey, 1988.

Ranchod-Nilsson, S. "'Educating Eve': The Women's Club Movement and Political Consciousness among African Women in Southern Rhodesia." Northwestern University. n.d. Mimeographed.

Ranger, T. O. "African Politics in Twentieth-Century Rhodesia." In *Aspects of Central African History,* ed. T. O. Ranger. Evanston: Northwestern University Press, 1968.

_____. "Bandits and Guerrillas: The Case of Zimbabwe." In *Banditry, Rebellion and Social Protest,* ed. Donald Crummey. London: James Currey, 1986.

_____. "Matabeleland since the Amnesty." *African Affairs* 88, no. 351 (April 1989).

_____. *Peasant Consciousness and Guerrilla War in Zimbabwe: A Comparative Study.* London: James Currey, 1985.

_____. "Tradition and Travesty: Chiefs and the Administration in Makoni District, Zimbabwe, 1960–1980." *Africa* 52 (1982).

Rapley, J. "New Directions in the Political Economy of Development." *Review of African Political Economy* 62 (1994).

Reno, W. "Who Really Rules Sierra Leone? Informal Markets and the Ironies of Reform." Ph.D. dissertation, University of Wisconsin, Madison, 1992.

Richards, P. *Fighting for the Rainforest: War, Youth and Resources in Sierra Leone.* Oxford: James Currey, 1996.

Riddell, R. *The Land Question.* From Rhodesia to Zimbabwe, vol. 2. Gwelo: Mambo Press, 1978.

Roberts, C. "Environmental Ethics and Wildlife Policy in Zimbabwe." B.A. thesis, Department of Religious Studies and Studies in the Environment Program, Yale University, 1991.

Robins, S. "Close Encounters at the "Development" Interface: Local Resistance, State Power, and the Politics of Land-Use Planning in Matabeleland, Zimbabwe." Ph.D. dissertation, Columbia University 1995.

Rohrbach, D. "A Preliminary Assessment of Factors Underlying the

Growth of Communal Maize Production in Zimbabwe." In *Food Security for Southern Africa*, ed. M. Rukuni and C. K. Eicher. Harare: University of Zimbabwe, Department of Agricultural Economics and Extension, UZ/MSU Food Security Project, February 1987.

Rukuni, M., and C. K. Eicher, eds. *Food Security for Southern Africa.* Harare: University of Zimbabwe, Department of Agricultural Economics and Extension, UZ/MSU Food Security Project, February 1987.

Sachikonye, L. "The Debate on Democracy in Contemporary Zimbabwe." *Review of African Political Economy*, no. 45/46 (1989).

———. "The 1990 Zimbabwe Elections: A Post-Mortem." *Review of African Political Economy*, no. 48, (Autumn 1990).

Sangpam, S. N. "The Overpoliticised State and International Politics: Nicaragua, Haiti, Cambodia and Togo." *Third World Quarterly* 16, no. 4 (1995).

———. "The Overpoliticized State and Democratization: A Theoretical Model." *Comparative Politics* 24, no. 4 (1992).

Saul, J. "The State in Post-Colonial Societies: Tanzania." *Socialist Register*, 1974.

Schmidt, E.. *Peasants, Traders and Wives: Shona Women in the History of Zimbabwe, 1870–1939.* London: James Currey, 1992.

Scoones, I. with C. Chibudu, S. Chikura, P. Jerenyama, D. Machaka, W. Machanja, B. Mavedzengo, B. Mombeshora, M. Mudhara, C. Mudziwa, F. Murimbarimba and B. Zirerezwa. *Hazards and Opportunities—Farming Livelihoods in Dryland Africa: Lessons from Zimbabwe.* London: Zed Books, 1996.

Scoones, I., and K. Wilson. "Households, Lineage Groups and Ecological Dynamics: Issues for Livestock Development in Zimbabwe's Communal Lands." In *People, Land and Livestock: Proceedings of a Workshop on the Socio-Economic Dimensions of Livestock Production in the Communal Lands of Zimbabwe*, ed. B. Cousins. Harare: University of Zimbabwe Centre for Applied Social Sciences, 1989.

Scott, J. C. *The Moral Economy of the Peasant: Subsistence and Rebellion in Southeast Asia.* New Haven: Yale University Press, 1976.

———. *Weapons of the Weak: Everyday Forms of Peasant Resistance.* New Haven: Yale University Press, 1985.

Seager, D. "A Salisbury Squatter Settlement: The Struggle for Shelter in an Urban Environment." *South African Labour Bulletin* 3, no. 6 (May 1977).

Shamuyarira, N. M. *Crisis in Rhodesia.* London: Andre Deutsch, 1965.

Shapiro, I. "Realism in the Study of the History of Ideas." *History of Political Thought* 3, no. 3 (Winter 1982).

Shipton, P. *Bitter Money: The Classification of Forbidden Commodities among the Luo of Kenya.* Washington, D.C.: American Ethnological Society, 1989.

Shopo, T. "Some Perspectives on Administrative Accountability for Nation Building and Development." Paper read to University of Zimbabwe Department of Rural and Urban Planning Workshop on Planning, February 1986.

Sibanda, A. "The Political Situation: Issues of Race, Class, State and Capital in Southern Africa." In *Zimbabwe's Prospects*, ed. C. Stoneman. London: Macmillan, 1981.

Sithole, M. "Zimbabwe: In Search of a Stable Democracy." In *Democracy in Developing Countries Vol II: Africa*, ed. L. Diamond, J. Linz, and S. Lipset. Boulder: Lynne Rienner, 1989.

————. "Zimbabwe's Eroding Authoritarianism." *Journal of Democracy* 18, no. 1 (1997).

Skocpol, T. *States and Social Revolutions: A Comparative Analysis of France, Russia and China.* Cambridge: Cambridge University Press, 1979.

Smith, G. A. "A Strategy for Rural Development: Savings Clubs and Package Programmes." University of Rhodesia, Institute of Adult Education, June 1974.

Stanning, J. "Household Grain Storage and Marketing in Surplus and Deficit Communal Farming Areas in Zimbabwe: Preliminary Findings." In *Food Security for Southern Africa*, ed. M. Rukuni and C. K. Eicher. Harare: University of Zimbabwe, Department of Agricultural Economics and Extension, UZ/MSU Food Security project, 1987.

Staunton, I. *Mothers of the Revolution.* London: James Currey, 1991.

Steele, M. C. "The Economic Function of African-Owned Cattle in Rhodesia." *Zambezia* 9, no. 2 (1981).

Stein, H., ed. *Asian Industrialization and Africa: Studies in Policy Alternatives to Structural Adjustment.* London: Macmillan, 1995.

Stepan, A. *The State and Society: Peru in Comparative Perspective.* Princeton: Princeton University Press, 1978.

Stocking, M. A. "The Relationship of Agricultural History and Settlement to Severe Soil Erosion in Rhodesia." *Zambezia* 6, no. 2 (1978).

Stoneman, C. ed. *Zimbabwe's Inheritance.* London: MacMillan, 1981.

Sylvester, C. "Unities and Disunities in Zimbabwe's 1990 Elections." *Journal of Modern African Studies* 28, no. 3 (1990).

_____. *Zimbabwe: The Terrain of Contradictory Development.* Boulder: Westview Press, 1991.

Tarrow, S. *Power in Movement: Social Movements, Collective Action and Politics.* Cambridge: Cambridge University Press, 1994.

Thomas, B. "Development through Harambee: Who Wins and Who Loses? Rural Self-Help Projects in Kenya." *World Development* 15, no. 4 (1987).

Thomas, S. J. "The Legacy of Dualism and Decision-Making: The Prospects for Local Institutional Development in 'Campfire.'" Paper prepared for the Second Annual Conference of the International Association for the Study of Common Property. Winnipeg: University of Manitoba, 1991.

Thompson, C. H., and H. W. Woodruff. *Economic Development in Rhodesia and Nyasaland.* London: Dennis Dobson, 1954.

Thompson, E. P. *Customs in Common: Studies in Traditional Popular Culture.* New York: Free Press, 1991.

Tilly, C. *From Mobilization to Revolution.* Reading, Mass.: Addison-Wesley, 1978.

Tribal Trust Lands Development Corporation (TILCOR). "Development in TILCOR." *Development,* February 1976 [reprint].

_____. *National Development: Proposals for the Under-Developed Parts of the Country.* December 1976.

_____. "Tilcor's Growth Point Policy." 22 June 1977. NAZ Gen/ Tri-p.

_____. *Urban Development at TILCOR Growth Points.* 25 June 1976. NAZ Gen/Tri-p.

Uphoff, N. "Grassroots Organizations and NGOs in Rural Development: Opportunities with Diminishing States and Expanding Markets." *World Development* 21, no. 4 (April 1993).

van den Pool, M., C. Jackson, R. Mula, M. Ning, O. P'Obwoya, and H. Thompson. *Changing Farming Systems in a Migrant Labour Economy.* International Course for development oriented Research in Agriculture (ICRA) Working Document Series, no. 9, 1989.

van Onselen, C. *Chibaro: African Mine Labour in Southern Rhodesia, 1900–1933.* London: Pluto, 1976.

von Freyhold, M. *Ujamaa Villages in Tanzania: Analysis of a Social Experiment.* New York: Monthly Review Press, 1979.

Wapner, P. "Politics beyond the State: Environmental Activism and World Civic Politics." *World Politics* 47, no. 3 (1995).

Weber, M. "Politics as a Vocation." In *From Max Weber: Essays in Sociology,* tr. and ed. H. H. Gerth and C. Wright Mills. New York: Oxford University Press, 1946.

Weinrich, A. K. H. *African Farmers in Rhodesia: Old and New Peasant Communities in Karangaland.* London: Oxford University Press, 1975.

———. *Black and White Elites in Rural Rhodesia.* Manchester: Manchester University Press, 1973.

———. "Strategic Resettlement in Rhodesia." *Journal of Southern African Studies* 3, no. 2 (April 1977).

Werbner, R. *Tears of the Dead: The Social Biography of an African Family.* Harare: Baobab Books, 1992.

Whitlow, R. "Environmental Constraints and Population Pressures in the Tribal Areas of Zimbabwe." *Zimbabwe Agricultural Journal* 77, no. 4 (1980).

Whitsun Foundation. *Agriculture in Rhodesia.* Salisbury: Whitsun Foundation, 8 March 1977.

Williams, G. "Growth, Equity and the State." *Africa* 52, no. 3 (1982).

———. "Taking the Part of Peasants: Rural Development in Nigeria and Tanzania." In *The Political Economy of Contemporary Africa,* ed. P. Gutkind and I. Wallerstein. Beverly Hills, Calif.: Sage Publications, 1985.

Wilson, K. B. "Trees in the Fields in Southern Zimbabwe." *Journal of Southern African Studies* 15, no. 2 (January 1989).

———. "Research on Trees in the Mazvihwa and Surrounding Areas." mimeograph, ENDA-Zimbabwe, 1987.

Wolf, E. R. *Peasant Wars of the Twentieth Century.* New York: Harper and Row, 1969.

Woollacott, R. C. "Community Boards." *Community Development and Local Government Bulletin,* no. 6 (May 1966).

Wood, E. M. "The Uses and Abuses of 'Civil Society.'" In *Socialist Register,* ed. R. Miliband and L. Panitch. London: Merlin Press, 1990.

World Bank. *Zimbabwe: Land Subsector Study.* Report no. 5878-ZIM. Washington, D.C.: World Bank, 30 September 1986.

Wrathall, J. J. "Developing the Tribal Trust Lands." *Rhodesian Journal of Economics* 2, no. 4 (December 1968).

Wright, A. *Valley of the Ironwoods.* Cape Town: Bulpin, 1972.

Wunsch, J. S., and D. Owolu, eds. *The Failure of the Centralized State: Institutions and Self-Governance in Africa.* Boulder: Westview Press, 1990.

Young, M. C. *The African Colonial State in Comparative Perspective.* New Haven: Yale University Press, 1994.

————. *Ideology and Development in Africa.* New Haven: Yale University Press, 1982.

————. "Patterns of Social Conflict: State, Class and Ethnicity." *Daedalus* 111 (1982).

————. "Zaire: Is There a State?" *Canadian Journal of African Studies* 18, no. 1 (1984).

Yudelman, M. *Africans on the Land: Economic Problems of Agricultural Development in Southern, Central, and East Africa, with Special Reference to Southern Rhodesia.* Cambridge, Mass.: Harvard University Press, 1964.

————. "Imperialism and the Transfer of Agricultural Techniques." In *Colonialism in Africa 1870–1960,* ed. P. Duignan and L. Gann Stanford: Hoover Institution Press, 1975.

ZANU(PF). *Zimbabwe at Five Years of Independence: Achievements, Problems and Prospects.* Harare: Nehanda Publishers, 1985.

Zehender, W., M. Draser, J. Elsäβer, G. Geier, B. Gnärig, and W. Schnell. *Options for Regional Development in the Pfura and Rushinga Districts, Zimbabwe.* Berlin: German Development Institute, 1984.

Zimbabwe Women's Bureau. *We Carry a Heavy Load: Rural Women in Zimbabwe Speak Out.* Report of a survey. Harare, 1981.

————. *We Carry a Heavy Load: Rural Women in Zimbabwe Speak Out.* Part 2: *1981–1991.* Summary of report on the follow-up survey. Harare, 1992.

Zolberg, A. *Creating Political Order: The Party-States of West Africa.* Chicago: Rand McNally, 1966.

Zweig, D. "Struggling over Land in China: Peasant Resistance after Collectivization, 1966–1986." In *Everyday Forms of Peasant Resistance,* ed. F. Colburn. Armonk, N.Y.: M. E. Sharpe, 1989.

Index

Monographs in International Studies

Titles Available from Ohio University Press

Southeast Asia Series

No. 56   Duiker, William J. Vietnam Since the Fall of Saigon. 1989. Updated ed. 401 pp. Paper 0-89680-162-4 $20.00.

No. 64   Dardjowidjojo, Soenjono. Vocabulary Building in Indonesian: An Advanced Reader. 1984. 664 pp. Paper 0-89680-118-7 $30.00.

No. 65   Errington, J. Joseph. Language and Social Change in Java: Linguistic Reflexes of Modernization in a Traditional Royal Polity. 1985. 210 pp. Paper 0-89680-120-9 $25.00.

No. 66   Binh, Tran Tu. The Red Earth: A Vietnamese Memoir of Life on a Colonial Rubber Plantation. Tr. by John Spragens. 1984. 102 pp. (SEAT*, V. 5) Paper 0-89680-119-5 $11.00.

No. 68   Syukri, Ibrahim. History of the Malay Kingdom of Patani. 1985. 135 pp. Paper 0-89680-123-3 $15.00.

No. 69   Keeler, Ward. Javanese: A Cultural Approach. 1984. 559 pp. Paper 0-89680-121-7 $25.00.

No. 70   Wilson, Constance M. and Lucien M. Hanks. Burma-Thailand Frontier Over Sixteen Decades: Three Descriptive Documents. 1985. 128 pp. Paper 0-89680-124-1 $11.00.

No. 71   Thomas, Lynn L. and Franz von Benda-Beckmann, eds. Change and Continuity in Minangkabau: Local, Regional, and Historical Perspectives on West Sumatra. 1985. 353 pp. Paper 0-89680-127-6 $16.00.

No. 72   Reid, Anthony and Oki Akira, eds. The Japanese Experience in Indonesia: Selected Memoirs of 1942–1945. 1986. 424 pp., 20 illus. (SEAT, V. 6) Paper 0-89680-132-2 $20.00.

* Southeast Asia Translation Project Group

No. 74   McArthur M. S. H. Report on Brunei in 1904. Introduced and Annotated by A. V. M. Horton. 1987. 297 pp. Paper 0-89680-135-7 $15.00.

No. 75   Lockard, Craig A. From Kampung to City: A Social History of Kuching, Malaysia, 1820–1970. 1987. 325 pp. Paper 0-89680-136-5 $20.00.

No. 76   McGinn, Richard, ed. Studies in Austronesian Linguistics. 1986. 516 pp. Paper 0-89680-137-3 $20.00.

No. 77   Muego, Benjamin N. Spectator Society: The Philippines Under Martial Rule. 1986. 232 pp. Paper 0-89680-138-1 $17.00.

No 79   Walton, Susan Pratt. Mode in Javanese Music. 1987. 278 pp. Paper 0-89680-144-6 $15.00.

No. 80   Nguyen Anh Tuan. South Vietnam: Trial and Experience. 1987. 477 pp., tables. Paper 0-89680-141-1 $18.00.

No. 82   Spores, John C. Running Amok: An Historical Inquiry. 1988. 190 pp. paper 0-89680-140-3 $13.00.

No. 83   Malaka, Tan. From Jail to Jail. Tr. by Helen Jarvis. 1911. 1209 pp., three volumes. (SEAT V. 8) Paper 0-89680-150-0 $55.00.

No. 84   Devas, Nick, with Brian Binder, Anne Booth, Kenneth Davey, and Roy Kelly. Financing Local Government in Indonesia. 1989. 360 pp. Paper 0-89680-153-5 $20.00.

No. 85   Suryadinata, Leo. Military Ascendancy and Political Culture: A Study of Indonesia's Golkar. 1989. 235 pp., illus., glossary, append., index, bibliog. Paper 0-89680-154-3 $18.00.

No. 86   Williams, Michael. Communism, Religion, and Revolt in Banten in the Early Twentieth Century. 1990. 390 pp. Paper 0-89680-155-1 $14.00.

No. 87   Hudak, Thomas. The Indigenization of Pali Meters in Thai Poetry. 1990. 247 pp. Paper 0-89680-159-4 $15.00.

No. 88   Lay, Ma Ma. Not Out of Hate: A Novel of Burma. Tr. by Margaret Aung-Thwin. Ed. by William Frederick. 1991. 260 pp. (SEAT V. 9) Paper 0-89680-167-5 $20.00.

No. 89   Anwar, Chairil. The Voice of the Night: Complete Poetry and Prose of Chairil Anwar. 1992. Revised Edition. Tr. by Burton Raffel. 196 pp. Paper 0-89680-170-5 $20.00.

No. 90   Hudak, Thomas John, tr., The Tale of Prince Samuttakote: A Buddhist Epic from Thailand. 1993. 230 pp. Paper 0-89680-174-8 $20.00.

No. 91   Roskies, D. M., ed. Text/Politics in Island Southeast Asia:

Essays in Interpretation. 1993. 330 pp. Paper 0-89680-175-6 $25.00.

No. 92   Schenkhuizen, Marguérite, translated by Lizelot Stout van Balgooy. Memoirs of an Indo Woman: Twentieth-Century Life in the East Indies and Abroad. 1993. 312 pp. Paper 0-89680-178-0 $25.00.

No. 93   Salleh, Muhammad Haji. Beyond the Archipelago: Selected Poems. 1995. 247 pp. Paper 0-89680-181-0 $20.00.

No. 94   Federspiel, Howard M. A Dictionary of Indonesian Islam. 1995. 327 pp. Bibliog. Paper 0-89680-182-9 $25.00.

No. 95   Leary, John. Violence and the Dream People: The Orang Asli in the Malayan Emergency 1948–1960. 1995. 275 pp. Maps, illus., tables, appendices, bibliog., index. Paper 0-89680-186-1 $22.00.

No. 96   Lewis, Dianne. *Jan Compagnie* in the Straits of Malacca 1641–1795. 1995. 176 pp. Map, appendices, bibliog., index. Paper 0-89680-187-x. $18.00.

No. 97   Schiller, Jim and Martin-Schiller, Barbara. Imagining Indonesia: Cultural Politics and Political Culture. 1996. 384 pp., notes, glossary, bibliog. Paper 0-89680-190-x. $30.00.

No. 98   Bonga, Dieuwke Wendelaar. Eight Prison Camps: A Dutch Family in Japanese Java. 1996. 233 pp., illus., map, glossary. Paper 0-89680-191-8. $18.00.

No. 99   Gunn, Geoffrey C. Language, Ideology, and Power in Brunei Darussalam. 1996. 328 pp., glossary, notes, bibliog., index. Paper 0-86980-192-6 $24.00.

No. 100   Martin, Peter W., Conrad Ozog, and Gloria R. Poedjosoedarmo, eds. Language Use and Language Change in Brunei Darussalam. 1996. 390 pp., maps, notes, bibliog. Paper 0-89680-193-4. $26.00.

Africa Series

No. 43   Harik, Elsa M. and Donald G. Schilling. The Politics of Education in Colonial Algeria and Kenya. 1984. 102 pp. Paper 0-89680-117-9 $12.50.

No. 45   Keto, C. Tsehloane. American-South African Relations 1784–1980: Review and Select Bibliography. 1985. 169 pp. Paper 0-89680-128-4 $11.00.

Monographs in International Studies

No. 46   **Burness, Don**, ed. Wanasema: Conversations with African Writers. 1985. 103 pp. paper 0-89680-129-2 $11.00.

No. 47   **Switzer, Les**. Media and Dependency in South Africa: A Case Study of the Press and the Ciskei "Homeland." 1985. 97 pp. Paper 0-89680-130-6 $10.00.

No. 51   **Clayton, Anthony and David Killingray**. Khaki and Blue: Military and Police in British Colonial Africa. 1989. 347 pp. Paper 0-89680-147-0 $20.00.

No. 52   **Northrup, David**. Beyond the Bend in the River: African Labor in Eastern Zaire, 1865–1940. 1988. 282 pp. Paper 0-89680-151-9 $15.00.

No. 53   **Makinde, M. Akin**. African Philosophy, Culture, and Traditional Medicine. 1988. 172 pp. Paper 0-89680-152-7 $16.00.

No. 54   **Parson, Jack**, ed. Succession to High Office in Botswana: Three Case Studies. 1990. 455 pp. Paper 0-89680-157-8 $20.00.

No. 56   **Staudinger, Paul**. In the Heart of the Hausa States. Tr. by Johanna E. Moody. Foreword by Paul Lovejoy. 1990. In two volumes., 469 + 224 pp., maps, apps. Paper 0-89680-160-8 (2 vols.) $35.00.

No. 57   **Sikainga, Ahmad Alawad**. The Western Bahr Al-Ghazal under British Rule, 1898–1956. 1991. 195 pp. Paper 0-89680-161-6 $15.00.

No. 58   **Wilson, Louis E.** The Krobo People of Ghana to 1892: A Political and Social History. 1991. 285 pp. Paper 0-89680-164-0 $20.00.

No. 59   **du Toit, Brian M.** Cannabis, Alcohol, and the South African Student: Adolescent Drug Use, 1974–1985. 1991. 176 pp., notes, tables. Paper 0-89680-166-7 $17.00.

No. 60   **Falola, Toyin and Dennis Itavyar**, eds. The Political Economy of Health in Africa. 1992. 258 pp., notes, tables. Paper 0-89680-166-7 $20.00.

No. 61   **Kiros, Tedros**. Moral Philosophy and Development: The Human Condition in Africa. 1992. 199 pp., notes. Paper 0-89680-171-3 $20.00.

No. 62   **Burness, Don.** Echoes of the Sunbird: An Anthology of Contemporary African Poetry. 1993. 198 pp. Paper 0-89680-173-x $17.00.

No. 64   **Nelson, Samuel H.** Colonialism in the Congo Basin 1880–1940. 1994. 290 pp. Index. Paper 0-89680-180-2 $23.00.

No. 66   Ilesanmi, Simeon Olusegun. Religious Pluralism and the Nigerian State. 1996. 336 pp., maps, notes, bibliog., index. Paper 0-89680-194-2 $23.00.

No. 67   Steeves, H. Leslie. Gender Violence and the Press: The St. Kizito Story. 1997. 176 pp., illus., notes, bibliog., index. Paper 0-89680195-0 $17.95.

Latin America Series

No. 9   Tata, Robert J. Structural Changes in Puerto Rico's Economy: 1947–1976. 1981. 118 pp. paper 0-89680-107-1 $12.00.

No. 13   Henderson, James D. Conservative Thought in Latin America: The Ideas of Laureano Gomez. 1988. 229 pp. Paper 0-89680-148-9 $16.00.

No. 17   Mijeski, Kenneth J., ed. The Nicaraguan Constitution of 1987: English Translation and Commentary. 1991. 355 pp. Paper 0-89680-165-9 $25.00.

No. 18   Finnegan, Pamela. The Tension of Paradox: José Donoso's *The Obscene Bird of Night* as Spiritual Exercises. 1992. 204 pp. Paper 0-89680-169-1 $15.00.

No. 19   Kim, Sung Ho and Thomas W. Walker, eds. Perspectives on War and Peace in Central America. 1992. 155 pp., notes, bibliog. Paper 0-89680-172-1 $17.00.

No. 20   Becker, Marc. Mariátegui and Latin American Marxist Theory. 1993. 239 pp. Paper 0-89680-177-2 $20.00.

No. 21   Boschetto-Sandoval, Sandra M. and Marcia Phillips McGowan, eds. Claribel Alegría and Central American Literature. 1994. 233 pp., illus. Paper 0-89680-179-9 $20.00.

No. 22   Zimmerman, Marc. Literature and Resistance in Guatemala: Textual Modes and Cultural Politics from El Señor Presidente to Rigoberta Menchú. 1995. 2 volume set 320 + 370 pp., notes, bibliog. Paper 0-89680-183-7 $50.00.

No. 23   Hey, Jeanne A. K. Theories of Dependent Foreign Policy: The Case of Ecuador in the 1980s. 1995. 280 pp., map, tables, notes, bibliog., index. paper 0-89680-184-5 $22.00.

No. 24   Wright, Bruce E. Theory in the Practice of the Nicaraguan Revolution. 1995. 320 pp., notes, illus., bibliog., index. Paper 0-89680-185-3. $23.00.

No. 25   Mann, Carlos Guevara. Panamanian Militarism: A Historical

Ordering Information

Individuals are encouraged to patronize local bookstores wherever possible. Orders for titles in the Monographs in International Studies may be placed directly through the Ohio University Press, Scott Quadrangle, Athens, Ohio 45701-2979. Individuals should remit payment by check, VISA, or MasterCard.* Those ordering from the United Kingdom, Continental Europe, the Middle East, and Africa should order through Academic and University Publishers Group, 1 Gower Street, London WC1E, England. Orders from the Pacific Region, Asia, Australia, and New Zealand should be sent to East-West Export Books, c/o the University of Hawaii Press, 2840 Kolowalu Street, Honolulu, Hawaii 96822, USA.

Individuals ordering from outside of the U.S. should remit in U.S. funds to Ohio University Press either by International Money Order or by a check drawn on a U.S. bank.** Most out-of-print titles may be ordered from University Microfilms, Inc., 300 North Zeeb Road, Ann Arbor, Michigan 48106, USA.

Prices are subject to change.

* Please add $3.50 for the first book and $.75 for each additional book for shipping and handling.

** Outside the U.S. please add $4.50 for the first book and $.75 for each additional book

Ohio University
Center for International Studies

The Ohio University Center for International Studies was established to help create within the university and local communities a greater awareness of the world beyond the United States. Comprising programs in African, Latin American, Southeast Asian, Development and Administrative studies, the Center supports scholarly research, sponsors lectures and colloquia, encourages course development within the university curriculum, and publishes the Monographs in International Studies series with the Ohio University Press. The Center and its programs also offer an interdisciplinary Master of Arts degree in which students may focus on one of the regional or topical concentrations, and may also combine academics with training in career fields such as journalism, business, and language teaching. For undergraduates, major and certificate programs are also available.

For more information, contact the Vice Provost for International Studies, Burson House, Ohio University, Athens, Ohio 45701.